D0803642

Naples &
the Amalfi Coast

Duncan Garwood
Cristian Bonetto

Published by Lonely Planet Publications Pty Ltd
ABN 36 005 607 983

Australia Head Office, Locked Bag 1, Footscray,
Victoria 3011, ☎ 03 8379 8000, fax 03 8379 8111,
talk2us@lonelyplanet.com.au

USA 150 Linden St, Oakland, CA 94607,
☎ 510 893 8555, toll free 800 275 8555,
fax 510 893 8572, info@lonelyplanet.com

UK 72–82 Rosebery Ave, Clerkenwell, London, EC1R 4RW,
☎ 020 7841 9000, fax 020 7841 9001,
go@lonelyplanet.co.uk

© Lonely Planet Publications Pty Ltd 2007
Photographs © Greg Elms and as listed (p271), 2007

Published April 2007
2nd Edition
First published April 2005

Printed by Colorcraft Ltd, Hong Kong

CONTENTS

ROCCO FASANO

SEARCHING FOR HAPPINESS ON THE AMALFI COAST

Naples is a double-shot espresso. Caught in the shadow of a snoozing Mt Vesuvius, it fronts each day with fatalistic intensity.

Teeming streets explode with high theatrics: lovers fight passionately, drivers dodge skilfully and counterfeit-Prada salesmen keep an eye out for police. From the hissing craters of the Campi Flegrei to the graphic ruins of Herculaneum and Pompeii, drama defines the details.

But Italy's hyperactive underdog is more than just mayhem and thin-crust margherita pizzas. This former regal diva boasts three royal palaces, a superlative archaeological museum, art collections spanning from the classics to Jeff Koons, and an ancient centro storico (historic centre) bursting with secret frescoed chapels and citrus-filled cloisters. Not bad for a city more renowned for bling-clad mafiosi.

Ironically, it is Naples' unfashionableness that has made it so cool. While other cities march to a globalised beat, Naples is keeping it real. Here, restaurants are family heirlooms and vintage tailors sew bratpack suits. The cutting edge exists but it lives side by side with the Naples of neorealist film director Vittorio de Sica's imagination – one of gesticulating crowds and Sophia Loren lookalikes.

A film star in its own right, the fabled Amalfi Coast rolls out to the south. Lush cliffs plunge into creamy-blue seas and chichi coastal towns read like a celebrity roll call. American heiresses prefer pastel Positano, day-trippers flock to Amalfi, and Gore Vidal once lived in elegant hillside Ravello. Across the Bay of Naples sits bewitching Capri, home to a neon-blue grotto and holidaying superstars. The island has always seduced the cream of the crop, from kinky Roman emperors to Jackie Onassis and Brigitte Bardot. Further west, steamy Ischia soothes the muscles with its thermal springs, while tiny Procida soothes the soul with its windswept villages and weathered, old fishermen.

Legendary coastlines, infamous ruins and a madcap metropolis to boot: welcome to Italy at its red-blooded best.

SUN, SEA & THE SILVER SCREEN

NAME	Antonietta de Lillo
AGE	47
OCCUPATION	Film-maker
RESIDENCE	Naples & Rome

What makes Naples queen of the Italian screen?

'Naples is an endless source of inspiration for me as a film-maker. There's an energy here that seems drawn from **Mt Vesuvius** itself. Like Caravaggio's chiaroscuro paintings, it's a place of extreme light and shadow. On one level there are the grand, sun-drenched castles of **Sant'Elmo**, **Castel Nuovo** and **Castel dell'Ovo**, and the sweeping views from **Posillipo**. But then there's a hidden Naples, the Naples of the **Quartieri Spagnoli** and **La Sanità**, where poverty and chaos sit side by side with grand baroque staircases, secret courtyards and forgotten palazzi. One of my favourite buildings in Naples is Luigi Vanvitelli's Palazzo Doria D'Angri on Piazza VII Settembre. It's considered one of Naples' finest 18th-century creations, and I used it as a location in *Resto di Niente,* a film set during the days of the Parthenopean Republic.

'Like any intriguing protagonist, Naples is complex and multilayered. Beneath its frantic streets sits an otherworld of catacombs, ancient cults and ruins. A fascinating way to explore it all is on a **Napoli Sotterranea tour**, which takes you underground into an eerie landscape of ancient passageways and caves. The sense of mystery continues at street level, where haunting little shrines and altars pay homage to various saints…and footballers. Naples is home to many cults, and our love of ritual and performance helps explain our rich

Mt Vesuvius looms behind Castel dell'Ovo (p83)   JEAN-BERNARD CARILLET

dramatic and musical legacy. Commedia dell'arte was born on these streets, and the **Teatro San Carlo** is one of the world's great opera houses.

'Once again, Naples shows a completely different side at **MADRE**, the city's new contemporary art gallery. I adore coming here for the contrast between the cutting-edge work on display and the weathered old city on the other side of the windows. It's a sharp paradox and what I love best about my home town. This, and the pastries at **Moccia**, of course. I have travelled the globe and am yet to find a *pasticceria* (pastry shop) as equally sublime. You can't sit down but it's a small price to pay for the world's best *caprese* (chocolate and almond cake).

> 'COMMEDIA DELL'ARTE WAS BORN ON THESE STREETS, AND THE TEATRO SAN CARLO IS ONE OF THE WORLD'S GREAT OPERA HOUSES'

'When I need inspiration (or just a break), I try to get away to **Procida**. This tiny island has inspired some great work, including Elsa Morante's bitter-sweet novel *L'Isola di Arturo* (Arthur's Island) and the wonderful film *Il Postino* (The Postman). My own film *Non e' Giusto* (It's Not Right) was shot here. With its fishermen and pastel-hued Arabesque houses, the island feels wilder and more authentic than neighbouring **Ischia** and **Capri**. A wonderful annual spectacle is Ischia's **Festa di Sant'Anna**, when the sea fills with boats and fireworks are set off at midnight in honour of the island's martyred protector. It's very beautiful to watch from Procida.'

Massimo Troisi in *Il Postino*   ALL STAR PICTURE LIBRARY

On the streets of Naples' Quartieri Spagnoli (p78)   JEAN-BERNARD CARILLET

INTERVIEW 2:
THEATRE, CURSES & FALLING CHURCHES

NAME	Francesco Sivo
AGE	32
OCCUPATION	Architect
RESIDENCE	Naples

If walls could talk, what would they say about Naples?

'To understand a city, you need only to look at its buildings. Each stone and each square offers a revealing insight into not just its history but also the soul of its people. In *La Perle et le Croissant*, the French writer Dominique Fernandez observes: 'Naples is resistant to bourgeois order, yet all the city is baroque…there is also baroque in the psychological fragility of the inhabitants, the very theatricality of each moment of existence.' Some of the most evocative examples of this dramatic sensibility are the city's old staircases. Particularly famous are the double-flighted creations of the 18th-century architect Ferdinando Sanfelice, which look fit for an opera. The best examples are in the **Palazzo Sanfelice** and the **Palazzo dello Spagnolo**. A recently restored baroque highlight is the **San Gregorio Armeno** in the centro storico (historic centre), with its lavish gilded interior and sumptuous marble sculptures and art.

Baroque *guglia* (obelisk) in Piazza San Domenico Maggiore (p73)   DALLAS STRIBLEY

Chiesa del Gesù Nuovo (p69) in Naples' centro storico   GREG ELMS

'Naples is also famous for its history of alchemy. An intriguing example of this is the diamond-stoned exterior of the **Chiesa del Gesù Nuovo**. The façade itself predates the church and was originally part of the 15th-century Palazzo dei Principi di San Severo di Sarno. Few people know that each stone is engraved with a mysterious esoteric symbol. Professors in ancient alchemy believe that these symbols were meant to bring good luck but for some unknown reason were engraved inversely on the stones, consequently cursing the building. According to legend, each one of its inhabitants was destined to be driven out. The first owner, Antonello Sanseverino, was forced to leave the palace by the Aragon ambassador. The second, Ferrante Sanseverino, was driven out in 1580 by Spanish king Philip II who sold the palace to the Jesuits. In 1767, they were thrown out and Franciscan monks moved in, only to be thrown out themselves in 1821 to allow the Jesuits back in. We're still waiting for the next ousting.

'Today, most of the bad luck that hits the city's buildings comes from a lack of funding for restoration works. Naples is packed with hundreds of lesser-known but sublimely beautiful buildings left run down and forgotten. One particularly sad example is the Chiesa di Santa Maria Delle Grazie a Caponapoli (Largo Santa Maria delle Grazie a Capo Napoli), next to the Ospedale dei Incurabili. Designed by Giovan Francesco di Palma, this Tuscan-inspired Renaissance church is exquisite. Decorated with hand-carved stones, it features a beautiful front door by Giovanni Donadio and is one of the most famous Neapolitan sculptures of the 16th century. Today, it's boarded up and decaying. Thankfully, the beautiful frescoed courtyard has been spared; it's now used as a laundry for the hospital next door.'

9

INTERVIEW 3:
NAME YOUR PRICE

NAME	Cinzia Boggia
AGE	32
OCCUPATION	Telecommunications Officer
RESIDENCE	Naples

Have you got what it takes to shop like a local?

'If you're up for a bargain, it's hard to beat the markets in Naples. You'll find almost anything here and it's usually very cheap. A great place to start is at **Poggioreale**. It's huge and *the* place for shoes. You can find everything from men's trainers to designer Italian stilettos. What might cost you €150 in a shop, you can get here for €20. The big names aren't fakes, just excess stock, which means that finding your size can be a question of luck. Try to come on a Sunday or Monday when all the stalls are open. As for haggling, always offer the vendor half their initial asking price. They'll always refuse, at which point you should feign disinterest and make to walk away. This is when you'll get that winning second offer that meets you halfway.

Market time (p140)

CRAIG PERSHOUSE

'Another great Neapolitan market is **La Pignasecca**. Here you'll find absolutely everything from discount perfume and linen to cheap CDs – and pickpockets, so leave your valuables at home. The designer clothes and bags are convincing copies and seriously cheap, so there's no need to haggle. But above all, this is the place for food, from fast-food *croccè* (potato mash breadcrumbed and fried, filled with mozzarella cheese) to fresh fish.

'For a totally different vibe, head to the **Bancarelle a San Pasquale** in Chiaia. This little market is very 'in' at the moment and a fabulous spot for cool clothes and unusual jewellery, bags and sarongs. Just don't

'THE DESIGNER CLOTHES AND BAGS ARE CONVINCING COPIES AND SERIOUSLY CHEAP'

haggle – it's not the done thing in this part of town. Up the hill in Vomero, check out the **Mercatino di Antignano** for good-quality Italian-made shoes, clothes and homewares.

'My personal favourite is the **Mercatino di Posillipo**. It's my local and a lot more chilled than the markets downtown. Towards the top of the hill on the right-hand side you'll find a stall that sells vintage clothes. Some of the pieces are really rare and beautifully tailored. Last-season or sample stock from Armani, Moschino, Dolce & Gabbana and Calvin Klein can go for as little as €10. The Gucci and Prada here are fakes, as are the Louis Vuitton bags sold at the bottom of the hill. That said, they're brilliant copies and the African vendors are always up for a haggle. Offer them half their asking price and expect to walk off with a bargain.'

INTERVIEW 4:
ISLAND LIFE

NAME	Claudia Verardi
AGE	37
OCCUPATION	Translator
RESIDENCE	Naples

What is it about Capri that keeps the A-list coming back?

'I have a true passion for Capri: all of my favourite memories as a child belong to this magical place. The long walks with my family, late-night chocolate gelato on the piazzetta, the trips to the **Grotta Azzurra**. These days, I head there with my dog Scooby and we just amble with no particular place to go. The soft light and heady scent of jasmine make me feel at peace with myself. Walking around, you never know who you might meet. In the 1950s and '60s, it was common to see the likes of Sophia Loren, Clark Gable and Vittorio de Sica on the piazzetta. Funnily enough, I saw de Sica's son Christian on the same square last summer. Days later, I spotted Tom Cruise outside the **Capri Palace**, a popular haunt for visiting stars. Naomi Campbell, another famous guest, is sometimes seen partying at **Musmè** and **Anema e Core**, two of Capri's most exclusive clubs.

Bathing boxes at Marina Piccola (p179), Capri

STEPHEN SAKS

The giant limestone pinnacles of Isole Faraglioni (p175), Capri   STEPHEN SAKS

'Of course, Capri had been courting the rich and famous long before the days of yachts and paparazzi. In the 1st century AD, Emperor Tiberius had 12 luxury villas built for himself here. The best preserved and most visited of them is **Villa Jovis**, although it's possible to visit some of the others with the help of a specialised guide.

'For icons of a different kind, head to the southeast coast, where the giant Faraglioni rocks rise from the water. Sculpted by wind and sea, the furthest of the three is home to the rare and beautiful *lucertola azzurra* (blue-tinted lizard). My favourite time to visit Capri is in the spring and early summer. The weather is warm, bougainvillea carpets the white-washed buildings and the summer crowds are still at bay. But before you pack your bikinis, make sure you watch *L'Imperatore di Capri* (The Emperor of Capri), a hilarious film about Capri starring the legendary comic Totò. It makes an interesting introduction.'

Marina Grande (p178), Capri   JONATHAN SMITH

INTERVIEW 5:
MYTHS & LEGENDS

NAME	Marcello Donnarumma
AGE	24
OCCUPATION	Tourism Researcher
RESIDENCE	Naples

Could the ancient Campi Flegrei be Naples' best-kept secret?

'I wrote my thesis on the **Campi Flegrei** and I'm forever blown away by it. There's something surreal and beautiful about the place, with its volcanic landscape, haunting ruins and ancient myths and legends. It feels like every stone has a tale to tell. In **Cuma**, you can see where Virgil's hero Aeneas sailed ashore and where he spoke with the Sibyl. Close by, **Lago d'Averno** is where Aeneas and later Dante, entered Hades – the underworld. Roman emperors spent their summers in decadent villas on these hills. And yet, the Campi Flegrei remains a little-known destination.

'To start exploring, catch the Cumana train from Montesanto station and get off at Arco Felice. Here you'll find **Monte Nuovo**, Europe's newest mountain. This is my favourite spot. I love the fact that it was formed just over 400-odd years ago. On its slopes, you'll find little holes exhaling volcanic steam. It's an easy climb to the top and the views over the Bay of Pozzuoli are amazing. Best of all, it's free.

Solfatara Crater (p104), Pozzuoli

MARTIN MOOS

Anfiteatro Flavio (p103), Pozzuoli

JEAN-BERNARD CARILLET

'Another little-known wonder is the **Piscina Mirabilis** in Bacoli. It's the largest Roman cistern in the world and one of Italy's most impressive archaeological sites. However, to visit it, you need to find Signora Filomena, an elderly local who lives down the street. She's the site's custodian and has keys to the place. This is wonderful because it feels so secret, like opening the doors to something really mysterious and mythical. While you're here, take a walk through Bacoli itself. It's like a slice of 1950s Italy and is a good place to go for a swim.

'Another great swimming spot is the **Spiaggia del Castello**, which lies right below the Castello di Baia. This tiny beach has a cute little lighthouse, and you can only get there by water taxi. Avoid it on summer weekends though, when half of Naples tries to cram onto it. After a swim, I sometimes walk up to the castle. Here you'll find the **Museo Archeologico dei Campi Flegrei**, which houses the famous ancient Roman Nymphaeum discovered under the sea in Baia.'

DUNCAN GARWOOD

Duncan first visited the Amalfi Coast on a wet weekend in May 1998. Driving a battered Ford Fiesta he crept his way along the coastal road, enjoying the endless grey horizons and praying that his car would make it up the hill to Ravello. Hooked on the area, he returned to research and write for the Lonely Planet *Italy* guide and then,

a couple of years later, to cover Naples for the first edition of this book. He currently lives near Rome but takes every opportunity to pop down the motorway for a blast of Neapolitan energy.

THE PHOTOGRAPHER
GREG ELMS

A contributor to Lonely Planet for more than 15 years, Greg finds shooting for city guides is like travelling with the fast-forward button pressed down. To maintain energy levels and to stay one jump ahead of Naples' manic drivers, he found himself devouring margherita pizzas, linguine alle vongole (linguine with clams) and making regular stops for gelato. The Amalfi Coast was more laid back, though the precipitous cliffs meant keeping one eye on the drop while the other framed a shot. Greg is based in Melbourne, Australia, and freelances for magazines, graphic designers, advertising agencies and book publishers.

CRISTIAN BONETTO

Much to the chagrin of Cristian's northern Italian relatives, his loyalties lie with Naples. Such affection seems only natural for a writer of farce and soap with a penchant for mussels and running red lights. Cristian's first taste of the city came in 1997 as a rookie backpacker. One moped ride along the lungomare (seafront) and he was hooked. In 2003 his play Il Cortile, which is set in Naples, toured Italy, and his musings on the city's bewitching contradictions have appeared in several Australian and UK travel magazines. Currently based in Melbourne, Cristian regularly returns to Naples for a fix of his favourite Neapolitan extreme sport –crossing the street.

v. Monte Rosa - p. ...
v.le della Resistenza - v. Labriola - v. ...
p. Tafuri (M.N.) - v. Dietro la Vigna - v. ...
v. Napoli - v. Vittorio Veneto - v. lanfo...
c. A. di Savoia - v. S.Teresa degli Scalz...
v. S.Teresa degli Scalzi - c. A. di Savoi...
v. Vittorio Veneto - v. Napoli - p. Tafur...
v. Brin - p. Garibaldi - p. Principio Umberto...
p. Cavour - p. Museo - v. S.Teresa degli Sca...
v.le Colli Aminei - v. Pansini - v. Guantai a C...
Eremo Camaldoli - v. L.Bianchi - v. Semmol...
v. Salvator Rosa - p. Dante - p. Carità - via ...
...Municipio - via Medina - c. Un...

GETTING STARTED

Naples and the Amalfi Coast couldn't be more different; the former is a high-octane burst of urban energy, the latter boasts Italy's most spectacular coastline.

The Amalfi Coast is one of the country's top tourist destinations. Most people arrive on the coast via Naples, either by train through Naples' Stazione Centrale or by air through Capodichino airport. Eight kilometres northeast of Naples' city centre, the airport is a 75-minute bus ride from Sorrento, the coast's western gateway. Once on the coast, travelling is relatively simple: there's a cheap, efficient and comprehensive year-round bus service, and between Easter and late September ferries connect the main coastal towns. A car is a mixed blessing, providing both freedom and headaches (think impossible parking) in equal measure.

If you're staying in Naples, there's no great need to book accommodation in advance unless you're arriving in peak season; on the coast, however, it's advisable throughout the year. In summer the area's main towns (Amalfi, Positano, Ravello and Capri) swell with holiday-makers, and in winter many places simply shut up shop.

WHEN TO GO

Naples is a destination for all season, even though some months are more popular (and expensive) than others. May is the busiest time of the year as thousands pour into the city for the annual Maggio dei Monumenti (May of the Monuments) festival. Similarly, the pre-Christmas period and Easter are considered peak season by city hoteliers. The best time to visit is spring (April to mid-June) when temperatures are bearable and the city is still in full swing. Arrive in August and you'll find Naples half-closed and most Neapolitans (along with most Italians) on the coast.

The low season (from April to mid-May and mid-September to October) is a good time for exploring the Amalfi Coast. The weather is usually pretty good, hotel rates are up to one-third cheaper than in high season and there are fewer tourists around. That said, June to September is the best time to catch some of the area's festivals (see p18).

Definitions of high and low season vary between hotels but expect to pay high-season rates at Easter, during summer (which on the coast runs from June to mid-September) and over the Christmas–New Year period. Note also that many coastal and island hotels close over winter, typically from November to March.

COSTS & MONEY

Your budget will almost entirely depend on where you stay. Naples is one of Italy's less-expensive cities, and accommodation (your greatest expense) is widespread and varied; in contrast, the Amalfi Coast is expensive with accommodation geared to a more moneyed market. In Naples, a realistic high-season budget covering accommodation in a comfortable

(Continued on page 20)

17

FEBRUARY

CARNEVALE
The lead up to Ash Wednesday involves a good deal of celebration and revelry: kids dress up in fancy costumes and throw *coriandoli* (coloured confetti) all over each other, and locals enjoy their last opportunity to indulge before Lent.

FESTA DI SANT'ANTONINO
Sorrento
Sorrento celebrates its patron saint on 14 February with musical processions through the centro storico (historic centre) and a huge fireworks display.

MARCH/APRIL

SETTIMANA SANTA
Easter's Holy Week in Naples and the surrounding area is marked by solemn processions and Passion plays. Particularly famous are the processions of Procida and Sorrento.

ADAM EASTLAND / ALAMY

SETTIMANA PER LA CULTURA
www.beneculturali.it
A nationwide initiative to celebrate Italy's national heritage. For the week of its duration, publicly owned galleries and museums are free.

MAY

FESTA DI SAN GENNARO
Duomo, Naples
Thousands gather in the Duomo on the first Sunday of the month to witness the saint's blood liquefy in its phials. This is a miracle said to save the city from potential disasters.

ADAM EASTLAND / ALAMY

MAGGIO DEI MONUMENTI
☎ 081 247 11 23; Naples
The city's premier cultural event offers a month-long programme of exhibitions, concerts, dance performances, guided tours and much more. Many buildings that are otherwise closed throw open their doors to the public.

JUNE

PALIO DELLE QUATTRO ANTICHE REPUBBLICHE MARINARE
Amalfi
The first Sunday of the month brings a procession of boats and a race between the four ancient maritime rivals: Pisa, Venice, Amalfi and Genoa. The event rotates between the four towns and will next be in Amalfi in 2009.

ESTATE A NAPOLI
☎ 081 247 11 23; www.napolioggi.it; Naples
All the city's a stage as music, film and dance take to the streets from June to September.

RAVELLO FESTIVAL
☎ 089 85 83 60; www.ravellofestival.com; Ravello
The Amalfi Coast's top cultural event boasts performances by world-class musicians from June to September in the gardens of Villa Rufolo.

JEAN-BERNARD CARILLET

JULY/AUGUST

FESTA DI SANT'ANNA
Ischia
The feast day of St Anne is marked on 26 July by the allegorical 'burning of the Castello Aragonese', along with a boat procession and fireworks.

FESTIVAL DELLE VILLE VESUVIANE
☎ 081 40 53 93; www.vesuviane.net; Ercolano
Open-air concerts are staged at Villa Campolieto, one of the 18th-century Ville Vesuviane in Ercolano.

MADONNA DEL CARMINE
Piazza del Carmine, Naples
The traditional celebration of the Madonna del Carmine, held in Piazza del Carmine on 16 July, culminates in a spectacular fireworks display.

NEAPOLIS ROCK FESTIVAL
www.neapolis.it; Bagnoli, Naples
Southern Italy's largest rock fest attracts top international acts. It's held west of Naples' city centre, down by the beach at Arenile di Bagnoli.

FERRAGOSTO
The busiest day of the beach year, the Feast of the Assumption is celebrated with concerts and local events on 15 August.

FESTA DI SAN GENNARO
Duomo, Naples
Repeat performance of San Gennaro's powder-to-blood miracle held in May.

LA NOTTE BIANCA
www.nottebiancanapoli.it (in Italian); Naples
A night-long bonanza of mainly free events, including open-air film screenings, concerts, art exhibitions and dance performances. Shops also stay open all night.

PIZZAFEST
☎ 081 420 12 05; www.pizzafest.net; Naples
Homage is paid to the city's most famous export as *pizzaioli* (pizza makers) from all over the country perform in various pizza-based events.

DECEMBER

FESTA DI SAN GENNARO
Duomo, Naples
Third running of the blood miracle of Naples' patron saint on 16 December.

NATALE
Christmas brings church concerts, exhibitions and a shopping frenzy, particularly around the shops selling *presepi* (nativity scenes) in Naples' Via San Gregorio Armeno.

CAPODANNO
Piazza del Plebiscito, Naples
Tens of thousands of Neapolitans pile into Naples' Piazza del Plebiscito for the traditional New Year's concert.

DALLAS STRIBLEY

SEPTEMBER

FESTA DI PIEDIGROTTA
Mergellina, Naples
Dedicated to the Madonna, this once-popular song festival is being revived. Centre of events is the Chiesa di Santa Maria di Piedigrotta in Mergellina from 5 to 12 September.

(Continued from page 17)

midrange hotel, two square meals a day, transport and admission to a museum would total about €115 per day per person. On the Amalfi Coast you'd be looking at €130 plus.

Land transport in the region is inexpensive: a bus ticket from Sorrento to Amalfi, for example, costs €2.40; a train ticket from Naples to Pompeii, €2.30. Car hire starts at about €55 per day, but to this you'll have to add the cost of petrol and parking, which can be very expensive on the Amalfi Coast. The price of ferry tickets depends on whether you take a regular ferry or a hydrofoil: a ferry from Sorrento to Capri costs €7.80, a hydrofoil costs €12.

To save money, look out for museum discounts – admission is often free to EU citizens under 18 and over 65 years, and discounted to those between 18 and 25. On the accommodation front, *agriturismi* (farm stays) are often good value, particularly for families, although without a car they can be difficult to get to.

TRAVEL LITERATURE

Naples and its environs have long fascinated foreign writers. In 1663 the great Spanish poet Cervantes described Naples as the best city in the world, a sentiment that Stendhal echoed 200 years later when he judged it the world's most beautiful. In 1775 the Marquis de Sade claimed, a little unbelievably, to be shocked by the habits of the Neapolitans, while in the mid-19th century Charles Dickens wrote of the theatrical life of the city's squalid streets. More recently, Virginia Woolf and her Bloomsbury set found solace in the rarefied air of Ravello, and Capri gained a reputation as a literary hideaway.

HOW MUCH?

Taxi from Capodichino airport to Stazione Centrale €12.50
1L of petrol €1.30
Mineral water (500ml) €0.50 to €2
Bottle of Peroni beer €1 to €5
Slice of pizza from €1.50
Souvenir T-shirt about €10
Naples bus ticket €1
Entry to Naples' Museo Archeologico Nazionale €6.50
Hydrofoil from Naples to Capri €14
Admission to Pompeii €11

GREG ELMS

Worth a read:

Falling Palace: A Romance of Naples (Dan Hofstadler) Naples' electric streets are brought to life in this evocative and loving portrayal of a city mired in romance and passion.

Capri and No Longer Capri (Raffaele La Capria) Acclaimed Italian author La Capria goes beyond the island's decadent reputation to present his slightly melancholic vision of modern Capri.

Italian Days (Barbara Grizzuti Harrison) With an acute eye and a baroque pen, Harrison travels Italy in search of her southern Italian roots.

The Story of San Michele (Axel Munthe) Swedish doctor and philanthropist Munthe falls in love with Capri, builds a villa in Anacapri and writes a breathless book about it.

Italian Journey 1786–1788 (Johann Wolfgang von Goethe) Naples as seen by the 37-year-old German poet and recorded in this, his classic Italian travelogue.

INTERNET RESOURCES

Campania Trasporti (www.campaniatrasporti.it) A comprehensive transport website with links to bus and ferry companies and a useful route planner (note that you need to insert Napoli not Naples when filling in your departure point or destination).

Capri (www.capri.net) The best of many websites dedicated to Capri, this site has accommodation lists, ferry schedules, suggested itineraries and a whole lot more.

Lonely Planet (www.lonelyplanet.com) Read up on Naples and the Amalfi Coast and speak to travellers who've already been there on the Thorn Tree forum.

Naples (www.inaples.it) The official site of the Naples tourist board with a wealth of information covering the city's major monuments, transport details, upcoming events and historical background.

Pompeii Sites (www.pompeiisites.org) All the latest info on the big archaeological sites – Pompeii, Herculaneum, Oplontis, Boscoreale and Stabiae – from the sites' managing body, the Soprintendenza Archeologica di Pompei.

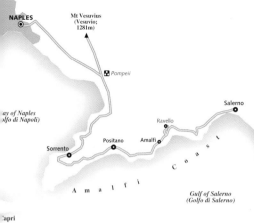

CLASSIC ROUTES
THE COASTAL RUN / TWO WEEKS

It's the compelling mix of chaos, culture and spectacular scenery that makes this whistle-stop coastal run such an eye-opener.

Start out by exploring **Naples** (p63) for a couple of days. Visit the **Museo Archeologico Nazionale** (p80) and wander Spaccanapoli's Dickensian streets; eat pizza in the city that created it and drink some of Italy's best coffee.

When the pace of the city starts to wear you down, jump on a train for **Pompeii** (p160), one of Italy's top tourist attractions. You'll need the best part of a morning to investigate the ancient streets, fossilised by ash from nearby **Mt Vesuvius** (p158). Looming menacingly overhead, the far-from-extinct volcano is now part of a national park crisscrossed with walking trails; the most popular route is to the summit crater.

Continuing round the Bay of Naples, **Sorrento** (p204) retains a genteel charm despite the foreign tourists who crowd the centre in summer. Perhaps it's the stunning views over the water to Mt Vesuvius. Push on from here to **Positano** (p221), the Amalfi Coast's westernmost town and a stunning picture of a place. Colourful houses cascade down the mountainside to two small beaches. The awe-inspiring coastal road ribbons its way along the dramatic coast to **Amalfi** (p230), the once proud capital of a powerful maritime republic. Once you've strolled the historic streets and perused the gaudy shops, take a trip up to **Ravello** (p237), the coast's aloof aristocrat. Famous for its villa gardens, it commands the coast's finest views. Last stop is **Salerno** (p244), a busy port city with an appealing medieval core.

> Two weeks might seem a long time to cover 110km, but few areas reward slow travel more than the coastline between Naples and Salerno. On the way you'll encounter an ancient ghost city and the volcano that reduced it to ruins, classical Mediterranean seascapes and views that will melt the heart of the most jaded traveller.

HOLLYWOOD ON THE MED / ONE WEEK

One of the few places that looks as good in real life as it does on celluloid, the Amalfi Coast is the ideal place for jetting from one film-set location to the next.

In 1953 John Huston and an unruly cast of Hollywood divas took over much of **Ravello** (p237) and **Atrani** (p230) for the crime caper *Beat The Devil*. Just down the road, **Amalfi** (p230) provides the backdrop to Mike Barker's 2004 light-hearted comedy *A Good Woman,* featuring Scarlett Johansson. Continuing west, **Positano** (p221) was an unlikely location for filming on the 2003 *Under the Tuscan Sun,* a classic do-up-a-Tuscan-villa flick. More action than art, Paul Greengrass' high-octane 2004 thriller, the *Bourne Supremacy,* stars Matt Damon as a CIA agent following leads through Berlin, Moscow and **Naples** (p63). Damon also stars in *The Talented Mr Ripley,* the 1999 film for which the Italian Tourist Board should be forever grateful. The list of locations for this film includes Naples' Teatro San Carlo, Ischia Ponte on **Ischia** (p188) and Marina Grande on **Procida** (p200). Still on Procida, Marina Corricella and Pozzo Vecchio beach were used for several scenes in Michael Radford's acclaimed 1994 hit, *Il Postino* (The Postman).

> 'Set jet' your way up the coast and discover just what it is that makes the area such a hit with international directors. This 120km route leads from Gore Vidal's former home town, Ravello, down the Amalfi Coast, up to Naples and its bay islands, before finishing at Caserta's monumental royal palace.

Back on shore, *Star Wars* fans will not want to miss the massive Palazzo Reale (known in Italy as the Reggia) in **Caserta** (p101) used by George Lucas for interior shots of Queen Amidala's residence in both *Star Wars Episode 1: The Phantom Menace* (1999) and *Star Wars Episode 2: Attack of the Clones* (2002).

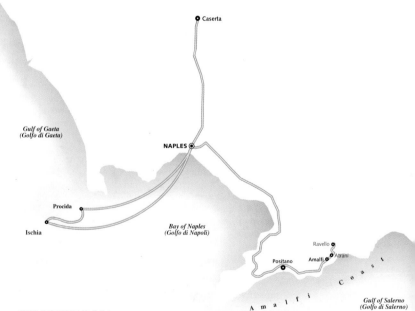

ISLAND HOP THE BAY / ONE WEEK

Capri, the most famous of Naples' three bay islands, has long exerted a powerful hold on the public imagination. But be sure to also explore Ischia and Procida; you'll be rewarded with stunning gardens, tumbledown fishing villages, beaches and castles.

From **Sorrento** (p204) jump on a ferry to glamorous **Capri** (p172), the day trip capital of the Med. Once you've explored diminutive **Capri Town** (p174) and visited the spellbinding **Grotta Azzurra** (p178), walk up to **Villa Jovis** (p176), the remains of Tiberius' main island residence. In **Anacapri** (p177) check out Axel Munthe's **Villa San Michele** (p177) and hitch a chair lift to the top of **Monte Solaro** (p177).

To the northwest, **Ischia** (p188) is an easy ferry crossing away. Best known for its thermal waters, the island boasts fine beaches and some spectacular scenery. In-

> From Capri's fabled caves and swish designer hang outs to Ischia's gardens and Procida's picturesque land-scapes, this 42km route could be done in three or four days. But give yourself a week, overnighting on each island, and you'll find yourself slowly relaxing into the pace of local life.

vestigate the landmark **Castello Aragonese** (p192) before heading over to Forio on the western coast. Here the gardens of **La Mortella** (p194) are considered among Italy's finest, with more than 1000 rare and exotic plants. For a dip in the sea, the **Spiaggia dei Maronti** (p194) near Barano is a scenic spot.

Procida (p200) is the least developed and smallest of the islands. Tourism has arrived but Procida's pastel-coloured villages and quintessential 'islandscape' retain an authenticity that is not always apparent elsewhere. Visit the **Abbazia di San Michele Arcangelo** (p201) and let the **Castello d'Avalos** prison (p201) give you the chills. Best of all, just hang out, potter around the pretty marinas, eat great seafood, or perhaps hire a boat for a day of leisurely beach-hopping.

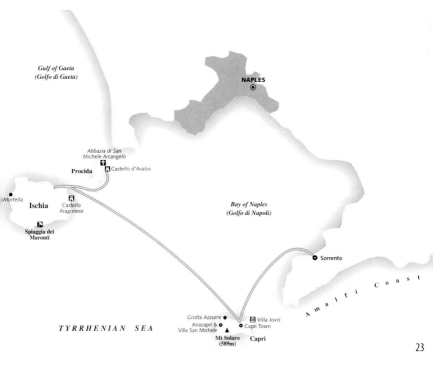

TAILORED TRIPS
THE ANCIENT COAST

Boasting some of Italy's finest archaeological sites, the coast southeast of Naples is rich in ancient Roman history. To get the best out of it, though, you'll need to ignore the urban sprawl that surrounds so many of the ruins.

To put yourself in the mood, start in **Naples** at the **Museo Archeologico Nazionale** (p80). Feast your eyes on mosaics stripped from Pompeii and check out the model of the doomed city.

Once your appetite has been suitably whetted, take the Circumvesuviana train to Ercolano Scavi, the stop for **Herculaneum** (p165). Much smaller than Pompeii, Herculaneum's well-preserved ruins cover an area of about 4.5 hectares and can easily be visited in a couple of hours. Next stop is Torre Annunziata where the centrepiece of the **Oplontis** (p157) site is Villa Poppaea, holiday home of Nero's second wife. Just down the road, **Pompeii** (p160) needs no introduction. The highlight of any archaeological trip, it provides fascinating insight into everyday ancient Roman life. Further south, the two villas at Castellammare di

Stabia are the only visible remains of ancient **Stabiae** (p157). Continuing down the coast and you'll eventually come to **Paestum** (p168) and its remarkable Greek temples. Forty-four kilometres away at Ascea (Velia) are the ruins of the ancient Greek settlement of **Elea** (p248).

SOUTHERN TASTES

As any Neapolitan will tell you, the pizza in **Naples** (p115) is the best in the world. The classic is the tomato, mozzarella and basil margherita. Other city treats include *babà*, a rum-sodden sponge cake, and coffee, served in short, deadly measures. Offshore, **Capri** (p172) lays claim to the ubiquitous lemon liqueur, *limoncello,* as well as the salad of tomato and mozzarella, *insalata caprese*. A short sail away, **Sorrento** (p204) is famous for *gnocchi alla sorrentina* (gnocchi baked in tomato sauce with mozzarella) and *limoncello*. Nearby, in **Vico Equense** (p215), you can order pizza by the metre at the restaurant where it was created, Pizzeria da Gigino.

It was in a convent in **Conca dei Marini** (p229) that *sfogliatella* (cinnamon-infused ricotta in a puff-pastry shell) was invented in the 18th century, and in a monastery above **Maiori** (p241) that *melanzane al cioc-colato* (chocolate aubergines) were con-ceived. Further east, **Cetara** (p242) is an important fishing centre, celebrated for its tuna and *colatura di alici* (anchovy seasoning). Pick some up at Sapori Cetaresi by the beach. For buffalo mozzarella you have two choices: either head up to **Caserta** (p101) or push south to **Paestum** (p168), where you can see it made at the Fattoria del Casaro buffalo farm.

HISTORY

Mosaic detail from Pompeii, displayed in the Museo Archeologico Nazionale (p80)

NEAPOLIS

Founded by Greek colonists, Naples was later adopted by swinging Roman holiday-makers in search of sun, sea and sin.

Little is known of Naples' early days. According to legend, Greek traders, possibly from Rhodes, established the city in about 680 BC on the island of Megaris, where today the Castel dell'Ovo stands (p83). Originally called Parthenope in honour of the siren whose body had earlier washed up there (she drowned herself after failing to seduce Ulysses), the city gradually spread to encompass Monte Echia on the mainland.

The Greeks' main Italian foothold, however, was 10km up the coast at Cuma, then known as Cumae. Founded in the 8th century BC, Cuma became the most important city in the southwest over the next 200 years: a rich commercial centre whose legendary Sibyl was said to be the mouthpiece of Apollo. In military terms, it was the key to the area, as the watching Etruscans understood only too well. Looking to expand southward from their Tuscan homeland, the Etruscans twice invaded and were twice repelled. After the second of these clashes, in 474 BC, the Cumaeans founded Neapolis (New Town, to distinguish it from Paleopolis, Old Town, the name by which Parthenope was then known) on the land that is now Naples' centro storico (historic centre).

The Etruscan battles had taken a toll, however, and in 421 BC the exhausted Greeks fell to the Samnites. They, in turn, proved no match for the Romans who took Neapolis in 326 BC.

ROMAN TIMES

Under the Romans, Neapolis and its environs bloomed into a successful Roman resort. Nero's second wife Poppea holidayed in Oplontis (p157) and Julius Caesar's father-in-law kept a home at Herculaneum. Neapolis' citizens, however, never completely gave in to their foreign occupiers. They refused, for example, to relinquish their language, traces of which remain in Neapolitan dialect. Then, during the Roman Civil War (88–82 BC), they opposed Rome, invoking the wrath of Cornelius Sulla who promptly took the city and slaughtered thousands of its citizens. In 73 BC slave leader Spartacus based his rebel army on the slopes of Mt Vesuvius.

GREG ELMS

Naples' fabled volcano Vesuvius exploded onto the stage in AD 79, drowning Pompeii and Herculaneum in a mix of molten lava, mud and ash. Coming just 17 years after a massive earthquake, it was a devastating blow for the rural area outside Neapolis, an area already in decline due to the effects of the earthquake and the import of cheap food from Rome's overseas colonies. Within the city walls, Neapolis was booming: General Lucullus built a massive villa on the spot where the Castel dell'Ovo now stands, and Virgil moved to the town for a period. Offshore, Capri became the centre of Emperor Tiberius' famously debauched operations.

The welfare of Neapolis was by then tied to that of the Roman Empire. When the last Roman emperor, Romulus Augustus, died in 476, the city passed into barbarian hands.

WHY BITE THE CARROT WHEN YOU'VE GOT THE GRAPES

Battered by a storm of volcanic debris and blasted by a white-hot wind, Pompeii's ancient victims didn't know what had hit them. Very few Romans knew that Vesuvius was volcanic, and those that did thought it was extinct. No-one today thinks Mt Vesuvius is extinct. Vulcanologists don't know when it'll go but they're pretty sure that one day it will, and when it does it could be devastating — some 600,000 people live within 7km of the crater.

In an attempt to clear Vesuvius' lower slopes, the Campania region launched Progetto Vesuvia in September 2003, a project offering a €30,000 carrot to anyone prepared to relocate.

Few residents, however, have taken up their offer. Their reasons range from the emotional ('this is my home and I'm not moving') to the financial (€30,000 will only buy about a quarter of a new two-bedroom flat in the outer suburbs of Naples) and the agricultural (the area's rich volcanic soil produces the region's best grapes and Italy's finest tomatoes).

JON DAVISON

KINGDOM OF THE TWO SICILIES

Art, culture and architecture thrive against a backdrop of invasion, rebellion, and occupation.

By the beginning of the 11th century, Naples was a prospering duchy. Industry and culture were thriving and Christianity had caught on in a big way. Outside the city walls, however, the situation was more volatile as the Normans began to eye up the Lombard principalities of Salerno, Benevento, Capua and Amalfi.

The Normans had arrived in southern Italy in the 10th century, initially as pilgrims en route from Jerusalem, later as mercenaries attracted by the money to be made fighting for the rival principalities and against the Arab Muslims in Sicily. And it was to just one such mercenary, Rainulfo Drengot, that the duke of Naples, Sergio IV, gave the contract to drive the Lombards out of Capua. Capua duly fell in 1062, followed by Amalfi in 1073 and Salerno four years later. By 1130 most of southern Italy, including Sicily, was in Norman hands and it was only a question of time before Naples gave in to the inevitable. It did so in 1139. The Kingdom of the Two Sicilies was thus complete.

The Normans maintained their capital in Sicily, and Palermo began to outshine Naples. Surprisingly, the Neapolitans seemed happy with their lot, and when the last of the Norman kings, Tancred, was succeeded by his enemy Henry Hohenstaufen of Swabia in 1194, the mood turned ugly. The Neapolitans despised their new Swabian rulers and were delighted when Charles I of Anjou routed them at the battle of Benevento in February 1265.

The French Angevins were determined to make Naples a sparkling artistic and intellectual centre. Charles built the Castel Nuovo (p83) in 1279, the port was enlarged, and in the early 14th century the third Angevin king, Robert of Anjou, constructed Castel Sant'Elmo (p91).

The last century of Angevin rule was marked by complex and often bloody politicking between family factions. Queen Joan I was suspected of murdering her husband and fled the city between 1348 and 1352, leaving her vengeful Hungarian in-laws to occupy Naples. Some 70-odd years later her namesake, Queen Joan II, could only stop her husband stealing the crown thanks to substantial popular support.

The time was ripe for the Spanish Aragonese to launch their attack.

top five
HISTORY READS

In the Shadow of Vesuvius:
A Cultural History of Naples
Jordan Lancaster (2005)
....
The Gallery
John Horne Burns (2004)
....
Naples '44:
An Intelligence Officer in the Italian Labyrinth
Norman Lewis (2002)
....
See Naples and Die:
The Camorra and Organised Crime
Tom Behan (2002)
....
The Bourbons of Naples
Harold Acton (1956)

THE ARAGONESE

After vicious fighting, Alfonso of Aragon took control of Naples in 1442. Known as *Il Magnanimo* (The Magnanimous), he did a lot for Naples, promoting art and science and introducing institutional reforms. But for all that, he could never live down the fact that he'd overthrown the popular Angevins.

In 1485 the city's barons took up arms against Alfonso's successor, Ferdinand I. Within a year, however, the ringleaders had been executed (in the Sala dei Baroni in Castel Nuovo) and peace restored. Peace didn't last long, and in 1495 King Charles VIII of France invaded. Supported by a small group of barons but fiercely opposed by the population, the French monarch occupied the city for four months. When he was forced out, the Neapolitans replaced him with the Aragonese Ferdinand II.

After Ferdinand II's death in 1496, the mutinous barons once again flexed their muscles, this time by crowning Ferdinand's uncle, Frederick, as king. This angered everyone: the Neapolitans, the French and the Spanish had all wanted Ferdinand II's widow Joan to succeed him. The upshot was the joint Franco–Spanish invasion of 1501. Frederick tried to hang on to power, but facing almost total opposition he skulked off, leaving Naples to the Spanish. Thus King Ferdinand of Spain became King Ferdinand III of Naples.

DON PEDRO & THE VICEROYS

Colonial wealth and construction define the character and cityscape of 16th- and 17th-century Naples.

As part of the Spanish empire, Naples prospered in the 16th century. Spain, wealthy on the back of its silver-rich American colonies, was enjoying a period of hitherto-unseen prosperity; confidence was running high throughout the empire. In Naples, the unruly barons were brought into line, order was imposed and the population continued to grow. In fact, by 1600 Naples was the biggest city in Europe with a population of 300,000. To house the ever-increasing masses, expansion became a priority.

To deal with the situation, viceroy Don Pedro de Toledo took drastic measures, moving the city walls westward and building an entire new quarter, the Quartieri Spagnoli. Yet housing was not enough; the new Neapolitans had spiritual needs to satisfy. Hundreds of new churches and monasteries sprung up, many of them designed by the city's new wave of architects and artists.

The most prolific of all Naples' architects was Cosimo Fanzago (1591–1678), whose Guglia di San Gennaro (p72) and Certosa di San Martino (p91) are considered high points of Neapolitan baroque. Painters were also having a rich time of it. Caravaggio arrived in town in 1606, and Giuseppe de Ribera, Massimo Stanzione, Luca Giordano and Francesco Solimena all made their names.

But the good times weren't to last, and in the early 17th-century economic depression descended, forcing Naples' viceroys to impose ever-increasing tax hikes. And it was this that drove the Neapolitans to rebellion.

Don Pedro de Toledo Kissing the Sword of Henry IV by Jean Auguste Dominique Ingres (1819) ©PRIVATE COLLECTION / THE BRIDGEMAN ART LIBRARY

THE MASANIELLO REVOLT

Already crippled by the sheer weight of taxes, the Neapolitans were becoming increasingly mutinous when the Spanish introduced a levy on fresh fruit in January 1647. It was one tax too many and on 7 July violence broke out on Piazza del Mercato (p76).

Led by an illiterate fisherman from Amalfi, Tommaso Aniello, aka Masaniello, the rebellion snowballed rapidly and grew out of control. On 16 July Masaniello was murdered in the Chiesa di Santa Maria del Carmine (p76) by extremists from within his own camp: they wanted to drive the Spanish out of Naples, he simply wanted an end to the fruit tax. The French then tried to cash in by sending the duke of Giusa to take the city; the duke failed, and on 6 April 1648 was captured by the new Spanish viceroy, the Count of Oñate. Order was soon reestablished, the rebel leaders were executed and life in Naples returned to a semblance of normality.

Naples' 17th-century woes were not all manmade. Nature played her hand to the full, striking three times in the space of 60 years.

The first of the triple whammy was the eruption of Mt Vesuvius in 1631. After almost 500 years of inactivity, it blew its top on the morning of 16 December, spewing out a molten mass of ash, gas and stone. The deadly torrent destroyed everything in its path, killing some 3500 people.

This death toll paled in comparison with that of the devastating plague epidemic that hit Naples and Campania in 1656. In a six-month period, up to three-quarters of Naples' population was killed and any hopes of economic recovery were buried with the dead. The horror that infected the city's squalid streets is graphically depicted in the paintings that hang in Room 37 of the Certosa di San Martino (p91).

The *coup de grâce* arrived 32 years later in the form of an earthquake. Although Naples was some distance from the epicentre in Benevento, the shock waves were clearly felt and the damage to the city was considerable.

THE BOURBONS

As revolution rocks France, Naples sparkles as Italy's Bourbon capital.

In little more than 100 years, the Bourbons transformed Naples into Europe's glitziest city. Between the accession of Charles VII to the Neapolitan throne in 1734 and Italian unification in 1860, Palazzo Reale di Capodimonte (p93) was built and Palazzo Reale (p85) enlarged, Teatro San Carlo (p87) became Europe's grandest opera house and Via Toledo its most sought-after address. Naples had never had it so good.

From all accounts Charles was not a particularly brilliant man. Neither a general – he apparently hated wearing a uniform – nor a great politician, he was nevertheless dutiful and felt honour-bound to do his best by Naples. Ruling through a Council of State, he ushered in the brightest of Naples' golden eras.

THE PARTHENOPEAN REPUBLIC

Naples' great republican experiment was a bloody and short-lived affair, sparked by events in faraway Paris.

As a monarchy, the Neapolitan court was hardly delighted to hear news of the 1789 French Revolution. However, it wasn't until word filtered down that Marie Antoinette, the sister of King Ferdinand's wife, Maria Carolina, had been guillotined that Naples joined the anti-French coalition.

Troops from Naples and revolutionary France eventually clashed in French-occupied Rome in 1798. The Neapolitans claimed the city but within 11 days were scurrying back south with the French in hot pursuit. In desperation King Ferdinand IV and Maria Carolina hotfooted it over to Palermo, leaving Naples to its own devices.

Bitterly opposed by most of the population, the French were welcomed by the Neapolitan nobility and bourgeoisie, many of whom had adopted fashionable republican ideas. And it was with the full backing of the French that the Parthenopean Republic was declared on 23 January 1799.

But it wasn't a success. The leaders were an ideologically rather than practically minded lot, and were soon in financial straits. Their efforts to democratise the city failed and the army was a shambles.

Over the water, the exiles in Palermo had not been sitting idle. Ferdinand and Maria Carolina dispatched Cardinal Fabrizio Ruffo to Calabria to organise an uprising. On 13 June he entered Naples and all hell broke loose as his men turned the city into

THE ODD COUPLE

They were a decidedly strange couple – he was an undereducated slob, and she was his beautiful and clever queen. He was Ferdinand IV, son of Charles VII and the Bourbon king of Naples; she was his Austrian wife, Maria Carolina.

One of 16 children of the Hapsburg empress of Austria, the 16-year-old Maria arrived in Naples in 1768 to marry Ferdinand. She was beautiful, calculating and ruthless, an unlikely partner for the famously uncouth dialect-speaking Ferdinand. She also had a serious political agenda (she wanted to distance Naples from Spain and forge closer links with Austria and Britain) unlike her husband who was happy to leave politics to her and her henchmen.

The first person to fall victim to Maria Carolina's ambition was Bernardo Tanucci, the man who had effectively been running Naples since 1759 when Ferdinand's father had left to take up the Spanish throne, leaving Naples to his eight year old son and trusted prime minister Tanucci.

An honest man, Tanucci ruled efficiently, abolishing feudal privileges, reducing tax revenue to the Church and steadfastly denying an education to Ferdinand. However, there wasn't much he could do to prevent Maria Carolina exercising her brain, which the young Austrian did with cut-throat precision.

In accordance with her marriage agreement, Maria Carolina joined Naples ruling Council of State on the birth of her first son in 1777. It was the position she'd been waiting for to oust Tanucci, which she promptly did, replacing him with a French-born English aristocrat, John Acton.

Acton quickly realised where the real power in Naples lay and wasted no time in ingratiating himself with Maria. He managed to win her over completely with his anti-Bourbon politics and authoritarian style, becoming her prime minister and, according to some, her lover. Under Acton, Naples joined the anti-French coalition, forcing Ferdinand and Maria Carolina to twice flee to Sicily to avoid French revolutionary forces.

It was in 1806, on the second of these self-imposed Sicilian exiles, that Maria Carolina met her nemesis, Lord William Bentinck, the British ambassador to Sicily and de facto ruler of the island. By now Maria Carolina's star was on the wane and, with Ferdinand little more than a bewildered spectator, Bentinck had her exiled to Austria in 1811. She died three years later in 1814. Ferdinand returned to Naples in 1816, reigning as King Ferdinand I of the Two Sicilies until his death in 1825.

a slaughterhouse. On 8 July Ferdinand and Maria Carolina returned from Sicily and embarked on a systematic extermination of republican sympathisers. More than 200 were summarily executed.

THE FRENCH DECADE

The failure of the Parthenopean Republic did not, however, signal the end of French interest in Naples. In 1806 French forces once again entered the city, forcing the royal family to flee to Sicily for a second time and in 1808 Joachim Murat, Napoleon's brother-in-law, was appointed king of Naples. From the Palazzo Reale di Capodimonte (p93), Murat launched a series of what should have been popular measures: he abolished feudalism and initiated a series of land redistribution programmes; he brought in foreign investment and kick-started local industry. And yet still he was hated. As a Frenchman and a revolutionary he could do no right in the eyes of the royalist masses, who were thrilled when he was finally ousted in 1815 and Ferdinand returned to claim his throne.

top five
HISTORICAL WORKS OF ART

Dionysiac Frieze (Anon.)
Villa dei Misteri, Pompeii (p164)

Tavola Strozzi (Anon.)
Certosa di San Martino (p91)

La Rivolta di Masaniello del 1647
(The 1647 Masaniello Revolt; Micco Spadaro)
Certosa di San Martino (p91)

Eruzione del Vesuvio dal Ponte Maddalena
(Eruption of Vesuvius from the Bridge of Maddalena; Pierre Jacques Volaire)
Palazzo Reale di Capodimonte (p93)

Ritratto di Maria Carolina di Borbone
(Portrait of Maria Carolina of Bourbon; Anon.)
Certosa di San Martino (p91)

Wartime Naples bombarded and in ruins, October 1943

WAR & PEACE

WWII vents its full force on Naples; the city is bombed to near destruction and the way is paved for organised crime.

Naples' postunification history makes for grim reading. Poverty forced hundreds of thousands to emigrate, and in 1884 a huge cholera epidemic swept through the city's overcrowded slums. In response to the epidemic, the municipal authorities launched a huge citywide cleanup. The worst slums near the port were destroyed, Corso Umberto I was bulldozed through the city centre, and developers constructed a sparkling new residential quarter on the Vomero.

The city's regeneration continued under Fascist rule. An airport was built in 1936, railway and metro lines were laid and the Vomero funicular was completed. The

GARIBALDI & HIS RED SHIRTS

A natural-born nationalist, Giuseppe Garibaldi was instrumental in the unification of Italy and the demise of Bourbon rule in Naples.

Buoyed by victory over Austrian troops in Piedmont, Garibaldi and his volunteer army of 1000 Red Shirts set sail for Sicily in May 1860. Waiting to oppose the nationalists was the 25,000-strong Neapolitan army. But despite their vastly superior numbers the Bourbon forces fought half-heartedly – morale was low due to the monarchy's consistent refusal to surrender any of its despotic powers to the Neapolitan parliament (constitutions had been granted in 1820 and 1848 but neither had lasted more than a year) – and Garibaldi prevailed.

Watching from over the water in Naples, King Francesco II hastily tried to appease his increasingly truculent population by agreeing to resurrect the 1848 constitution. But it was too little too late. Garibaldi had already crossed over to the Italian mainland and was marching relentlessly towards Naples. True to the family spirit, Francesco fled the city, taking refuge with 4000 loyalists behind the River Volturno, about 30km north of Naples. On 7 September Garibaldi marched unopposed into Naples, and was welcomed as a hero.

But it wasn't quite over for Francesco. More in hope than anything else, the Bourbon loyalists launched a series of last-ditch attacks on the rebel army, only to be defeated at the Battle of Volturno over the first two days of October. Naples was now well and truly in Garibaldi's hands, and on 21 October the city voted overwhelmingly to join a united Italy under the Savoy monarchy.

Mostra d'Oltremare exhibition space was inaugurated in 1937 by Mussolini to celebrate Italy's great colonial victories. But no sooner had many of these buildings gone up than they were hit by the full force of WWII.

Its importance as a port meant Naples suffered horrendously during the war. Heavy aerial bombing by the Allies left more than 20,000 people dead and destroyed large amounts of the city centre.

Events came to a head in 1943. Bombardments were at their worst in preparation for the Allied invasion and the Germans had taken the city. The Nazis didn't last long, though, being forced out by a series of popular uprisings between 26 and 30 September; these were led by local residents in particular by young *scugnizzi* (a Neapolitan word for the young boys who used to hang out on the city streets) and ex-soldiers. Known as the Quattro Giornate di Napoli (Four Days of Naples), the street battles paved the way for Allied troops to enter the city on 1 October.

Greeted as liberators, the Allies set up their provisional government in Naples. By this stage the city had become an anarchic mass of humanity, with Allied troops, German prisoners of war and bands of Italian fascists all competing with the city's starving population for food. Then in 1944, when it looked like it couldn't get any worse, Mt Vesuvius erupted.

Faced with such circumstances the Allied authorities turned to the underworld for assistance. In return for the Allies turning a blind eye towards their black market activities, criminal organisations such as the Camorra were willing to help and began to flourish.

American troops in Naples during WWII

MODERN TIMES

Described as the Città Perduta (Lost City), Naples is still struggling to contain its feuding criminal families.

Dubbed the Neapolitan Renaissance, the rebirth of Naples over the past 15 years has been little short of spectacular. Under the charismatic mayor Antonio Bassolino, the city shed its fearsome reputation and bloomed into a gleaming model of urban regeneration.

But what is now history must have looked almost impossible when Bassolino took the reins of civic power in 1993. Naples was in a mess. The Camorra was in rude health, its bosses publicly partying with the city's iconic football star Diego Armando Maradona, *abusivismo* (illegal construction) was flourishing and public services had virtually ceased to exist. The grim situation was not unique to Naples – corruption and cronyism were rife across the country.

By the early 1990s the time was ripe for change, and in 1992 the nationwide Mani Pulite (Clean Hands) anticorruption crusade kicked into gear. Naples voted its approval by electing Bassolino whose promises to smarten up the city and fight corruption were exactly what the weary Neapolitans wanted to hear.

In the seven years that followed, Naples began to clean up its act. After being used as a huge car park for years, Piazza del Plebiscito (p86) was pedestrianised; a new arts festival, the Maggio dei Monumenti, was inaugurated; and Naples' new metro stations were treated to a dash of modern art. In 1994 world leaders met in Naples for the G7 summit.

After winning a second term in 1997, Bassolino couldn't keep up the momentum he'd created, and the pace of change began to slow. In 2000 he was elected president of the Campania region, a move that many people considered a political fudge to remove him from the day-to-day running of the city.

Into his shoes stepped Rosa Russo Jervolino, a former interior minister and Naples' first female mayor. Elected on a centre-left ticket firstly in 2001, and then for a second term in May 2006, she hasn't had an easy time of it. In April 2002 political chaos ensued after eight policemen were arrested on charges of torturing antiglobalisation protestors arrested at a 2001 government conference. In 2003 Naples' street corners were submerged in rubbish as authorities struggled to sort out the city's refuse contracts. Three years later and it was the same story all over again as a strike in July 2006 left many suburbs mired in rotting refuse.

Worst of all, however, was the return of the Camorra to the limelight. In late 2004 and early 2005 a bloody turf battle erupted on the streets of Scampia and Secondigliano, two tough suburbs in the north of the city. In just four months, up to 47 people were gunned down as rival clans fought for control of the city's lucrative drugs trade.

A year on in 2006 Italian journalists continued to highlight the city's crime profile. In September the leading news weekly *L'Espresso* ran a major article on Naples under the headline *Città Perduta*, which described life among the city's gangs of thieves. Whether the return of organised crime is a momentary hiccup in the city's roller-coaster history, or heralds a descent into the bad old days, remains to be seen.

WORD ON THE STREETS

- 'We pay €250 a year in rubbish tax and still they don't do a bloody thing.' (Rubbish strikes continue to plague the city.)
- 'They say the metro will be finished by 2008. They're having a laugh.' (Few Neapolitans believe the revised opening date for the metro.)
- 'Yeah, well, she's not doing a bad job, all things considered.' (Jervolino is reelected mayor in May 2006).
- 'Next year Serie A, the year after that the Champions League.' (Napoli football team hovers midtable in Serie B after winning promotion from the third division.)
- 'It never used to be so muggy in summer.' (Neapolitans love to grumble that the weather is worse than it was.)

CULTURE

INCO
Barbiere

SOUTHERN SAVVY

Consummate performers and as *furbo* (cunning) as they come, Neapolitans are justifiably famous for their ingenuity.

Only in Naples will you hear of street entrepreneurs selling secondhand newspapers to lovers so that they can cover their car windows. Or of vendors flogging T-shirts printed with a diagonal seat-belt design so as to fool short-sighted traffic cops. Even the authorities have the knack for invention: in 2006 they launched Operation Bandit Mockery, which involved handing out plastic watches to tourists in order to trick Rolex-hungry thieves. This is a city where the black market thrives and counterfeit goods line the streets.

THE CAMORRA

Fans of the Fascist dictator Benito Mussolini still talk about one of his great successes – the eradication of the Mafia and its local incarnation the Camorra. But although the great criminal organisations of the south had a tough time of it under the Fascist regime, they weren't quite destroyed for good. Down but not out, they were quick to grasp the window of opportunity that WWII provided. Following the 1943 Allied invasion, the British and American command turned to the flourishing underworld as the best way to get things done. The black market thrived and slowly the Camorra began to spread its roots again. Postwar reconstruction provided plenty of business, as the need for cheap housing ran roughshod over such niceties as gaining planning permission and obeying the law.

The earthquake of 23 November 1980, which killed more than 2700 people in the region, signalled the start of a boom period. By now skilled in the art of siphoning off government and European grants, the Camorra made a lot of money – and they flaunted it. Bosses Carmine and Luigi Giuliano, for example, became famous for their lavish parties.

Nowadays, the bosses prefer to keep a lower profile but the coffers continue to swell. To their core activities of racketeering, drug smuggling and controlling the city's fruit-and-veg markets, the families have added the lucrative businesses of counterfeiting (CDs, designer clothes etc) and waste disposal. Occasionally, tension between rival clans explodes in bloody displays of vengeance. In 2005, the notorious districts of Secondigliano and Scampia witnessed the murder of 47 gang members and their families over a period of three months. Experts estimate that the drug trade they were fighting over is worth €500,000 a day.

DALLAS STRIBLEY

top five
DOS & DON'TS

- Make an effort with the local lingo. Even the worst broken Italian will win you a few local fans.

- Cover up when visiting churches and religious sites. Singlet tops and shorts are forbidden.

- Never touch window displays. They're a source of pride for shopkeepers and not to be ruined by your dirty mitts!

- Steer clear of chrysanthemums when buying flowers for a local. In Italy they're only used to decorate graves.

- Focus on the city's positives, not its negatives. Although Neapolitans are the first to criticise their city's shortcomings, criticism from outsiders can cause offence.

- Don't tell a Neapolitan you're a fan of the Lega Nord (Northern League), a northern Italian separatist party much loathed in the south.

Tough times have forced Neapolitans to become who they are today. For much of its history the city was fought over, occupied and invaded by foreign powers whose interests were purely selfish. The lot of the city's population was irrelevant as long as they paid their taxes. Consequently the Neapolitans learned early to fend for themselves and to get by on what they had. The art of *arrangiarsi* (getting by) is not a uniquely Neapolitan skill, but it's one at which the city's residents excel. Despite a per-capita income of around €14,500, well below the Italian average of €22,000, Neapolitans still manage to shop hard, play harder and enjoy *la dolce vita* (the sweet life).

Neapolitans know that many of the stereotypes foreigners hold of Italians – noisy, theatrical, food-loving, passionate and proud – refer to them. And they revel in it. Nowhere else in Italy are the people so conscious of their role in the theatre of everyday life and so addicted to its drama and intensity. Everyone has an opinion to give, a line to deliver or a sigh to perform. Eavesdropping is a popular pastime and knowing everyone else's business is a source of pride. Neapolitans joke that if you were to collapse on the street a local would first want to know exactly what happened, and only after that would they think of calling an ambulance. In a city with a population density of 2613 people per sq km (nearly 14 times higher than the national average), this penchant for curiosity makes sense. For the most part, life is lived on the street and privacy is a luxury many can't afford.

In addition to these dramatics and passion for life is a strong distrust of authority. The state has done little for Neapolitans and Neapolitans feel justified in doing nothing in return. Tax evasion is widespread and *abusivismo* (illegal building) rampant. And where the state hasn't provided, the Camorra (see opposite) has stepped in. Organised crime is a fact of life in Naples. It's something that lurks behind the scenes, emerging occasionally as gangs violently settle their accounts, but otherwise silently getting on with its business of making money. While resenting this element of life, most Neapolitans accept it as they've accepted many of their past ills – with a resigned shrug and a melancholy nod of the head. Life goes on.

DALLAS STRIBLEY

SAINTS & SUPERSTITIONS

Superhero saints and cursing evil eyes – the Catholic and the cultish walk hand in hand.

In Naples, saints are celestial celebrities. Fireworks explode in their honour, fans flock to kiss their marble feet and newborn *bambini* (children) take on their saintly names. Neapolitans often celebrate their *giorno omastico* (name day) with as much gusto as they do their own birthdays. In fact, forgetting a friend's name day is considered a bigger faux pas than forgetting their birthday because everyone knows (or should know) the most important saints days.

For the city's religiously inclined, saints play a more important role in their spiritual life than God. While the Almighty is seen as stern and distant – the typical old-school Italian father – saints take on a more familial role, that of intercessor and confidant. This preference is not supported by everyone in the Church: a sign inside the Santissima Annunziata (p77) austerely asks visitors to pay homage to Christ at the altar before sidling off to the saints' side-chapels. Despite the request, the faithful keep marching straight to the saints.

Different saints have different specialisations. Infertile couples head to the former apartment of Santa Maria Francesca at Vico Tre Re a Toledo 13 in the Quartieri Spagnoli. Here, they sit on a holy chair once belonging to the stigmatic and ask for her intercession in their having a child. In the Chiesa del Gesù Nuovo (p69), entire rooms are dedicated to Dr Giuseppe Moscati, a much-loved local medic canonised in 1987. Covering the walls are miniature silver body parts representing the miracle cures put down to the good doctor's advocacy.

Not all petitions to one's haloed chums are of a grave or spiritual nature, either. It's not unusual to hear insouciant requests for a lucky lottery ticket or help with scoring a date.

That Gennaro is the most common boy's name in the city is no surprise; San Gennaro is Naples' patron saint and without doubt the city's heavenly hero. Every year thousands of Neapolitans cram into the Duomo (p75) to witness the blood of San Gennaro miraculously liquefy in the phial that contains it. Of course, very few believe that it's a real miracle, and science has a ready explanation. Apparently, it's all to do with thixotrophy, which is the property of certain compounds to liquefy when shaken and then to return to their original form when left to stand. To verify this, however, scientists would have to analyse the blood, something the Church has effectively blocked by refusing permission to open the phial.

Still, the fact remains that when the blood liquefies the city breathes a sigh of relief – it symbolises another year safe from disaster. A coincidence maybe, but when the miracle failed in 1944 Mt Vesuvius erupted, and when it didn't happen again in 1980 an earthquake struck the city on 23 November of that year.

The whole miracle scenario illustrates the way in which religion and superstition have become entangled in this city. Here, votive shrines flank shops selling shiny red horns to ward off curses, bulbs of garlic hang from the odd balcony to stave off bad vibes, and the same Neapolitan who makes the sign of the cross when passing a church will make the sign of the horns (by extending their thumb, index finger and little finger) to ward off *mal'occhio* (the evil eye). Even the Chiesa del Gesù Nuovo has a superstitious twist – its diamond-stoned façade was designed to deflect bad luck. In Naples, the Catholic and the cultish walk hand in hand.

The Cult of the Purgative Souls is one of the most macabre examples of this alliance. Widely practised until the 1970s, it involved adopting a skull at the infamous Cimitero delle Fontanelle (Fontanelle Cemetery; p96), where thousands of plague victims were unceremoniously dumped and forgotten. Cult followers would lavish their adopted skull with gifts and prayers, hoping to release its soul from purgatory and earn themselves good fortune in return. So popular was this practice that until the 1950s a tram serviced the cemetery, which was packed with flower-laden devotees. In 1969 Cardinal Ursi officially banned the cult, branding it fetishistic. And yet, some say this cult is far from dead.

LOTTERY DREAMS

In every visible aspect the Neapolitan lottery is the same as every other lottery – tickets are bought, numbers marked and the winning numbers pulled out of a closely guarded hat. It differs, however, in the way that Neapolitans select their numbers. They dream them, or rather they interpret their dreams with the aid of *La Smorfia*, a kind of dream dictionary. According to the good book, if you dream of God or Italy you should pick number one; for a football player choose number 42 (Maradona, a football-playing god, is 43). Other symbols include dancing (37), crying (21), fear (90) and a woman's hair (55). Some leave the interpreting to the lotto-shop expert by whispering their dreams into the shop owners' ears (no-one wants to share a winning combination) and letting them choose the numbers. According to the locals, the city's luckiest *ricevitoria* (lotto shop) is the one at Porta Capuana. Run by the same family for more than 200 years, the shop's current owner's grandmother was considered a dream-theme expert. To this day, people bring their dreams here from as far afield as the US, Spain and Switzerland.

JEAN-BERNARD CARILLET

PORT OF CALL

Punchinello-selling Poles and Chinese *pizzaioli* (pizza makers) – welcome to new-millennium Naples.

Like the rest of Italy, Naples is fast becoming a multiethnic melting pot. Camorra is making way for curry in the Quartieri Spagnoli, Chinese paper lanterns are spreading across Mercato, and Polish delis are popping up on Piazza Garibaldi. Officially, Naples and its province are home to 45,000 foreign-born residents. Americans and Canadians form the largest group (8000), many working at the city's NATO base. Close behind are Sri Lankans and Filipinos (7500), followed by Moroccans, Tunisians and Algerians (4000), as well as sizable communities from West Africa, Eastern Europe and the Dominican Republic. In reality, the numbers are higher, with thousands of *clandestini* (illegal immigrants) living in limbo across the region.

While an increasing number of Chinese and Eastern Europeans are opening their own small businesses, the majority of immigrants are employed by the locals – in factories, on construction sites and in private homes. Indeed, 70% of immigrants in Naples work as housekeepers, baby-sitters or domestic carers for the elderly. In the 1970s and 1980s, housekeeping was a veritable dream job for the newly arrived. Having a maid was the ultimate status symbol for the city's rich, and as a result many immigrant workers enjoyed long-term job security and friends in high places. Since the 1990s, however, increased demand has come from the time-pressed middle class. Unlike their upper-class counterparts, most of these newer clients can't afford to offer workers the same economic and legal perks. What was once a relatively secure job is now fraught with risk.

More precarious is the life of the street sellers, many of whom are *clandestini* from Senegal. Known as *vù cumprà* – named for their trademark catchphrase, 'Do you want to buy?' – they sell counterfeit goods displayed on sheets along the pavement. When the police cruise by, the sellers swoop up their stock and flee, fearing arrest and possible deportation.

Outside the city the situation is worse for *clandestini*, who mostly find short-term seasonal work in the agricultural sector. The work is hard and lowly paid, and some employers are more than happy to exploit their illegal employees' vulnerable position.

The paradox of immigration in Naples is that the most invisible in the system are the most visible in the community. Marginalised and poor, they are often the ones caught begging, scamming or stealing, creating bad PR for immigrants at large and fuelling a mostly right-wing sentiment that Italy and immigration are a bad match.

Even more ironic is that while an increasing number of foreigners move in, a growing number of young university-educated Neapolitans move out, in a case of *fuga dei cerveli* (brain drain). Faced with a 20.9% unemployment rate and underfunded universities, some of the city's brightest minds are heading north and abroad in search of better career prospects in their chosen fields.

Not that Naples is a stranger to exodus. Between 1876 and 1976, a staggering 2,700,000 people from Naples and Campania left their motherland behind in search of better opportunities across borders and seas. So monumental was this chapter in the city's history that it became a major theme in many a Neapolitan song, the most famous of which is the melancholic 'Santa Lucia Luntana'. Indeed, the huge Neapolitan diaspora managed to turn Neapolitan song into the most internationally recognisable form of Italian music. When the sheet music to the Italian national anthem was lost at the 1920 Olympic Games in Antwerp, the orchestra broke into 'O Sole Mio' instead… It was the only Italian melody that everyone knew.

THE GOOD, THE BAD & THE TYPECAST

Neapolitans proudly see themselves as a tolerant bunch. Centuries of foreign influence and rule have created a city with a knack for absorbing and appropriating the distant and the exotic. Yet, as in any society, commonly held prejudices about foreigners exist. Some cultures fascinate, others provoke suspicion or just plain resentment. The undisputed darlings of the city's foreign set are the Americans. Despite growing support for the 'no-global' movement, most Neapolitans refer to Uncle Sam's own as *gli alleati* (the allies); indeed, many local WWII survivors still call them *i liberatori* (the liberators). Of the poorer immigrants, the Sri Lankans and Filipinos are considered the most diligent, honest and hard-working. A soft spot is reserved for the Senegalese and Ghanans, seen as friendly and willing to integrate into the mainstream. Indeed, Neapolitans will proudly point out that many of their West African neighbours master Nnapulitano (Neapolitan dialect) long before they ever learn Italian. More mysterious to the Neapolitans are the Chinese, whose community is tightknit and relatively self-sufficient. Some locals see them as an economic threat because cheap Chinese imports saturate the market. Less favourably considered are the Eastern Europeans. It's not uncommon to hear Ukrainian and Polish women described as 'home-wrecking gold-diggers' and Eastern European men as 'public drunks'. But at the bottom of the barrel are the North Africans and Roma. Marginalised and much maligned, their reputation for petty theft and crime has earned them few fans in the shadow of Vesuvius.

SEXUAL POLITICS

Sisters are (almost) doing it for themselves…

In the first vignette in Vittorio de Sica's 1963 film *Ieri, Oggi, Domani* (Yesterday, Today, Tomorrow), Sophia Loren plays Adelina. Caught selling contraband cigarettes to support herself and her layabout husband (Marcello Mastroianni), she is arrested and thrown into jail. When her husband discovers that under Italian law a woman cannot be imprisoned until six months after childbirth, they seize the moment to produce a string of babies. Despite the comic opportunism, Adelina encapsulates the 'ideal' Neapolitan woman in many ways. She is fertile, earthy, shrewd and fiercely devoted to her husband and children. She defines herself through motherhood and marriage.

Neapolitan families are still among Italy's largest; their average size is 3.23, compared to the national average of 2.6. It's still the norm to live at home until you marry and one-third of husbands still visit their mothers every day. Yet, despite this old-school picture, gender norms are changing. Twenty years ago most Neapolitan men couldn't fry an egg; today you can find them cooking dinner for their working wives. In 2004, Italian women owned 25% of the country's companies, up from 15% in 1993, and today Naples has a female mayor, Rosa Russo Jervolino. A narrow job market has seen women's educational careers lengthen; there are more women than men studying medicine in the city, and 40% of Neapolitan women are enrolled in universities compared to 31% of men.

But, while women are moving forward, obstacles remain. Although more women graduate than men, only 53.7% of them find employment within three years of receiving their degree compared to 69.2% of men. Furthermore, men receive roughly 10% more in their pay packet than their female counterparts. Antidiscrimination laws are slowly making a difference, although some employers still see women as a risk, likely to ditch their jobs to raise a family. Indeed, ineffective childcare infrastructure makes work and motherhood an often stressful combination for many Neapolitan women. These days, Adelina may carry a briefcase, but her frantic juggling act is still in evidence and far from being relegated to celluloid history.

ACTION-PACKED CLOSETS

The hedonistic islands off the coast of Naples have long been a hit with gay pleasure-seekers. On Capri, Emperor Tiberius entertained a legion of male escorts, while WH Auden ruled the roost over Ischia's gay expat colony. On the conservative mainland, however, sexuality is a more ambiguous affair. While gay clubs teem with happy punters, few of the clubbers tell their *mammas* where they are going. Although attitudes are changing, double lives are still common and it's not unusual for gays and lesbians to play happy hetero couples with each other to keep the family off their back. As in much of southern Italy, the Catholic Church remains a powerful sociopolitical force. Yet, few cities are so erotically charged as Naples. Lingering looks fill the streets and propositions pop up in the strangest of places – from shop counters to taxis. Switch that gaydar into overdrive – you're in for a lusty ride.

top five

PLACES TO FALL IN LOVE

Marechiaro (p99)

Borgo Marinaro (p83)

Lungomare (p88)

Piazza Bellini (p72)

Teatro San Carlo (p87)

ARTS &
ARCHITECTURE

Tempio di Apollo (p163), Pompeii   MARTIN MOOS

THE ANCIENTS

Greek temples, Roman amphitheatres and erotic frescoes testify to the skill and creativity of the ancient artists and architects.

People have been building in Naples and the surrounding countryside for almost three thousand years. First the Greeks came and went, and then the Romans arrived, developing the area into a trendy holiday destination until Vesuvius erupted in AD 79. In terms of classical archaeology, there are fewer areas on earth as rich as Naples and the Amalfi Coast.

Considered to be among the best examples of classical Greek architecture in Italy, the temples at Paestum are a legacy of Magna Grecia, the Greek colony that covered much of southern Italy until the 3rd century BC. Further north the ruins at Cuma tell of a thriving settlement and a superstitious population; it was in the Antro della Sibilla Cumana (Cave of the Cumaean Sibyl; p106) that the Sibyl is said to have made her prophecies.

Little remains of the art that must once have adorned these great Greek cities. Notable exceptions are the *Tomba del Truffatore* (Tomb of the Diver) frescoes of the 5th-century BC in the museum at Paestum (p168).

Evidence of Roman life is more widespread. In Naples the centro storico (historic centre) is based on the three *decumani* (main streets) of the Roman city of Neapolis. You can still see plenty of evidence of the ancient city, especially if you head underground.

Duck beneath the Chiesa di San Lorenzo Maggiore (p70) and you'll find yourself walking down an eerily quiet Roman street. Similarly, the Duomo (p75) stands atop a series of Graeco-Roman remains, and the network of tunnels beneath Piazza San Gaetano dates to ancient times. Recently, workers on Naples' new metro unearthed a 2nd-century AD Roman spa and parts of temple near Piazza del Municipio (see p86) from the same period.

The real archaeological gems, however, are not in Naples itself but peppered throughout the surrounding region. To the north, the Anfiteatro Flavio (p103) in Pozzuoli is the third largest amphitheatre in Italy; to the southeast Pompeii and Herculaneum need little introduction. Nearby, in Torre Anunziata, Villa Poppaea is a stunning example of the holiday homes that upmarket Romans maintained at Oplontis (p157). On Capri enough remains of Tiberius' Villa Jovis (p176) to sense the scale of the Roman emperor's lifestyle.

Impressive as they both are, Pompeii and Herculaneum would look far grander if they hadn't been systematically pillaged since they were unearthed in the 18th century. Today many of their greatest mosaics are in Naples' Museo Archeologico Nazionale (p80). Happily you can still see one of the ancient world's largest paintings, the *Dionysiac Frieze,* in the Villa dei Misteri (p162).

The Romans used painting and mosaic work, legacies from the Etruscans and Greeks, to decorate houses and palaces from about the 2nd century BC. Many of the mosaics from Pompeii date from this period, created by skilled craftsmen from Alexandria. Similarly, many early Roman sculptures were either made by Greek sculptors or were copies of imported Greek works. A classic example is the 3rd-century AD *Toro Farnese* (Farnese Bull) in the Museo Archeologico Nazionale.

CHURCH FROWNS ON ANCIENT PORN

The Catholic Church's role in Italian art is an important one. Historically a major patron, it's still a force in the art world today. The Vatican's collection is among the most spectacular in Italy, and the wealth of art housed in the nation's churches is staggering.

Naturally the Church's tastes are conservative and the cassocked authorities take a dim view of anything they consider corrupting, which is exactly how they regarded the opening of the *Gabinetto Segreto* (Secret Chamber) in the Museo Archeologico Nazionale (p80) in 2000.

Central to the controversy was the museum's collection of 250 works of erotic art. Pillaged from Pompeii and Herculaneum, the collection includes a number of paintings that depict sex acts, numerous figurines of small men with large phalluses, and a small but perfectly formed statue of Pan caught in flagrante delicto with a goat. Originally unearthed in the mid-19th century, the collection had been kept under royal lock and key for some 170 years – and would have remained so if the Church had had its way.

A year on from this opening and the Church was once again spluttering with fury. In December 2001 a series of seven explicit panels were revealed to the public for the first time (one is pictured at right). The frescoes, which had been discovered in the 1950s in the Terme Suburbane in Pompeii (p158), where they remain to this day, depict what is perhaps the only lesbian sex scene in ancient art.

GREG ELMS

45

THE CITY ON CANVAS

Brash, arrogant and full of fire, Naples' 17th-century artists brushed aside artistic tradition as the city was rebuilt around them.

The 17th and 18th centuries were exciting times for Naples. Under Spanish rule, the city became Europe's biggest, until plague decimated up to three-quarters of the population, economic depression provoked rebellion and Vesuvius erupted. Later, the Bourbons transformed Naples into *the* place to live. Against this background, art flourished and a new wave of aggressive young painters rewrote the rule books.

The main influence on 17th-century Neapolitan art was Caravaggio (1573–1610). A controversial character, he escaped to Naples in 1606 after killing a man in Rome, and although he only stayed for a year his impact was huge. Caravaggio's dramatic depiction of light and shade, his supreme draughtsmanship and his naturalist style had an electrifying effect on the city's younger artists. Take a look at his *Flagellazione* (Flagellation) in the Palazzo Reale di Capodimonte (p93) or *Le Sette Opere di Misericordia* (Seven Acts of Mercy) in the Pio Monte della Misericordia (p73) and you'll understand why.

One of Caravaggio's greatest fans, Giuseppe de Ribera became the city's most influential painter. His style, a combination of shadow, colour and gloomy naturalism, proved hugely popular with Naples' wealthy patrons and earned him the artistic recognition he urgently sought (see below). Of Ribera's many works, the *Pietà* in the Certosa di San Martino (p91) is considered his masterpiece.

LO SPAGNOLETTO

The leading light of Naples' mid-17th-century art scene was an aggressive, bullying Spaniard, known as much for his ruthless behaviour as for his art. Giuseppe (or Jusepe) de Ribera (1591–1652) arrived in Naples in 1616, seven years after he'd left his native Spain for Rome.

Once settled in Naples, his career took off, thanks largely to his marrying the daughter of Giovanni Battista Azzolini, an important art dealer. According to legend, Azzolini sold his son-in-law's talent to the Spanish viceroy by displaying Ribera's depiction of *The Martydom of St Bartholomew* (right), now in Madrid's Prado, on the family balcony. It was the break Ribera had been waiting for and the commissions began to flow in.

Success did nothing to diminish Ribera's vicious streak. Along with the Greek artist Belisiano Crenzio and local painter Giambattista Caracciolo, Lo Spagnoletto (The Little Spaniard, as Ribera was known) formed a cabal to stamp out any potential competition. Merciless in the extreme they shied away from nothing to get their way. Ribera is said, for example, to have won a commission for the Cappella del Tesoro in the Duomo by poisoning his rival Domenichino (1581–1641) and wounding the assistant of a second competitor, Guido Reni (1575–1642). The cabal eventually broke up when Caracciolo died in 1642.

Mystery surrounds Ribera's last years. Some say that he left Naples in 1648 and simply disappeared from circulation; others claim that he died peacefully in Naples in 1652.

Volaire's *Eruzione del Vesuvio dal Ponte Maddalena*   GETTY IMAGES

top five

ARTS READS

Palaces of Naples
Donatella Mazzoleni (2003)

Jusepe de Ribera
Michael Scholz-Hansel (2001)

Baroque Naples 1600–1800
Jeanne Chenault Porter (ed.; 2000)

In the Shadow of Vesuvius: Views of Naples from Baroque to Romanticism 1631–1830
Silvia Cassani (ed.; 1990)

Eros in Pompeii: The Erotic Art Collection of the Museum of Naples
Michael Grant (1975)

Naples-born Luca Giordano (1632–1705) took Ribera's naturalism further and added his own vibrant touch. An exceptionally prolific artist, Giordano's works can be seen in churches throughout the city, including the Certosa di San Martino and the Chiesa del Gesù Nuovo (p69). A contemporary of Giordano, Francesco Solimena (1657–1747) was also influenced by Ribera, although his use of shadow showed a clearer link with Caravaggio.

Artists continued to be in demand after the accession of the Bourbons to the Neapolitan throne in 1734. As Charles VII set about building the Reggia di Caserta (p101) and refurbishing the Palazzo Reale (p85), his wife Maria Amalia began decorating the family properties. To do so, she turned to a willing group of painters, which included Francesco de Mura (1696–1782), Domenico Antonio Vaccaro (1678–1775) and Giuseppe Bonito (1707–89).

The master sculptor of the age was Giuseppe Sanmartino (1720–93), whose technical brilliance reached its apogee in the sensational 1753 *Cristo Velato* (Veiled Christ), now in the Cappella Sansevero (p68).

MARTIN MOOS

DALLAS STRIBLEY

Ceramic-tile detail from the Basilica di Santa Chiara JEAN-BERNARD CARILLET

FALLING PALACES

The innate Neapolitan extravagance found its soul mate in the baroque of the 17th and 18th centuries.

top five
MUSEUMS

Certosa di San Martino (p91)

MADRE Museo d'Arte Contemporanea Donnaregina (p75)

Museo Archeologico Nazionale (p80)

Palazzo Reale (p85)

Palazzo Reale di Capodimonte (p93)

Synonymous with excess, the baroque burst onto the Neapolitan cityscape in the mid-17th century. A sensual and highly emotional style, it provided the architectural and decorative vehicle for the city's Spanish-inspired face-lift, begun under the rule of the 17th-century viceroys and continued in the 18th century under the Bourbon monarchs. But more than the Spanish authorities it was the Catholic Church that set Naples' baroque bandwagon in motion.

Determined to reaffirm their authority in the wake of the Protestant Reformation, the Catholic Church turned to baroque art and architecture to conquer the hearts and minds of the masses. The result was an ecclesiastical building boom – up to 900 churches were built between 1585 and 1650 – and the make-over of some of the city's showcase churches. Most famously, the Certosa di San Martino (p91) was given a major overhaul by Cosimo Fanzago (1591–1678), the undisputed master of Neapolitan baroque. The result was a gleaming baroque design: a kaleidoscopic medley of polychrome marble, frescoed ceilings and lavish stucco work, with dark, naturalist paintings and ornate sculpture, all flooded in natural light and designed to overwhelm.

The Certosa also boasts one of Naples' most impressive collection of *presepi* (nativity scenes). The use of *presepi* and locally produced majolica tiling was a distinguishing feature of the Neapolitan baroque. A stunning case in point is the Basilica di Santa Chiara (p67), whose ceramic-tiled cloister garden was landscaped by one of the leading architects of the day, Domenico Antonio Vaccaro (1678–1745).

BOURBON BAROQUE & NEOCLASSICISM

Under the 18th-century Bourbons, Naples became one of Europe's most glamorous capitals, a model of modern baroque splendour. Royal palaces were commissioned, piazzas were designed and aristocratic palazzi sprung up across town. The architectural climax of the era, however, was celebrated 25km north of Naples in Caserta. Designed by Luigi Vanvitelli (1700–73), the monumental Palazzo Reale (usually known as the Reggia; p101) is generally considered one of the greatest examples of Italian baroque. Begun in 1752 and modelled on the French palace of Versailles, it was reputedly the largest building in 18th-century Europe. Highlights include Vanvitelli's grand staircase, a masterpiece of vainglorious baroque featuring many of the genre's telltale hallmarks – acres of inlaid marble, allegorical statues set into wall niches, raised columns and an unbridled sense of the theatrical.

The early 18th century also bore witness to a renewed interest in antiquity, largely inspired by the discovery of Herculaneum in 1709 and Pompeii in 1748. The architectural manifestation of this was the early 19th-century neoclassicist style. Marking a return to the symmetrical lines and colonnades so beloved of the ancients, it found its most obvious expression in the design of Piazza del Plebiscito and the Chiesa di San Francesco di Paola (p86), an unapologetic homage to the Pantheon in Rome.

CERTOSA DI SAN MARTINO

The most visible building in Naples, the Certosa di San Martino (right) has stood on the Vomero hill since the early 14th century. Home to one of the city's best museums, it's also a beautiful ensemble of architectural styles: originally Gothic, it was enlarged in the late 16th century and given a baroque make-over a century later.

The original monastery was commissioned in 1325 by Charles, duke of Calabria and protector of the Neapolitan order of Carthusians. Built and designed by Francesco de Vito and Tino di Camaino, it was consecrated in 1368 in honour of San Martino (St Martin; AD 316/7–397), the bishop of Tours.

But despite its Gothic origins, it owes most of its fame to two subsequent overhauls: the first, in the late 16th century, by the mannerist architect Giovanni Antonio Dosio; the second a century later by the grandmaster of Neapolitan baroque, Cosimo Fanzago.

Dosio modified the monastery's church, closing two of the three original aisles and adding six lateral chapels. He also designed two cloisters, the Chiostro dei Procuratori and the stunning Chiostro Grande, although this was later reworked by Fanzago, who added the statues above the portico, the ornate corner portals and the white balustrade around the monks' cemetery.

Fanzago started work on the complex in 1623 and continued on and off for 33 years. His crowning glory, and indeed one of the finest examples of Neapolitan baroque in existence, is the sumptuous church, whose exuberant façade he designed and whose opulent marble-clad interior contains works by most of Naples' major 17th- and 18th-century artists.

For more on the Certosa, see p91.

NEAPOLITAN THEATRICS

There's nowhere more theatrical than Naples, a city in which everyday transactions become minor performances and traffic jams give rise to impromptu klaxon concerts.

The drama is not confined to the streets. The city enjoys a unique musical and theatrical heritage: commedia dell'arte was born in 16th-century Naples, playwrights Eduardo de Filippo and Roberto de Simone have achieved international recognition, and Neapolitan songs have featured in adverts across the world.

COMMEDIA DELL'ARTE

With its origins in the earthy ancient Roman comedy theatre of *Fabula Atellana* (Atellan Farce), commedia dell'arte dates back to the 16th century. Like its Roman inspiration, commedia dell'arte featured a set of stock characters in masks acting out a series of semistandard situations. Based on a recipe of adultery, jealousy, old age and love, performances were often used to satirise local situations.

Commedia dell'arte was performed on temporary streetside stages by troupes of travelling actors and proved popular and accessible. It gave birth to a number of legendary characters, including the Harlequin and Punchinello.

Nowadays the Punchinello, the ubiquitous symbol of Naples, is a complex figure. In his white costume and black beak-nosed mask, he is exuberant and optimistic, cynical, lazy and melancholic. As a street philosopher, he is antiauthoritarian and is often seen beating the local copper with a stick (hence the term slapstick). At home, however, his wife's the beater and he's the victim, much like his English descendant Mr Punch.

Naples' great tradition of popular theatre grew out of the commedia dell'arte. It was a tradition in which the great dramatist Raffaele Viviani (1888–1950) was firmly rooted. His use of dialect and his subject matter – the Neapolitan working class – won him local success and the enmity of the Mussolini regime.

MODERN THEATRE

The most important figure in Neapolitan theatre was Eduardo de Filippo (1900–84). The son of a famous Neapolitan actor, Eduardo Scarpetta (1853–1925), de Filippo made his stage debut at the age of four and

top five
NEAPOLITAN TRACKS

Facendo La Storia
99 Posse

Il Rock di Capitano Uncino
Edoardo Bennato

'Napul é
Pino Daniele

Salvamm'o munno
Enzo Avitabile

Sanacore
Almamegretta

GETTY IMAGES

LA CANZONE NAPOLETANA

Ask for a list of Italian stereotypes and you'll get the usual answers – pasta, pizza, opera and Ferrari. Ask for an Italian song and nine times out of 10 you'll get Giovanni Capurro's 1898 hit 'O Sole Mio'. Yet this Neapolitan classic is just one of the many that the early-20th-century Italian immigrants took with them to the far corners of the world.

The defining moment for *la canzone napoletana* (Neapolitan song) came in 1839 when 'Te Voglio Bene Assaje' ('I Love You Loads') was released. Written by Raffaele Sacco and set to music by Donizetti, it became an instant sensation – more than 180,000 copies of the song's lyrics were sold and witnesses tell of pandemonium verging on mass hysteria. Subsequent Neapolitan hits included 'O Sole Mio' and 'Funiculì Funiculà'.

The success of the songs was largely based on their catchy melodies and lyrics, generally sung in dialect, which spoke of love and death, passion and longing.

The genre is still thriving. Kept alive by the likes of Roberto Murolo (1912–2003) and Sergio Bruni (1921–), it's been given a commercial pop sound by, among others, Nino D'Angelo (1957–) and Gigi Alessio (1967–). As a visitor, you're more likely to hear it performed by one of the many buskers who traipse around the city's restaurants doing a lucrative trade in tableside concerts.

over the next 80 years became a hugely successful actor, impresario and playwright. His body of often bittersweet work includes the classics *Il Sindaco del Rione Sanità* (The Mayor of the Sanità Quarter) and *Sabato, Domenica e Lunedì* (Saturday, Sunday and Monday). Today Eduardo's son Luca (1948–) is a highly regarded theatre actor.

Roberto de Simone (1933–) is another great Neapolitan playwright. He's made less of an international impact than de Filippo, as much of his work is in dialect and loses some effect in translation, but his masterpiece *La Gatta Cenerentola* (The Cat Cinderella) nevertheless enjoyed a successful run in London in 1999.

Naples' contemporary theatre scene is fairly hit and miss. The leading light is Enzo Moscato (1948–), whose work fuses a vibrant physicality with skilful use of dialect and music. His most famous work is the 1991 multiple-award-winning *Rasoi* (Razors). Moscato is often found hanging out at the Galleria Toledo (p134), Naples' leading experimental theatre.

OPERA

Emotional and highly theatrical, opera has always been close to the Neapolitan heart. In fact in the 18th century Naples was the capital of the opera world, and its sparkling Teatro San Carlo (p87) attracted Europe's greatest composers.

Naples' greatest composer, Alessandro Scarlatti (1660–1725), was one of the most prolific of the early 18th century. He wrote some 100 operas, and as one of the leading lights of the Neapolitan school he helped establish the conventions of *opera seria* (serious opera). Opera buffs owe the *aria da capo* and the three-part overture to Scarlatti and company.

Running parallel to the formal *opera seria* was the more popular *opera buffa* (comic opera). Taking its cue from the Neapolitan commedia dell'arte it was often written in dialect with the emphasis on comedy rather than the love, duty and honour so favoured by *opera seria*.

THE SILVER SCREEN

Intense, introvert and darkly funny, Neapolitan cinema holds a mirror to the harsh realities of this most visual of cities.

Feted for his 1948 neorealist masterpiece *Ladri di Biciclette* (Bicycle Thieves), Vittorio de Sica (1901–74) was a master at depicting the bittersweet struggle at the heart of so much Neapolitan humour. His two Neapolitan classics, *L'Oro di Napoli* (The Gold of Naples; 1954) and *Ieri, Oggi, Domani* (Yesterday, Today, Tomorrow; 1963), delighted audiences throughout the country but nowhere more so than in Naples, his adopted city, where filmgoers thrilled to the sight of Sophia Loren (1934–) in top form.

More than anyone though, it was Antonio de Curtis (1898–1967), aka Totò, who best depicted the *furbizia* (cunning) for which Neapolitans are famous. Born in the working class Sanità district, he appeared in more than 100 films, typically playing the part of a hustler living on nothing but his quick wits. It was a role that ensured Totò's cult status in a city where the art of *arrangiarsi* (getting by) is a way of life.

Inheriting Totò's mantle, Massimo Troisi (1953–1994) is best known abroad for his role in *Il Postino* (The Postman). Within Italy, however, he was adored for his unique brand of rambling humour. In his debut film of 1980, *Ricomincio da Tre* (I'm Starting from Three), he humorously tackles the problems faced by Neapolitans who are forced to head north for work. Sadly the message is still relevant 25 years later.

In recent times a new wave of Neapolitan directors, including Antonio Capuano (1945–), Mario Martone (1959–) and Pappi Corsicato (1960–), have turned their cameras on the city and its difficulties in films such as Capuano's critically acclaimed *Luna Rossa* (Red Moon) of 2001. Antonietta de Lillo (1960–) has also been making waves with her personal, graceful take on city life.

A FILM FOR ALL SEASONS

L'Oro di Napoli (The Gold of Naples; 1954; Vittorio de Sica)
A who's who of Neapolitan greats – Totò, Sophia Loren, Eduardo de Filippo and Vittorio de Sica – star in six episodes of city life.

Le Mani Sulla Città (Hands Over the City; 1963; Francesco Rosi)
Rod Steiger leads an amateur cast in this powerful condemnation of Naples' corrupt postwar building boom.

Libera (Free; 1992; Pappi Corsicato)
Often compared to Pedro Almodóvar, Corsicato is flamboyant, bizarre and colourful. His debut film features, in three short stories, a cast of transsexual parents, unwitting porn stars and wedding singers.

Il Resto di Niente (The Remains of Nothing; 2003; Antonietta de Lillo)
Lillo's intense take on Naples' doomed Parthenopean Republic centres on the psychological complexities of Eleonara Pimental de Fonseca, one of its tragic heroines.

Sophia Loren, June 1965 · GETTY IMAGES

FOOD FOR LIFE

Steeped in folklore, Neapolitan cuisine is a celebration of the tried and tested, of combinations that work and tastes that never tire.

It's also a culmination, a colourful *minestra* (soup) of foreign influence and local creativity. In its 3000-year history Naples has been a Roman holiday resort, a cosmopolitan centre of medieval culture and a glittering European capital. As the foreign rulers have come and gone, they've left their mark – on the art and architecture, on the local dialect and on the food.

In the very early days, it was the Greeks who introduced olive trees, grape vines and durum wheat to Italy. Later on, the Byzantines and Arab traders from nearby Sicily brought with them pine nuts, almonds, raisins and honey that they used to stuff their vegetables. They also brought what was to become the mainstay of the Neapolitan diet and, in time, Italy's most famous food – pasta.

Although it was first introduced in the 12th century, pasta really took off in the 1600s when it established itself as the poor man's food of choice. Requiring only a few simple ingredients – just flour and water at its most basic – pasta proved a life saver as the city's population exploded in the 17th century. The invention of a mechanised press further eased the situation and allowed for increased production at lower costs. The nobility, however, continued to shun pasta until Gennaro Spadaccini invented the four-pronged fork in the early 18th century.

During Naples' Bourbon period (1734–1860), two parallel gastronomic cultures developed: that of the opulent Spanish monarchy, and that of the streets – the *cucina povera* (cuisine of the poor). As much as the former was elaborate and rich, the latter was simple and healthy.

The food of the poor, the so-called *mangiafoglie* (leaf eaters), was largely based on pasta and vegetables grown on the fertile volcanic plains around Naples. Aubergines (eggplants), artichokes, courgettes (zucchini), tomatoes and peppers were among the staples, while milk from sheep, cows and goats was used to make cheese. Flat breads imported from Greek and Arab lands, the forebear of the pizza, were also popular. Meat and fish were expensive and reserved for special occasions.

Meanwhile, in the court kitchens, the top French cooks of the day were working to feed the insatiable appetites of the Bourbon monarchy. The headstrong queen Maria Carolina, wife of King Ferdinand I, was so impressed by her sister Marie Antoinette's court in Versailles that she asked to borrow some chefs. The French cooks obviously took

JEAN-BERNARD CARILLET

top five
FOODIE READS

The Food Lover's Companion to Naples and the Campania Carla Capalbo (2005)
Exactly what it says it is: an encyclopedic guide to the region's food producers, what they make and where they serve it.

Guiliano Bugialli's Food of Naples and Campania Guiliano Bugialli (2003)
Prolific Italian-cookery writer Bugialli leads readers on a culinary journey through the region.

La Pizza: The True Story from Naples Nikko Amandonico and Natalia Borri (2005)
Sumptuously illustrated history of the pizza, set in Naples' kaleidoscopic streets.

David Ruggerio's Italian Kitchen: Family Recipes from the Old Country David Ruggerio (2004)
Son of a Neapolitan mum and a Sicilian father, Ruggerio shares the secrets and atmosphere of a Neapolitan kitchen.

Naples at Table: Cooking in Campania Arthur Schwartz (1998)
Learn how *zuppa inglese* (a trifle of cream, chocolate and sponge) got its name; cook from a selection of 250 recipes.

to the Neapolitan air, creating among other things highly elaborate *timballi di pasta* (pasta pies) and a new potato tart known as *gattò di patate*.

CULTURE

Loud, crowded and exhilarating, Naples' great food markets are a technicolour testament to the importance Neapolitans place on their food. To watch the hard-to-please hagglers bullying vendors into giving them precisely what they want is to understand that food really matters in Naples. And it's these people, the *nonne* (grandmothers) and *casalinghe* (housewives), who are keeping the city's great culinary traditions alive.

For proof, step into a local home, preferably on a Sunday. Here you'll taste great pasta dishes – try the *pasta al ragù* (pasta with tomato and meat sauce) – and magnificent main courses such as *costata alla pizzaiola* (veal cutlet served in a tomato and oregano sauce). It's also in the home that you'll see the uninhibited pleasure locals take in eating a good meal in good company.

Neapolitan cuisine is also about street food. You might not find kiosks doling out *maccheroni* (macaroni) and tomato sauce anymore, but you'll find plenty of takeaway shops serving freshly cooked focaccia, deep-fried vegetables, pizza, *arancini* (large rice balls stuffed with meat sauce) and a whole host of other delicious nibbles.

Just don't come to Naples hoping to lose weight. To many people the south of Italy is synonymous with the Mediterranean diet – that winning combination of fruit, vegetables and olive oil. And yes, the quantity and quality of the fruit and veg served in Naples is impressive, but it takes an iron will to choose the boiled courgette over the lightly fried version, or to turn down the selection of artfully decorated desserts.

Restraint is not a Neapolitan characteristic, and when confronted with temptation the locals know which choice to make. Unfortunately, the results are showing: child obesity currently runs at an alarming 16% in Naples.

CAFÉ SOCIETY

Short, dark and very, very strong, Neapolitan coffee enjoys cult status in this city of a million aficionados.

Nowhere else in Italy does coffee enjoy the iconic standing it has in Naples. Neapolitans will proudly tell you that their coffee is the best in the country, and they may have a point. Although many bars and cafés use the same machines that are used in the rest of the country, the espresso that drips out of the Neapolitan models seems somehow darker and richer than anywhere else. It's because of the water, they'll tell you, or the air.

More than a simple drink, *caffè* (coffee) is the city's great social lubricant, a part of life that cuts through all social barriers. Camorra bosses drink it, just as do judges and police officers; intellectuals swoon over it and students wake up to it. Elsewhere you might be asked out for a beer or for lunch; in Naples you're invited to go for a coffee. And your host will know just where to take you. Every true coffee aficionado, and there are about a million in Naples, has a favourite bar where *'fanno un buon caffè'* ('they make a good coffee').

GREAT EATS

Get your teeth into Naples with these city classics:

Mozzarella di bufala On pizza, in a salad or simply on its own, there's no beating Campania's great buffalo cheese.

Pizza margherita Connoisseurs swear you can't beat the traditional tomato, mozzarella and basil topping.

Spaghetti alla puttanesca Spaghetti with a sauce of tomatoes, olives, capers and anchovies.

Sfogliatella Cinnamon-infused ricotta in a puff-pastry shell.

Espresso Hit the mark with a shot of almost pure caffeine.

JEAN-BERNARD CARILLET

ALAN BENSON

Surprisingly, the coffee ritual is a brief affair. The coffee itself is tiny – little more than a drop – and you'll almost certainly have it standing at the bar rather than seated at a table. But the speed with which it's consumed does not diminish the importance of its quality.

According to experts, a good coffee depends on five criteria: the mix of the beans; the roasting of the beans – too much and the coffee tastes burnt, too little and it lacks body; the grinding of the beans – the resulting powder should be fine enough to ensure perfect solubility; the coffee machine; and the cup in which the coffee's served – it should be big enough to absorb some of the liquid's heat, but not so big that it absorbs too much. The human element also counts: a practised hand will always make a better coffee than a novice.

Neapolitans were not the first Italians to take coffee to their heart. Italy's first coffee house opened in 1640 in Venice, some 70 years after a certain Prospero Alpino of Padua had brought some coffee beans over from Egypt. It was an expensive luxury, and for much of the 18th century coffee remained an upper-class curiosity. Slowly it caught on, however, and by the mid-19th century coffee-drinking had become a universal habit.

Today there are any number of coffee combinations served in Naples, but the most common are: *un caffè* (a very strong espresso served in a hot cup and already sugared);

top five
PLACES TO BE SEEN

Intra Moenia (p119)
Bohemian centro storico café

Caffè Mexico (p120)
Cool café with hot coffee

Caffè Gambrinus (p120)
Prince of Neapolitan cafés

Moccia (p124)
Trendy Chiaia pasticceria (pastry shop)

Pintauro (p121)
The place for sfogliatelle (cinnamon-infused ricotta in a puff-pastry shell).

JEAN-BERNARD CARILLET

un caffè macchiato (an espresso with a drop of milk); and a cappuccino (generally served lukewarm rather than hot). For a more watered-down coffee ask for a *caffè lungo* or a *caffè americàno*. In summer a *cappuccino freddo* (cold cappuccino) is a wonderfully refreshing drink.

SWEETS & PASTRIES

No celebration, be it a birthday party or Sunday lunch, is complete without a traditional tray of delicious Neapolitan pastries.

The city's most famous cake is the *sfogliatella*, a flaky seashell-shaped pastry filled with cinnamon-infused ricotta and candied fruit. Debate rages about its origins: some say it was created by French chefs for the king of Poland in the 18th century, others that it was invented by 18th-century nuns in Conca dei Marini, a small village on the Amalfi Coast. Nowadays it comes in three forms: soft and doughy, deep-fried, and the justifiably popular crispy version.

The *babà* is another favourite. Invented by the French chefs sent to Maria Carolina from Versailles, it's a delicious mushroom-shaped sponge cake soaked in rum and sugar.

To celebrate the feast of San Giuseppe (19 March), Neapolitans eat *zeppole,* deep-fried doughnuts stuffed with custard.

For more on cakes, pastries and sweets see p121.

CUCINA POVERA

Pizza and pasta encapsulate Naples' earthy attitude to food – keep it simple, keep it local and keep it coming.

Food fashions come and go but some things never change. Naples will always be Italy's pasta and pizza capital. Ever since pasta was used to feed the city's burgeoning 17th-century population, it's been a mainstay of *cucina povera* and the foundation on which Naples' gastronomic reputation stands. Pizza, already a popular snack by the 16th century, may not have been invented in Naples, but the city has long claimed it for its own – and nowhere does it better.

Although the Neapolitans profess to have created spaghetti, no-one is quite sure who first made pasta. The generally accepted view is that it was Arab traders who developed it for use on their desert caravans. And certainly pasta arrived in Naples via Sicily where it had first been introduced by Arab merchants. The dry windy Campanian climate was later found to be ideal for drying pasta, and production took off in a big way, especially after the 1840 opening of Italy's first pasta plant in Torre Annunziata.

Pasta is divided into *pasta fresca* (fresh pasta), which is eaten within a few days of purchase, and *pasta secca* (dried pasta), which can be stored for as long as you want. Naples is famous for its *pasta secca,* the most obvious examples of which are spaghetti, *maccheroni,* penne (smallish tubes cut at an angle) and rigatoni (similar to penne but with ridges on them).

Pasta secca is, and always has been, made from *semolino* (durum wheat) flour and water, and is often served (*al dente*, of course) with vegetable-based sauces, which are generally less rich than the traditional *pasta fresca* sauces.

Of the vegetables that Neapolitans consume with such gusto, none is acclaimed more than the simple tomato. Discovered by Spanish colonialists in the New World, it was first introduced to Naples by the city's 16th-century Spanish viceroys. Some five centuries later, it's not only a mainstay of the local cuisine but also of the region's

top five
DOS & DON'TS

As a foreigner, any faux pas you make will be forgiven as long as you've enjoyed your meal and done so visibly. There are, however, some dos and don'ts to observe when eating in Naples.

Pasta is eaten with a fork only.

Bread is not eaten with pasta – unless you're cleaning up the sauce afterwards.

It's fine to eat a pizza with your hands.

If in doubt, dress smart.

If you're invited to someone's home, the traditional gift is a tray of *dolci* (sweets) from a *pasticceria* (pastry shop).

ALAN BENSON

ALAN BENSON

THE QUEEN OF PIZZA

Naples' most famous contribution to world cuisine is startlingly simple. Yet, over the centuries, pizza has become the stuff of gastronomic legend: there are museums dedicated to it, festivals held in its honour and websites devoted to it. Italians debate its merits and are split between those who favour the thin-crust Roman variant, and those who go for the thicker Neapolitan version. Whatever your choice, the fact remains that the pizza they make in Naples is quite superb.

A derivation of the flat breads of ancient Greece and Egypt, it was already a common street snack by the time the city's 16th-century Spanish occupiers introduced the tomato to Italy. And it was this, the addition of tomato, that ensured the pizza's huge popularity. *Pizzerie* (pizza restaurants) began to appear across the city – the first to open was Port'Alba (p119) in 1738 – and *pizzaioli* (pizza makers) became minor celebrities.

During a visit to Naples in 1889, the Italian king Umberto I and his wife Queen Margherita were so curious to try pizza that they summoned the city's top *pizzaiola*, Raffaelle Esposito, to cook for them. In order to impress the royal couple, Esposito based his creation of tomato, mozzarella and basil on the red, white and green flag of the newly unified Italy. The resulting topping met with the queen's approval and was subsequently named in her honour.

More than a hundred years later, traditionalists claim you really can't top Esposito's classic combo when made by a true Neapolitan *pizzaiola*. Nor when it's made by Makoto Onishi, the 31-year-old Japanese cook who was voted Naples' best pizza maker at the 2006 Pizzafest.

agricultural income. The most famous and most cultivated tomato in Italy is grown in the volcanic soil near the small Vesuvian town of San Marzano. Its sauce, *conserva di pomodoro,* is made from super-ripe tomatoes, which are cut and left to dry in the sun for at least two days to concentrate the flavour. This is the sauce that adorns so many of Naples' great pasta dishes.

A classic Neapolitan dish is *maccheroni al ragù* (macaroni in a tomato and meat sauce), with the *ragù* left to simmer for hours before serving. Another favourite is *pasta al forno* (baked pasta), a combination of macaroni, tomato sauce, mozzarella and, depending on the recipe, hard-boiled egg, meatballs and sausage. The most colourfully named pasta dish in Naples is *spaghetti alla puttanesca* (whore's spaghetti), which is spaghetti served with a sauce of tomatoes, black olives, capers and anchovies. Some cooks like to tart this up with a dash of red chilli. Tomatoes also make the local *parmigiana di melanzane* (fried aubergines layered with hard-boiled eggs, basil, tomato sauce, onion and mozzarella) indecently good.

Seafood is often used with pasta, and you'll rarely find a restaurant that doesn't offer *spaghetti alla vongole* (spaghetti with clams) or *alle cozze* (with mussels). *Acciughe* (anchovies) also crop up in a number of local dishes.

Before leaving Naples you should also try some of the fabulous *mozzarella di bufala.* It's the high fat content and protein in the buffalo milk that gives the distinctive, pungent flavour so often absent in the versions sold abroad. Mozzarella made from cow's milk has a milder taste and is known as *fior di latte* (flower of milk).

CAMPANIAN WINES

Revered by the Romans, loved by Renaissance writers and snubbed by modern critics, Campanian wine is making a comeback.

Despite wine-making traditions that date back to the 4th century BC, Campanian wine was for a long time disregarded by critics. This is no longer the case. Regional wine makers have recently raised their game and are now producing exciting wines that the experts cannot ignore.

Producers such as Feudi di San Gregorio, Mastroberardino, Terredora di Paolo and Mustilli have returned to their roots by cultivating grape varieties that have flourished in the region's volcanic soils since Greek and Roman times. The red Aglianico grape is thought to be the oldest cultivated grape in Italy; the whites – Falanghino, Fiano and Greco – were all growing long before Mt Vesuvius erupted in AD 79. As if to labour the point, in 2003 Mastroberardino presented the first wine produced in Pompeii's ancient vineyards in 2000 years, a robust limited edition red called Villa dei Misteri.

Campania's three main wine-producing zones are centred around Avellino, Benevento and Caserta. And it's in the high hills east of Avellino that the region's best red is produced. Taurasi, a full-bodied Aglianico wine, sometimes known as the Barolo of the south, is one of southern Italy's best known labels and one of only three in the region to carry Italy's top quality rating, DOCG (Denominazione di Origine Controllata e Garantita; Controlled & Guranteed Denomination of Origin). The other two wines that carry this rating are Fiano di Avellino and Greco di Tufo, both whites and both from the Avellino area.

Wine is also produced on the Amalfi Coast and Capri, although here you're more likely to come across *limoncello,* the canary-yellow lemon liqueur. A simple concoction of lemon peel, water, sugar and alcohol, it's traditionally served in a frozen glass after dinner. But don't let the sweet, syrupy taste fool you: this is a powerful liqueur that should be treated with the utmost respect.

PICK YOUR PLONK

To help you navigate Campania's ever-growing wine list, here are some of the region's top wines:
Taurasi A DOCG since 1991, this dry, intense red goes well with boiled and barbecued meat.
Fiano di Avellino A dry, fresh DOCG white wine, this is one of Campania's historic wines. Ideal with seafood.
Greco di Tufo Another long-standing favourite, this DOCG white comes in both dry and sparkling versions.
Falerno del Massico Its red and white versions originate from the volcanic slopes of Mt Massico in the north of the region.
Aglianico del Taburno Good all-round red, white and rosé from near Benevento.

EAT YOUR WORDS

USEFUL PHRASES

I'd like to reserve a table.	Vorrei riservare un tavolo.	vo·*ray* ree·ser·*va*·re oon *ta*·vo·lo
I'd like the menu, please.	Vorrei il menù, per favore.	vo·*ray* eel me·*noo* per fa·*vo*·re
Do you have a menu in English?	Avete un menù in inglese?	a·*ve*·te oon me·*noo* een een·*gle*·ze
What would you recommend?	Cosa mi consiglia?	*ko*·za mee kon·*see*·lya
May I see the wine list, please?	Mi fa vedere la lista dei vini, per favore?	mee fa ve·*de*·re la *lis*·ta day *vee*·nee per fa·*vo*·re
Can you recommend a good local wine?	Ci può consigliare un buon vino locale?	chee pwo kon·*see*·*lya*·re oon bwon *vee*·no lo·*ka*·le
Please bring the bill.	Mi porta il conto, per favore?	mee *por*·ta eel *kon*·to per fa·*vo*·re
I'm a vegetarian.	Sono vegetariano/a. (m/f)	*so*·no ve·je·ta·*rya*·no/a
I'm a vegan.	Sono vegetaliano/a. (m/f)	*so*·no ve·je·ta·*lya*·no/a
I'm allergic (to peanuts/to shellfish).	Sono allergico/a (alle arachidi/ ai crostacei). (m/f)	*so*·no a·*ler*·jee·ko/a (al·le a·ra·*kee*·dee/ *a*·ee kros·*ta*·che·ee)

Basics

cameriere/a ka·mer·*ye*·re/ra	waiter (m/f)
cena *che*·na	dinner
coltello kol·*te*·lo	knife
cucchiaio koo·*kya*·yo	spoon
forchetta for·*ke*·ta	fork
(non) fumatori (non) foo·ma·*to*·ree	(non) smoking
pranzo *pran*·dzo	lunch
prima colazione *pree*·ma ko·la·*tsyo*·ne	breakfast
spuntini spun·*ti*·ni	snacks

Staples

aceto a·*che*·to	vinegar
acqua *ak*·wa	water
aglio *a*·lyo	garlic
burro *bu*·ro	butter
formaggio for·*ma*·jo	cheese
latte *la*·te	milk

limone lee·*mo*·ne	lemon
miele *mye*·le	honey
olio *o*·lyo	oil
olive o·*lee*·ve	olive
pane *pa*·ne	bread
panna *pan*·na	cream
peperoncino pe·pe·ron·*chee*·no	chilli
riso *ree*·so	rice
rucola *roo*·ko·la	rocket
sale *sa*·le	salt
uovo/uova *wo*·vo/*wo*·va	egg/eggs
zucchero *dzoo*·ke·ro	sugar

Cooking Methods

arrosto/a a·*ros*·to	roasted
bollito/a bo·*lee*·to/ta	boiled
cotto/a *ko*·to/ta	cooked
crudo/a *kroo*·do/da	raw

61

fritto/a *free*·to/ta — fried

alla griglia a la *gree*·lya — grilled (broiled)

Meat, Fish & Seafood

acciughe a·*choo*·ge — anchovies

agnello a·*nye*·lo — lamb

aragosta a·ra·*go*·sta — lobster

bistecca bi·*ste*·ka — steak

calamari ka·la·*ma*·ree — squid

capretto kap·*re*·to — kid (goat)

coniglio ko·*nee*·lyo — rabbit

cozze *ko*·tse — mussels

fegato *fe*·ga·to — liver

frutti di mare *froo*·tee dee *ma*·re — seafood

gamberoni gam·be·*ro*·nee — prawns

granchio *gran*·kyo — crab

manzo *man*·dzo — beef

merluzzo mer·*loo*·tso — cod

ostriche *os*·tree·ke — oysters

pesce spada *pe*·she *spa*·da — swordfish

pollo *pol*·lo — chicken

polpi *pol*·pee — octopus

salsiccia sal·*see*·cha — sausage

sarde *sar*·de — sardines

seppia *se*·pya — cuttlefish

sgombro *sgom*·bro — mackerel

tonno *ton*·no — tuna

trippa *tree*·pa — tripe

vitello vee·*te*·lo — veal

vongole *von*·go·le — clams

Fruit & Vegetables

arancia a·*ran*·cha — orange

asparagi as·*pa*·ra·jee — asparagus

carciofi kar·*chyo*·fee — artichokes

carota ka·*ro*·ta — carrot

cavolo *ka*·vo·lo — cabbage

ciliegia chee·*lye*·ja — cherry

cipolle chee·*po*·le — onions

fagiolini fa·jo·*lee*·nee — green beans

finocchio fee·*no*·kyo — fennel

fragole *fra*·go·le — strawberries

funghi *foon*·gee — mushrooms

mela *me*·la — apple

melanzane me·lan·*dza*·ne — aubergine/eggplant

patate pa·*ta*·te — potatoes

pepe *pe*·pe — pepper

peperoni pe·pe·*ro*·nee — capsicum

pera *pe*·ra — pear

pesca *pes*·ka — peach

piselli pee·*se*·lee — peas

pomodori po·mo·*do*·ree — tomatoes

spinaci spee·*na*·chee — spinach

uva *oo*·va — grapes

Drinks

birra *bee*·ra — beer

caffè ka·*fe* — coffee

tè te — tea

vino rosso *vee*·no *ro*·so — red wine

vino bianco *vee*·no *byan*·ko — white wine

QUARTERS

JEAN-BERNARD CARILLET

NAPLES

Sandwiched between a sleeping volcano and the steaming Campi Flegrei, Naples is a rumbling mass of contradictions.

Extremes are something Naples does impressively well. Grimy streets hit palm-fringed boulevards, crumbling façades hide baroque ballrooms and cultish shrines flank cutting-edge clubs. One minute you're in dusty Tangiers, the next you're thinking of Paris.

Stepping onto Piazza Garibaldi from Stazione Centrale, your impression will probably be of the former. Wild traffic, shabby street stalls and smooth-talking African salesmen make for an intense introduction. To the south and southwest, the Mercato quarter is a high-octane spectacle of rough-and-ready markets, multiculturalism and poverty.

A few blocks west of Piazza Garibaldi begins the centro storico (historic centre). Dense, dark and intoxicating, its ancient Greek streets teem with tourists, scooters, shrines and secret hidden treasures.

At its western edge, shop-heavy Via Toledo stretches from Piazza Trieste e Trento in the south to Parco di Capodimonte in the north; its chic southern end is a favourite haunt for *sfogliatella*-munching shopaholics. Immediately to the west lie the mean, washing-strung streets of the Quartieri Spagnoli.

South of Via Toledo, regal Santa Lucia boasts the mighty Piazza del Plebiscito, Palazzo Reale and world opera great Teatro San Carlo. Close at hand, Castel Nuovo (Maschio Angioino) looms over Piazza del Municipio like a giant toy castle.

Looking down on it all is middle-class Vomero, a leafy concoction of gorgeous Liberty villas, soulless apartment blocks and the hulking Castel Sant'Elmo.

West of Piazza del Plebiscito, upmarket Chiaia is Naples' heart of cool, its sleek shops and bars stretching west towards the bobbing-boat port of Mergellina. From here, posh Posillipo climbs the promontory separating the Bay of Naples from the Bay of Pozzuoli. Beyond it lies the Campi Flegrei, a volcanic sprawl of classical ruins, sulphurous steam and sexy summertime beach clubs.

CAMPANIA ARTECARD

If you're planning on spending three days or more in Naples, it's worth getting the **Campania artecard** (☎ 800 600 601; www.campaniartecard.it). For more details on this museum-and-transport ticket see p252.

ORGANISED TOURS

Outside of the city, **CIMA Tours** (Map pp280–1; ☎ 081 20 10 52; cimatour@tin .it; Piazza Garibaldi 114) and **Tourcar** (Map pp280–1; ☎ 081 552 19 38; Piazza G Matteotti 1) organise excursions to the Bay of Naples islands, the Amalfi Coast and Pompeii, Herculaneum and Vesuvius. A half-day tour to Pompeii costs about €50, including admission costs.

CITY SIGHTSEEING NAPOLI MAP PP280-1

☎ 081 551 72 79; www.napoli.city-sightseeing.it;
Via Parco del Castello, Piazza del Municipio; adult/
child/family €20/10/60

City Sightseeing Napoli operates a hop-on, hop-off bus service for tourists. There are three routes, all of which depart from Piazza del Municipio Parco Castello. Route A (*I Luoghi dell'Arte*, or Art Tour) covers the city's major art sites including Piazza del Gesù Nuovo, Piazza Dante, the Museo Archeologico Nazionale, Museo di Capodimonte, the Catacomba di San Gennaro, Piazza Bellini, Porta Capuana and Piazza Bovio. The 1¼-hour circular tour departs every 45 minutes between 9.45am and 6pm daily.

Route B (*Le Vedute del Golfo*, or Bay of Naples) follows the sea westwards passing through Santa Lucia, Piazza Vittoria, Villa Pignatelli, Mergellina and Posillipo. Departures are every 45 minutes between 9.30am and 6.30pm daily. The tour takes 1¼ hours.

Route C (San Martino) runs up to Vomero, with stops in Via Santa Lucia, Piazza dei Martiri, Piazza Amedeo, Piazza Vanvitelli, Largo San Martino (for the Certosa di San Martino), Via Salvator Rosa and Piazza Dante. Tours last 1¾ hours and depart every two hours between 10am and 6pm Saturday and Sunday.

Tickets, which are available on the bus, are valid for 24 hours for each of the three routes. Tour commentaries are provided in eight languages, including English.

NAPOLI SOTTERRANEA MAP PP280-1

Underground Naples; ☎ 081 29 69 44; www
.napolisotterranea.org; Piazza San Gaetano 68;
tours €9.30; ☉ 2hr tours noon, 2pm & 4pm Mon-Fri,
extra tours 10am & 6pm Sat & Sun, 9pm Thu

This company organises guided underground tours that take you 40m below the city to explore an eerie network of ancient passages and caves. The passages were originally hewn by the Greeks to extract the soft tufa stone for construction, and then extended by the Romans as water conduits. Clogged up with illegally dumped refuse over the centuries, they were used as air-raid shelters in WWII.

IT'S FREE

Villa Comunale (p89)
Duomo (p75)
Chiesa di Sant'Anna dei Lombardi (p79)
Views from Largo San Martino in front of the
Certosa di San Martino (p49)
PAN Art Gallery (p89)

LEGAMBIENTE MAP PP280-1

☎ 081 420 31 61; www.napolisworld.it, in Italian;
Vico della Quercia 7

A national environmental organisation offering made-to-measure tours in the centro storico and in less explored areas such as the Sanità district.

NAPOLIJAMM MAP PP278-9

☎ 081 562 13 13; www.napolijamm.it; Via Sannio 9;
adult/child €30/free

Napolijamm runs four walking tours covering the centro storico (red tour); castles and historic palazzi (green tour); sites of famous miracles and mysteries (blue tour); and the *centro storico* by night (pink tour). With the exception of the three-hour pink tour, all tours last four hours. Departure is at 9.30am from one of the two meeting points: Piazza del Gesù Nuovo or outside Caffè Gambrinus in Piazza Trieste e Trento. You should book at least 24 hours in advance.

CENTRO STORICO & MERCATO

Eating p118; Shopping p139; Sleeping p148; Walking Tours p107

Secret cloisters, cultish shrines and bellowing *baristi* in tiny old-school bars: the centro storico is a bewitching urban blend.

On its greasy streets, renegade scooters dodge handsome young waiters, bronze skulls guard dusty chapels and beer-clutching students chill and chat on cobbled stones.

Running dead straight from east to west, its three *decumani* (main streets) follow the original street plan of ancient Neapolis. The most famous of the three is the decumanus inferior, affectionately called Spaccanapoli (Break Naples). Comprising Via Benedetto Croce, Via San Biagio dei Librai and Via Vicaria Vecchia, it cuts right through the heart of the old city. One block to the north, Via dei Tribunali is the ancient decumanus maior. Most of the major sites are grouped around these two parallel streets, from the macabre Cappella San Severo to the majolica-tiled beauty of the Basilica di Santa Chiara. The northernmost of these three ancient strips, the decumanus superior, is made up of Via Sapienza, Via Anticaglia and Via Santissimi Apostoli. Just to its north is the city's hottest new art space, MADRE.

South and east of the centro storico, the Mercato district is a fast and filthy mix of cheap hotels, cheaper market stalls, Chinese spice shops and retro porn cinemas. At its eastern end, Piazza Garibaldi is the city's tattered welcome mat, home of Stazione Centrale and a long-distance bus hub. Think Harlem with date palms, where Ghanaian men sell fake D&G, Moroccan kids flog bootleg CDs and surly Russian belles serve freshly squeezed OJ. Mind your bags and dive into the market at its western end for dirt-cheap threads and local kitsch.

highlights
CENTRO STORICO & MERCATO

❶ Basilica di Santa Chiara (below)

❷ Cappella Sansevero (p68)

❸ Chiesa e Scavi di San Lorenzo Maggiore (p70)

❹ Duomo (p75)

❺ MADRE Art Gallery (p75)

❻ Porta Nolana (p77)

Cloister paintings, Basilica di Santa Chiara   JEAN-BERNARD CARILLET

South of smog-choked Corso Umberto I sits Piazza Nolana, its 15th-century city gate, Porta Nolana, and one of the city's wildest morning markets. Further west, you will hit the Borgo degli Orefici (Goldsmiths' Quarter), Naples' medieval heart of bling.

SPACCANAPOLI

The main streets in the centro storico are Via San Biagio dei Librai (becoming Via Benedetto Croce to the west and Via Vicaria Vecchia to the east) and Via Tribunali one block to the north. Lined with historic churches and palazzi, most of the main sites are either on these streets or not far off them.

BASILICA DI SANTA CHIARA
MAP PP280-1

☎ 081 195 759 15; Via Benedetto Croce; cloisters €4; basilica ⏰ 9am-1pm & 4.30-7.30pm Mon-Sat, 8am-1pm & 5.30-7.30pm Sun, cloisters ⏰ 9.30am-5.30pm Mon-Sat, 9.30am-2pm Sun; 🚌 R4 to Via Monteoliveto
Simple, vast and severe, the bare Gothic interior that you see today is not the genuine

14th-century article, but a brilliant recreation of Gagliardo Primario's original design. Commissioned by Robert of Anjou for his wife Sancia di Maiorca, this hulking complex was built to house around 200 monks and the tombs of the Angevin royal family. Adhering to the Gothic principles of the day which equated height with vicinity to God, the original design met with a lukewarm reaction in some quarters – Robert's son Charles of Anjou brusquely dismissed it as nothing more than a 'stable'. Four centuries later, it was given a luscious baroque makeover by Domenico Antonio Vaccaro, Gaetano Buonocore and Giovanni Del Gaizo.

It all went up in flames on 4 August 1943 when the church took a direct hit during an Allied air raid on 4 August 1943. However, thanks to the skill and dedication of a small army of experts it has been largely restored to its original Franciscan simplicity. Features that survived the fire include part of a 14th-century fresco to the left of the main door and a chapel containing the tombs of the Bourbon kings from Ferdinand I to Francesco II.

To the left of the church, the famous tiled **cloisters** are a soothing getaway from the chaos outside. While the Angevin porticoes date back 14th century, the cloisters took on their current look in the 18th century thanks to the landscaping work of Domenico Antonio Vaccaro. The walkways that divide the central garden of lavender and citrus trees are lined with

72 ceramic-tiled octagonal columns connected by benches. Painted by Donato e Giuseppe Massa, the colourful tiles depict various scenes from rural life, from hunting and fishing to languid peasants posing. The four internal walls are covered with softly coloured 17th-century frescoes of Franciscan tales.

Adjacent to the cloisters is a small **museum** with an elegant display of ecclesiastical bits and bobs, including some impressive 14th-century busts and 17th-century tabernacles.

CAPPELLA E MUSEO DEL MONTE DI PIETÀ MAP PP280-1

☎ 081 580 71 11; Via San Biagio dei Librai 114; church ☉ 9am-2pm daily, gallery ☉ 9am-2pm Sat & Sun; 🚌 CS to Via Duomo

An imposing 16th-century complex, the Cappella e Museo del Monte di Pietà was originally home to the Pio Monte di Pietà, an organisation set up to issue interest-free loans to impoverished debtors. Ironically, it now houses sumptuous paintings, embroidery and silverware belonging to the Banco di Napoli (Bank of Naples). Most impressive, however, is the perfectly preserved mannerist **chapel** and its four richly decorated side rooms. Flanking the entrance to the single-barrel chapel are two sculptures by Pietro Bernini, while above sits Michelangelo Naccherino's *Pietà*. Inside, it is the striking 17th-century frescoes by Belisario Corenzio that take the breath away.

CAPPELLA SANSEVERO MAP PP280-1

☎ 081 551 84 70; Via de Sanctis 19; admission €6; ☉ 10am-5.40pm Wed-Mon; 🚌 R4 to Via Monteoliveto

For sheer 'how the hell did he do that' impact, the *Cristo Velato* (Veiled Christ) sculpture takes some beating. Giuseppe Sanmartino's incredible depiction of Jesus lying covered by a thin sheet is so realistic that it's tempting to try to lift the veil and look at Christ underneath. The magnificent centrepiece of this opulent building is one of three works that defy belief. Similarly lifelike, Francesco Queirolo's *Disinganno* (Disillusion) shows a man trying to untangle himself from a net, while *Pudicizia* (Modesty) by Antonio Corradini is a deliciously salacious veiled nude. Above them all you'll find riotously colourful frescoes by Francesco Maria Russo.

Originally built around the end of the 16th century to house the tombs of the de Sangro family, this Masonic-inspired temple was

given its current baroque fit-out by the bizarre Prince Raimondo de Sangro. Between 1749 and 1766 he commissioned the top artists of the day to decorate the interior, while he quietly got on with the task of embalming his dead servants. Determined to crack the art of human preservation, Raimondo was regarded with considerable fear by the local population. You can judge for yourself whether they were right by going down the stairs and checking out the two meticulously preserved human arterial systems.

CASTEL CAPUANO MAP PP280-1

☎ 081 223 72 44; Piazza Enrico De Nicola; Ⓜ Garibaldi

This Norman castle has been the seat of the city's civil courts since 1540, and the crowd of noisy families, slick lawyers and menacing police around the main entrance is a permanent feature. The fort was built in 1165 by William I to guard the nearby city gate Porta Capuana. Later enlarged by the Swabian king Frederick II and fortified by Charles I of Anjou, it remained a royal residence until the 16th century when Don Pedro de Toledo made it the city court. The castle is not open to the public.

Across the square, the imposing **Porta Capuana** (Map pp278–9) was one of the city's main medieval gates. Built on the orders of Ferdinand II of Aragon in 1484, the two cylindrical towers, named Honour and Virtue, flank a white marble-clad triumphal arch. Giuliano da Maiano oversaw the addition of Emperor Charles V's intricately decorated coat of arms in 1535.

CENTRO MUSEI SCIENZE NATURALI MAP PP280-1

☎ 081 253 51 60; www.musei.unina.it; Via Mezzocannone 8; admission each museum €1.50, all four €3; ☉ 9am-1.30pm & 3-5pm Mon & Thu, 9am-1.30pm Tue & Fri, 9am-1pm Sat & Sun; 🚌 R2 to Corso Umberto I

Housed at the university, this fascinating natural science centre features four museums. The Museo della Mineralogia, one of Italy's most important, features some 30,000 minerals, meteorites and quartz crystals collected from as far afield as Madagascar.

A hit with kids is the Museo della Zoologia, with its colourful collection of butterflies, birds and creepy insects.

Across the courtyard, the Museo della Antropologia boasts an eclectic collection of prehistoric relics including a grinning Palaeo-lithic skeleton from Puglia and a cute Bolivian mummy. Dinosaur bones await at the nearby Museo di Paleontologia.

CHIESA DEL GESÙ NUOVO MAP PP280-1

☎ 081 551 86 13; Piazza del Gesù Nuovo; ⏲ 7am-1pm & 4-7.30pm; 🚌 R4 to Via Monteoliveto

The Chiesa del Gesù Nuovo, on the northern side of the piazza, is one of the city's greatest examples of Renaissance architecture. Consecrated by the Jesuits in the 16th century, its diamond-shaped stone façade actually belongs to the 15th-century Palazzo Sanseverino, which was converted to create the church. Legend has it that the carved markings on the *piperno* (volcanic rock) stones are inversed esoteric symbols that have cursed the building (p8).

The exterior itself was desiged by Giuseppe Valeriani, while a series of big-name baroque artists, including Francesco Solimena, Luca Giordano and Cosimo Fanzago, transformed the barrel-vaulted interior into the frescoed wonder that you see today.

In sharp contrast to the opulence of the main church is a small **chapel** dedicated to the much-loved local saint Giuseppe Moscati. Here you'll find walls covered with *ex votos* (including golden syringes) and a recreation of the great man's study, complete with the armchair in which he died. Canonised in 1977, Moscati (1880–1927) was a local doctor who spent his life helping the city's poor.

CHIESA DEL GESÙ VECCHIO MAP PP280-1

☎ 081 552 66 39; Via Giovanni Paladino 38; ⏲ 7.30am-noon & 3.45-6pm Mon-Sat, 7.30am-noon Sun; 🚌 R2 to Corso Umberto I

Baroque cranked up to the max, step inside for sumptuous statues by Cosimo Fanzago and frescoes by Francesco Solimena and Battista Caracciolo. Established in 1570 and completely rebuilt in the 17th century, this is Naples' oldest Jesuit church.

CHIESA DI SAN DOMENICO MAGGIORE MAP PP280-1

☎ 081 45 91 88; Piazza San Domenico Maggiore 8a; 🚌 R4 to Via Monteoliveto

Rudely giving its back to the Piazza, this vast Gothic number features a double flight of marble steps leading up to the apse. Completed in 1324 on the orders of Charles I of Anjou, it was built onto the medieval church

High-impact façade, Chiesa del Gesù Nuovo   JEAN-BERNARD CARILLET

of San Michele Arcangelo as the royal church of the Angevins.

The church's three-nave interior, a cross between baroque and 19th-century neo-Gothic, has undergone various facelifts, leaving little of the original Gothic design. Of the few 14th-century remnants, the frescoes by Pietro Cavallini in the **Cappella Brancaccio** take the cake. In the **Cappellone del Crocifisso**, the 13th-century *Crocifisso tra La Vergine e San Giovanni* is said to have spoken to St Thomas Aquinas, asking him: *'Bene scripsisti di me, Thoma; quam recipies a me pro tu labore mercedem?'* ('You've written good things about me, Thomas, what will you get in return?') – *'Domine non aliam nisi te'* ('Nothing if not you, O Lord'), Thomas replied diplomatically.

The softly lit sacristy contains a beautiful ceiling fresco by Francesco Solimena and 45 coffins of Aragon princes and other nobles. Curiously enough, the first bishop of New York, Richard Luke Concanen (1747–1810), is also buried here.

CHIESA DI SAN PAOLO MAGGIORE
MAP PP280-1

☎ 081 45 40 48; Piazza San Gaetano 76; ⏲ 9am-5.30pm Mon-Sat, 11am-noon Sun; 🚇 CS to Via Duomo
Leading up to the entrance of this baroque beauty is a grand double staircase built by Francesco Grimaldi in 1603. Situated on the site of a Roman temple to Castor and Pollux, of which the two columns flanking the entrance are the only visible sign, the church dates to the 8th century but was almost entirely rebuilt at the end of the 16th century. A huge gold-stuccoed interior features paintings by Massimo Stanzione and Paolo De Matteis and stunning frescoes by Francesco Solimena tucked away in the sacristy to the right of the altar.

CHIESA DI SANT'ANGELO A NILO
MAP PP280-1

☎ 081 420 12 22; entrance at Vico Donnaromita 15; ⏲ 9am-1pm & 4-6pm Mon-Sat, 9am-1pm Sun; 🚇 R4 to Via Monteoliveto
Benignly presided over by a quartet of tubby gilt cherubs, this modest 14th-century church contains one of the first great artworks to grace the Neapolitan Renaissance – the majestic tomb of Cardinal Brancaccio, the church's founder. Although considered a part of Naples' artistic heritage, the sarcophagus was actually sculpted by artists in Pisa. Donatello, Michelozzo and Pagno di Lapo Partigiani spent a year chipping away at it before shipping it down to Naples in 1427.

CHIESA E CHIOSTRO DI SAN GREGORIO ARMENO MAP PP280-1

☎ 081 420 63 85; Via San Gregorio Armeno 44; church ⏲ 8.30am-noon Mon & Wed-Sat, 9.30am-12.30pm Tue & Sun; 🚇 CS to Via Duomo
There are churches and then there is the Chiesa e Chiostro di San Gregorio Armeno. Zealously run by a posse of snappy nuns, the recently restored 16th-century church boasts a jaw-dropping baroque interior designed by Nicolò Tagliacozzi Canale. Highlights include sumptuous wood and papier-mâché choir stalls, a 17th-century marble altar by Dionisio Lazzarn and lavish frescoes by Paolo de Matteis and Luca Giordano, whose masterpiece *The Embarkation, Journey and Arrival of the Armenia Nuns with the Relics of St Gregory* recounts the 13th-century exile of nuns fleeing persecution in Constantinople. Once in Naples, the sisters set up this church, naming it after the Bishop of Armenia, San Gregorio, whose earthly

remains they were carrying with them. More famously, though, they also kept the relics and dried blood of Santa Patrizia (St Patricia) who, having escaped from Constantinople, died in Naples some time between the 4th and 8th centuries. Patricia's powdered blood is said to liquefy every Tuesday, unlike that of Naples' patron saint San Gennaro, who can only manage it three times a year.

The peaceful, citrus-filled cloisters are accessible by a gate on nearby Vico G Maffei.

CHIESA E SCAVI DI SAN LORENZO MAGGIORE MAP PP280-1

☎ 081 211 08 60; www.sanlorenzomaggiorenapoli.it; Via dei Tribunali 316; excavations & museum adult/child €5/3; ⏲ 9am-5.30pm Mon-Sat, 9.30am-1.30pm Sun; 🚇 CS to Via Duomo
Soaring, vast and bathed in light, this French Gothic masterpiece was commenced in 1270 by French architects who built the apse. Local architects took over the following century, recycling ancient columns in the nave. Victim of a baroque makeover in the 17th- and 18th centuries, it was stripped back to its original Gothic splendour in the mid-20th century, although a concession was made for Ferdinando Sanfelice's petite baroque façade

Catherine of Austria, who died in 1323, is buried here in a beautiful mosaiced tomb. Legend has it that this was where Boccaccio first fell for Mary of Anjou, the inspiration for his character Fiammetta, while the poet Petrarch called the adjoining convent home in 1345.

Beneath the church are some extraordinary **scavi** (excavations) of the original Graeco-Roman city. Stretching the length of the underground area is a 54m-long road lined with ancient bakeries, wineries and communal laundries. At the far end of the *cardo* (road) there's a *cryptoporticus* (covered market) with seven barrel-vaulted rooms. There are very few signs to explain the patchwork of crumbling walls and alleyways but this takes little away from the experience – simply let your imagination do the job. (You can, however, buy a glossy leaflet explaining the excavations in Italian or English for €1.50.)

Back upstairs, the recently opened **Museo dell'Opera di San Lorenzo Maggiore** houses a fascinating collection of local archaeological finds, including Graeco-Roman sarcophagi, ceramics and crockery from the digs below. Other treasures include vivid 9th-century ceramics, Angevin frescoes, paintings by Giuseppe Marullo and Luigi Velpi, and camp ecclesiastical drag for 16th-century bishops.

Under the archways of Chiesa di San Lorenzo Maggiore

JEAN-BERNARD CARILLET

CHIESA SANTA CATERINA A FORMIELLO MAP PP278-9

☎ 081 44 42 97; Piazza Enrico de Nicola 65; ⏰ 8.30am-8pm Mon-Sat, 8.30am-1pm Sun; Ⓜ Garibaldi

Despite the grime, this richly decorated Renaissance church is one of Naples' most beautiful. Harmoniously proportioned and softly lit, it boasts a series of exceptional frescoes by Luigi Garzi, as well as the relics of the martyrs of Otranto. The martyrs were all killed in 1480 when Turkish invaders swept into the Puglian coastal town after a lengthy siege and vented their bloody fury by killing 800 citizens.

Dedicated to Alexandrian martyr Santa Caterina, the church was completed in 1593. For 300 years it belonged to the Dominicans, but in the 19th century they moved out and the military moved in, transforming it into a wool factory.

CHIESA SANTA MARIA DELLE ANIME PURGATORIO AD ARCO MAP PP280-1

☎ 081 29 26 22; Via dei Tribunali 39; ⏰ 9am-2pm Mon-Sat; 🚌 CS to Via Duomo

Guarded by three bronze skulls, this 17th-century church is macabre. Inside, two winged skulls stare out from either side of the main altar. Built by a congregation dedicated to praying for souls in purgatory, the church became a centre for the Neapolitan cult of the dead which, although officially banned, is said to be far from extinct. Cult practices included lavishing care and gifts on a skull as a means of keeping in touch with an absent loved one. Below the church in the **hypogeum** (currently closed) you can still see a dusty hoard of skulls and bones.

On a lighter note, the church boasts some fine paintings by Massimo Stanzione and Luca Giordano.

CHIESA SANTA MARIA DONNAREGINA VECCHIA MAP P286

☎ 081 29 91 01; Vico Donnaregina 25; ⏰ 9am-12.30pm Sat by appointment only; 🚌 CS to Via Duomo

Home to Naples University's architectural restoration department, this beautiful 14th-century church was built at the behest of Mary of Hungary, wife of Charles II of Anjou. Featuring a light-filled pentagonal apse, its walls and fan-vaults reveal traces of Giotto-esque frescoes, decorated with Angevin lilies and the red and white stripes of Hungary. Above the choir, coffered ceilings drip with beautiful frescoes by Pietro Cavallino, while Mary's spectacular marble tomb (created by Tina da Camaino between 1326 and 1327) sits along the left-side wall.

71

CHIESA SANTA MARIA MAGGIORE
MAP PP280-1

Via dei Tribunali 16; 🕙 **9am-1pm Mon-Sat;** 🚌 **CS to Via Duomo**

The full title of this church, Santa Maria Maggiore alla Pietrasanta, is a reference to a 17th-century practice of kissing the church's *pietrasanta* (holy stone) to gain indulgences. Dating to the 6th century, the church was originally built by San Pomponio, the Bishop of Naples. According to legend, he did so to appease worried locals, who reported sightings of the devil in the form of a pig on the site. The church was modified in the 17th century by Cosimo Fanzago, whose dome is visible from miles around. The Romanesque **campanile** (bell tower) is one of Naples' oldest, built sometime between the 10th and 11th centuries. Adjacent to the church, the 15th-century **Cappella Pontano** boasts an exquisite majolica-tiled floor.

CHIESA SAN PIETRO A MAIELLA
MAP PP280-1

☎ **081 45 90 08; Piazza Luigi Miraglia 25;** 🕙 **7.30am-noon & 5.30-7.30pm Sun-Fri, 5-7.30pm Sat;** Ⓜ **Dante**

Not many churches are dedicated to hermits. But not many hermits go on to become popes as Pietro del Morrone did when, in 1294, he was named Pope Celestine V. The typically Gothic interior dates to the 14th century, but the ceiling is pure baroque, with 10 superlative round paintings by Mattia Preti. Along with the impressive gilded wooden ceilings, they were discovered under stucco during a late-19th-century restoration. Further baroque touches are provided by Cosimo Fanzago and Massimo Stanzione, whose *Madonna Appearing to Celestine V* hangs in one of the side chapels on the right.

Soak it all up to the sound of Bach; since 1826, Naples' Conservatory – one of Italy's finest music schools – has been housed in the adjoining **convent**.

GUGLIA DI SAN GENNARO MAP PP280-1

Piazza Riario Sforza; 🚌 **CS to Via Duomo**

The oldest of the three obelisks in the centro storico, the Guglia di San Gennaro was dedicated to the city's patron saint in 1636. And like the Guglia di San Domenico it was a token of gratitude, only this time to San Gennaro for protecting the city from the 1631 eruption of Mt Vesuvius. The stonework is by Cosimo Fanzago, the bronze statue at the top by Tommaso Montani.

LARGO SAN GIOVANNI MAGGIORE
MAP PP280-1

🚌 **R2 to Corso Umberto I**

This fetching little square heaves with students, who drink and groove at Kestè (p130). Dominating the square's western flank is Giovanni da Nola's impressive 16th-century **Palazzo Giusso**, home to the Istituto Universitario Orientale. Facing this is the **Chiesa San Giovanni Pappacoda** (Map pp280–1), whose original 15th-century structure barely survived the attentions of an 18th-century makeover. Antonio Baboccio's Gothic portal remains, along with a bell tower constructed out of tufa, marble and *piperno* stone.

OSPEDALE DELLE BAMBOLE
MAP PP280-1

☎ **339 587 22 74; Via San Biagio dei Librai 81;** Ⓜ **Dante**

You may not have a Barbie in need of a facelift while in Naples, but the city's legendary doll hospital is worth an emergency visit – hanging dolls' heads, injured saints, flower-sprouting mannequins and fairy lights. All that's missing is a puppet called Pinocchio.

PALAZZO SPINELLI DI LAURINO
MAP PP280-1

Via dei Tribunali 362; 🚌 **CS to Via Duomo**

Dodge past the porter patrolling the entrance to this Renaissance palazzo and you'll find an unusual oval-shaped courtyard. This, together with the imposing double staircase, was the work of architect Ferdinando Sanfelice, whose hallmark staircase design was a must-have for 18th-century Neapolitan nobility.

On the 1st floor, Parisian Natalie de Saint Phalle exhibits the cutting-edge work of her artists-in-residence in one week exhibitions commencing 23 March, 23 June and 23 September.

PIAZZA BELLINI
MAP PP280-1

Ⓜ **Dante**

Just to the north of the western end of Via dei Tribunali, lively Piazza Bellini is a hotspot for the city's bohemians. Each night, its ivy-clad cafés and bars hum with jazz-loving writers, left-leaning students and a healthy dose of flirtatious glances. At its centre, 4th-century ruins of the Greek **city walls** add a classical touch.

JEAN-BERNARD CARILLET

PIAZZA DEL GESÙ NUOVO MAP PP280-1

Ⓜ Dante

Flanked by the spiky **Chiesa del Gesù Nuovo** (p69) and the **Basilica di Santa Chiara** (p67), this lively square is one of Naples' most beautiful. For hundreds of years it was the principal western entrance to the city. But it wasn't until two major modifications in the 16th century that the piazza took on its current proportions. Firstly, Ferrante Sanseverino knocked down the houses that were blocking his beautiful 15th-century palazzo (later to become the Chiesa del Gesù Nuovo) and in one fell swoop cleared the square's northern flank. Some years later, Spanish viceroy Don Pedro de Toledo demolished the Angevin city gate and once again moved the city walls westwards.

At its centre soars Giuseppe Genuino's ornate **Guglia dell'Immacolata** (Map pp280–1), built between 1747 and 1750. On 8 December, the Feast of the Immacolata, firemen scramble up to the top to place a wreath of flowers at the Virgin Mary's feet.

PIAZZA SAN DOMENICO MAGGIORE

MAP PP280-1

Ⓜ Dante

For some unexplained reason, this airy square is a hit with dreadlocked Spaniards. Along with local students and foreign tourists, they flock here for a late-night beer, cigarette and chat.

Headed by the **Chiesa di San Domenico Maggiore** (p69) and flanked by imposing **palazzi**, the piazza was a series of humble kitchen gardens until the 15th century when the Aragonese decided to make San Domenico their royal church. In the 17th century, various aristocrats built their townhouses around the square. At its centre sits the very baroque **Guglia di San Domenico** (Map pp280–1). Decorated by Cosimo Fanzago and completed in 1737 by Domenico Antonio Vaccaro, it was a token of gratitude to San Domenico for ridding the city of the plague epidemic of 1656.

PIO MONTE DELLA MISERICORDIA

MAP PP280-1

☎ 081 44 69 44; Via dei Tribunali 253; gallery admission €5; church ⏰ 9am-2pm daily, gallery ⏰ 8.30am-2pm Thu-Tue; 🚌 CS to Via Duomo

Caravaggio's masterpiece *Le Sette Opere di Misericordia* (The Seven Acts of Mercy) is considered by many to be the single most important painting in Naples. And it's here that you'll see it, hung above the main altar of this small octagonal church. The painting magnificently demonstrates Caravaggio's chiaroscuro style that had a revolutionary impact in Naples (see p46). A disturbing image, it depicts two angels reaching down towards a group of shadowy Neapolitan characters, while on the right a hungry grey-bearded man is breast-fed by a young woman.

On the 1st floor of the 17th-century church, a small **art gallery** boasts a fine collection of Renaissance and baroque paintings by names such as Francesco de Mura, Giuseppe de Ribera and Paul van Somer.

73

PORT'ALBA MAP PP280-1

Via Port'Alba; Ⓜ Dante

A Mediterranean Diagon Alley, Port'Alba is an atmospheric porthole into the centro storico. Crammed with vintage bookshops and stalls, this is the place for leather-bound classics, dog-eared Manzoni or obscure 1950s sci-fi novels. The gate, which leads through to Piazza Dante, was opened in 1625 by Antonio Alvárez, the Spanish viceroy of Naples. At the eastern end of Via Port'Alba, southbound Via San Sebastiano boasts the world's greatest concentration of musical instrument shops alongside 49th St in New York.

STATUA DEL NILO MAP PP280-1

Piazzetta Nilo, Via Nilo; 🚌 R4 to Via Monteoliveto

This rather grim statue of the ancient Egyptian river god Nilo was put up by the city's Alexandrian merchants, who lived in the area during Roman times. When they moved out the statue disappeared, eventually turning up minus its head in the 15th century. Renamed *Il Corpo di Napoli* (The Body of Naples), it remained headless until the end of the 18th century when a great bearded bonce was added.

VIA SAN GREGORIO ARMENO
MAP PP280-1

🚌 CS to Via Duomo

Naples is famous for its traditional *presepi* (nativity scenes) and Via San Gregorio Armeno is where Italians come to buy theirs. Running off Spaccanapoli, the street heaves with artisan studios and shops in which crib-makers craft an eclectic range of figurines and crib pieces, from beautiful hand-carved baby saviours to cutting celebrity caricatures. Popular after Silvio Berlusconi's election defeat was a figurine of the media mogul carrying his head and testicles on a platter.

VIA DUOMO

Built as part of the late 19th-century Risanamento (slum-clearance programme), Via Duomo connects Corso Umberto I with Via Foria and more or less runs parallel to Via Toledo.

BASILICA DI SAN GIORGIO MAGGIORE MAP PP280-1

☎ 081 28 79 32; Via Duomo 237; 🕑 8.15am-noon & 5-7.30pm Mon-Sat, 8.30am-1.30pm Sun; 🚌 CS to Via Duomo

Standing on the site of a pagan temple, the austere Basilica di San Giorgio Maggiore is one of Naples' oldest churches, built by St Severus in the 4th century. Despite a thorough restyling by designaholic Cosimo Fanzago in the mid-17th century, the earthy Palaeo-Christian apse survives. Less fortunate was the right-hand nave of the church, demolished to make way for Via Duomo in the late 19th century. The third chapel features frescoes by Francesco Solimena.

CHIESA E PINACOTECA DEI GIROLAMINI MAP PP280-1

☎ 081 44 91 39; Via Duomo 142; 🕑 church varies, cloisters & gallery 9.30am-12.30pm Mon-Sat; 🚌 CS to Via Duomo

Opposite the Duomo is the entrance to the Chiesa dei Girolamini, also called San Filippo

ALTAR TO THE MARADONA

Opposite the Statua del Nilo there's an altar to an altogether more temporal deity. Argentine football player Diego Armando Maradona is worshipped throughout the city and so it's only natural that he should have his own shrine. Displayed on the wall outside the Bar Nilo, the **Maradona altar** (Map pp280–1) a small glass case containing a number of artefacts relating to the great man. Stuck to an epic poem written in his honour is a small wiry black hair – 'Kapel Original of Maradona' reads the English label, a direct translation of the Italian *Capello Originale di Maradona*. You can also admire a small container full of genuine Maradona tears. And shame on anyone who suggests it's only water.

Neri, a rich baroque church of two façades. The more imposing 18th-century façade is closed for restoration. The adjoining 17th-century convent features a raffish cloister, complete with rambling lemon trees and faded majolica tiles. A small **gallery** on the convent's 1st floor features superb local art, including works by Luca Giordano and Battista Caracciolo.

DUOMO MAP PP280-1

☎ 081 44 90 97; www.duomodinapoli.com; Via Duomo 147; ⏲ 8am-12.30pm & 4.30-7pm Mon-Sat, 8.30am-1pm & 5-7pm Sun; 🚍 CS to Via Duomo

Every year in May, September and December thousands gather in the Duomo to pray for a miracle – that the blood of the city's patron saint San Gennaro, kept here in two phials, will liquefy and save Naples from any potential disaster. When the miracle failed to occur in 1944, Vesuvius erupted. When it failed in 1980, the city was hit by a devastating earthquake.

Vast and stunning, Naples' spiritual centre-piece sits on the site of earlier churches, themselves preceded by a pagan temple to Neptune. Begun by Charles I of Anjou in 1272 and consecrated in 1315, it was largely destroyed in a 1456 earthquake. Copious nips and tucks over the centuries, including the addition of a late-19th-century neo-Gothic façade, have created a melange of styles and influences.

Topping the huge central nave is a gilded coffered ceiling studded with late-mannerist art. The high sections of the nave and the transept were decorated by Luca Giordano.

The 17th-century baroque **Cappella di San Gennaro** (Chapel of St Januarius; also known as the Chapel of the Treasury) was designed by Giovanni Cola di Franco and completed in 1637. It features a fiery painting by Giuseppe de Ribera and a bevy of silver busts and bronze statues depicting all the saints of Naples' churches. Above them, a heavenly dome glows with frescoes by Giovanni Lanfranco. Hidden away in a strongbox behind the altar is a 14th-century silver bust in which sits the skull of San Gennaro and the two phials which hold his miraculous blood.

The next chapel eastwards contains an urn with the saint's bones and a cupboard full of femurs, tibias and fibulas. Below the high altar is the **Cappella Carafa**, a Renaissance chapel built to house yet more of the saint's remains.

On the north aisle the **Basilica di Santa Restituta** sits one of Naples' oldest basilicas, dating to the 4th century. Incorporated into the main cathedral, it was subject to an almost complete

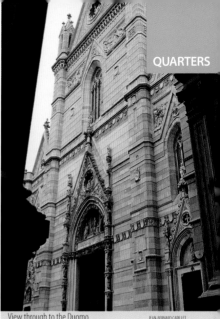

View through to the Duomo   JEAN-BERNARD CARILLET

makeover following damage incurred in an earthquake in 1688. Beyond this is the Duomo's **archaeological zone** (admission €3; ⏲ 9am-12pm & 4.30-7pm Mon-Sat, 9am-12.30pm Sun). The tunnels beneath lead down into the fascinating remains of the site's original Greek and Roman buildings and roads. Here, too, is the baptistry, the oldest in Western Europe, with its glittering 4th-century mosaics.

MADRE (MUSEO D'ARTE CONTEMPORANEA DONNAREGINA) MAP P286

☎ 081 562 45 61; www.museomadre.it; Via Settembrini 79; €7; ⏲ 10am-9pm Mon-Thu & Sun, 10am-midnight Fri & Sat; Ⓜ Cavour

The hottest gallery in town, MADRE is to Naples what MoMA is to Manhattan. Housed in the historic Donnaregina Palace, this world-class art space was designed by Portuguese architect Alvaro Siza y Vieira and boasts the city's best collection of contemporary art. While the ground and 2nd floors host cutting-edge temporary exhibitions, the 1st floor houses the museum's permanent collection. Highlights include Jeff Koons' über-kitsch *Wild Boy and Puppy*, Rebecca Horn's eerie collection of synchronised skulls and moving mirrors *Spirits,* and a perspective-warping installation by Mumbai-born artist Amish Kapok.

FOR CHILDREN

Centro Musei Scienze Naturali (p68)
Edenlandia (p106)
Città della Scienza (p106)
Stazione Zoologica (p89)
Catacomba di San Gennaro (p93)
Anfiteatro Flavio, Pozzuoli (p103)
Solfatara crater, Pozzuoli (p104)

MUSEO DEL TESORO DI SAN GENNARO MAP PP280-1

☎ 081 29 49 80; Via Duomo 149; admission €5.50;
🕑 9am-6.30pm Mon-Sat, 10am-5pm Sun; 🚌 CS to Via Duomo

The city's love affair with San Gennaro is well documented at this savvy museum at the Duomo's southern end. Two floors glimmer with precious ex voto gifts made to the saint, from bronze busts and sumptuous paintings to silver ampullas and a gilded 18th-century sedan chair used to shelter the saint's bust on rainy procession days. Included in the price of the ticket is a multilingual audioguide.

MERCATO

East of Via Pietro Colletta and south of Corso Umberto I lie the shabby and lively streets of the Mercato district. This is the place for rough-and-ready markets, fashion fakes, dusty baroque and streetside kebabs.

CHIESA DI SAN PIETRO MARTIRE
MAP PP280-1

☎ 081 552 68 55; Piazzetta Bonghi 1; 🕑 7am-1pm & 5-7pm; 🚌 R2 to Corso Umberto I

Originally commissioned to help clean up the crime-packed port in the 13th century, this Dominican church and monastery received an elegant cloister by Giovan Francesco di Palma in the 16th century. During the decade of French rule (1806–15) the monks were kicked out and the monastery became a tobacco factory. It remained so until 1978 when, after a major revamp, the professors of the faculty of Literature and Philosophy at University of Naples moved into their new, and current, home.

CHIESA DI SANTA MARIA DEL CARMINE MAP PP280-1

☎ 081 20 11 96; Piazza del Carmine; 🕑 6.30am-12.30pm Mon-Sat, 6.30am-2pm Sun; 🚌 152 to Via Nuova Marina

One of Naples' oldest churches, Santa Maria del Carmine plays a starring role in Neapolitan folklore. When Conrad (Corradino) of Swabia was charged for attempting to depose the king in 1268, his mother Elisabetta di Baviera desperately tried to collect the money to pay Charles I of Anjou a ransom for her son's life. But the money arrived too late and Conrad was beheaded for treason. Grief-stricken, she gave the money to the church, on the condition that the Carmelite brothers prayed for him every day. They agreed and the cashed-up brothers built the church you see today. There's a monument to Conrad in the transept.

However, it's the 13th-century Byzantine icon behind the main altar, the *Madonna della Bruna,* that is the star attraction here. Attributed with miraculous powers, the Madonna is celebrated every year on 16 July when crowds flock here to see the 17th-century **campanile** lit up by fireworks. The city's tallest bell tower, its onion-dome design is the work of Giacomo di Conforto and Giovanni Donzelli.

Further myth (and miracle) surrounds a wooden crucifix that hangs in a tabernacle under the church's main arch. According to legend, a cannonball fired at the church in 1439 during the war between Alfonso of Aragon and Robert of Anjou flew into the church and headed straight for the crucifix. In the nick of time Jesus ducked and the cannonball sailed harmlessly past.

History rather than tradition records that it was from this church that Tommaso Aniello (Masaniello) harangued the mob into rising against the Spanish rulers. Defeated and killed by the Spanish, he is said to be buried in an unmarked tomb in the church.

At the southern end of the square, on the opposite side of busy Via Nuova Marina, stand remnants of the city's 14th-century medieval fortress, **Castello del Carmine**.

PIAZZA DEL MERCATO MAP PP280-1

🚌 C55 to Corso G Garibaldi

Where cars now park, heads once rolled. For centuries, this scruffy square was the site of gruesome public executions, including that of Conrad of Swabia, whose mother paid for the nearby **Chiesa di Santa Maria del Carmine** (left), and those of over 200 ill-fated supporters of the 1799 Parthenopean Republic. Equally grim is its honour as the starting spot for the devastating plague of 1656.

The square sits at the easternmost point of the city's old medieval wall. To the north

Porta Nolana market

GREG ELMS

shines the green- and yellow-tiled dome of the boarded-up Chiesa di Santa Croce al Mercato, while in the southwest corner you will find a bizarre pyramid supported by four curious creatures. Only one remains intact – with the head of puffy-cheeked girl and the body of a lion.

One block west along Via Sant'Eligio stands the starkly gothic **Chiesa Sant'Eligio** (Map pp280–1; ☎ 081 553 84 29; Via Sant'Eligio; ⏰ 8-12.30pm Mon-Fri, 8am-12.30pm & 5-6.30pm Sat, 10am-1.30pm Sun). The first Angevin church in Naples, Sant'Eligio was built in 1270 by Charles I of Anjou and features a beautiful external clock arch complete with a (working!) 15th-century clock.

PORTA NOLANA & MERCATO
MAP PP280-1

Via Sopramuro; ⏰ R2 to Corso Umberto I
At the head of Via Sopramuro stands the 15th-century Porta Nolana, one of the medieval city gates. Two cylindrical towers, optimistically named Faith and Hope, support an arch decorated with a bas-relief of Ferdinand I of Aragon on horseback. Under and beyond it, sits the most vivacious street market in all of Naples (see the boxed text, p140). Street theatre at its rawest, it's an intoxicating scene of glistening seafood, buxom vegetables,

plump cheeses, contraband cigarette stalls and pink inflatable dolphins.

SANTISSIMA ANNUNZIATA MAP PP280-1
☎ 081 254 26 08; Via dell'Annunziata 34; ⏰ 7.30am-noon & 4.30-7.30pm Mon-Sat, 7.30am-1pm Sun; ⏰ R2 to Corso Umberto I
This 14th-century religious complex is as well known for its former orphanage as it is for its jasmine-scented, light-filled basilica. Designed by Carlo Vanvitelli (son of the better-known Luigi) at the end of the 18th century, the basilica's white and light-grey interior is a bold affair with some 44 Corinthian columns lining the nave and a soaring 67m-high dome. The third chapel on the left features the wooden statue of the Virgin Mary, one of the few remnants from the original 14th-century church. Affectionately known as *mamma chiatta* (chubby mother), its image was once reproduced on the leaden medals worn by the children left at the former orphanage to the left of the basilica (☎ 081 28 90 32; ⏰ 9am-6pm Mon-Sat).

Hear you can still see the infamous **ruota** (wheel) set in the orphanage wall. In use up until the 1980s, desperate parents would place the baby in a hollow in the wheel and turn it. On the other side of the wall sat a nun ready to take the baby, wash it in the adjacent basin and record its time and date of entry.

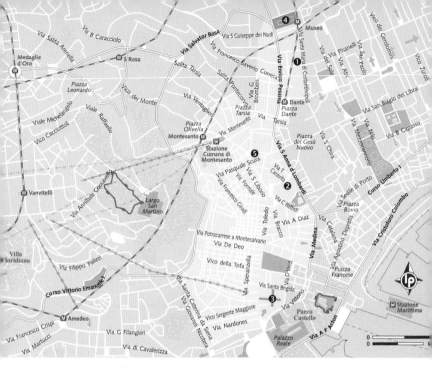

TOLEDO & QUARTIERI SPAGNOLI

Eating p120; Shopping p141; Sleeping p150

In the 19th century, Grand Tour travellers swooned at its grand design. Today, the masses hit the strip to swoon over new-season threads and decked-out locals.

On the night that Italy won the 2006 World Cup, hundreds of thousands of flag-wrapped fans poured onto Via Toledo to blow their horns, let off firecrackers and make fun of their frog-eating opponents. Since its construction by Spanish viceroy Don Pedro de Toledo in the 16th century, this palazzo-flanked high street (also known as Via Roma) has pulled a crowd. Its pedestrianised southern end is the place for trend-savvy shopping, with old-school shops and kitsch further up near Piazza Dante. From here, Via Toledo becomes Via Enrico Pessina as it continues north to the booty-packed Museo Archeologico Nazionale and beyond. East of Via Toledo, along Via A Diaz, the city takes a brutal turn with colossal fascist classics like the Palazzo delle Poste.

Immediately west, however, are the razor-thin, criss-crossing streets of the Quartieri Spagnoli. Originally built to house Don Pedro's Spanish troops, the area is better known as a hotbed of crime and urban malaise. The infamous *bassi* (one room, ground-floor houses) became, and still are, home to entire families, while the mean streets provided fertile ground for the spread of the Camorra (the Neapolitan Mafia); that said, a run-in with the Godfather is highly unlikely. With an eye on your bag, venture in for some daytime exploration. The district might be low on sites per se but its washing-strung streets harbour hidden delights, from classic trattorie and century-old artisan workshops, to the unmissable Pignasecca market.

highlights

TOLEDO & QUARTIERI SPAGNOLI

❶ Accademia di Belle Arti (below)
....
❷ Chiesa di Sant'Anna dei Lombardi (right)
....
❸ Galleria Umberto I (right)
....
❹ Museo Archeologico Nazionale (p80)
....
❺ La Pignasecca Market (p140)

Galleria Umberto I   GREG ELMS

ACCADEMIA DI BELLE ARTI MAP PP280-1

☎ 081 44 42 45; Via Santa Maria di Costantinopoli
107; admission €5; ☼ 10am-2pm Mon-Thu, 2-6pm Fri,
10am-2pm Sat; Ⓜ Dante

Buzzing with brush-clutching art students,
this academy was once the convent of San
Giovanni Battista delle Monache. Built in
the 17th-century, it was given a thorough
makeover in 1864 by architect Enrico Alvino,
who gave the building a neoclassical façade,
grand staircase, and two noble lions to guard
the main entrance. The 1st-floor gallery houses
an important collection of mainly 19th-
century Neapolitan work, many by former
academy alumni, including watercolourist
Giacinti Gigante and sculptor Vincenzo
Gemito. That so many of Gemito's busts were
created in 1874 is not a coincidence – he
frantically chipped away to pay his way out
of military service.

CHIESA DI SANT'ANNA DEI LOMBARDI MAP PP280-1

☎ 081 551 33 33; Piazza
Monteoliveto; ☼ 8.30am-12.30pm
Mon-Fri; ➡ R4 to Via Monteoliveto

The Chiesa di Sant'Anna dei Lombardi is a
sanctified stunner. In fact, it's often spoken
of as more a museum of Renaissance art
than a church; a fact that owes much to the
close links that existed between the Neapolitan Aragonese and the Florentine Medici
dynasty.

The main, but by no means only attraction
is Guido Mazzoni's spectacular *Pietà*. Dating to
1492, the terracotta ensemble is made up of
eight life-size terracotta figures surrounding
the dead body of Christ. Originally the figures
were painted, but even without colour they
make quite an impression.

The **Sacrestia** is a work of art in itself. The
walls are lined with gloriously inlaid wood
panels by Giovanni da Verona, while the
ceiling is covered by Giorgio Vasari's 16th-
century frescoes depicting the Allegories and
Symbols of Faith.

Across Via Monteoliveto from the church is
the 16th-century **Palazzo Gravina** (Map pp280–
1), the seat of Naples University's architecture
faculty.

GALLERIA PRINCIPE DI NAPOLI
MAP PPP280-1

☎ 081 44 42 45; Piazza Museo Nazionale; Ⓜ Museo

Naples' oldest shopping arcade has seen
better days. Now abandoned, it was designed
by Nicola Briglia and built between 1876 and
1883. Its soaring neoclassical look is almost
identical to that of its younger, better-loved
sibling Galleria Umberto I, located at the lower
end of Via Toledo.

GALLERIA UMBERTO I MAP PP280-1

Via San Carlo; ➡ R2 to Via San Carlo

Doppelgänger of Milan's Galleria Vittorio
Emanuele, the trick to appreciating this
mammoth glass-and-steel masterpiece is
to walk with your head tilted up: its grand
central dome soars to a lofty 56 metres. The
mysterious stars of David imbedded in the
glasswork are said to suggest local Jewish
investment in the building. Complete with a
sumptuous marble floor, the Galleria makes
a surreal setting for impromptu late-night
soccer games.

Pompeii's *La Battaglia di Alessandro Contro Dario* mosaic, now in Museo Archeologico Nazionale   JEAN-BERNARD CARILLET

MUSEO ARCHEOLOGICO
NAZIONALE MAP P286

☎ 081 44 01 66; www.marketplace.it/museo
.nazionale; Piazza Museo Nazionale 19; admission
€6.50; 🕘 9am-7.30pm Wed-Mon; Ⓜ Museo

Even if the idea of an archaeology museum usually sends you to sleep, this place will amaze you. With many of the best finds from Pompeii and Herculaneum on display, as well as hundreds of classical sculptures and a trove of ancient Roman porn, the Museo Archeologico Nazionale is world museum heavyweight. You could easily spend a couple of days exploring the museum, although it is possible to do an abridged tour in a morning.

Originally a cavalry barracks and later the seat of the city's university (Palazzo dei Regni Studi), the museum was established by the Bourbon king Charles VII in the late 18th century to house the rich collection of antiquities he had inherited from his mother, Elisabetta Farnese. However, he never lived to see its inauguration; he died in 1788, 28 years before the Reale Museo Borbonico (Royal Bourbon Museum) was opened by his successor Ferdinand IV. Forty-four years later, in 1860, the museum became the property of the new Italian state.

The museum is spread over five floors. Before you venture into the galleries (numbered in Roman numerals), it's worth investing €7.50 in the *National Archaeological Museum of Naples* quick-guide or, to concentrate on the highlights, €4 for an audioguide in English.

Starting in the basement you'll find the Borgia collection of Etruscan and Egyptian relics, while it's on the ground floor that the Farnese collection of colossal Greek and Roman sculptures is displayed. The two highlights of classical sculpture are the world-famous *Toro Farnese* (Farnese Bull) in Room XVI and the gigantic *Ercole* (Hercules). Sculpted in the

early 3rd century AD and noted in the writings of Pliny, the *Toro Farnese*, probably a Roman copy of a Greek original, depicts the death of Dirce, Queen of Thebes. According to Greek mythology she was tied to a wild bull by Zeto and Amphion as punishment for her treatment of their mother Antiope, the first wife of King Lykos of Thebes. Carved from a single colossal block of marble, the sculpture was discovered in 1545 near the Baths of Caracalla in Rome and was restored by Michelangelo, before eventually being shipped to Naples in 1787.

Ercole (Room XI) was discovered in the same Roman dig and like the *Toro Farnese* remained in Rome until 1787. Originally without legs, Ercole had a new pair made for him by Guglielmo della Porta. In fact, the story goes that the Farnese were so impressed with della Porta's work that they refused to reinstate the original legs when they were subsequently found. The Bourbons, however, had no such qualms and later attached the originals to their rightful place. You can see the della Porta legs displayed on the wall behind *Ercole*.

Continuing up the grand staircase, the mezzanine floor houses exquisite mosaics from Pompeii and ancient smut in the Gabinetto Segreto (Secret Chamber). Of the series taken from the Casa del Fauno in Pompeii, it is *La Battaglia di Alessandro Contro Dario* (The Battle of Alexander against Darius) in Room LXI that stands out. The best-known depiction of Alexander the Great, the 20-sq-metre mosaic was probably made by Alexandrian craftsmen working in Italy around the end of the 2nd century BC. Of the other mosaics in the collection, that of a cat killing a duck in Room LX impresses with its portrayal of feline ferocity, while in Room LXIII, the study of Nile River animals combines art with zoology.

Beyond the mosaics is the **Gabinetto Segreto** and its small but much-studied collection of ancient erotica. The room was only reopened to the public in 2000 after decades of being accessible only to the seriously scientific, although you still need to book at the front desk to see it. Guarding the entrance is a marble statue of a lascivious-looking Pan draped over a very coy Daphne. Pan is then caught in the act, this time with a nanny goat, in the collection's most famous piece – a small and surprisingly sophisticated statue taken from the Villa dei Papiri in Herculaneum. There is also a series of nine paintings depicting erotic positions, which served as a menu for brothel clients.

Originally the royal library, the **Sala Meridiana** (Great Hall of the Sundial) on the 1st floor is enormous. Measuring 54m long and 20m high, it contains the Farnese *Atlante,* a statue of Atlas carrying a globe on his shoulders, and various paintings from the Farnese collection. The rest of the 1st floor is largely devoted to a treasure trove of discoveries from Pompeii, Herculaneum, Stabiae and Cuma. Items range from huge murals and frescoes to a pair of gladiator's helmets, household items, ceramics and glassware – even egg cups. Rooms LXXXVI and LXXXVII house an extraordinary collection of vases of mixed origins, many carefully reassembled from fragments.

Finish your tour up on the 2nd floor, where there are various engraved coppers and Greek vases.

PALAZZO DELLE POSTE MAP PP280-1
☎ 081 551 14 56; Piazza G Matteotti 3; ⏰ 8.15am-6.30pm Mon-Fri, 8am-noon Sat; 🚍 R4 to Via Monteoliveto

Looking like a giant, graffitied UFO, Naples' main post office is a striking fascist concoction. Product of an urban renewal programme that wiped out the San Giuseppe quarter, it was designed in 1935 by Giuseppe Vaccaro and features a number of fascist architectural hallmarks: most notably its foreboding scale and black marble columns – a reference to the black armbands worn by Mussolini and his right-wing posse. Predictably, the front steps are a popular rallying spot for young neofascists.

PIAZZA DANTE MAP PP280-1
🚍 Dante

On hot summer evenings, Piazza Dante turns into a communal living room, packed with entire families who stroll, eat, smoke, play cards, chase balloons, whinge about the in-laws or simply sit and stare.

Dominating the eastern flank of the square is the enormous pink façade of the **Convitto Nazionale**. Now housing a boarding school, shops and cafés, it was the piece-de-resistance of Luigi Vanvitelli's spectacular 18th-century square. Dedicated to the Bourbon king Charles VII, it was known as the Foro Carolino until Italian unification in 1860 when it was renamed Piazza Dante. At the centre of the square, a sand-blasted marble Dante looks out over anarchic Via Toledo in arm-raised disbelief.

Below it all, the **Dante metro station** doubles as a cutting-edge art space with installations from some art-world heavyweights. As you head down on the escalator, look up and catch Joseph Kosuth's *Queste Cose Visibili* (These Visible Things) above you. Huge and eye-squintingly neon, it's an epic quotation from Dante's *Il Convivio*. Along the wall at the bottom of the escalator you'll find artist Jannis Kounellis's renegade train tracks running over abandoned shoes (Locals have been known to add a pair of their own trainers to the mix.) Right behind you, above the second set of escalators, sits *Intermediterraneo,* Michelangelo Pistoletto's giant mirror map of the Mediterranean Sea.

EYE FOR AN EYESORE

Infamous home of self-serving politicians and devil-may-care developers, Naples is home to a fair share of aesthetic atrocities. Here's the best of the worst.

Centro Direzionale (Map pp278–9; Corso Meridionale) Designed by Japanese architect Kenzo Tange in the 1980s, this soulless minicity of dated glass towers and wind tunnels features a freaky-looking church that resembles a party hat.

Jolly Hotel (Map pp280–1; Via Medina 70) Neapolitans love to hate this 30-storey block. Looking like a lanky concertina, it has been a cyst on the city skyline since 1960. Not surprisingly, the city council that rubber-stamped it has since been discredited.

Cinema di Santa Lucia (Map pp284–5; Via Generale Orsini 37) This once glorious cinema is now a luxury carpark. Under its art deco ceiling, A-list cars rest their glossy wheels for €3/hr. At the time of writing, plans were underway to convert the front part of the cinema into a discount supermarket.

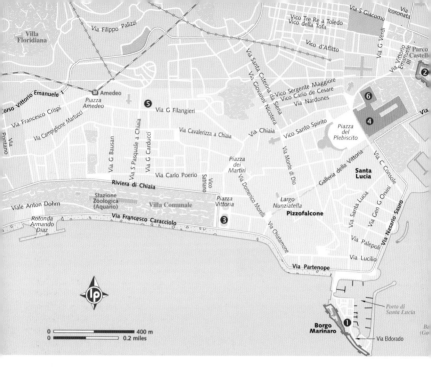

SANTA LUCIA & CHIAIA

Eating p122; Shopping p141; Sleeping p151; Walking Tours p110

Santa Lucia is a scene-stealing combo of sweeping squares and fur-clad *signore* in chandeliered cafés. Further west, neoclassical Chiaia cranks up the style.

At the heart of Santa Lucia lies Piazza dei Plebiscito, a sprawling sea of cobblestones and colonnades. Flanking its eastern edge is the Palazzo Reale, former royal downtown pad and a decadent mass of gilded thrones and crystal chandeliers. Behind the palace sits the legendary Teatro San Carlo and bulky Castel Nuovo (Maschio Angioino), one-time home of Angevin kings, imprisoned barons and a hungry renegade crocodile.

Directly south, ferries dock at Stazione Marittima while further southwest candlelit diners tuck into seafood at portside Borgo Marinaro. The district's main street is Via Santa Lucia, a palazzo-flanked strip of pizzerie, bars and legend – Prince Rainier of Monte Carlo once strolled here arm-in-arm with Princess Grace and mafia boss Lucky Luciano dropped by for a bite to eat. Until the 19th century, the sea reached the fishermen's houses tucked behind its western flank. Soaring above their peeling façades is Monte Echia and the Pizzofalcone district, inhabited since the 7th century BC and a little-known warren of dense, dark streets, macabre votive shrines and knockout views over city and bay.

Further west, and a figurative world away, Chiaia is a mix of designer boutiques, slick sushi bars and glammed-up bars and clubs. Stock up on Prada on Via Calabritto, fashion mags on Piazza dei Martiri and *aperitivo* cocktails on Vico Belledonne. This is where you'll find the hot new PAN art gallery, former Rothschilds pad Villa Pignatelli (now a museum) and Europe's oldest aquarium, elegantly poised in Villa Comunale, the city's famous seaside park.

❶ Borgo Marinaro & Castel dell'Ovo (below)

❷ Castel Nuovo (right)

❸ Lungomare (p88)

❹ Palazzo Reale (p85)

❺ PAN Art Gallery (p89)

❻ Teatro San Carlo (p135)

The 12th-century Castel dell'Ovo   DALLAS STRIBLEY

where the Greeks first settled the city in the 7th century BC, calling the island Megaris. A humble fishing hub in the 19th and early 20th centuries, Borgo Marinaro is now a lively mix of bars, restaurants and cocktail-sipping night-owls, all in the shadow of the looming Castel dell'Ovo.

SANTA LUCIA

No overhead washing here, just Naples at its blue-blooded best: peep into royal boudoirs, sit where Oscar Wilde once sipped and take a deep breath on an elegant square.

ACQUEDOTTO MAP PP284-5

☎ 081 40 02 56; www.lanapolisotterranea.it; Piazza Trieste e Trento; admission €10; 🕑 1½hr guided tours 10am, noon, 6pm Sat, 10am, 11am, noon, 6pm Sun, 9pm Thu; 🚊 R2 to Piazza Trieste e Trento

Deep below Naples' royal quarter lies a series of Graeco-Roman tunnels that were once part of the city's aqueduct system. Used as air-raid shelters in WWII, the tufa-rock tunnels run below Via Chiaia.

Guided tours are organised by La Napoli Sotterranea, run in Italian and depart from Caffè Gambrinus at the times listed above.

BORGO MARINARO MAP PP284-5

🚊 C25 to Via Partenope

According to legend, this small island of volcanic rock is where the heartbroken siren Partenope washed ashore after failing to seduce Ulysses with her song. This is also

CASTEL DELL'OVO MAP PP284-5

☎ 081 240 00 55; Borgo Marinaro; 🕑 9am-6pm Mon-Fri, 9am-1pm Sat & Sun; 🚊 C25 to Via Partenope

According to myth, the Castel dell'Ovo owes its improbable name – Castle of the Egg – to Virgil. The Roman poet was said to have buried an egg on the site where the castle now stands, ominously warning that when the egg breaks the castle (and Naples) will fall. Killjoys prefer to say that the name of the castle is due to its oval shape.

Built in the 12th century by the Normans, the castle is the city's oldest. Its particular position had long been appreciated – originally by the Roman general Lucullus, who had his villa here – and it became a key fortress in the defence of Campania. It was subsequently used by the Swabians, Angevins and Alfonso of Aragon, who modified it to suit his military needs.

Today the castle is invaded by tourists, taffeta-clad brides and dictatorial wedding photographers all out for the perfect sea-view shot.

The in-house **Museo di Etnopreistoria** (Map pp284-5; ☎ 081 764 53 43; 🕑 10am-1pm Mon-Fri by appointment only) features a cool collection of prehistoric tools, fossils and ceramics.

CASTEL NUOVO (MASCHIO ANGIOINO) MAP PP280-1

Piazza Municipio ☎ 081 795 58 77; admission €5; 🕑 9am-7pm Mon-Sat; 🚊 R2 to Piazza del Municipio

Known to Neapolitans as the Maschio Angio-ino (Angeyin Keep) and to everyone else as the Castel Nuovo, this imposing 13th-century castle is one of Naples' most striking buildings.

When Charles I of Anjou took over Naples and the Swabians' Sicilian kingdom, he found himself in control not only of his new southern Italian acquisitions, but also of possessions in Tuscany, northern Italy and Provence (France). It made sense to base the new dynasty in Naples, rather than Palermo in Sicily, and Charles launched an ambitious construction programme to expand the port and city walls.

His plans included converting a Franciscan convent into the castle that still stands in Piazza del Municipio.

Christened the Castrum Novum (New Castle) to distinguish it from the older Castel dell'Ovo and Castel Capuano, it was erected in three years from 1279. A favourite royal residence, it was a popular hang-out for the leading intellectuals and artists of the day. Petrarch, Boccaccio and Giotto all stayed here, the latter repaying his hosts by painting much of the interior. However, of the original structure only the Cappella Palatina remains; the rest is the result of renovations by the Aragonese two centuries later, as well as a meticulous restoration effort prior to WWII. The heavy grey stone that dominates the castle was imported from Mallorca. The two-storey Renaissance triumphal arch at the entrance, the Torre della Guardia, commemorates the triumphal entry of Alfonso I of Aragon into Naples in 1443.

Now the venue of city council meetings, the stark stone **Sala dei Baroni** (Hall of the Barons) is named after the barons who were slaughtered here in 1486 for plotting against King Ferdinand I of Aragon. Its striking ribbed vault fuses ancient Roman and Spanish late-Gothic influences.

The walls of the **Cappella Palatina** were once graced by Giotto frescoes, of which only fragments remain on the splays of the Gothic windows. Above the chapel's elegant Renaissance doorway is a beautiful Catalan-style rose window.

The cappella forms part of the **museum**, spread across several halls on three floors. The 14th- and 15th-century frescoes and sculptures on the ground floor are of the most interest.

The other two floors mostly display paintings, either by Neapolitan artists, or with Naples or Campania as subjects, covering the 17th to the early 20th centuries. Worth seeking out is Guglielmo Monaco's 15th-century bronze door, complete with a cannonball embedded in it. The Sala Carlo V hosts temporary exhibitions of contemporary art.

In the summer months the castle's courtyard is often used for outdoor concerts, including productions from the nearby Teatro San Carlo.

CHIESA DELLA PIETÀ DEI TURCHINI MAP PP280-1

☎ 081 552 04 57; Via Medina 19; ⏱ varies; 🚌 R2 to Via Medina

Originally a poorhouse, this modest 16th-century church takes its name from the *turchino* (deep blue) uniforms the children used to wear. Fashion aside, it's known as a historic conservatory and birthplace of the famous Neapolitan musical group Pietà dei Turchini (see p133). One of the conservatory's most famous alumni was the composer Alessandro Scarlatti (1660–1725).

CHIESA SANTA MARIA INCORONATA MAP PP280-1

Via Medina 60; ⏱ 9am-5pm Mon-Sat; 🚌 R2 to Via Medina

The beautiful Gothic arches of the Chiesa Santa Maria Incoronata date to the mid-14th century. Situated on the sunken site that Charles I of Anjou had earmarked for his planned Castel Nuovo, the church was built on the wishes of Giovanna of Anjou, who wanted somewhere to conserve a fragment of her most precious relic – Jesus' crown of thorns.

Now used an exhibition space, it's worth a stop for the 14th-century frescoes by Roberto Oderisi.

THE CROCODILE HUNTED

Every hulking castle needs a legend. While the Castel dell'Ovo has its hidden egg (p83), the **Castel Nuovo** (p83) had a very peckish crocodile. Philosopher and writer Benedetto Croce recounts the tale in his 1919 publication *Storie e Leggende Napoletane* (Neapolitan Stories and Legends). The story takes us down into the dark, dank dungeon beneath the Angevin-built fortress. In here, the king would accommodate his imprisoned enemies, who included the conspirators in the infamous Baron's Plot of 1486. A seemingly impenetrable structure, bewilderment ensued when prisoners started disappearing Houdini-style. When security was beefed up, guards made a shocking discovery. Through a discreet hole entered a crocodile that would snap up prisoners and drag them out to sea. It's assumed that the sneaky beast made it to Naples on a ship from Egypt. Efficient, clean and cruel, the hungry croc fell in favour with the king for a while. Alas, its own days were numbered: lured into the pit with a slab of horse meat, the snappy Egyptian was impaled, stuffed and hung above the castle's second entrance door. According to Croce, it remained there until the mid 19th-century. Where it went after that, and just how reliable the legend is, remains an urban mystery.

FONTANA DELL'IMMACOLATELLA
MAP PP284-5

Via Partenope; 🚌 C25 to Via Partenope

Diva of the local fountain scene, the Fontana dell'Immacolatella is a grand three-arched affair. Known also as the Fontana del Gigante, it was built by Michelangelo Naccherino and Pietro Bernini in 1601. Two minor arches, under which stand statues of river gods, flank a grand central arch topped by a look-at-me collection of obelisks, cherubs and coats of arms.

FONTANA DI NETTUNO MAP PP280-1

Via Medina; 🚌 R2 to Via Medina

A studly Neptune tops this baroque ensemble by Cosimo Fanzago, Michelangelo Naccherino and Pietro Bernini, father of the more famous Gian Lorenzo Bernini. Under the glistening god, a cast of lions and spewing creatures complete the lavish picture. Built in 1601, this city favourite has had several addresses. Its last move came when work on the metro forced a transfer from Piazza Bovio to its current position. Will it stay or will it go? Only the Gods know.

PALAZZO REALE MAP PP284-5

☎ 081 40 04 54; entrance on Piazza Trieste e Trento; admission €4, audioguide €4; 🕙 9am- 7pm Thu-Tue; 🚌 CS to Piazza Trieste e Trento

Former downtown royal pad, this sprawling palace was built around 1600. Envisaged as a monument to Spanish glory (Naples was under Spanish rule at the time), it was designed by local architect Domenico Fontana and completed two long centuries later in 1841.

From the courtyard, an ego-boosting double staircase leads to the royal apartments which house the **Museo del Palazzo Reale**, a rich and eclectic collection of baroque and neoclassical furnishings, porcelain, tapestries, statues and paintings.

First stop at the top of the stairs is the Teatrino di Corte (1768), a lavish private theatre created by Ferdinando Fuga to celebrate the marriage of Ferdinando IV and Maria Carolina of Austria. Incredibly, Angelo Viva's statues of Apollo and the Muses set along the walls are made of papier-mâché.

Snigger smugly in Sala (Room) XII, where the 16th-century canvas *Gli Esattori delle Imposte* (The Tax Collectors) by Dutch artist Marinus Claesz Van Roymerswaele confirms that attitudes to tax collectors have changed

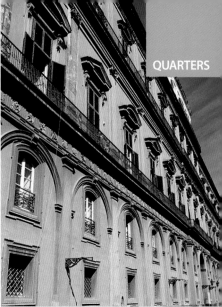

Monumental Palazzo Reale   JEAN-BERNARD CARILLET

little in 500 years (think two hideous-looking creatures gleefully recording their day's takings in a ledger).

The next room, Sala XIII, used to be Joachim Murat's study in the 19th-century but was used as a snack bar by Allied troops in WWII. Meanwhile, what looks like a waterwheel in Sala XXIII is actually a nifty rotating reading desk made for Maria Carolina by Giovanni Uldrich in the 18th century.

The *Cappella Reale* (Royal Chapel) houses a colossal 18th-century *presepe* (nativity scene). Impressively detailed, its cast of wise men, busty peasants and munching mules were crafted by a series of big-name Neapolitan artists including Giuseppe Sanmartino, creator of the legendary *Cristo Velato* in the Cappella Sansevero (see p68).

Extending out from Sala IX, the once-impressive hanging gardens are still closed for restoration, although a sweet smile at the staff member on duty might score you a peek. Otherwise, head to the picture-perfect garden to the left of the palace's main ground-floor entrance. Entry is free and there are bay views to boot.

The palace also houses the **Biblioteca Nazionale** (National Library; ☎ 081 781 92 31; 🕙 9am-7.30pm Mon-Fri, 9am-1pm Sat), which includes at least 2000 papyruses discovered at Herculaneum and fragments of a 5th-century Coptic Bible. Bring ID or miss out.

PIAZZA DEL PLEBISCITO MAP PP284-5

🚌 CS to Piazza Trieste e Trento

Until the world's G7 bigwigs landed in Naples for their 1994 summit, the city's largest piazza was also Europe's most impressive car park. Today, legs substitute wheels and this vast cobbled space is a hotspot for New Year revellers and World Cup celebrations.

The piazza's undisputed star is this colossal **Chiesa di San Francesco di Paola** (Map pp284–5; ☎ 081 74 51 33, ⏰ 8am-noon & 3.30-6pm Mon-Sat, 8am-1pm Sun), a later addition to the colonnade of columns that formed the highlight of Joachim Murat's original piazza (1809). A neoclassical copy of the Pantheon in Rome, the church is striking more for its size than any artistic merit; its dome measures 34m in diameter and 53m in height. Designed by architect Pietro Banchini, it was commissioned by Ferdinand I in 1817 to celebrate the restoration of his kingdom after the Napoleonic interlude.

Facing the church is the Palazzo Reale (p85), with its eight statues of past kings. The royal theme continues centre square with Antonio Canova's statue of a galloping Bourbon king Charles VII and a nearby statue of his son Ferdinand I by Antonio Calí.

PIAZZA DEL MUNICIPIO MAP PP280-1

🚌 R2 to Piazza del Municipio

Dominated by the iconic Castel Nuovo (Maschio Angioino), Piazza Municipio is not looking its best at the moment as construction work continues on the new metro system (see the boxed text, below). At the head of the square stands the 19th-century **Palazzo San Giacomo**. Attached to it is the 16th-century **Chiesa**

Piazza del Plebiscito

MARTIN MOOS

di **SanGiacomo degli Spagnoli** (☎ 081 552 37 59; Piazza Municipio 27; ⏰ 7.30-11am Mon-Fri, 10.30am-1pm Sun), burial place of the 16th-century Spanish viceroy Don Pedro de Toledo (p29) and his wife Maria. On the northern flank stands the Teatro Mercadante (p134), a local theatre heavyweight.

PIAZZA TRIESTE E TRENTO MAP PP284-5

🚌 CS to Piazza Trieste e Trento

Cocktail-sipping poseurs and packs of flirting teens make this an essential city pitstop. Grab a lemon granita from the hole-in-the-wall

RUINING SCHEDULES

In January 2004, construction workers in **Piazza del Municipio** (above) struck archaeological gold. Working on the extension of Metro Line 1, they accidentally unearthed three perfectly-preserved Roman vessels. In nearby Via Armando Diaz, excavation work on the new Toledo station uncovered a 2nd-century Roman spa complete with frescoed coffered ceilings. Further east, on Piazza Nicola Amore, detailed parts of a 2nd-century Roman temple were found, as well as statues of the Imperial Roman family.

For historians and archaeologists, the extension of Metro Line 1 has been a gift from the Gods, revealing parts of ancient Neapolis they would never have reached alone. Indeed, due to Naples' hilly topography, the city's metro system is one of the world's deepest, and just the ticket for some hardcore archaeology.

For many commuters, however, the discoveries have simply meant more delays for the long-overdue project, set to connect Piazza Dante and Via Toledo to Stazione Centrale. Yet, despite the setbacks, few doubt the wait will be worth it. What had been planned as standard stations for hurried commuters are now set to become train-stopping showpieces of archaeological booty. So when will you be sneaking a peek? According to the city's transit authority, 2008. According to commuters... *l'anno mai, il mese poi* (the twelfth of never).

acquaiolo (drink stall) and take in the famous locals, which include the Palazzo Reale, Teatro San Carlo and legendary Caffè Gambrinus.

Squeezed into its northeast corner is the **Chiesa di San Ferdinando** (☎ 081 41 81 18, 8am-noon Mon-Sat, 9.30am-1pm Sun), which features ceiling frescoes of the good-living Jesuits and a fine marble tomb by Tito Angelini in which lies Lucia Migliaccio, the Duchessa di Floridia and wife of King Ferdinand I. Designed by Giovan Giacomo di Conforto in the early 17th century, it was modified by Cosimo Fanzago.

RACCOLTA DE MURA MAP PP284-5

☎ 081 795 77 36; Piazza Trieste e Trento; admission free; 9am-1.30pm Mon-Fri; CS to Piazza Trieste e Trento

Hidden among the chairs of the Bar del Professore (next to the Caffè Gambrinus) is an entrance to an underpass. Go down it and you'll hit one of the city's best-kept secrets – a tiny gallery dedicated to Neapolitan song and dance. Hanging on its pink-tiled walls is a fetching collection of old music-hall programmes and posters, vintage photos of the Festa di Piedigrotta and models of Punchinello (Naples' original version of Mr Punch). Stereo speakers provide a suitable background of warbling Neapolitan crooners.

TEATRO SAN CARLO MAP PP284-5

☎ 081 797 21 11, tour bookings ☎ 081 66 45 45; www.teatrosancarlo.it; Piazza Trieste e Trento, Via San Carlo 98; tours €5; R2 to Via San Carlo

The stuff of tenors' dreams, the sumptuous Teatro San Carlo is Italy's largest and oldest opera house. Inaugurated on 4 November 1737 by King Charles VII, it burnt down in 1816 before rising from the ashes courtesy of Antonio Niccolini, who'd added the neoclassical façade a few years earlier. Utterly deceiving, its straight-laced exterior gives few clues to the red and gold opulence waiting inside, which includes six gilded levels and pitch-perfect acoustics.

Twenty-minute guided tours depart from the theatre's main entrance between 9am and 6pm Monday to Sunday (excluding August) and are conducted in various languages, including English. Book between 9am and 2pm on the tour bookings number listed above.

MONTE ECHIA

Rising up behind Piazza del Plebiscito, Monte Echia is the oldest part of Naples, once forming the ancient city of Parthe-

The illuminated Piazza Trieste e Trento   MARTIN MOOS

nope. Today it's an area of few sites but remarkable views. The top spot to enjoy them is from the unkempt garden at the top of Via Egiziaca a Pizzofalcone: from Piazza Carolina (behind the columns on the northern side of Piazza del Plebiscito) head up the hill until you reach Via Egiziaca a Pizzofalcone, turn left and carry on all the way to the top of the steep hill. You'll know when you get there.

CHIESA SANTA MARIA DEGLI ANGELI MAP PP284-5

☎ 081 764 49 74; Piazza Santa Maria degli Angeli; 7.30-11.30am & 5.30-7pm Mon-Sat, 8.30am-1.30pm & 6-7.30pm Sun; C22 to Via Monte di Dio

This yellow-hued baroque church was financed by Costanza Doria del Carretto, a noble lady with a deep purse and pious heart, and donated to the priests of the Teatini order.

Step inside for works by Neapolitan stalwarts Massimo Stanzione and Luca Giordano, as well as Francesco Grimaldi's famous dome.

LA NUNZIATELLA MAP PP284-5

☎ 081 764 15 20; Via Generali Parisi 16; C22 to Via Nunziatella

A hulking red heap perched high above Chiaia, the convent of Nunziatella is home to the sharp, preened cadets of Italy's prestigious Royal Military Academy of the Nunziatella.

Built in 1588, the convent was donated to the Jesuits by its benefactor, noblewoman Anna Mendozza Marchesana della Valle. It was used as a novitiate until the Jesuits were kicked out of town in the mid-18th century.

The adjacent church is also part of the academy. Famous for its beautiful 17th-century baroque interior – frescoes by Francesco de Mura, an altar by Sanmartino, the floor by Ferdinando Sanfelice – it's open to civilians by appointment only.

CHIAIA

Chiaia is Naples' 'It' spot – preferred playground of fashionistas, soap stars and tie-clad *bella gente* (beautiful people). At night, the chic cobbled streets west of Piazza dei Martiri buzz with crowds who hit the city's coolest restaurants, bars and clubs for some designer *dolce vita* (sweet life).

CHIESA SANTA MARIA IN PORTICO MAP PP284-5

☎ 081 66 92 94; Via Santa Maria in Portico 17;
⏲ 8-11am & 4.30-7pm; 🚍 C25 to Riviera di Chiaia

Craving baroque? This 17th-century church should hit the spot. Check out the fabulous

Taking a dip at the *lungomare*   DALLAS STRIBLEY

frescoes by Fabrizio Santafede (a good name for a church painter – 'Santafede' means 'holy faith'), Paolo De Matteis, Giovan Battista and Fedele Fischetti. In the sacristy there's a life-size 17th-century *presepe*, while the stuccowork and high altar is by Domenico Antonio Vaccaro. The *piperno* stone façade is by Arcangelo (another apt name – it means 'archangel') Guglielminelli and not, as was previously believed, Cosimo Fanzago.

LUNGOMARE MAP PP284-5

🚍 C25 to Via Partenope

Strolling the *lungomare* (seafront) is as Neapolitan as lunch at Nennella (p121). Running the length of Via Partenope and Via Francesco Carrociolo, this 2.5km seaside stretch is particularly beautiful as the sun sets and the light over the sea takes on an orange hue – picture Capri on the horizon, Mt Vesuvius looming to the south and you hopelessly smitten. On Sunday mornings, hit Via Francesco Carrociolo for a car-free passing parade of sexy skaters, gym-fit joggers and gelato-licking *flâneurs*.

MUSEO PIGNATELLI MAP PP284-5

☎ 081 761 23 56; Riviera di Chiaia 200;
admission €2; ⏲ 8.30am-1.30pm Wed-Mon;
🚍 C25 to Riviera di Chiaia

In the early 19th century, Naples was gripped by classical fever. If it was Doric or Ionic, it was *in*. So when Ferdinand Acton, a minister at the court of King Ferdinand IV (1759–1825), asked Pietro Valente to design Villa Pignatelli in 1826, Valente whipped up this striking Pompeiian lookalike, complete with English garden.

Bought and extended by the Rothschilds in 1841, it became home to the Duke of Monteleone, Diego Aragona Pignatelli Cortes in 1867, before his granddaughter Rosina Pigna telli donated it to the state, which opened it (and its treasures) to the public.

The museum is a mix of opulent furniture, art and hunting paraphernalia (including a collection of royal whips). Highlights include the Meissen and Viennese porcelain in the Salotto Verde (Green Room) and the leather-lined smoking room.

The 1st floor features mainly 18th- to 20th-century Neapolitan paintings and busts from the Banco di Napoli's extensive art collection, including Francesco Guarino's chiaroscuro-rich *San Giorgio* (1645–1650).

The adjoining **Museo delle Carrozze** contains a collection of 19th- and 20th-century carriages, but is currently closed for restoration.

PAN (PALAZZO DELLE ARTI NAPOLI)
MAP PP284-5

☎ 081 795 86 05; www.palazzoartinapoli.net, in Italian; Via dei Mille 60; admission free; ⏲ 9.30am-7.30pm Mon & Wed-Sat, 9.30-2.30pm Sun; Ⓜ Amedeo
One of the city's two new hotbeds of contemporary art – the other being MADRE (p75) – PAN is the brainchild of European art curator and critic Lóránd Hegyi. Three slick white minimalist floors host three innovative exhibitions per year, spanning everything from painting, photography and sculpture to multimedia, design and architecture. Past exhibitions have included a retrospective of the work of set designer Dean Tavoularis (Rumble Fish, Peggy Sue Got Married), as well as cutting-edge art from names like Anselm Kiefer, Katerina Vincourova and Jiri Černičký. Housed in a pink 16th-century palace once belonging to Francesco di Sangro, PAN also boasts an experimental art lab, multimedia library, archive and slick café and bookshop.

PIAZZA DEI MARTIRI MAP PP284-5

🚌 C25 to Piazza dei Martiri
If Chiaia is Naples' drawing room, Piazza dei Martiri is its sultry chaise longue. Anyone worth their Gucci shades heads here for caffè and languid outdoor lounging. Get a crash course in both at squareside café **La Caffettiera** (p123).

Taking centre stage on the square is Enrico Alvino's 19th-century monument to Neapolitan martyrs, with four lions representing the anti-Bourbon uprisings of 1799, 1820, 1848 and 1860.

On the western flank of the square, at No 58, **Palazzo Partanna** (Map pp284–5) is a neoclassical update of an original 18th-century edifice, while at No 30, **Palazzo Calabritto** (Map pp284–5) is a Luigi Vanvitelli creation.

Culture of a readable nature is on hand at **Feltrinelli** (p142), Naples' best bookshop, in the northeastern corner of the square.

STAZIONE ZOOLOGICA (AQUARIO)
MAP PP284-5

☎ 081 583 32 63; www.szn.it; Viale Aquario 1; adult/child €1.50/1; ⏲ 9am-5.30pm Mon-Fri, 9am-6pm Sat, 9am-7.30pm Sun; 🚌 C25 to Riviera di Chiaia
Europe's oldest aquarium is more 'vintage' than 'cutting-edge' with its dripping tanks of spooky

squid and nervous little Nemos. Housed in an elegant neoclassical building designed by Adolf von Hildebrandt, its 23 tanks contain some 200 species of marine flora and fauna exclusively from the Bay of Naples, while its biology library is one of the largest of its kind in the world. Founded in 1872 by German naturalist Anton Dohrn, its research centre plays a vital role in rehabilitating Loggerhead sea turtles injured by ships in the bay.

VIA CHIAIA MAP PP284-5

🚇 CS to Piazza Trieste e Trento, 🚌 C25 to Piazza dei Martiri
Linking Piazza Trieste e Trento with Piazza dei Martiri (and Santa Lucia with Chiaia), pedestrianised Via Chiaia is a lively mix of trendy boutiques, imposing palazzo and perma-tanned fashion slaves. Built in the 16th century, it follows the line of the natural divide that separates the hills of Pizzofalcone and Mortella. Towards the western end of the street you pass under what looks like a triumphal arch but is, in fact, a bridge built in 1636 to connect the two hills.

The most famous kid on the block is at the 16th-century **Palazzo Cellamare** (Via Chiaia 149). Built as a summer residence for Giovan Francesco Carafa, close friend of the Spanish viceroy Don Pedro de Toledo, it later housed Bourbon monarchy guests, including Goethe and Casanova.

VILLA COMUNALE MAP PP284-5

☎ 081 761 11 31; Piazza Vittoria; ⏲ 7am-midnight; 🚌 C25 to Riviera di Chiaia
Another Luigi Vanvitelli production, this long, leafy seaside strip was originally built for Bourbon royalty. Called the Passeggio Reale (Royal Walkway), it was off-limits to the plebs except on 8 September, the day of the **Festa di Piedigrotta** (see p19). Rumour has it that taking one's wife to the park on that day was a clause in many a marital contract. Husbands across the city must have heaved a sigh of relief when the park finally went public in 1869.

Dividing the Riviera di Chiaia from Via Francesco Caracciolo and the sea, this urban oasis boasts a vintage aquarium, bandstand, tennis club and at least eight fountains. Named after the ducks that used to swim in it, the Fontana delle Paperelle (Duck Fountain) replaced the famous Toro Farnese which, in 1825, was transferred to the Museo Archeologico Nazionale (p80).

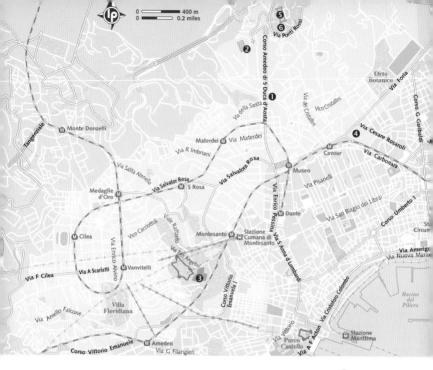

VOMERO, CAPODIMONTE & LA SANITÀ

Eating p125; Shopping p144; Sleeping p153; Walking Tours p113

Home to *professori* and their polo-shirted teens, Vomero is the city's middle-class heartland, while La Sanità is its impoverished underbelly.

A respectable 250m above the raffish city centre, tree-lined avenues, Liberty villas and chic boutiques set the scene for bourgeois Neapolitan living. Wedged in between it all are some of the city's ugliest post-war apartment blocks, which tumble down the hill like oversized pastel boxes. At Vomero's heart sits Piazza Vanvitelli, fringed by vintage cafés, voguish *palazzi* and a funky art-clad metro station.

While not a tourist hotspot per se, this is where you'll find the bulky Castel Sant'Elmo, the must-see Certosa di San Martino and the manicured sprawl of Villa Floridiana and its Museo Nazionale della Ceramica Duca di Martina.

Loftier ambitions await further northeast at Capodimonte. Transformed by Charles VII of Bourbon from a hopeless hill to a royal hunting reserve, the Parco di Capodimonte is a lavish sprawl of lawns, lakes, woods and pedal-happy cyclists. At its southern end, Charles' extravagant hunting lodge, the Palazzo Reale di Capodimonte, houses one of Italy's greatest art collections, with names like Caravaggio, Bellini, Botticelli and Warhol in an obscenely impressive line-up.

Immediately to the south, squeezed between Via Foria and Via Santa Teresa degli Scalzi, the impoverished, overpopulated streets of La Sanità are a bewitching mix of crumbling tufa façades, garish market stalls, creaking overhead clotheslines and curious *bambini* (children). Comedy great Totò was born here (at Via Santa Maria Antesaecula 109, to be precise!), Vittorio de Sica's *Ieri, Oggi, Domani (Yesterday, Today, Tomorrow)* was partly filmed here and tens of thousands of skeletons lie waiting to meet you in the catacombs below.

JEAN-BERNARD CARILLET

VOMERO

All roads might lead to Rome, but all Neapolitan funiculars lead to Vomero. Hop on and head on up for knockout views, top-notch art and a chilled out preppy-vibe.

CASTEL SANT'ELMO MAP P283

☎ 081 578 40 30; Via Tito Angelini 22; admission €3; ⌚ 8.30am-7.30pm Thu-Tue, 9am-6.30pm Sun; Ⓜ Vanvitelli, Funicular Montesanto to Morghen

It might look strong and mean, but this hulking star-shaped heap has seen little military action. The biggest blow it received came in 1587 when a bolt of lightning hit the castle's stock of gunpowder, killing some 150 people. It has, however, seen plenty of prisoners, as its dungeons were used as a military prison until the 1970s.

Originally, however, it was neither a castle nor a fort that topped the tufa rock, but a church. Dedicated to St Erasmus (from which the name Elmo is derived), it rested on the top of Vomero hill for some 400 years before Robert

of Anjou turned it into a castle in 1349. In 1538, Spanish viceroy Don Pedro de Toledo had it further fortified, giving it its present look.

Somewhat emasculated, it's now mainly used as an exhibition and conference centre. Although you can visit the castle's roof (for the best view in town) most of the castle is closed if there's no exhibition on. Admission times and price vary according to the exhibition.

CERTOSA DI SAN MARTINO MAP P283

☎ 081 578 17 69; Largo San Martino 5; admission €6; ⌚ 8.30am-7.30pm Thu-Tue; Ⓜ Vanvitelli, Funicular Montesanto to Morghen

The Certosa di San Martino and its **Museo Nazionale di San Martino** are, in a word, unmissable. Barely 100m from the castle, this former Carthusian monastery houses one of the city's richest collections of Neapolitan art and history, wisely collected by its resident monks. From precious frescoes and sculpture to vintage *presepi* and pumpkin-style carriages, the museum is a crash course in Neapolitan art and soul.

Originally built by Charles of Anjou in 1325, the Certosa (charterhouse) has been decorated, adorned and altered over the centuries by some of the greats of Italian art

In the park at Villa Floridiana   GREG ELMS

scene in an ornately decorated eggshell – to the colossal Cuciniello creation, which covers one wall of what used to be the monastery's kitchen. Angels fly down to a richly detailed landscape of rocky houses, shepherds and local merry-makers, all carved out of wood, cork, papier-mâché and terracotta.

The Quarto del Priore (Prior's Quarter) in the southern wing houses the bulk of the picture collection, as well as one of the museum's most famous pieces, Pietro Bernini's tender *La Vergine col Bambino e San Giovannino* (Madonna and Child with the Infant John the Baptist).

A pictorial history of Naples is told in the section *Immagini e Memoria dell Città* (Images and Memories of the City). Here you'll find portraits of historic characters (Don Pedro de Toledo in Room 33, Maria Carolina di Borbone in Room 43); antique maps, including a 35-panel copper map in Room 45; and rooms dedicated to major historical events such as the Revolt of the Masaniello (Room 36) and the plague (Room 37). Room 32 boasts the beautiful Tavola Strozzi (Strozzi Table), whose fabled depiction of 15th-century maritime Naples is one of the city's most celebrated historical records.

VILLA FLORIDIANA & MUSEO NAZIONALE DELLA CERAMICA DUCA DI MARTINA MAP P.283

☎ 081 578 84 18; Via Domenico Cimarosa 77; ☼ park 8.30am-1hr before sunset daily, museum ☼ 8.30am-2pm Wed-Mon; admission museum €2.50, park free; Ⓜ Vanvitelli

Not one for understated gift giving, King Ferdinand I had the elegant Villa Floridiana and its stately gardens built for his second wife, the Duchess of Floridia. Purchased by the Italian government in 1919, the gardens were opened to the public and the villa turned into a ceramics museum. In a city short on space, the park is a soothing tonic of oaks, palms and terraces looking out over city and sea.

Sitting snugly at the bottom of the park in the Villa Floridiana, the Museo Nazionale della Ceramica Duca di Martina boasts a 6000-piece collection of European, Chinese and Japanese china, ivory, enamels and Italian majolica.

The Oriental collection, including Chinese Ming (1368–1644) ceramics and Japanese Edo (1615–1867) vases, is displayed in the basement, while upstairs on the ground floor you'll find Renaissance majolica pottery. Continue up to the 1st floor for European ceramics, which include sumptuous Meissen pieces.

and architecture, most importantly Giovanni Antonio Dosio in the 16th century and baroque master Cosimo Fanzago a century later.

The monastery's church and the rooms that flank it contain a feast of frescoes and paintings by some of Naples' greatest 17th-century artists. In the *pronaos* (a small room flanked by three walls and a row of columns), Micco Spadaro's frescoes of Carthusian persecution seem to defy perspective as figures sit with their legs hanging over nonexistent edges. Elsewhere in the chapel you'll find works by Francesco Solimena, Massimo Stanzione, Giuseppe de Ribera, Luca Giordano and Battista Caracciolo.

Adjacent to the church, the elegant **Chiostro dei Procuratori** is the smaller of the monastery's two cloisters. A grand corridor on the left leads to the larger **Chiostro Grande** (Great Cloister), considered one of Italy's finest. Originally designed by Giovanni Antonio Dosio in the late 16th century and added to by Fanzago, it's a sublime composition of white Tuscan-Doric porticoes, manicured gardens and marble statues. The sinister skulls mounted on the balustrade were a light-hearted reminder to the monks of their own mortality.

One of the many museum highlights is the Sezione Presepiale, which houses a whimsical collection of rare Neapolitan *presepi* (nativity scenes) carved in the 18th and 19th centuries. These range from the miniscule – a nativity

CAPODIMONTE

Sitting at the northern end of Via Toledo (which is known as Corso Amedeo di Savoia Duca d'Aosta by this stage), the hill of Capodimonte is home to the Parco di Capodimonte and its art-heavy Palazzo Reale. Down below on its southern slope sit the macabre catacombs of San Gennaro, ancient home of skulls, cults and Palaeo-Christian frescoes.

CATACOMBA DI SAN GENNARO MAP P286

☎ 081 741 10 71; Via Capodimonte 16; adult/child €5/3; ⏱ guided tours 9am,10am, 11am, noon, 2pm, 3pm Tue-Sun; 🚌 24 to Via Capodimonte

The oldest and most famous of Naples' ancient catacombs, the Catacomba di San Gennaro date to the 2nd century. Originally they belonged to a noble family, but when San Gennaro's body was interred here in the 5th century they became a hotspot for Christian pilgrims. Naples' bishops were also buried here until the 11th century.

Spread over two levels, the catacombs house a mix of tombs, corridors and broad vestibules held up by columns and arches. The crumbling walls are decorated with 2nd-century Christian frescoes and 5th-century mosaics, including the oldest known portrait of San Gennaro.

To reach the catacombs, go through the gates to the left of the Chiesa di Madre di Buon Consiglio; the ticket office is in a small ivy-clad building. Tours (in Italian) last about 45 minutes but only depart if there are more than two people.

CHIESA DI MADRE DI BUON CONSIGLIO MAP P286

☎ 081 741 49 45; Via Capodimonte 13; ⏱ 8am-12.30pm & 4.30-7.30pm Mon-Sat, 8am-1pm & 5-7.30pm Sun; 🚌 24 to Via Capodimonte

Feel like you've seen this church before? It may be because it's a snack-size replica of the Basilica di San Pietro in Rome. But unlike the real thing, this Neapolitan version is still a relative tot. Designed by Vincenzo Vecchia and completed in 1960, it took 40 years to build. Inside you'll find numerous works of art transferred here after the earthquake of 1980. While none are likely to excite art buffs, the mock-Vatican exterior warrants a quick kitsch Polaroid.

OSSERVATORIO DI CAPODIMONTE MAP P286

☎ 081 557 51 11; www.na.astro.it; Salita Moiariello 16; ⏱ 9am-1.30pm by appointment; 🚌 24 to Via Capodimonte

Overcast skies never faze the crew at Italy's oldest observatory – they simply look earthward for some of the best sea and skyline views in town. Perched high above the city, this elegant neoclassical number was founded by King Ferdinand I of Bourbon in 1819 and built according to the designs of astronomers Giuseppe Piazzai and Federico Zuccari. The in-house museum features an interesting collection of astronomical instruments and its stunning location makes a heavenly setting for occasional music concerts throughout the year. Check the website for upcoming events.

PALAZZO REALE DI CAPODIMONTE MAP P286

☎ 081 749 91 11; Parco di Capodimonte; adult/child €7.50/free, adult 2-5pm €6.50; ⏱ 8.30am-7.30pm Thu-Tue; 🚌 24 to Via Capodimonte

Believe it or not, this colossal peachy pad was meant to be a hunting lodge. At least that's what Charles VII of Bourbon had asked for when construction began in 1738. But it seems that size really did matter to the king, whose plans for the place kept getting grander and grander. By 1759, the city had a new palace. Just as well, really, for when Charles inherited his mother Elisabetta Farnese's hefty art collection, space was at a premium. Indeed, so impressive was this collection that artists and 17th-century travellers flocked from all over Europe to eruditely 'ooh' and 'ahh'.

However, visits were abruptly halted during the decade of French rule (1806–15) when the palace became the official residence of Joseph Bonaparte and Joachim Murat. The history of the museum proper resumed in 1860 when a Galleria d'Arte Moderna was established. Today, the palace boasts one of the best and most extensive art collections in Italy.

The museum is spread over three floors and 160 rooms. The 1st floor is dominated by the Galleria Farnese and the Appartamento Reale (Royal Apartment); the 2nd floor contains the Galleria delle Arti a Napoli; while the top floor is dedicated to modern art. Before you embark on the museum, consider forking out €4 for an audioguide – the English and Italian commentary is interesting.

Palazzo Reale di Capodimonte

To do the whole museum in one day is impossible – you'd need at least two to start getting to grips with the place. For most people, though, a full morning is sufficient for a shortened best-of tour.

First-floor highlights are numerous. In Room 2 you can see family portraits of the Farnese by Raphael and Titian; depictions of Cardinal Alessandro Farnese (later Pope Paul III), show a thin, rather weedy-looking man. Next door in Room 3 the *Crocifissione* (Crucifixion; 1426) by Masaccio is one of Capodimonte's most famous pieces. Botticelli's *Madonna con Bambino e Angeli* (Madonna with Baby and Angels; Room 6), Bellini's *Trasfigurazione* (Transfiguration; Room 8) and Titian's *Danae* (Room 11) are all must-see pieces, while Pieter Bruegel's disturbing 16th-century canvases make an eerie impression in Room 17. In Room 20, a glum-looking Hercules has a hard time choosing between a stern-looking Virtue and a fun-loving Vice in Annibale Carracci's 16th-century painting *Ercole al bivio* (Hercules at the Crossroads).

In the **Galleria delle Cose Rare** (Gallery of Rare Objects) you can imagine how the dinner table of Cardinal Alessandro Farnese might have looked. His blue majolica table service has his coat of arms embossed in gold on every piece, while the elaborate centrepiece depicting Diana the huntress can be used as a goblet by taking off the stag's detachable head.

A study in regal excess, the **Appartamento Reale** (Royal Apartment) occupies Rooms 31 to 60. Huge, sumptuous rooms heave with valuable Capodimonte porcelain, heavy curtains and shiny inlaid marble. Meet your knight in shining armour in Room 46 then hit the **Salotinno di Porcellana** (Room 52) for a study in tasteless extravagance – think 3000 pieces of porcelain stuck to the wall or hanging from the ceiling. Created between 1757 and 1759 for the Palazzo Reale in Portici, it was transferred to Capodimonte in 1866. The 1st-floor Appartamento Reale is also home to Volaire's *Eruszione del Vesuvio dal Ponte Maddalena* (Eruption of Vesuvius from the Bridge of Maddalena).

The 2nd floor is no less rich than the 1st, and is packed to its elegant rafters with works produced in Naples between the 13th and 18th centuries. The first room you come to, however, is lined with a series of gigantic 16th-century Belgian tapestries depicting episodes from the Battle of Pavia.

Simone Martini's work *San Ludovico di Tolosa* (1317) is brilliantly displayed in Room 66. Considered the museum's finest example of 14th-century art, Martini's golden work portrays the canonisation of Ludovico, brother of King Robert of Anjou.

The piece that many come to Capodimonte to see, *Flagellazione* (Flagellation; 1607–10) hangs in reverential solitude in Room 78, at the

Narrow passages characterise underground Naples   JEAN-BERNARD CARILLET

Within the park walls there are five lakes, a wood, and various 18th-century buildings, including the **Palazzo Porcellane**, where porcelain was once produced. Those after more peace than people watching should head for its northern reaches. The easiest entrance is through the Porta Grande on Via Capodimonte.

LA SANITÀ

Positioned outside the city walls until the 18th century, La Sanità (despite its name, which means 'healthy') was for centuries where the city buried its dead. Below its grimy streets lies a macabre otherworld frozen in time. Authentic and raw, La Sanità is also a little edgy, so it's best not to loiter here after dark.

ALBERGO DEI POVERI MAP PP278-9

Piazza Carlo III; Ⓜ Cavour
Not impartial to a spot of PR, Bourbon king Charles VII built this giant poorhouse at a main city entrance to promote himself as enlightened and compassionate. It was a grand gesture indeed – the Albergo dei Poveri (Hostel of the Poor) is Europe's largest public building. If all had gone according to architect Ferdinando Fuga's plans, though, it would have been bigger. His original designs called for a façade 600m long, with five internal courtyards. When construction came to a halt in 1829, however, he settled for the smaller version that you see today. The façade measures a mind-blowing 349m, there are three internal courtyards and the whole edifice covers 103,000 sq metres. Undergoing a slow restoration, it currently houses 85 families, by now the descendants of needy families housed there after WWII. According to locals, they share the place with a number of luminous ghosts.

end of a long corridor. Caravaggio's dramatic and subliminally homoerotic image of Jesus about to be flogged was originally painted for the de Franchis family chapel in the Chiesa di San Domenico Maggiore. And like his other great Neapolitan work *Le Sette Opere di Misericordia* (The Seven Acts of Mercy; see p73), its intensity and revolutionary depiction of light was to have a huge influence on his contemporaries.

Continue through the 28 rooms that remain on the 2nd floor for works by Ribera, Giordano, Solimena and Stanzione. If you have any energy left, the small **gallery of modern art** on the 3rd floor is worth a quick look, if nothing else for Andy Warhol's poptastic Mt Vesuvius.

But you're not finished yet. On the ground floor, the **Gabinetto Disegni e Stampe** (Drawing and Print Room) contains some 27,000 pieces, including several sketches by Michelangelo and Raphael. All done, pick up a few art books in the well-stocked gift shop.

PARCO DI CAPODIMONTE MAP P286

🕙 9am-1hr before sunset; 🚌 24 to Via Capodimonte
Like Hampstead Heath with sunshine, this 130-hectare park was designed by Ferdinando Sanfelice in 1742 as a hunting reserve for King Charles VII. In order to provide the proper environment for the prey he wished to hunt, the grounds were turned into a botanical wonderland; a fact not lost on Neapolitans, who flock here for a spot of weekend R&R.

CHIESA SANTA MARIA DELLA SANITÀ & CATACOMBA DI SAN GAUDIOSO MAP P286

☎ 081 544 13 05; www.santamariadellasanita.it; Via della Sanità 124; catacombs adult/child €5/3; church 🕙 8.30am-12.30pm & 5-8pm Mon-Sat, 8.30am-1.30pm Sun, catacombs guided tours 🕙 9.30am, 10.15am, 11am, 11.45am, 12.30pm; Ⓜ Cavour
Topped by a green-and-yellow tiled dome, the much-loved Basilica Santa Maria della Sanità is known also as the Chiesa di San Vincenzo,

in honour of the cult of San Vincenzo Ferreri. Gracing dusty Piazza della Sanità since the 17th century, its architectural highlight is a sumptuous double stairway leading up to a raised altar. Below the altar sits the 5th-century **Cappella di San Gaudioso**, entrance to the catacombs below.

Burial site of San Gaudioso, a North African bishop who died in Naples in AD 452, these eerie catacombs reveal traces of mosaics and frescoes from various periods; the earliest from the 5th century, while later examples are from the 17th and 18th centuries. But it's not so much the art that strikes you, as the gruesome history that the catacombs tell.

The damp walls reveal two medieval methods of burying the dead. The first involved burying the corpse in the foetal position in the belief that you should depart this world as you enter it. The second method, and the one favoured by the 17th-century rich, was to be buried upright in a niche with one's head cemented to the wall. Once sapped of fluids, the headless body would be buried and the skull set over a fresco of the dearly departed.

Tours of the catacombs last about an hour, while an atmospheric night tour features costumed actors and local produce to feast on (€25). Book ahead for an English-speaking guide.

CHIESA SAN GIOVANNI A CARBONARA MAP PP278-9

☎ 081 29 58 73; Via Carbonara 5; ⏲ 9am-6pm Mon-Sat; Ⓜ Cavour

This fabulous Gothic cluster comprises a church, a chapel and a cloister, fronted by an 18th-century double-flight staircase by stair-meister Ferdinando Sanfelice. While the chapel is currently closed, the wooden-beamed church is a treasure-trove of stunning marble sculpture.

Standing at 18m behind the main altar, the colossal monument to King Ladislas (built in 1428) is a sublime mix of Renaissance and Gothic styles.

Other important works include the *Crocifisso* (Crucifixion; 1545) by Giorgio Vasari, the early 16th-century *Monumento Miroballo* by Tommaso Malvito and Jacopo dell Pila, and the *Cappella Caracciole del Sole* with its vintage majolica-tiled floor and colourful 15th-century frescoes. In this beautiful round chapel you'll also find the tomb of Gianni Caracciolo, the ambitious lover of King Ladislas' sister Queen Joan II of Naples. Caracciolo's increasing political power led the queen to plot his demise and in 1432 he was stabbed to death

in the Castel Capuano. The tomb is the work of Leonardo da Besozzo.

CIMITERO DELLE FONTANELLE
MAP P283

☎ 081 29 69 44; Piazza Fontanella alla Sanità 154; ⏲ currently closed; Ⓜ Museo

The perfect place to sneak up on someone, this creepy underground cemetery heaves with the skulls and bones of some 40,000 Neapolitans. First used during the plague of 1656, it became the city's main burial site during the cholera epidemics of 1835 and 1974.

At the end of the 19th century it became a cult spot for the worship of the dead. Adherents would adopt a skull, pray for its soul and lavish it with treats in the hope of a little good fortune. When condensation formed on the skull, it was seen a sign of good fortune for its custodian. Dry bones, however, were seen as a sign of impending doom. Some custodians were so attached to their bony friend that they would encase it in a glass shrine for protection.

So popular was the cult that a tram line served the cemetery and its gift-bearing devotees up until the 1950s. In 1969, a fed-up Cardinal Ursi banned what was becoming an increasingly fetishistic practice and contrary to Catholic doctrine.

Although the site is normally only open during the **Maggio dei Monumenti** (May of the Monuments; p18), at the time of writing there were plans to reopen it permanently. Contact Napoli Sotterranea (☎ 081 29 69 44) for updates.

ORTO BOTANICO MAP PP278-9

☎ 081 44 97 59; Via Foria 223; ⏲ 9am-2pm Mon-Fri by appointment only; Ⓜ Cavour

Slap-bang on gridlocked Via Forio, Naples' botanical garden has its work cut out for it. Yet, in spite of the fumes, the vegetation stands tall, lush and utterly inviting.

Founded by Joseph Bonaparte between 1807 and 1819, the gardens belong to Naples University, hence the need to request a look. But it's worth asking nicely – if for no other reason than to stretch out under a So-Cal palm and breathe away that road-rage stress.

Dedicated botanists will be impressed with an oxygen-rich collection of plants from the major American, African, Asian and Australian deserts, an arboreal fern section and an ancient citrus orchard.

Decorative dome inside the Chiesa San Giovanni a Carbonara

JEAN-BERNARD CARILLET

PALAZZO SANFELICE MAP P286

Via della Sanità 2; M Cavour

Don't let yourself be fooled by the run-of-the-mill exterior and scruffy La Sanità address. When Ferdinando Sanfelice built this pile for his family in 1726, it quickly became an avant-garde icon. The main talking point was the wildly theatrical double-ramped staircase in the second internal courtyard. From here onward, there was no stopping Sanfelice, who perfected his dramatic staircase design in various palazzi across the city. Unmissable is the one in the **Palazzo dello Spagnolo** (Map p286; Via Vergini 19).

While technically neither of these two buildings is open to the public, the porter should let you go through if you ask nicely. Porters generally work office hours, so avoid going in the early afternoon if you want to find someone there to let you in.

PORTA SAN GENNARO MAP P286

Via Foria; M Cavour

This city gate was rebuilt in its current position in the 15th century after the expansion of the city walls. Named after San Gennaro because it marks the beginning of the route up to the Catacomba di San Gennaro, it retains traces of a 17th-century fresco by Mattia Preti. The artist decorated all the major city gates to give thanks for the end of the plague epidemic in 1656.

NAPLES ALLA NAPOLETANA

Crafty pickpockets, scooter-riding bandits, smooth-talking scammers: Naples' reputation as a den of iniquity too often upstages the city's many virtues. While petty theft and scams are rife, following a few local rules should have you staving off the bad guys:

- Dress down. Leave that Rolex in the hotel safe. Also, avoid carrying large amounts of money on you, especially in easy-to-reach pockets.
- Keep handbags and small backpacks under your arm (not over your shoulder) and never leave bags unattended.
- Avoid dodgy districts. While much of central Naples is generally safe during the day, areas like the Quartieri Spagnoli, La Sanità, Mercato and Piazza Garibaldi can be edgy at night. Be vigilant and stick to well-lit, crowded areas.
- Know your surroundings. Hotel and hostel staff are a great source of local wisdom. Ask them for tips on navigating the area safely, carry their number and address on you and know how to get back safely.
- Be weary of scams. A notorious one on Piazza Garibaldi involves scammers placing fake bets on guessing under which cup a ball is hiding. They always get it right, unlike unsuspecting travellers, who are set up to lose. At Stazione Centrale, be wary of strangers who insist on seeing you onto the right train. Once on the platform, they may demand a €10 'tip'.

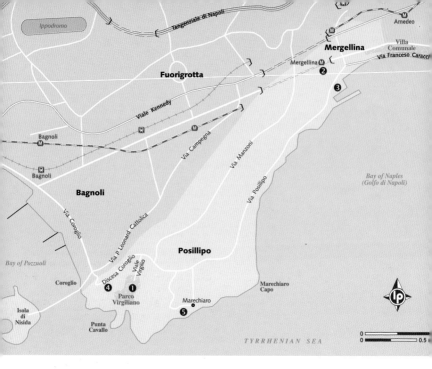

MERGELLINA & POSILLIPO

Eating p126; Sleeping p154

Rambling elegantly, Mergellina exudes an air of faded grandeur. But for a taste of the high-life head up to Posillipo – Naples' version of Beverly Hills.

Lemon-hued Liberty palazzi line the slightly scruffy seafront, slinky palms catch a southerly breeze and elegant elderly widows walk their miniature Dachshunds in the afternoon sun.

Before the Riviera di Chiaia was built in the 17th century, this was little more than a quaint fishing village on the city's outskirts. Today it's Naples' second port and an important transport hub. Dominating Piazza Piedigrotta, its Art Nouveau train station serves both metro and regional lines. At Mergellina's hydrofoil terminal, thousands of people set off every day for the islands, while nearby in Piazza Sannazzaro traffic roars through a fume-choked tunnel linking central Naples to suburban Fuorigrotta. The piazza itself is named for Mergellina-born Renaissance poet Jacopo Sannazzaro. Labelled the Christian Virgil, his verses influenced the development of modern-day Italian. The real Virgil's tomb is in nearby Parco Virgiliano.

Mergellina's star attraction, however, is its waterfront. On balmy nights, its kitsch bars and vintage ice-cream parlours, known as Chalets (Map pp284–5), pull huge crowds for a languid slice of *la dolce vita* (the sweet life).

Set on the headland dividing the Bay of Naples from the Bay of Pozzuoli, Posillipo is the place for lush leafy streets, sprawling villas, secret swimming coves and chichi restaurants filled with Sophia Loren lookalikes. For star-worthy views, head to Parco Virgiliano at the western tip of the cape, where dizzying panoramas take in the bay, Mt Vesuvius and the little island of Nisida where Brutus is said to have conspired against Julius Caesar.

highlights

MERGELLINA & POSILLIPO

❶ Parco Virgiliano (p100)

❷ Chiesa Santa Maria di Piedigrotta (right)

❸ Porticciolo (p101)

❹ Grotta di Seiano (right)

❺ Marechiaro (right)

Porticciolo at Mergellina (p101)   JEAN-BERNARD CARILLET

CHIESA SANTA MARIA DEL PARTO MAP PP284-5

☎ 081 66 46 27; Via Mergellina 21; ☼ 8am-12.30pm & 4-7pm; Ⓜ Mergellina

Founded by poet Jacopo Sannazzaro, this Renaissance favourite was built on land donated to him by King Frederick of Aragon in 1497. The church was completed shortly before the poet died in 1530. Sannazzaro's tomb sits behind the altar.

Created in 1537 by Giovanni Angelo Montorsoli, Bartolomeo Ammannati and Francesco del Taddain, it features various mythological gods, including Apollo, Minerva, Pan and Mars in a depiction of Arcadia.

Another resident icon is Leonardo da Pistoia's painting of *St Michael Vanquishing the Devil*, also known as the *Devil of Mergellina*. Tradition holds that the devil in question was a lusty local lass who had made a move on the unwavering bishop Diomede Carafa.

CHIESA SANTA MARIA DI PIEDIGROTTA MAP PP284-5

☎ 081 66 97 61; Piazza Piedigrotta 24; ☼ 7am-noon & 5.30-8pm Mon-Sat, 7am-1.30pm & 5.30-8pm Sun; Ⓜ Mergellina

The fishing families of Mergellina had already built a church on this site when, in 1353, the Virgin Mary appeared to a Benedictine monk, a nun and Pietro the Hermit (later to become Pope Celestine V; (see Chiesa San Pietro a Maiella on p72) telling them to build her a church. She was taken at her word and the church was consecrated within the year. Since then, the church has remained the central focus of the Festa di Piedigrotta (p19), celebrated on 8 September.

Originally, the façade faced the rock, or *grotta*, to which the church owes its name (*piedigrotta* means 'foot of the cave'), but in 1553, it was reversed to face the city. In 1853, Enrico Alvino added the current neoclassical façade.

Inside, it's the 13th-century wooden statue of the *Madonna con Bambino* (Madonna with Baby) that the faithful come to see.

GROTTA DI SEIANO OFF MAP P287

☎ 081 230 10 30; Discesa Coroglio 36; 🚌 140 to Via Posillipo

At the bottom of a long, steep and exhausting descent (Discesa Coroglio), the Grotta di Seiano is not, in fact, a cave but a 1st-century tunnel linking the Roman Villa Pausilypon to Pozzuoli. Ventilated by three air ducts opening onto the sea, it was dug out of the tufa rock by Cocceius, the same Roman engineer who built the Crypta Neapolitana in Parco Vergiliano (p100). When the villa's owner Publio Vedio Pollione died in 15 BC, he bequeathed his clifftop pad to friend and emperor, Augustus.

Both the villa and the tunnel are currently closed for restoration.

MARECHIARO MAP P287

Via Marechiaro; 🚌 140 to Via Posillipo

Immortalised in a traditional 19th-century Neapolitan song 'Marechiaro' (Clear Sea) by Salvatore di Giacomo and Francesco Paolo Tosti, the little fishing village of Marechiaro is one for die-hard romantics. Complete with its own church, the Chiesa di Santa Maria del Faro, this is *the* place for candle-lit meals by lapping seas.

To get here, get off the bus on Via Posillipo and head down Via Marechiaro on the left. It takes about 30 minutes on foot.

PALAZZO DONN'ANNA MAP P287
Largo Donn'Anna 9; 🚌 140 to Via Posillipo
The most famous unfinished palazzo in Posillipo, Palazzo Donn'Anna takes its name from Anna Carafa, for whom it was built as a wedding present from her husband Ramiro Guzman, the Spanish viceroy of Naples. When Guzman hot-footed it back to Spain in 1644 he left his wife heartbroken in Naples. She died shortly afterwards and Cosimo Fanzago gave up the project. The semiderelict palazzo is not open to the public.

Not far from Palazzo Donn'Anna are the ruins of Villa Hamilton, the former residence of the British ambassador to the Kingdom of Naples. Sir William Hamilton is remembered less as a diplomat than as a wronged husband – his wife Emma was the long-time mistress of Lord Horatio Nelson.

PARCO VERGILIANO MAP PP284-5
☎ 081 66 93 90; Salita dell Grotta 20; ⏰ 9am-1hr before sunset Tue-Sun; Ⓜ Mergellina
Squeezed in between a railway bridge and the cliffs of Posillipo hill, this shady urban oasis hides two historical treasures; Virgil's tomb and the world's longest Roman tunnel.

The exact whereabouts of Virgil's body is a mystery. He died in Brindisi in 19 BC, and legend has it that his remains were then brought to Naples. Buried in a vault dating to the Augustan age, his tomb lies at the top of an exceedingly steep flight of stairs above the entrance to the closed **Crypta Neapolitana**. Built in the 1st century AD to connect Naples with Pozzuoli, this 700m-long feat of ancient engineering is the world's longest Roman tunnel and one of the best places to catch a cool draft on a hot summer's day.

Also buried in the park is the 19th-century poet Giacomo Leopardi.

PARCO VIRGILIANO MAP P287
Viale Virgilio; ⏰ 9.30am-11.30pm; 🚌 140 to Via Posillipo
Playground of the city's well-heeled denizens, this 9600 sq-metre park sits high above the shimmering sea on the westernmost tip of posh Posillipo hill. Kick back on a terrace and soak up the views; from Capri to the south, Nisida, Procida and Ischia to the southwest, to the Bay of Pozzuoli and Bagnoli to the west. Open 14 hours a day, this leafy getaway features swings and slides for the kids and

---

STEAMY WINDOWS

Head to any city lookout after 10pm and chances are you'll find a small sea of parked cars happily rocking and rolling. Windows covered up with newspaper, they harbour lust-struck couples in the mood for *lurve*. In Naples, most backseats have a saucy tale (or more) to tell. Indeed, you'd be hard pressed to find any Italian under 60 who doesn't fondly remember fumbling in the back of a Fiat. Shagging in the car is as Italian as pizza, Prada and dodgy politicians. Indeed, when Fiat CEO Gianni Agnelli died in 2003, then prime minister Silvio Berlusconi fondly reminisced about how many Italians experienced their 'first kiss' on those squeaky backseats.

Yet, the reason behind this tight-fit tradition is more a case of necessity than kink. A recent study by the EU revealed that a staggering 64% of Italians aged between 18 and 35 still live at home with their parents, compared to 21% in Germany and 12% in Finland. A case of spoilt *mammoni* (mummies boys... and girls)? Although many non-Italians like to think so, the truth has more to do with economics than immaturity. Italy's chronic lack of employment and high taxes make the prospect of moving out impossible for many young adults. In Naples, where youth unemployment is over 60%, the problem is acutely amplified. As a result, many young lovers simply have no choice but to hit the backseat for a bit of privacy.

Despite its celebrated status, shagging in the car can land lovebirds in legal hot water. In 1999, a young couple caught in the act was charged with committing a lewd act in public. Since then, blackening out the windows with newspaper has given new meaning to the term 'safe sex'.

Feeling kinky? Then park your car at one of these classic make-out spots:
Largo San Martino (Map pp278–9)
Stunning city views and the occasional police patrol, so don't forget the newspaper.
Parco Virgiliano (Map p287)
Daytime home to the respectable Mercatino di Posillipo (see the boxed text, p140), this car park is Naples' number-one spot for after-dark backseat antics.
Via Coroglio (Map p287)
Close to beachside club L'Arenile di Bagnoli (see the boxed text, p132) the car parks here are a hit for summertime love.
Via Manzoni (Map p287)
High up in Posillipo, the views of Bagnoli and the Bay of Pozzuoli make for the perfect lip-locking backdrop.

MARTIN MOOS

low-key bars for the grown-ups. The trendy Posillipo market takes place outside the main gates on Thursdays (p140).

PORTICCIOLO MAP PP284-5

Via Francesco Caracciolo; 🚌 **140 to Via Francesco Caracciolo**

Once home to the area's fishing fleet, Mergellina's marina is now a crowd-pulling combo of anchored yachts and kitsch Neapolitan **Chalets**; neon-lit gelaterie and bars right on the water's edge. On summer evenings, families, love-struck teens and the odd worn-out tourist flock here for gelati, cocktails and a spot of double parking.

STAZIONE MERGELLINA MAP PP284-5

☎ **081 761 21 02; Piazza Piedigrotta;** Ⓜ **Mergellina**

In the 1920s and '30s, Stazione Mergellina was *the* station to be seen alighting a train. Currently under the surgeon's knife, it's set to steal the scene again. Designed by Gaetano Coast in 1925, its beaux-arts style is a flouncy combo of glass and iron framework, grand classical columns and high camp extravagance, including two depictions of Mercury languidly posing above the station entrance.

VILLA ROSEBERY MAP P287

Via Ferdinando Russo 26; 🚌 **140 to Via Posillipo**

In an area famed for its blue-ribbon real estate, Villa Rosebery is a star resident. Built in the 18th century, its history is both romantic and epic. It was used by Luigi of Bourbon in the early 19th century for his trysts with the dancer Amina Boschetti, and it was from here that King Vittorio Emanuele III left Italy in 1946 after the abolition of the monarchy.

The complex consists of three buildings – the Palazzina Borbonica, the Piccolo Foresteria and the Cabina a Mare – surrounded by lush, extensive waterside gardens.

During the Maggio dei Monumenti (p18), the estate is sometimes open to the public, who flock here in droves to see what their taxes can buy.

WORTH A TRIP

An easy 25km north of Naples sits the modest town of Caserta (Map p171) and its colossal **Palazzo Reale** (Royal Palace; ☎ 0823 44 80 84; Via Douhet 22, Caserta; admission €6; 🕐 8.30am-7pm Wed-Mon). More commonly known as the Reggia di Caserta, this Unesco-listed pad is considered one of the greatest – and last – achievements of Italian baroque architecture. It is also where Tom Cruise shot scenes for *Mission: Impossible 3* and where George Lucas filmed the interior shots of Queen Amidala's royal residence in *Star Wars Episode 1: The Phantom Menace* and *Star Wars Episode 2: Attack of the Clones*.

Work on palace began in 1752 after Charles VII of Bourbon, ruler of Naples, wanted a palace to rival Versailles. Neapolitan Luigi Vanvitelli was commissioned for the job and built a palace not just equal to Versailles, but even bigger – think 1200 rooms, 1790 windows, 34 staircases and a 250m-long façade. You enter by Vanvitelli's immense staircase and follow a route through the royal apartments, richly decorated with tapestries, furniture and crystal. Beyond the library is a room containing a vast collection of *presepi* composed of hundreds of hand-carved nativity pieces.

To clear the head afterwards, take a walk in the elegant **landscaped grounds** (🕐 8.30am-2hr before sunset, last entry 1hr before closing Wed-Mon). They stretch out for some 3km to a waterfall and fountain of Diana and the famous **Giardino Inglese** (English Garden; tours every hr Wed-Mon) with its intricate pathways, exotic plants, pools and cascades. The weary can cover the same ground in a pony and trap (from €5) or for €1 you can bring a bike into the park. A picnic is another good idea. Within the palace there's also the **Mostra Terrea Motus** (admission free with palace ticket; 🕐 9am-6pm Wed-Mon), illustrating the 1980 earthquake that devastated the region. All done, revive yourself in the palace's cafeteria and restaurant and start drawing up those home extension plans.

CPTC buses connect Caserta with Naples' Piazza Garibaldi (€2.80) about every 30 minutes between 8am and 8pm. Some Benevento services also stop in Caserta. Trains from Naples also reach the town (€2.80). Both bus and train stations are near the Palazzo Reale entrance, signposted from each. If you're driving, follow the signs for 'Reggia'.

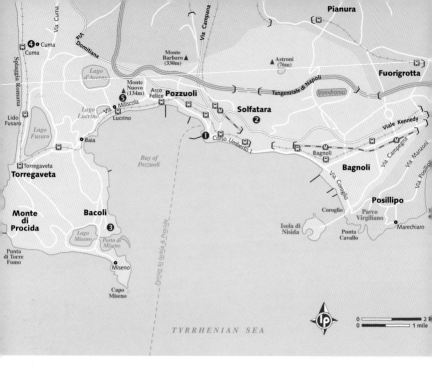

CAMPI FLEGREI

Sleeping p154

Steaming, bubbling and volcanic, the Campi Flegrei (Fiery Fields) are Naples' best-kept secret.

Stretching west from Posillipo Hill to the Tyrrhenian Sea, this pock-marked landscape of craters, lakes and fumaroles heaves with ancient myths and legends. This is where Icarus plunged to his death with melted wings, where Aeneas sought the Sibyl's advice, and where Roman emperors came to soak, swim and indulge. Hillsides are littered with thermal baths, sunken villas lie under the sea and unassuming streets hide some of Italy's finest archaeological sites.

Predating the city of Naples, the Greek settlements of the Campi Flegrei are the oldest in Italy. Cuma, the first mainland stronghold in the area, was already a thriving city in the 7th century BC when the Greeks founded Parthenope (the area around Pizzofalcone in Naples) in 680 BC. Pozzuoli, the area's main centre, was founded around 530 BC while Neapolis (where Naples' centro storico now stands) sprung up in 470 BC. Beneath Pozzuoli's streets, you can roam the ancient port's alleys and taverns. Nearby, you can climb Europe's newest mountain (Monte Nuovo), let nature freak you out at the hissing Solfatara Crater and look for the mythical entrance to hell at peaceful Lago d'Averno.

Before exploring the area it's worth stopping at the **tourist office** (☎ 081 526 66 39; Piazza G Matteotti 1a; ⏰ 9am-2pm & 2.30-3.40pm Mon-Fri Oct-May, 9am-1pm & 4-7.30pm daily Jun-Sep) in Pozzuoli to pick up a copy of the very useful leaflet *Welcome to the Campi Flegrei*. Also a good idea is the €4 cumulative ticket that covers the Tempio di Serapide and the archaeological sites of Baia and Cuma.

highlights
CAMPI FLEGREI

❶ Rione Terra (p104)

❷ Solfatara Crater (p104)

❸ Piscina Mirabilis (p105)

❹ Acropoli di Cuma (p106)

❺ Monte Nuovo (see the boxed text, p104)

Solfatara Crater (p104), Pozzuoli   JEAN-BERNARD CARILLET

POZZUOLI

Pozzuoli has had its fair share of ups and downs – literally. A victim of *bradeyism* (the slow upward and downward movement of the earth's crust), its seabed rose a dramatic 1.85m between 1982 and 1984, rendering its harbour too shallow for large vessels. An earthquake in October 1983 saw 40,000 residents evacuated, many permanently.

Founded by political exiles from the Aegean island of Samos, the town was initially under Cuman control. It came into its own under the Romans, who in 194 BC colonised it, renamed it Puteoli (Little Wells), and turned it into a major port. It was here that St Paul is said to have landed in AD 61, that San Gennaro was beheaded and that screen goddess Sophia Loren spent her childhood.

Today, Pozzuoli's future is looking up again – so to speak. Cranes dot the skyline, property values are soaring and frazzled Neapolitans are moving in for fresher air and seafood. Chilled-out, ancient and an easy 13kms from Naples, it's worth dropping in for some laid-back exploration.

The tourist office (opposite) is five minutes' walk downhill from the metro station.

ANFITEATRO FLAVIO MAP P288
☎ 081 526 60 07; Via Terracciano 75; admission €4; ⏰ 9am- 1hr before sunset Wed-Mon; 🚉 Cumana to Pozzuoli, Ⓜ Pozzuoli

The third-largest amphitheatre in Italy, the Anfiteatro Flavio could hold over 20,000 spectators and was occasionally flooded for mock naval battles. Wanted by Nero and completed by Vespasian (AD 69–79), its best-preserved remains lie under the main arena. Wander among the fallen columns and get your head around the complex mechanics involved in hoisting the caged wild beasts up to their waiting victims through the overhead 'skylights'. In AD 305 seven Christian martyrs were thrown to the animals by the emperor Diocletian. They survived, only to be later beheaded. One of the seven was San Gennaro, the patron saint of Naples.

Today the Anfiteatro hosts a summer season of theatre and concerts – contact the tourist office (opposite) for details.

The ancient Anfiteatro Flavio   GREG ELMS

RIONE TERRA MAP P288

☎ 848 80 02 88; Largo Sedile di Porto; admission €3; ☺ 9am-6pm Sat & Sun; ⊕ Cumana to Pozzuoli, Ⓜ Pozzuoli

Rising 33m above sea level at the western end of the seafront, Rione Terra is the Pozzuoli's oldest quarter and ancient Puteoli's acropolis. During the age of Augustus, an existing *Capitolium* here was lavishly restructured in white marble by architect Lucius Cocceius Auctus. Renamed the Temple of Augustus, it famously rivalled the temples of Rome.

Between the late 5th century and the early 6th century, the temple was again re-structured, becoming Pozzuoli's Duomo. In 1632, the cathedral was dedicated to San Procolo and given a baroque revamp by Bartolomeo Picchiatti and Cosimo Fanzago. When it caught fire in 1964, the temple was revealed once more and now both structures are undergoing an ambitious restoration, due for completion in 2008.

Indeed, the Tempio-Duomo project is one part of a major restoration of the quarter, which was abandoned en masse in the 1970s due to severe *bradeyism*. Ironically, this mass abandonment was a blessing for archaeologists, who unearthed fascinating parts of the ancient port.

Visitors can now head underground into an archaeological wonderland of ancient Roman roads, shops and even a brothel. You can walk down the decumanus maximus, check out ancient taverns, peer into millers' shops (complete with intact grindstones) and decipher graffiti written by the poet Catullus in a dingy slaves' cell.

SOLFATARA CRATER MAP P288

☎ 081 526 23 41; Via Solfatara 161; admission €5.50; ☺ 8.30am-7pm; Ⓜ Pozzuoli

Unnerving and surreal, this geological freakshow is a vivid reminder of just how active the ground below here is. Called Foro Vulcani (home of the god of fire) by the Romans, the crater's acrid steam, bubbling mud and sulphurous water have been lauded as health cures for thousands of years. At the far end of the crater you can see the **Stufe**, in which two ancient grottos were excavated at the end of the 19th century to create two brick *sudatoria* (sweat rooms). Christened Purgatory and Hell, they both reach temperatures of up to 90°C.

To get here, catch any city bus heading uphill from the metro station and ask the driver to let you off at Solfatara.

MOUNTAIN, ANYONE?

It's not every week that a mountain just appears on the scene. But this is exactly what happened just west of Pozzuoli in 1538. It all began in the early 1530s, when the area began experiencing an unusual level of seismic activity. Meanwhile, locals began noticing a dramatic uplift of the land between Lake Averno, Monte Barbaro and the sea, which displaced the coast by several hundred metres. Little did they know that under them a **Monte Nuovo** (New Mountain; Map p287; ☎ 081 804 14 62; Via Virgilio; ☺ 9am-1hr before sunset; ⊕ Cumana to Arco Felice) was getting set for its grand debut. At 8pm on 29 September 1538, a crack appeared in the earth near the ancient Roman settlement of Tripergole, spewing out a violent concoction of pumice, fire and smoke over six days. By the end of the week, Pozzuoli had a new 134m-tall neighbour. Today, Europe's newest mountain is a lush and peaceful nature reserve. Off the tourist track, its shady sea-view slopes are the perfect spot for a chilled-out stroll or picnic

TEMPIO DI SERAPIDE MAP P288

Via Serapide; ⊕ Cumana to Pozzuoli, Ⓜ Pozzuoli

Just east of the port, sunken in a leafy piazza, stands the Tempio di Serapide (Temple of Serapis). Despite its name, it wasn't a temple at all, but rather an ancient *macellum* (town market). Named after a statue of the Egyptian god Serapis found here in 1750, its ancient toilets (at either side of the eastern apse) are considered works of ancient ingenuity. Badly damaged over the centuries by *bradeyism*, the *tempio* is occasionally flooded by sea water.

BAIA

About 7km west of Pozzuoli, Baia takes its name from Baios, a shipmate of Ulysses who died and was buried here. An upmarket Roman holiday resort, it acquired something of a reputation as a sordid centre of sex and sin. Today much of the ancient town is under water (*bradeyism* again) and modern development has left what is effectively a built-up, ugly and uninspiring coastal road. It does, however, boast a dramatic castle that is home to the area's best archaeological museum.

A further 4km south sits the sleepy fishing town of Bacoli, where you'll find the magical Piscina Mirabilis.

LAGO D'AVERNO MAP P287

Via Lucrino Averno; 🚉 Cumana to Lucrino, 🚌 Sepsa to Lucrino

If someone tells you to go to hell, Lago d'Averno (Lake Averno) is a good place to start. In Virgil's *Aeneid*, it's from here that Aeneas descends into the underworld.

In 37 BC the Roman general Marcus Vipsanius Agrippa linked the crater lake to nearby Lake Lucrino and subsequently to the sea, turning it into a strategic naval dockyard.

While the battleships have gone, the ruins of the **Tempio di Apollo** (Temple of Apollo) remain. Built during the reign of Hadrian in the 2nd century AD, this thermal complex once boasted a domed roof almost the size of the Pantheon in Rome. Today, only four great arched windows remain.

This chilled-out, vine-fringed lake is an easy 1km walk north of Lucrino train station.

MUSEO ARCHEOLOGICO DEI CAMPI FLEGREI MAP P287

☎ 081 523 37 97; Via Castello; admission €4; ⏲ 9am-7pm Tue-Sat, 9am-1 hr before sunset Sun; 🚉 Cumana to Lucrino, 🚌 Sepsa to Baia

Packed with local ancient booty, this is where you will find the bewitching *Nymphaeum*, dredged up from underwater Baiae and skilfully reassembled. Monuments consecrated to the nymphs, *nymphaeums* were a popular spot to the tie the proverbial knot. Other finds include a bronze equestrian statue of the Emperor Domitian (altered to resemble his more popular successor Nerva upon his deposition) and recent finds from Rione Terra (opposite).

The museum sits in the Castello di Baia, built in the late 15th century by the Aragonese as a defence against possible French invasion. Later enlarged by Naples' Spanish viceroy Don Pedro de Toledo, it served as a military orphanage for most of the 20th century. The views over the bay are sublime.

PARCO ARCHEOLOGICO DI BAIA MAP P287

☎ 081 868 75 92; Via Sella di Baia 22, Bacoli; admission €4; ⏲ 9am-5pm Tue-Sun; 🚉 Cumana to Lucrino & then 🚌 Sepsa to Baia

In Roman times, this 1st-century BC palace and spa complex was hot – literally and figuratively. Emperors would entertain themselves and their splash-happy guests in a series of lavishly decorated thermal baths that descended to the sea. While the hedonists have long gone,

some of its treasures remain; including some exquisite floor mosaics, a beautifully stuccoed *balneum* (bathroom), outdoor theatre and the impressive Tempio di Mercurio, with its domed swimming pool filled with giant goldfish. In the summer months, the outdoor theatre is occasionally used for opera performances by the Teatro San Carlo (p135).

PISCINA MIRABILIS MAP P287

☎ 081 523 31 99; Via Piscina Mirabilis; ⏲ varies; 🚌 Sepsa to Bacoli

An archaeological pièce de résistance, the Piscina Mirabilis (Exquisite Pool) lies tucked away in a Bacoli backstreet. To access it, contact custodian Signora Filomena at No 9. Awaiting underground is the world's largest Roman cistern. Featuring 48 soaring pillars and a barrel-vaulted ceiling, it resembles a great subterranean cathedral, eerily bathed in shafts of sunlight. Erected in the Augustan age, its 12,600 cubic-metre water supply served the military fleet at nearby Miseno. Fresh water flowed into the cistern from the Serino river aqueduct which was then raised up to the terrace with hydraulic engines, exiting through doors in the central nave. To this day,

ATLANTIS, ITALIAN STYLE

Just off the coast of Baia, submerged in the sea, lie the mesmerising ruins of ancient Baiae. The former holiday hotspot for cashed-up Romans, it eventually fell victim to *bradeyism*, sinking into obscurity for hundreds of centuries. In 1956, celebrity diver Raimondo Bucher discovered the ruins. While many of the finds are now displayed in the Museo Archeologico dei Campi Flegrei (left), this underwater treasure trove still shimmers with beautiful mosaics and ruins, including parts of Emperor Claudius' summer villa. From the port at Baia, CYMBA operates tours of the **Città Sommersa** (Underwater City) on a glass-bottomed boat (☎ 349 497 41 83; prenotazioni@baiasommersa.it; ⏲ Tue-Sun; tours €10/7). Tour times change sporadically, so call ahead.

engineers marvel at the cistern's sophistication: its pounded terracotta walls and floor are still emulated today. Admission is free but save face and tip the Signora – €1 will do.

CUMA

The stuff of legends, Cuma exerted a powerful sway on the ancient imagination. Its sun melted Icarus' wings and its shores received Trojan hero Aeneas.

Ancient Cumae was the earliest Greek colony on the Italian mainland, founded in the 8th century BC by Greek colonists from the island of Euboea. The Romans took control in the 3rd century BC and built the impressive Grotta di Cocceio (closed), a straight-line tunnel connecting Cuma to the inland harbour at Lago di Averno.

ACROPOLI DI CUMA MAP P287

☎ 081 854 30 60; Via Montecuma; €4; 🕘 9am-2hrs before sunset; 🚌 12 from Pozzuoli

The centre of the ancient settlement of Cuma was the *acropoli* (acropolis). Situated at the base of the acropolis, the **Tempio di Apollo** (Temple of Apollo) was built on the site where Daedalus is said to have flown into Italy. According to Greek mythology, Daedalus and his son Icarus took to the skies to escape King Minos in Crete. En route Icarus flew too close to the sun and plunged to his death as his wax-and-feather wings melted from the heat.

At the top of the acropolis stands the **Tempio di Giove** (Temple of Jupiter). Dating to the 5th century BC it was later converted into a Christian basilica, of which the remains of the altar and the circular baptismal font are visible.

However, it's the haunting **Antro della Sibilla Cumana** (Cave of the Cumaean Sibyl) that steals the show. Hollowed out of the tufa bank, its eerie 130m-long trapezoidal tunnel leads to the echo-filled vaulted chamber where the oracle was said to pass on messages from Apollo. The poet Virgil, probably inspired by a visit to the cave himself, writes of Aeneas coming here to seek the Sibyl, who directs him to Hades (the underworld), entered from nearby Lago d'Averno (p105). Less poetic are the recent studies that maintain the tunnel was originally built as part of Cuma's defence system.

If you plan on coming here by bus, take the P12R operated by CTP (www.ctpn.it in Italian). It's also worth asking the driver for departure times back to Pozzuoli; it'll save yourself a long and tedious wait by the roadside later.

ELSEWHERE

The city's northwest Fuorigrotta district is home to the Edenlandia amusement park and the Stadio San Paolo (p134) football stadium. Close by you'll find the huge exhibition space, the **Mostra d'Oltremare** (Map p287; ☎ 081 725 80 00; Piazzale Tecchio 52; 🚌 152) built by Mussolini between 1937 and 1940.

For information on Vesuvius, Pompeii and the Amalfi Coast see the Amalfi Coast and Ancient Sites chapters.

CITTÀ DELLA SCIENZA MAP P287

Science City; ☎ 081 735 21 11; www.cittadellascienza.it; Via Coroglio 104, Bagnoli; adult/child €7/5; 🕘 9am-5pm Tue-Sat, 10am-7pm Sun, extended hr Jul; Ⓜ Bagnoli, 🚌 C9/C10

Part of a major redevelopment of the Bagnoli steelworks area, this huge, high-tech museum takes the 'geek' out of science. Get clued up on physics at the science gym, walk through constellations in the high-tech planetarium (€2) or just go plain silly pressing lots of funky buttons.

EDENLANDIA MAP P287

☎ 081 239 40 90; Viale Kennedy 76; adult/child under 1.1m €2/free, rides €1.50 each; 🕘 varies, call ahead; 🚇 Cumana to Edenlandia

Fabulously kitsch and loads of fun, the Edenlandia amusement park boasts over 200 attractions, including dodgem cars, a fairy-tale castle, high-tech 3D cinema and flight simulator. The €2 admission covers the cinema, variety show and children's theatre.

WALKING
TOURS

WALKING TOURS

If you know one thing about Naples, it's probably that you don't want to drive here. Ever.

Italians will warn you not to take a car into Naples; Neapolitans will tell you (with just a hint of swagger) that you only need to get used to the road conditions. But unless you're staying for about 18 years you don't have time to get used to anything. The solution is simple – walk.

Even walking is not without its hazards. Scooters shoot past, brushing you as they go, parked cars block the pavements, and no car will ever stop at a pedestrian crossing unless physically forced to do so. The best advice is to cross the road with a local (ideally a nun) between you and the oncoming traffic.

Naples is a big city but it can easily be divided into manageable areas and explored on foot. The itineraries we describe here will take you through the heart of the city and give you an appetising taste.

SPACCANAPOLI & THE CENTRO STORICO

This tour takes you through the centro storico (historic centre), concentrating on its two main streets, Via San Biagio dei Librai and Via dei Tribunali.

Starting from **Piazza Garibaldi**, head a short way down Corso Umberto I before turning right into Via Ranieri and then left into Via dell'Annunziata. A little way down on your left you'll see the **Santissima Annunziata** 1 (p77), famous for its orphanage. It's a sad but moving experience to see the *ruota,* the wooden wheel where babies were once abandoned. Continue down the street and turn right down Via Forcella. After crossing Via Pietro Colletta, follow the street as it veers left and merges into Via Vicaria Vecchia. Where it meets the busy cross street, Via Duomo, stands the **Basilica di San Giorgio Maggiore** 2 (p74) on your left and, two blocks northwest up Via Duomo, the **Duomo** 3 (p75). Thousands gather at the Duomo in May, September and December to witness San Gennaro's dried blood miraculously liquefy. Over the road from the cathedral is the entrance to the **Chiesa e Pinacoteca dei Girolamini** 4 (p74).

Double back down Via Duomo until you meet Via dei Tribunali. Known to the Romans as the *decumanus maior,* this street runs parallel to the decumanus inferior, aka Spaccanapoli, aka Via San Biagio dei Librai. Before heading right into the heart of the centro storico, quickly nip left to admire Caravaggio's masterpiece *Le Sette Opere di Misericordia* (The Seven Acts of Mercy) in the **Pio Monte della Misericordia** 5 (p73). Before you retrace your steps to Via Duomo, have a quick look at the baroque **Guglia di San Gennaro** 6 (p72) in the small square opposite the church.

After you've crossed Via Duomo make for Piazza San Gaetano, about 150m down on the right. The tiny square where the Roman forum once stood is now dominated by the imposing **Chiesa di San Paolo Maggiore** 7 (p70). Tucked away to the side is **Napoli Sotterranea** 8 (p65). It is here that you enter Naples' extensive underworld. Some 30m to 40m under the surface, the ancient network of tunnels was originally cut out by the Greeks to extract the tufa stone, but the tunnels were used in WWII as air-raid shelters. Back on the surface, opposite the piazza, is the **Chiesa di San Lorenzo Maggiore** 9 (p70). A stark but beautiful Gothic church, it stands atop yet more Roman *scavi* (excavations) and is one of the highlights of the centro storico.

It's at this point that you leave Via dei Tribunali and head down **Via San Gregorio Armeno** 10 (p74). In December people come from all over Italy to visit the shops that line this street. They specialise in the *presepi* (nativity scenes) that no traditional Italian house is without at Christmas. Along this street you'll also find the **Chiesa di San Gregorio Armeno** 11 (p70), famous for its extravagant baroque décor and weekly miracle – the blood of Santa Patrizia is said to liquefy here every Tuesday.

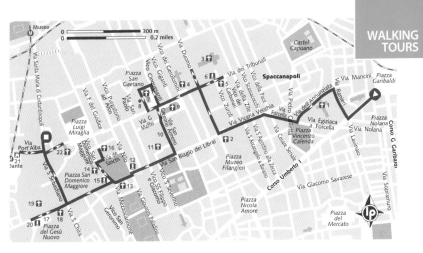

WALK FACTS

Start Piazza Garibaldi
End Piazza Bellini
Distance 3km
Duration 4 hours
Transport Ⓜ Garibaldi

Chiesa di San Paolo Maggiore (p70)   JEAN-BERNARD CARILLET

At the end of the road you hit Via San Biagio dei Librai. Turn right and after about 250m you will pass the **Statua del Nilo** 12 (p74) on your right. Less imposing is the altar to footballer Maradona on the wall opposite the statue. Further down on the left, the **Chiesa di Sant'Angelo a Nilo** 13 (p70) is entered from the small sidestreet Vico Donnaromita.

The rear of the imposing **Chiesa di San Domenico Maggiore** 14 (p69) abuts onto the café-fringed, pedestrianised **Piazza San Domenico Maggiore** (p73). At the heart of the square is the **Guglia di San Domenico** 15 (p73), topped by a statue of the good saint himself. The not-to-be-missed **Cappella Sansevero** 16 (p68) is just off this square in a lane east of the church. A jewel of a chapel, it's home to the stunning Cristo Velato (Veiled Christ), as beautiful a sculpture as any in Naples.

Back on Via San Biagio dei Librai, the road becomes Via Benedetto Croce and continues west to **Piazza del Gesù Nuovo** 17 (p73), the scene of much nightly revelry. The lively piazza is flanked by the **Basilica di Santa Chiara** 18 (p67) and the **Chiesa del Gesù Nuovo** 19 (p69), while in the centre the **Guglia dell'Immacolata** 20 (p73) is a study in baroque excess. The majolica-tiled cloisters of Santa Chiara provide one of the few peaceful spots in the centro storico, while the adjoining church stands as testament to the skill of Naples' restoration experts after it was almost completely destroyed by WWII bombs.

Backtrack from the square to the first intersection and turn left along Via S Sebastiano. At the next intersection on your left a short street leads down to book-lined **Port'Alba** 21 (p74), a city gate built in 1625, then to Piazza Dante.

Back on route and ahead of you is **Piazza Bellini** (p72) and, to the right, Piazza Luigi Miraglia, flanked by Naples' conservatory and the **Chiesa San Pietro a Maiella** 22 (p72). A great place to rest your weary feet is in one of Piazza Bellini's several cafés. While you're at it you could inspect the remains of the ancient Greek city walls under the square.

ROYAL SITES & SPECTACULAR VIEWS

The royal Santa Lucia district features some of the city's most recognisable landmarks, while Vomero boasts the city's highest point and best views. This tour covers both areas from the Castel Nuovo on the seafront to the Certosa di San Martino 250m up. But don't worry, you don't have to climb all the way to the top (although there is a long, steep stairway that leads up to the Certosa) – the funicular will haul you up to Vomero in about two minutes.

Piazza del Municipio (p86) is a big, brash place that's Naples in a nutshell. Traffic thunders past, spewing out clouds of black fumes; people crowd the pavements simultaneously eating gelati, smoking and shouting into mobile phones; tourists traipse past on their way to the ferry port. Overlooking all of this is **Castel Nuovo** 1 (p83). Known to Neapolitans as the Maschio Angioino, this sturdy castle dates to the 13th century and now houses a museum. From the castle, cross over the square and turn left towards Via Medina where you'll find the **Fontana di Nettuno** 2 (p85), one of Naples' finest baroque fountains. At the head of the piazza stands the **Chiesa San Giacomo degli Spagnoli** 3 (p86), where Naples' 16th-century Spanish viceroy Don Pedro de Toledo is buried. Next door the mayor has her office in **Palazzo San Giacomo** 4 (p86).

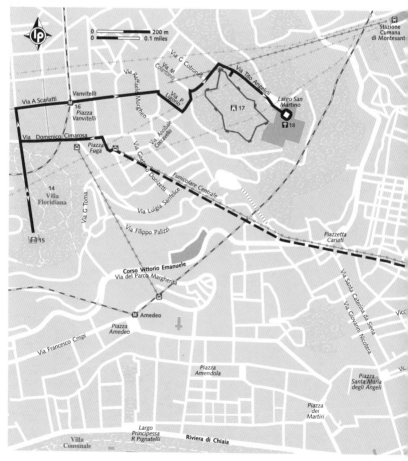

110

Following Via G Verdi south you emerge onto Via S Carlo and the **Teatro San Carlo** 5 (p87). Italy's largest opera house, it predates Milan's La Scala by 41 years. Opposite the theatre is one of four entrances to the **Galleria Umberto I** 6 (p79), the 19th-century shopping centre that, like Teatro San Carlo, compares to a similar building in Milan, the Galleria Vittorio Emanuele II.

Continuing down Via S Carlo brings you to the massive **Palazzo Reale** 7 (p85), home to the national library and some richly furnished royal apartments. The entrance to the royal palace is on **Piazza Trieste e Trento** 8 (p86), a magnet for thirsty tourists keen to try the coffee at **Caffè Gambrinus** 9 (p120). From the pavement in front of the café, stairs lead down to an unexpected and original gallery, **Raccolta de Mura** 10 (p87), dedicated to traditional Neapolitan music and theatre.

Fuelled with coffee, hop across to the huge **Piazza del Plebiscito** 11 (p86) where you'll find Naples' own version of the Roman Pantheon, the **Chiesa di San Francesco di Paola** 12 (p86). From here backtrack to Piazza Trieste e Trento, continue past the **Chiesa di San Ferdinando** 13 (p86), and about 150m up Via Toledo you'll see a funicular station on the left. Jump on any funicular and you'll be headed for Vomero.

When you get out at the top, walk down Via Domenico Cimarosa for **Villa Floridiana** 14 (p92), one of the city's rare patches of green and a good spot for a picnic. At the bottom of the park is the **Museo Nazionale della Ceramica Duca di Martina** 15 (p92). When you're done with ceramics, exit the park and take Via Giovanni Merliani as far as the first crossroad, Via A Scarlatti. Turn right and follow Vomero's main drag through **Piazza Vanvitelli** 16 as far as it will go. Keep on going straight, up the stairs near the Morghen funicular station, and turn left into Via Colantonio. Turn left again into Via Annibale Caccavello and at the end of the street you'll come out on Via Tito Angelini. Here you'll find **Castel Sant'Elmo** 17 (p91) and about 100m further down the road the **Certosa di San Martino** 18 (p91). Dating to the 14th century, this stunning monastery houses a fabulous museum and art gallery. And if all that's not enough, just look at the views – they're the best in town.

WALK FACTS

Start Piazza del Municipio
End Certosa di San Martino
Distance 4km (excluding funicular)
Duration 4 hours
Transport R2 to Piazza del Municipio & Funicular Centrale Via Toledo to Fuga

Piazza Trieste e Trento (p86)

MARTIN MOOS

111

A SEAFRONT STROLL

Starting at the Borgo Marinaro and the wonderfully named Castel dell'Ovo (Castle of the Egg), this route leads up to Piazza del Plebiscito, and round Via Chiaia to Piazza dei Martiri. From here you head seawards to pick up Villa Comunale and the *lungomare* (seafront) as it curves round the bay to Mergellina. The seafront is a favourite Neapolitan walk that is particularly enjoyable in the cool of a summer evening.

Start on the island of volcanic rock known to the ancient Greeks as Megaris and to modern Neapolitans as the **Borgo Marinaro** (p83). Naples' oldest castle, **Castel dell'Ovo** 1 (p83) has stood here since the 12th century. Returning to the mainland you'll see a row of luxurious hotels across the busy seafront road Via Partenope. Before you cross the road, however, take a second to admire the dramatic **Fontana dell'Immacolatella** 2 (p85) a few metres down on your right.

From the fountain cross Via Partenope, turn left and take the second right into Via Santa Lucia. Make your way up this attractive street to the top, turn left, and after about 200m you'll find yourself at **Piazza del Plebiscito** 3 (p86). Traverse the square and bear left into Via Chiaia. Cobbled and smart, this historic street cuts through to Via S Caterina and **Piazza dei Martiri** 4 (p89), the centre of the upmarket Chiaia district, dominated by a 19th-century obelisk. This is a good place to stop for a coffee.

Refreshed, continue down Via Calabritto, pausing to shop or look in the expensive designer shops, until you reach Piazza Vittoria and the entrance to **Villa Comunale** 5 (p89). This smart park of palms, statues and swings is home to Europe's oldest aquarium, the **Stazione Zoologica** 6 (p89). For more greenery and some priceless porcelain make for the **Museo Pignatelli** 7 (p88), on the inland side of the park.

To get back to the *lungomare,* retrace your steps over the Riviera di Chiaia and Villa Comunale to Via Francesco Caracciolo, the extension of Via Partenope. From here it's a pleasant and relaxing walk around the bay to Mergellina. This stretch of the route has no sites per se but if you look out to sea you'll spot the distinctive shape of Capri in the distance. When you get to Mergellina – you'll know you're there once you pass the **Porticciolo** 8 (p101) – make a beeline for the bars and gelaterie (ice-cream parlours) known as the **Chalets** 9 (p101). Here you can rest up and either call it a day or, if you've energy left, push on for a short final leg.

WALK FACTS

Start Borgo Marinaro
End Parco Vergiliano
Distance 5km
Duration 4 hours
Transport 🚌 C25 to Via Partenope

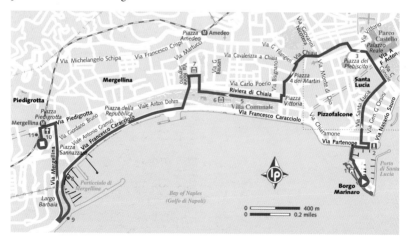

If you can tear yourself away from beer and ice cream cross over the main road to pick up Via Mergellina, which heads north, becoming Salita Piedigrotta after Piazza Sannazzaro. At the top of the short incline you will see the **Chiesa Santa Maria di Piedigrotta** 10 (p99) on your left and across the road Mergellina train and metro station. At the church, go left, hold your breath as you walk under the railway bridge, and you'll come to the **Parco Vergiliano** 11 (p100) on your left. A small but well-tended park, this is where Virgil is said to be buried.

FROM CATACOMBS TO CAPODIMONTE

This tour takes in two museums, three catacombs, a few churches and a park. From the Museo Archeologico Nazionale located on Piazza Museo Nazionale, the route rises through the little-explored La Sanità district and continues up to the Palazzo Reale di Capodimonte before finishing up at the Catacomba di San Gennaro.

You don't need to be an archaeologist to appreciate that the collection at the **Museo Archeologico Nazionale** 1 (p80) is something special. Highlights include the *Toro Farnese* (Farnese Bull) sculpture and the incredible mosaics, many of which once adorned noble houses in Pompeii.

From Piazza Museo Nazionale follow the traffic along Via Foria, passing Piazza Cavour (the grand name for a strip of bald grass) until shortly after the Cavour metro station. Take a left at Via Vergini and enter the Sanità district.

Known as La Sanità (which means 'healthy'), this area of crumbling buildings and impoverished streets was for centuries where the city buried its dead. The network of catacombs that runs underground is the main reason to come here.

At the end of Via Vergini the road forks. Follow the left-hand street, Via Arena della Sanità, which becomes Via della Sanità as it approaches Piazza della Sanità. On the square, the **Chiesa Santa Maria della Sanità** 2 (p95) is the entrance to the dark and dank **Catacomba di San Gaudioso**. Here you'll find mosaics and frescoes from the 5th century and learn the secrets of medieval inhumation.

Back in the open air and with your back to the church, turn left down Via San Severo a Capodimonte towards the Chiesa di San Severo. Under the 16th-century church lies Naples' first bishop, buried in the **Catacomba di San Severo** 3 in AD 410.

The road, or rather alleyway, now turns north. The Salita Capodimonte rises to the left of Piazzetta San Severo. At the top of the steps, head left and follow the street as it carves its winding way up to Via Capodimonte and, over the road, to the **Parco di Capodimonte** 4 (p95). Enter through the gate and follow the path round to the **Palazzo Reale di Capodimonte**

WALK FACTS

Start Piazza Museo Nazionale
End Catacomba di San Gennaro
Distance 3km
Duration 4 hours
Transport [M] Cavour

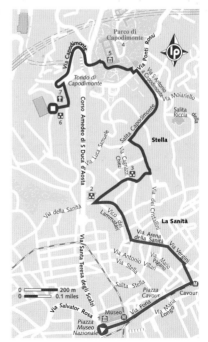

113

5 (p93). This majestic Bourbon palace houses one of Italy's most important art collections. Paintings by artists ranging from Caravaggio to Warhol line some 160 rooms spread over three floors.

To get to the last port of call, the **Catacomba di San Gennaro** 6 (p93), you can either walk down Via Capodimonte, or jump on a bus (any going downhill from outside the park gate) for the quick trip down to the catacombs. Get off the bus by the impossible-to-miss **Chiesa di Madre di Buon Consiglio** 7 (p93) on the right-hand side. The catacombs are the last resting place of San Gennaro and are known for their Palaeo-Christian frescoes and mosaics.

CLIMB THE ANCIENT HILL

Rising behind Piazza del Plebiscito, Monte Echia and the Pizzofalcone district is the oldest inhabited part of Naples. Greeks founded the city of Parthenope here in the 7th century BC, predating Neapolis (New Town) by some 300 years. Although the short tour outlined here does not include a whole host of must-see sites, it's an atmospheric (and relatively peaceful) walk that offers some fine views. Be warned though that it does involve a fairly steep climb and a hairpin descent.

Behind the columns on the northern side of Piazza del Plebiscito, **Piazza Carolina** 1 is the starting point for the climb up to Monte Echia. Rising up the hill are two narrow

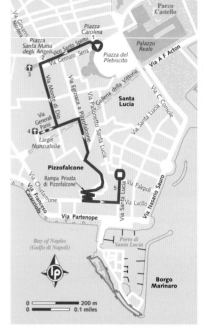

WALK FACTS

Start Piazza Carolina
End Via Santa Lucia
Distance 1.5km
Duration 2 hours
Transport 🚌 CS to Piazza Trieste e Trento

streets – Vico Santo Spirito di Palazzo and Via Gennaro Sorra. Take one of these, it doesn't matter which, and head up to **Piazza Santa Maria degli Angeli** 2. A small, undistinguished square, it takes its name from the yellow-fronted **Chiesa Santa Maria degli Angeli** 3 (p87). A baroque church, its most impressive feature is its huge dome.

From the square continue upwards along Via Monte di Dio until, on your right, you come to Via Generali Parisi. At the end of this short street is **La Nunziatella** 4 (p87), one of Italy's most prestigious military schools.

Backtracking to Via Monte di Dio, continue straight down Via Nunziatella until the first crossing. Turn right up Via Egiziaca Pizzofalcone and head uphill. The street is dark and atmospheric and the climb comfortable. At the top, continue straight up the Salita Echia and carry on until you come to the shabby gardens at the top. From here the views are your reward.

To return to sea level you can either go back the way you've come or follow the path that leads right off the garden terrace. Technically a private road, the Rampa Privata di Pizzofalcone zigzags its steep way down the side of the rock face until it flattens out into Via Chiatamone. As you descend notice the houses carved into the rock. Once you get to the bottom turn left and after a few metres you'll find yourself on **Via Santa Lucia** 5, an ideal place to plonk yourself at a pavement table and order a pizza.

THE EATING SCENE

While chefs in Seattle and Sydney fuss about with fusion, Neapolitan cooks remember what their mammas taught them: keep it simple, seasonal and fresh.

See Naples and diet. These city streets are a foodie's promised land. Market crates heave with voluptuous peppers, lobsters wriggle in plastic tubs, delis burst with spicy salami and the scent of freshly fried *pesce* (fish) fills the air. Street stalls sell Italy's best (and cheapest) fast food – from golden *arancini* (large rice balls stuffed with meat sauce) and *crocchè* (fried mashed-potato balls filled with mozzarella) to *pizza fritta* (deep-fried pizza stuffed with ham, mozzarella or seaweed) and *frittatine di pasta* (deep-fried pasta balls stuffed with minced pork, béchamel sauce and peas).

Home cooking rules, especially at family-run trattorie and *osterie* (casual-dining restaurants similar to trattorie), where classics such as *pasta e fagioli* (pasta and beans stew) and *spaghetti alla vongole* (spaghetti with clams) are filling, delicious and affordable. Some of the oldest and best lie tucked away in the dark streets of the centro storico (historic centre) and Quartieri Spagnoli.

HOW MUCH?

Eating out in Naples is generally cheaper than in Venice or Rome, with many restaurants catering to locals rather than tourists. For really cheap eats, go for street food, pizza or simple pasta dishes. Make sure you check the drink prices; a beer can easily cost €3 to €4 at fancier restaurants. Also, be wary when ordering fish that has to be weighed; ask for a quote *before* it hits the flame. Most restaurants will add an additional *coperto* (bread and cover charge) to your bill; this can range from €1.50 to €3 per person.

All of the eating options listed here are rated using three budget categories: € (€1 to €15), €€ (€15 to €30) or €€€ (€30+). Unless otherwise specified, 'meals' denotes the average cost of a first and second course plus dessert per person, excluding wine and cover charge.

THE BEST...

Sfogliatella Pintauro (p121)
Coffee Caffè Mexico (p120)
Pizza Da Michele (p118)
Pasta Donna Teresa (p125)
Gelato Scimmia (p122)
Seafood Dora (p123)
Vibe Nennella (p121)
Cheap eat Di Girolamo Giuseppe (p126)

Sfogliatelle   JEAN-BERNARD CARILLET

Do not be fooled by the dodgy décor, either – here, the emphasis is on food, not fashion. Of course, glammed-up options do exist, many concentrated around the old fishing quarter of Santa Lucia, where fresh *zuppa di pesce* (fish soup) is served with a side of bobbing boats.

As for the city's most famous export, pizza, it's the real deal; soft and thin in the middle and deeper around the edge. The margherita is the undisputed classic, simply topped with oil, basil, tomatoes and buffalo mozzarella. The pizza *marinara* has no seafood: its fishy name stems from its popularity with fisherfolk. Always go for the Vera Pizza sign, with its Punchinello (Punch) figure, a designation awarded to places that make their pizzas to strict traditional methods.

When not devouring the above, Neapolitans can be found huddled around bar counters and café tables scoffing down local pastries such as *sfogliatella* (a flaky pastry filled with sweet, cinnamon-infused ricotta) to *babà* (sponge soaked in rum). The croissantlike *cornetto* (filled with Nutella, cream or jam) is a popular way to start the day and end a big night out, with hordes of partied-out clubbers stopping off at late-night bars for a freshly baked batch. As for the city's gelato, it's mostly made on site and is lip-lickingly good.

Restaurants usually open for lunch from noon to 3pm and for dinner from 7pm to around 11pm. Many restaurants in the commercial centro storico close on Sunday, while others will close on Monday. Roughly half of Naples' restaurants close in August.

Where opening times are listed in reviews, this indicates that they vary from the usual opening times. Where no opening hours appear, assume that the standard hours given here apply.

Booking a table is generally not possible in a simple trattoria or pizzeria, although it is advisable at midrange to top-end restaurants, especially over the weekend.

Always check your bill carefully – if it includes a service charge of 10% to 15%, don't feel obliged to tip. If generosity gets the better of you, a tip of between 5% to 10% is appreciated, although Neapolitans often don't bother to leave anything at all.

The best news, however, is that smoking is now banned in Italian restaurants. Somewhat surprisingly, the usually do-as-I-please Neapolitans have generally accepted (and respect) this law.

For more information about specific food and drinks, see p53.

Tucking in at Da Michele pizzeria (p118)   GREG ELMS

CENTRO STORICO & MERCATO

Start your culinary adventure on the corner of Via dei Tribunali and Via San Paolo, with its daily fruit-and-vegetable stalls. Wander down Tribunali in either direction for a nonstop feast of tiny pizzeria, snack stalls, bakeries and heavenly scented delis. In Mercato, head straight to the market at Porta Nolana (see the boxed text, p140) for glistening fish, fresh pasta, small goods and minisized pizzas.

ANTICA GASTRONOMIA FERRIERI
MAP PP280-1   SNACK BAR €

☎ 081 554 01 65; Piazza Garibaldi 82-88; snacks from €2; ☻ daily; Ⓜ Garibaldi

Opposite Stazione Centrale, this snack bar draws everyone from surly Russian maids to cautious American backpackers. Side by side they scoff down moreish snacks such as herb focaccia and *pagniottiello*, a hybrid pizza/bread roll filled with aubergine, tomatoes and ricotta. There's a self-service restaurant upstairs.

ANTICA TRATTORIA DA CARMINE
MAP PP280-1   TRATTORIA €€

☎ 081 29 43 83; Via dei Tribunali 330; meals €17; ☻ lunch & dinner Wed-Sat, lunch only Tue & Sun, closed Mon; Ⓜ Dante

This homely haven houses the rarest of native species: the patient waiter. Beneath vintage Neapolitan photographs, he guides the indecisive through keep-the-faith classics such as juicy grilled squid and a delectable *penne alla sorrentina* (penne, mozzarella and tomatoes). Propose a toast to the well-priced house wine.

top five

CENTRO STORICO & MERCATO

Bellini (right)

Campagnola (right)

Da Michele (right)

Europa Mattozzi (right)

La Sfogliatella (opposite)

AVELLINESE
MAP PP280-1   TRATTORIA €

☎ 081 28 91 64; Via Silvio Spaventa 31-35; meals €15; ☻ daily; Ⓜ Garibaldi

Energy-boosting serves of pasta, meat and fish dishes. Go for the latter (unless it's Monday); there's a fish market around the corner. The service is brisk and businesslike and there's an outdoor terrace. The district is a little dodgy so don't wave that Prada handbag around after dark.

BELLINI
MAP PP280-1   RISTORANTE €€€

☎ 081 45 97 74; Via Santa Maria di Costantinopoli 79-80; meals €30; ☻ lunch daily, 7.30pm-1am Mon-Sat; Ⓜ Dante

Bellini sets the scene for *lurve*, with its candlelit terrace, cobbled streetscape and vintage cummerbund waiters. Get acquainted with just-caught fish or tuck into obscenely copious bowls of pasta – the *linguine ai frutti di mare* (pasta with fresh seafood) is heroic.

CAMPAGNOLA
MAP PP280-1   TRATTORIA €€

☎ 081 45 90 34; Via dei Tribunali 47; meals €16; ☻ lunch only; Ⓜ Dante

Hidden out the back of a wine shop, Campagnola looks like a poker room – sallow light and a wizened owner dealing out cards to his chums. The diners? Mostly an afterthought. So why do the famished keep flocking? Try the *spaghetti alla maccheronata* (fresh tomatoes, basil and *pecorino* cheese) and you'll see. Expect weekend queues.

DA MICHELE
MAP PP280-1   PIZZERIA €

☎ 081 553 92 04; Via Cesare Sersale 1; pizzas from €3.50; ☻ Mon-Sat 11am-11pm, closed Sun; ❿ R2 to Corso Umberto

King of the pizza brat pack, vintage Da Michele keeps things plain and simple: unadorned marble tabletops, brisk service and two types of pizza – margherita or *marinara*. Both are superlative and guaranteed to turn you into a pizza snob. Just show up, take a ticket and wait your turn.

EUROPA MATTOZZI
MAP PP280-1   RISTORANTE €€

☎ 081 552 13 23; Via Campodisola Marchese 4; meals €29; ❿ R2 to Corso Umberto I

This celebrated low-key classic has been on the scene for over a century. Adorned with colourful wall plates and prints, its elegant, well-versed staff serve up gems such as buffalo mozzarella with marinated octopus and fried zucchini, and nourishing pasta with parsley and chickpeas.

IL CAFFÈ ARABO MAP PP280-1   CAFÉ €
☎ 081 442 06 07; Piazza Bellini; snacks from €3; daily; M Dante

Arab by name, Arab by nature. This funky bolthole dishes out good-value falafel, hummus, *fuul* (a bean-based dip) and kebabs. Heartier fare includes a vegetarian couscous and a brave attempt at curry (more like a mild vegetable stew). The wine is the cheapest on the piazza.

INTRA MOENIA MAP PP280-1   CAFÉ €€
☎ 081 29 07 20; Piazza Bellini 70; snacks from €8; daily; M Dante

Lattes and literature live side by side at this free-thinking café/bookshop/publishing house. It's a hit with the left-leaning and artistically inclined, who feed their souls on the *misto di formaggi* (mixed cheese platter) and fruit salad with honey and muesli. The house wine costs €4 a glass.

LA CANTINA DELLA SAPIENZA
MAP PP280-1   TRATTORIA €€
☎ 081 45 90 78; Via della Sapienza 40; meals €17; Mon-Sat, lunch only; M Cavour

No culinary acrobatics here, just pared-down classics such as *parmigiana di melanzane* (slices of baked aubergine with decadent layers of tomato and parmesan) and *pizza bianco*, topped with nothing more than a drizzle of extra-virgin olive oil and crunchy sea salt. *Babà* fans take note – there's a different type baked each day.

LA SFOGLIATELLA
MAP PP280-1   PASTICCERIA €
☎ 081 28 56 85; Corso Novara 1; daily; M Garibaldi

Diet? What diet? Lose all self-control at this buzzing *pasticceria*, famed for its *sfogliatelle* and house specialities: *zeffiro all'arancia* (orange delicacy), chocolate and rum cakes, and *riccias millefeuilles* (pastry with an apple-custard filling).

LOMBARDI A SANTA CHIARA
MAP PP280-1   RISTORANTE €€
☎ 081 552 07 80; Via Benedetto Croce 59; meals €29; Tue-Sun; M Dante

Spaghetti alla vongole   JEAN-BERNARD CARILLET

From J-Lo lookalikes to cantankerous *nonni* (grandmothers), Neapolitans clamber to get into this faded favourite. *Perche?* For classic pizza, hearty pasta and finger-licking seafood. Vegetarians are spoilt for choice, with satisfying salads and an artfully combined platter of courgettes, artichokes and buffalo mozzarella. Weekend queues are long, so book ahead.

PORT'ALBA MAP PP280-1   PIZZERIA €
☎ 081 45 97 13; Via Port'Alba 18; pizzas from €5, meals €15; Thu-Tue; M Dante

Possibly the oldest pizzeria in the world ('twas founded in 1738), this doughy stalwart sits snugly on a cobbled street of secondhand bookshops. Sit outside under Port'Alba itself and choose from a dizzying selection of pizza and pasta. Fed and full, settle the bill and head to nearby Intra Moenia (left) for laid-back coffee and culture.

TRIANON MAP PP280-1   PIZZERIA €
☎ 081 553 94 26; Via Pietro Colletta 42-46; pizzas from €3; daily; R2 to Corso Umberto I

A Neapolitan institution – film director Vittorio de Sica and comic Totò used to eat here – this few-frills pizzeria has been tossing pizzas with the best of them since 1923. Today, burly labourers, boisterous families and giggling Japanese girlfriends come to chew in communal bliss.

TOLEDO & QUARTIERI SPAGNOLI

Hit the southern end of Via Toledo for *fin de siècle* cafés and restaurants, where fellow 'sippers and suppers' might include an opera great from nearby Teatro San Carlo. To the west, Quartieri Spagnoli keeps it real with quick-eat kiosks and old-style grub in earthy trattorie.

ANTICA TRATTORIA DON PEPPINO
MAP PP284-5   TRATTORIA €€

☎ 081 551 28 54; Vico 1 Gravina 7-10; meals €25; 🚌 R1 to Via Monteoliveto

This snug spot has a head-bonking array of rustic artefacts hanging from its ceiling – brass pots, dried corn and ropes of garlic and peppers. Equally loveable are its bountiful offerings, which include hearty seafood risotto and *carne al ragù* (beef cooked slowly in a rich tomato sauce).

BRANDI MAP PP284-5   PIZZERIA €€

☎ 081 41 69 28; Salita S Anna di Palazzo 1; pizzas from €5; 🕐 Wed-Mon; 🚌 R2 to Piazza Trieste e Trento

Everything about Brandi promises a pizza slice above the ordinary, from the table-top roses to the multilingual flyers that claim this was where the pizza margherita was invented in 1889. While this claim is contestable, Brandi's huge perfect pizzas are not. Alternatively, hunker down à la carte with pasta, fish and meat choices of lofty quality (and price).

CAFFÈ GAMBRINUS MAP PP284-5   CAFÉ €

☎ 081 41 75 82; Via Chiaia 1-2; 🕐 daily; 🚌 R2 to Piazza Trieste e Trento

The grand Gambrinus is Naples' oldest and most venerable café. Oscar Wilde knocked back a few here and Mussolini had some of the rooms shut down to keep out left-wing intellectuals. It's now suitably decked out in marble, antiques and the odd mock-Grecian statue, and the snooty staff serve pricey coffees, cocktails and snacks to golden-skinned posers and smitten out-of-towners.

CAFFÈ MEXICO MAP PP280-1   CAFÉ €

☎ 081 549 93 30; Piazza Dante 86; 🕐 7am-8.30pm Mon-Sat; Ⓜ Dante

Classic diner fit-out and shocking-orange espresso machine set the scene for the city's meanest coffee. Once hooked, stock up on freshly roasted beans all vintage cool in retro

top five
TOLEDO & QUARTIERI SPAGNOLI

Brandi (left)

Ciro a Santa Brigida (below)

Kukai (below)

Nennella (opposite)

Scimmia (p122)

1950s packaging. There's another branch at Piazza Garibaldi 70.

CIRO A SANTA BRIGIDA
MAP PP280-1   RISTORANTE €€€

☎ 081 552 40 72; Via Santa Brigida 71-74; meals €35; 🕐 Mon-Sat; 🚌 R2 to Piazza Trieste e Trento

After a night at nearby Teatro Augusteo, styled-up theatre buffs head here for classic service and soul food. Discuss the plot over *pasta e fagioli* or *pizza ai frutti di mare* (seafood pizza).

FRIGGITORIA FIORENZANO
MAP PP280-1   SNACK BAR €

☎ 081 551 27 88; Piazza Montesanto; snacks from €1; 🕐 8am-11pm Mon-Sat; Ⓜ Montesanto

Slap-bang in market country, this majolica-tiled veteran serves Italian-style tempura such as crunchy deep-fried aubergines and artichokes (in season), and prosciutto-and-mozzarella-stuffed croquets. Wolf them down by the counter or dive back into the market throng.

KUKAI MAP PP284-5   SUSHI BAR €€

☎ 081 41 19 05; Via Carlo de Cesare 55-56; meals €19; 🕐 1-3pm & 7pm-midnight daily; 🚌 R2 to Piazza Trieste e Trento

Sick of spaghetti? Then join the urban-savvy for fresh sushi and real-deal *temaki*. Sip green tea and choose from a menu that a Tokyoite couldn't falter. As for the takeaway and delivery service – it's as brisk as a Bullet Train.

LA SFOGLIATELLA MARY

MAP PP280-1   KIOSK €

☎ 081 40 22 18; Galleria Umberto 1, Via Toledo 66;
🕐 Tue-Sat 8am-8.30pm, closed Mon; 🚇 CS to Via
Toledo

Never short of a clambering crowd, this hole-in-the-wall kiosk serves up some of the steamiest, creamiest *sfogliatelle* in town. Start off with the minisized one for a mere €0.60 before hitting the hard stuff. Top off your sugar fix with a mini Moretto (€0.60), a dreamy chocolate *babà* filled with decadent cocoa cream.

MA TU VULIVE'A PIZZA

MAP PP280-1   PIZZERIA €

☎ 081 551 44 90; Via S Maria la Nova 46; pizzas from
€3.50; 🚇 CS to Via Toledo

Lively and packed; come here for epic pizzas and heaving *calzoni*. Tuck into the salubrious *calzone Terra Mia*, stuffed with vegetables, *provola* cheese, black olives and capers (€4.70) as you eavesdrop on student conversations about politics, travel and who's hot or not. In the evening, head to nearby Piazza Santa Maria la Nova for late-night boho chilling.

NENNELLA

MAP PP280-1   TRATTORIA €

☎ 081 41 43 38; Vico Lungo Teatro
103-105; meals €10; 🕐 Mon-Sat;
Ⓜ Montesanto

Classic and chaotic, this legend is unmissable. Write your name and number of guests on the list by the door and wait for the boisterous manager to call you in, boot camp–style. Inside, roguish waiters shout orders across the floor, patriarchs propose toasts and Rolexed studs dine with Mafia mistresses. Tuck into crispy fried sardines, lip-smacking *spaghetti con lupine* (spaghetti with lupins) or *insalatona nennella* (rocket, bresaola and radish salad).

PINTAURO MAP PP280-1   PASTICCERIA €

☎ 081 41 73 39; Via Toledo 275; 🕐 Mon-Sat Sep-Jul;
🚇 CS to Via Toledo

Follow your nose and join the queue for the city's best *sfogliatella*. But don't stop there. This legendary *pasticceria* does a mean *babà* and melt-in-your-mouth *biscotti di mandorla* (almond biscuits).

EATING LA DOLCE VITA

Creamy *sfogliatella*, trickling *babà* – the Neapolitan *pasticceria* (pastry shop) gives new meaning to the catchphrase *la dolce vita*. There's a pastry or cake for every occasion and feast day, and no Sunday lunch is complete without a tray of fresh pastries on the dining room table. Not sure where to begin? Here's the lowdown:

Babà
A yeasty mushroom-shaped sponge soaked in sugar and rum. Look out for a cocoa version filled with chocolate cream. According to legend, it was created by French chefs for the King of Poland in the 18th century.

Cassatina
The Neapolitan version of the Sicilian cassata, this mini cake is made with *pandispagna* (sponge), ricotta and candied fruit, and covered in glazed sugar.

Paste Reali
Cleverly crafted miniatures of fruit and vegetables, these sweets are made of almond paste and sugar (marzipan) and gobbled up at Christmas.

Pastiera
Traditionally baked at Easter, this latticed tart is made of shortcrust pastry and filled with ricotta, cream, candied fruit and cereals flavoured with orange-blossom water.

Rafioli & Roccocò
Traditional Christmas biscuits. While *rafioli* are hard and made with almonds, *roccocò* are a sweeter, softer concoction of sponge and marzipan sprinkled with icing sugar.

Sfogliatella
Naples' most typical pastry comes in two types: *frolla* (shortcrust pastry) and *riccia* (puff pastry), the latter considered the most classic. Both are shell-shaped, filled with sweet ricotta and candied fruit, and baked to golden perfection.

Torta di Ricotta e Pera
The cake of the moment, this ricotta-and-pear concoction is light, tangy and dangerously moreish. Best of all, it's available year-round.

Zeppole
Traditionally baked for the feast of San Giuseppe in March, these Neapolitan doughnuts are filled with custard and topped with bitter cherries.

SCIMMIA MAP PP280-1 GELATERIA €
☎ 081 552 02 72; Piazza Carità 4; ⊗ 10am-midnight Apr-Oct & Dec, 10am-10pm Jan-Mar & Nov, closed Wed Jan & Feb; Ⓜ Montesanto

The best of the much-loved Scimmia outlets. Locals flock here rain, hail or shine for creamy made-on-the-premises ice cream. Go the *zabaglione* (made with eggs and sweet Marsala wine) or a tangy orange sorbet and swing your hips to samba on the Latino-flavoured square.

TRIPPERIA FIORENZANO
MAP PP280-1 SNACK BAR/TRATTORIA €
☎ 349 781 01 46; Via Pignasecca 14; ⊗ 8.30am-8.30pm Mon-Sat; snacks from €1; Ⓜ Montesanto

Beneath languorous strips of hanging tripe, fifth-generation *trippaio* (tripe seller) Antonio and his son busily prepare take-home orders for hurried housewives. Behind the counter, five tables and a neon-blue shrine to Christ set the scene for sit-down adventures. Be brave and try the *zuppa di carne cotta* (tripe broth, €4) or the quintessentially Neapolitan tripe with tomato and basil. You might surprise yourself.

SANTA LUCIA & CHIAIA

Despite the over-sized yachts, hotels and limousines, dining in Santa Lucia needed cost a helipad. Head for the vintage fishing quarter of Borgo Marinaro for superlative (and justifiably priced) seafood and seductive sea and city views. To the west, savvy Chiaia offers a high-density clash of chichi cafés, slick sushi bars and homely trattorie serving *just-like-mamma* classics.

top five

SANTA LUCIA & CHIAIA

La Bersagliera (right)

Dora (opposite)

Jap-One (opposite)

La Cantinella (p124)

Umberto (p124)

ANTICA OSTERIA DA TONINO
MAP PP284-5 OSTERIA €€
☎ 081 42 15 33; Via Santa Teresa a Chiaia 47; mains €18; ⊗ lunch daily, dinner Fri & Sat only Ⓜ Amedeo

Popular? It's a wonder the door hasn't come off its hinges. At the front, time-pressed *signore* pick up their takeaway orders and a bottle of red. At the few packed tables, Borrelli suits, old-timers and the odd Nobel Prize winner (Dario Fo ate here) tuck into hearty grub such as *pasta ragù e ricotta*.

LA BERSAGLIERA MAP PP284-5 RISTORANTE €€€
☎ 081 764 60 16; www.labersagliera.it; Borgo Marinaro 10-11; meals €45; ⊗ noon-3.30pm, 7.30pm-midnight Wed-Mon, closed 2 weeks in Jan; 🚌 C25 to Via Partenope

This harbourside diva has wined and dined the best of them – there are photos of Salvador Dali and Sophia Loren to prove it. Waterfront views and a lavish dining room set the scene for star-worthy dishes such as clam and mussel soup and *taglierini* (fine ribbon pasta) with baby octopus, black olives and tomatoes.

CASTELLO MAP PP284-5 OSTERIA €€
☎ 081 40 04 86; Via Santa Teresa a Chiaia 38; set lunches €12, meals €26; ⊗ Mon-Sat; Ⓜ Amedeo

It could be the *vino* lining the walls, the piles of cookbooks or Norah Jones crooning in the background, but this place feels like home. Kick back with a steamy bowl of *pappardelle* (wide ribbon pasta) with courgette flowers and mussels or *filetto al castello* (veal in a creamy courgette sauce). Equally divine is the homemade *zeppola*, a doughy pie filled with fresh berries and custard.

CIRO MAP PP284-5 RISTORANTE €€€
☎ 081 764 60 06; Borgo Marinaro 29-30; meals €35; ⊗ Thu-Tue; 🚌 C25 to Via Partenope

More bobbing boats and roaming Romanian musicians. Yacht owners and envious tourists clamber for a spot on the terrace (get here early), where classic waiters serve equally classic dishes. Stick with the award-winning pizzas and fresh seafood; the linguine with crustaceans and shellfish (€18) is pricey perfection.

DA PIETRO MAP PP284-5 TRATTORIA €€
☎ 081 807 10 82; Via Lucilliana 27; meals €19; ⊗ Tue-Sun; 🚌 C25 to Via Partenope

Flanked by its grander neighbours, but sharing the same five-star harbour view, Da Pietro is simple and modest, right down to the plastic tableclothes, chalked-up daily menu and mildly harassed staff. Keep it real with spaghetti with tomato and basil, and filthy fresh bowls of mussels. A combination of competitive prices and few tables means you should expect to queue.

DI BRUNO MAP PP284-5 RISTORANTE €€€
☎ 081 251 24 11; Riviera di Chiaia 213-14; meals €36; ⏲ Tue-Sun; 🚌 C25 to Riviera di Chiaia

Discerning palates saunter here for upper-crust Italian fare, a 200-strong wine list and impeccable service. Seafood is the undisputed star, with offerings such as *carpacci tagliati di pesce crudo* (raw fish drizzled in olive oil and parmesan) guaranteed to please the picky. The pasta is made from scratch, as are the desserts, which feature a can't-stop-at-one ricotta and pear tart.

DORA MAP PP284-5 RISTORANTE €€€
☎ 081 68 05 19; Via Ferdinando Palasciano 30; meals €45; 🚌 C25 to Riviera di Chiaia

Dishing up the best fish in town, humble Dora hides its celebrity status behind a tatty shop front on a forlorn street. Don't be fooled. Inside, an empty seat is as rare as a mediocre meal. Under hospital-bright light, loveable waiters dish up gems such as juicy char-grilled prawns, and linguine with crustaceans. The owner is known to break out in song. Book or miss out.

JAP-ONE MAP PP284-5 JAPANESE RESTAURANT €€€
☎ 081 764 66 67; Vico Santa Maria a Cappella Vecchia 30/I; meals €45; ⏲ closed Sun; 🚌 C25 to Piazza dei Martiri

Giving **Kukai** (p120) stiff competition in the sushi stakes, this über-trendy bolthole is hidden away down a series of 'where-am-I' laneways. Inside, fashionistas with savvy palates nibble on faultless sashimi, nigori and tempura in a suitably minimalist setting of polished concrete, steel and cocoa-coloured furnishings.

LA CAFFETTIERA MAP PP284-5 CAFÉ €
☎ 081 764 42 43; Piazza dei Martiri 30; ⏲ daily; 🚌 C25 to Piazza dei Martiri

Waiters in waistcoats serve potent espresso and cool Camparis to cross-legged businessmen and chichi shopaholics. Take a seat on the terrace (no-one can see you inside, sweetie) order a slice of the *torta di mandorla* (almond cake) and compare shopping bag sizes.

GREG ELMS

GREG ELMS

LA CANTINELLA MAP PP284-5   RISTORANTE €€€
☎ 081 764 86 84; Via Cuma 42; meals €51;
⏰ Mon-Sat; 🚌 C25 to Via Partenope

Fussy foodies flock here for sophisticated twists on classic dishes. At crisp linen tables they savour the likes of beef fillet with Marsala sauce and pork liver served with Saracen flour flan (€28), and encrusted pork with apples and Parma ham drizzled in an Armagnac sauce (€24). Desserts are equally luxe, and the lengthy and interesting wine list yields some excellent quaffs.

LA FOCACCIA MAP PP284-5   SNACK BAR €
☎ 081 41 22 77; Vico Belledonne a Chiaia 31; focaccias from €1.60; ⏰ 11am-3pm Tue-Sun; 🚌 C25 to Piazza dei Martiri

The young, the hip and the just-plain-starving cram into this funky red spot for fat focaccia squares stacked with lip-smacking combos such as aubergine, *pecorino* cheese and smoked ham.

L.U.I.S.E. MAP PP284-5   DELI €
☎ 081 41 77 35; Piazza dei Martiri 68; snacks from €1.20, meals €10; ⏰ 7.30am-8.30pm Mon-Sat;
🚌 C25 to Piazza dei Martiri

This chic little deli is a gourmand's playpen – think fat cheeses and sausages, homemade foodstuffs and bottles of luscious wine. In the back room, lunching 9-to-5ers tuck into warming osso bucco, nourishing *risotti* and homemade gnocchi. Busy travellers can take theirs away. Try the freshly fried *pizza fritta*, crisp *arancini* and sugar-dusted *pasticcini crema amarena* (pastries filled with cherry cream).

MAKTUB MAP PP284-5 RISTORANTE €€
☎ 081 764 73 37; Vico Satriano 8C; meals €26, set lunches Mon-Fri €7.50; ⏰ Mon-Sat; 🚌 C25 to Riviera di Chiaia

Mandolins and wall plates? Try yellow paper lanterns and a gnarled tree trunk growing out of the dining room floor. Add barrel-vaulted ceiling, evening candlelight, DJ and a laid-back crowd, and you start to get the picture. Go for *scialatielli con pomodorino, zucchini e pancetta* (pasta with tomato, corgettes and bacon) and *filetto di manzo in salsa di grana Padana* (beef fillet with Grana Padana sauce) and the naughty *sbriciolona di Nutella* (chocolate salami).

MOCCIA MAP PP284-5   PASTICCERIA €
☎ 081 41 13 48; Via San Pasquale a Chiaia 21-22;
⏰ Wed-Mon; 🚌 C25 to Riviera di Chiaia

With gleaming displays of dainty strawberry tartlets, liqueur-soaked *babà* and creamy gelato (try a watermelon and peach combo), no-one is safe at this chichi pastry peddler – blow-waved matriarchs, peckish professionals or waif-thin Chiaia princesses. The *caprese* (chocolate and almond cake) is the best in town.

UMBERTO MAP PP284-5   RISTORANTE €€
☎ 081 41 85 55; Via Alabardieri 30-31; meals €25;
⏰ 10.30am-3.30pm & 7.30pm-midnight; 🚌 C25 to Piazza dei Martiri

Gluten-intolerant diners can feast on allergy-friendly fare, such as a refreshing orange, almond and fennel salad and perfectly pan-fried swordfish with cherry tomatoes, olives and capers. The cheaper gourmet pizzas include a fabulous *prosciutto crudo*, rocket, mozzarella and parmesan combo.

VOMERO, CAPODIMONTE & LA SANITÀ

Don't let Vomero's building-block air fool you – the streets around Piazza Vanvitelli harbour some soulful restaurants, trattorie and snack bars. Less packed with options is La Sanità, though its tangle of backstreets hides one or two gems. If you're heading to Capodimonte, pack a picnic or opt for one of the options listed here.

ACUNZO MAP P283 TRATTORIA €€
☎ 081 578 53 62; Via Domenico Cimarosa 64; meals €18; ✆ Mon-Sat; Funicular Centrale to Fuga

Old-school cooking, heady aromas, vintage décor and one very satisfied clientele. Tuck into simple, satisfying classics such as the homemade gnocchi, paper-thin pizzas topped with cherry tomatoes, mozzarella and fresh rocket leaves, or the hearty *calzoni* stuffed with beans.

top five

VOMERO, CAPODIMONTE & LA SANITÀ

Acunzo (above)

Angolo de Paradiso (right)

Donna Teresa (right)

Antica Cantina de Sica (right)

Starita (p126)

Fried nibbles for sale at Friggitoria Vomero JEAN-BERNARD CARILLET

ANGOLO DE PARADISO
MAP P283 PIZZERIA €
☎ 081 556 71 46; Via Michele Kerbaker 152; ✆ Tue-Sun; pizzas from €3; Ⓜ Vanvitelli

Beneath the ubiquitous row of old photographs, time-tested regulars tackle steamy hot pizzas served by affable pin-striped wait staff. Indecisive taste buds can have it all with the pizza Paradiso (€5); five good-sized slices with toppings such as Neapolitan sausage, salami, aubergine and spinach. The wine is dangerously cheap.

ANTICA CANTINA DI SICA
MAP P283 RISTORANTE €€
☎ 081 556 75 20; Via Bernini 17, meals €29; ✆ Wed-Mon; Ⓜ Vanvitelli

Rustic yet chic (think softly lit vaulted ceilings, dark wooden furniture and bottle-lined honeycomb walls), Antica Cantina serves up classic Neapolitan fare made with salutary attention to detail. Among the winners are the *pasta patata e provola* (pasta, potato and *provola* cheese) and the *ziti alla genovese* (pasta with rich onion and meat sauce). Ditch the *vino locale* for a bottled wine instead – it's cheaper.

DONNA TERESA MAP P283 OSTERIA €
☎ 081 556 70 70; Via Michele Kerbaker 58; meals €14; ✆ Mon-Sat; Ⓜ Vanvitelli

This swing-a-cat-sized dining room – there are only eight tables – has an epic reputation for solid home cooking. Mamma Teresa's photo looks on approvingly as diners tuck into classics such as *spezzatini al ragù* (meat stew) and *salsicce al sugo* (sausages with tomato sauce). The menu is limited, changes daily and pulls in the hordes, so book or go hungry.

FRIGGITORIA VOMERO
MAP P283 SNACK BAR €
☎ 081 578 31 30; Via Domenico Cimarosa 44; snacks from €1; ✆ Mon-Sat; Funicular Centrale to Fuga

This worn corner snack bar keeps punters happy with superb *fritture* such as deep-fried aubergines, potatoes and *zeppole*. Located opposite the funicular, it's a good place to stock up before legging it to Castel Sant'Elmo.

I GIARDINI DI CAPODIMONTE
MAP P286 RISTORANTE €€
☎ 081 744 51 36; Via Capodimonte 19; meals €25; ✆ daily; 🚌 24 to Via Capodimonte

Like a merciful mate, this shady terraced number waits at the top of the steep steps leading from Tondo di Capodimonte. Be good to yourself with a bowl of *gnocchetti al limone* (gnocchi with lemon; €7) or the decadent *risotto allo champagne* (champagne risotto). Gurgling fountain and sultry Neapolitan song complete the soothing picture.

STARITA MAP P286 PIZZERIA €

☎ 081 557 46 82; Via Materdei 28; pizzas from €4; ☺ Tue-Sun; M Materdei

They don't get more Neapolitan than this pizzeria. Set in a washing-strung street, the giant fork and ladle hanging on the wall were used by Sophia Loren in *L'Oro di Napoli* – the kitchen made the *pizze fritte* (fried pizzas) sold by the actress in the film. Get indecisive over the 53 pizzas or trust in the owner's favourite, *fiorilli e zucchini* (€5.50), with its zucchini, zucchini flower and *provola* topping.

MERGELLINA & POSILLIPO

These two seaside places get packed out with large noisy families at weekends, especially on Sunday in summer. As well as the restaurants listed here, Mergellina is ice cream heaven. The best places boast the longest queues. Posillipo will give you a taste of the Amalfi Coast; the seafood restaurants are comparable in quality to those in Mergellina but are generally cheaper.

A LAMPARA MAP P287 RISTORANTE €€€

☎ 081 575 64 92; Via Discesa Coroglio 79; meals €30; ☺ Thu-Tue; ☐ 140 to Via Posillipo

Short of spruiking it on a street corner, perma-tanned locals pledge allegiance to this homely haven, where the *ravioli alla bolognese* is an education in bolognese brilliance. Enjoy it on the voyeuristic streetside terrace. The wine list brims with decent local drops, and the summertime Sunday buffet draws a preppy league of loyal fans – so get in early.

CIBI COTTI MAP PP284-5 TAVOLA CALDA €

☎ PHONE; Via F Galliani 30; meals €7; ☺ 12-4pm daily; M Mergellina

The gruff old chap in the Godfather sunglasses is Vittorio and deep down he's a softie. His little white-tiled eatery is an in-the-know gem, tucked away in a raffish market arcade. Conversations bounce from table to laminex table as regulars feed on simple, filling and supercheap choices such as *sardine fritte* (fried sardines) and rice with octopus, rocket and cherry tomatoes.

DI GIROLAMO GIUSEPPE
MAP PP284-5 SNACK BAR €

☎ 081 66 44 98; Via Mergellina 55E; pasta from €1; ☺ 8am-3pm & 5-11pm daily; M Mergellina

Run by charming elderly gentlemen in retro diner hats, this loveable nook serves up tasty grub at rock-bottom prices. *Pizza a taglio* (pizza by the slice) combos include mozzarella and spinach, and pumpkin tomato basil and olives. There's also *pizza fritta*, focaccia and ready-to-eat plates of pasta. Plonk yourself down on a bar stool and fill up to the sounds of Burt Bacharach.

SALVATORE MAP PP284-5 RISTORANTE €€€

☎ 081 68 18 17; Via Mergellina 4A; meals €35; ☺ Thu-Tue; M Mergellina

The key to happiness? Balmy nights, bay views and filthy-fresh seafood. You're guaranteed at least the last two at this buzzing favourite, with its *dolce vita* terrace and blingy indoor chandeliers. Culinary clichés make way for *cecinielle* (fried fish patties), comforting *minestra in brodo* (thick noodle broth) and *calamaretti con uva passa* (baby squid with pine nuts and raisins). Owner Tonino is a serious wine buff.

ENTERTAINMENT

NAPLES NIGHTLIFE

An unruly insomniac, Naples is a high-voltage jolt of teeming piazzas, thunderous opera, and sexy, sweat-soaked dance floors.

Naples has been tagged everything from filthy to fabulous. One thing it's not is boring. The Neapolitans' infamous Bacchanalian bent makes *divertirsi* (enjoying oneself) a high priority. For many, it's as simple as an evening *passeggiata* (stroll), when locals hit the streets en masse to chat, smoke and lick gelato (ice cream). For many more, it's an evening spent sipping, supping and socialising on the city's cobbled piazzas. Particularly buzzing are the cosy little squares in the centro storico (historic centre), filled with philosophical students, joint-smoking punks and jazz-loving bohemians.

For languid seaside lounging, head west to the restaurants and bars on Borgo Marinaro, where yachting types, hopeless romantics and scooter-happy teens kick back and eye the passing throng. The *lungomare* (seafront) itself is a hugely popular spot for strolling and smooching and at its Mergellina end the Chalets serve up some epic ice cream concoctions to boisterous families and first-date teens.

Pleasure-seeking fashionistas hang out in upmarket Chiaia, home to Naples' best *aperitivo* (happy hour) scene (see the boxed text, p123). Most of the action takes places west of Piazza dei Martiri, where minimalist bars sit alongside chichi restaurants, *enoteche* (wine bars) and A-list clubs fit for Prada kit. Less known to visitors is the Vomero bar scene, which features a small string of funky little drinking spots on Via Aniello Falcone. Popular in the spring and summer, this is where Vomero's Polo Ralph Lauren set drinks beer, kicks back and gazes out over city and bay.

In the summer months, the clubbing scene moves west to the beaches of Bagnoli and Campi Flegrei. Here, cabanas, A-list acts and waterside bars and dance floors make for heady summer nights.

Of course, Naples is more than beach babes, bars and clubs. A packed cultural calendar includes the biggest rock music event in southern Italy, an all-night art and shopping festival and world-class opera at the legendary Teatro San Carlo. Each May, people flock to the city for the Maggio dei Monumenti (see p18), a month of concerts and cultural activities in museums and monuments around town, most of which are free. In summer, the Amalfi Coast and Bay of Naples islands host a range of festivals, chief of which is the world-famous Ravello Festival (see p238 for details). For more festival dates, see p18.

The monthly *Qui Napoli* (in Italian and English) and local newspapers (in Italian) are the best guides to what's on when, or ask at tourist offices for details.

For background information on many aspects of Naples' arts scene, see p43.

GREG ELMS

top five
BARS

Kestè (p130) A student hot spot with DJs, cool pop art and a buzzing square to boot.

Enoteca Belledonne (right) The wine bar of choice for the city's chic.

S'Move (p130) Funky fit-out, acid jazz and slinky scrubbed-up drinkers.

White Bar (p131) Minimalist, modern and white, the music is lounge and the vibe cool and laid-back.

Al Barcadero (right) An unpretentious spot to sip by the sea.

DRINKING

Neapolitans are not big drinkers, so don't expect boozy English-style pubs. In fact, in the centro storico many people simply buy a bottle of beer from the nearest bar and hang out on the streets.

Here, the biggest concentration of bars is found around Via Cisterno dell'Olio, Piazza Bellini, Piazza del Gesù Nuovo and Piazza San Domenico Maggiore. The proximity of the university ensures a vibrant atmosphere.

In upmarket Chiaia, head to the area around Via Ferrigni and the nearby Vicoletto Belledonne for the city's most stylish bars.

Uphill in Vomero, a string of eclectic little bars on Via Aniello Falcone mixes a preppy crowd with toast-worthy views.

Cafés usually open from about 7am until about 1am. Bars either open for apéritifs, at around 6pm, or directly for the evening shift at 10pm. Closing is rarely much before 2am or 3am. Many city centre bars close for a month over the summer.

AL BARCADERO MAP PP284-5
☎ 333 222 70 23; Banchina Santa Lucia 2; 🚌 C25 to Via Partenope

Turn left down the steps as you walk towards Borgo Marinaro and you'll find this unpretentious waterfront bar. Grab a beer and watch boat-rowing fishermen and a menacing Mt Vesuvius.

ARET'A'PALM MAP PP280-1
☎ 339 848 69 49; Piazza Santa Maria La Nova 14; 🕐 6pm-2.30am Mon-Sun; 🚌 CS to Via Diaz

Red velvet curtains, a soaring palm on the piazza and a laid-back crowd of artists, actors and academics who flock here as much for the jazz and blues as for the inspiring wine list. On summer evenings, an elderly man sets up a stall in the piazza and sells cheap beer for those with more thirst than money.

CHANDELIER MAP PP284-5
☎ 333 252 81 77; Vico Belledonne a Chiaia 34/5; 🕐 6.30pm-2am daily; 🚌 C25 to Piazza dei Martiri

Chandelier is a slick pic of shiny white floors, black walls and a bright-yellow motorbike on show beside the bar. Popular for evening *aperitivo*, its perma-tanned clientele nibble and chill to house, pop and R&B.

ENOTECA BELLEDONNE MAP PP284-5
☎ 081 40 31 62; Vico Belledonne a Chiaia 18; 🕐 4.30pm-2am Mon, 10am-2pm & 4.30pm-2am Tue-Sat; 🚌 C25 to Riviera di Chiaia

Exposed brick walls, ambient lighting and bottle-lined shelves set the elegant scene at Naples' best-loved wine bar. Grab the savvy wine list and swirl, sniff and sip your way to bliss.

S'Move bar, Chiaia   GREG ELMS

FARINELLA MAP PP284-5
☎ 081 423 84 55; Via Alabardieri 10; ⏱ 12pm-late daily; 🚌 C25 to Piazza dei Martiri
Skip the restaurant and head straight for the chocolate-toned bar. Here, style-savvy locals nibble on *aperitivo* gems such as steamy risotto and tapas and kick back with fruity Martini Pleasers.

FUSION BAR 66 MAP PP284-5
☎ 081 41 50 24; Via Bisignano; ⏱ 6pm-3am daily; 🚌 C25 to Riviera di Chiaia
Vintage Turkish lanterns and gilded gold and silver chairs give this place a funky ethnic vibe. A 30-plus crowd spills out onto the street, living it up to jazz, lounge and the occasional live bossa nova act.

GROOMING MAP PP278-9
☎ 081 193 607 00; Via Aniello Falcone 346; ⏱ 9pm-2am daily; 🚌 C28 to Parco Lamaro
One in a row of quirky bars, Grooming is a hit with Vomero's rich kids. Under its hanging African masks, they sip apéritifs, snack on *panini* (sandwiches) and gaze out over city and sea. Head in early for food as it tends to run out.

KESTÈ MAP PP280-1
☎ 081 551 39 84; Largo San Giovanni Maggiore 26/7; ⏱ 8.30am-7.30pm Mon & Tue, 8.30am-3am & 8.30pm-3am Sat & Sun; 🚌 R2 to Corso Umberto I
A student hot spot, with tables spilling onto the square and a pop painting of San Gennaro above the DJ deck. Monday to Saturday, punters bop to pop, electronica and world beats. Sunday features live blues, folk and jazz.

KINKY BAR MAP PP280-1
☎ 081 552 15 71; Via Cisterna dell'Olio 21; ⏱ 10.30pm-3am daily Oct–mid-Jun; Ⓜ Dante
No whips and chains here – just a funky smoky cellar pumping out dub and reggae, man. A mainly student crowd packs the place, with the overspill packing out the bar-lined street outside.

LONTANO DA DOVE MAP PP280-1
☎ 081 549 43 04; Via Bellini 3; ⏱ 5pm-late Tue-Sun Sep-Jul; Ⓜ Dante
Literary types head here to sip espresso, talk Baudelaire and tap their fingers to Chet Baker. Close to Piazza Bellini, this erudite café also hosts poetry readings. Turtleneck sweaters are optional.

S'MOVE MAP PP284-5
☎ 081 764 58 13; Vico dei Sospiri 10a; ⏱ 12pm-2am Mon-Sat, 7pm-3am Sun Sep-Jul; 🚌 C25 to Riviera di Chiaia
A local favourite. Wine-red lounges and slick retro lamps draw a friendly crowd of the glam and the corporate. *Aperitivo* is served between 7pm and 9pm and DJs spin nu-jazz, acid jazz, electro and funk.

ST TROPEZ MAP PP278-9
☎ 081 64 44 37; Via Aniello Falcone 336B; ⏱ 10am-2am, closed Mon; 🚌 C28 to Parco Lamaro
Looking like a tiny Buddha Bar with its red paper lanterns and zebra-print bar stools, this intimate bar soothes with its retro, lounge and house tunes. *Aperitivo* starts at 7pm. Dig in with a rum-and-pear cocktail.

TRINITY BAR MAP PP280-1

☎ 081 551 45 69; Calata Trinità Maggiore 5; ☼ 7am-4am daily; 🚃 R1 to Via Monteoliveto

Trinity Bar looks like any other café on the block, but for some mysterious reason it draws the biggest crowds on Piazza del Gesù Nuovo. So grab a beer and join the throng.

WHITE BAR MAP PP284-5

☎ 081 64 45 82; Vico Satriano 3B; ☼ 10pm-4am Thu-Sun; 🚃 C25 to Riviera di Chiaia

Bar-hopping fashionistas always make time for White. Stark and minimalist, it never upstages their Capri tans and catwalk threads. Join the moneyed masses for lounge tunes and one of the city's best *aperitivo* spreads.

YACHTING BAR MAP PP284-5

☎ 328 944 67 53; Via Mergellina 2B; ☼ 10am-late Tue-Sun; 🚃 140 to Via Mergellina

Pumped-up studs and down-to-earth dykes head here for drinks, snacks and languid chill-out tunes. On the weekend, DJs burn it up with thumping commercial house.

CLUBBING

Most of the big clubs are out of town and out of reach of public transport. Central clubs tend to be small and eclectic, from cavernous reggae bolteholes to galleries-cum-discos.

Venues usually open at 10.30pm or 11pm but don't fill up until after midnight. Many clubs close in summer (July to September), some transferring themselves to out-of-town beach locations (see the boxed text, p132).

Admission charges vary, but expect to pay between €5 and €25, which may or may not include a drink.

The student-dense centro storico and yuppie-centric Chiaia are clubbing hot spots. Pick up a free copy of mini-mag *Zero* in bars and for up-to-date listings.

DEPOT CRUISING BAR

☎ 081 780 95 78; www.depotmilano.com; ☼ 10pm-3am Tue-Thu, 10pm-6am Fri & Sat, 8pm-3am Sun; Via della Veterinaria 72; admission €10; 🚃 C55 to Albergo dei Poveri

This gay playpen attracts men with one thing on their mind, and it's not Kylie – think skin flicks, cruising maze and dark private cabins.

ENTERTAINMENT

Check the website for themed leather, uniform and naked nights. The club is located just off edgy Piazza Carlo III, so catch a cab home.

FREELOVERS @ EDENLANDIA MAP P287

☎ 328 307 11 05; www.freelovers.it; Viale Kennedy 76; ☼ 12.30am-late Sat Jun-Sep; admission €12; 🚃 Cumana to Edenlandia

Set in a Disney-style theme park, this is a queer summertime favourite. Groove under the stars beside a fairytale castle or crash into a cutie on the dodgem cars. Music is pop-ish and the vibe is fun. You'll need a taxi to get back into town.

FREEZER MAP PP278-9

☎ 081 750 24 37; www.freezerstereobar.it; Via F Lauria 6, Centro Direzionale, Isola G6; ☼ 11pm-3am Sat & Sun Sep-Jul; admission €13; Ⓜ Garibaldi

Blue neon and acid-green walls set the postmodern scene at this Berlin-style bolthole. Dressed to kill in latex and plastic creations, a mixed crowd of extravagant clubbers hits the floor for high-octane house and electronica.

LA MELA MAP PP284-5

☎ 081 41 02 70; Via dei Mille 40/bis; ☼ Thu-Sat; 🚃 C25 to Riviera di Chiaia

Chiaia's 30-something 'It' crowd saunters here for civilised clubbing after drinks at Farinella (opposite). DJs spin mainstream sounds and the look is über-chic. Dress to impress or face rejection at the door.

top five

CLUBS

Velvet Zone (p132) Hot and funky grooving in the centro storico.

La Mela (above) Elegant clubbing for the seriously chic.

Rising South (p132) Art-house flicks, drum 'n' bass and a savvy boho crowd.

Free Lovers @ Edenlandia (above) Fabulous gay fun in a fairytale setting.

L'Arenile di Bagnoli (see the boxed text, p132) Live acts, DJs and Caipirinhas on the beach.

TWISTING BY THE BEACH

Not that long ago, summertime Naples was a clubbing wasteland. When the city's nightclubs closed in June, party people were left counting the days to October. Times are changing, however, as a growing number of beachside venues turn the coast west of Naples into a bite-sized Ibiza. Four of the best:

L'Arenile di Bagnoli (Map p287; ☎ 081 570 60 35; www.larenile.it in Italian; Via Coroglio 14B, Bagnoli; 🚃 C9) The biggest and oldest of the clubs. Tan on the beach, order a pizza, chill at the bar, catch a band (BB King has performed here) or hit the beachside dance floor for thumping house under the stars.

Lido L'Altro (Map p287; ☎ 335 879 04 28; www.altro-lab.com in Italian; Via Coroglio, Bagnoli; 🚃 C9) More sun beds, comfy lounges and a funky four-sided bar. The crowd is fun and mixed and the music retro and commercial dance.

Vibes on the Beach (Map p287; ☎ 081 523 28 28; Via Miseno 52, Capo Miseno, Bacoli; 🚃 SEPSA to Bacoli) DJs spin languid lounge to an older crowd. The frozen daiquiris are legendary and Sunday features brunch on the beach.

Nabilah (Map p287; ☎ 335 527 81 89; www.nabilah.it in Italian; Via Spiaggia Romana 15, Cuma; 🚋 Cumana to Torregaveta)
Cranks up the style factor (and bar prices) with candles and sofas on the sand and big-name DJs such as Moloko and DJ Ravin from Buddha Bar in Paris.

    As these venues are out of town and serviced by limited transport, your best bet for getting there and back is in a cab. Budget for €35 one way from Naples to Bagnoli and €55 from Naples to Bacoli. Share and save.

MUTINY REPUBLIC MAP PP280-1
☎ 335 732 10 34; Via Bellini 45; 🕐 Tue–Sun; Ⓜ Dante
Artful clubbing awaits at this funky centro storico newie. A friendly, boho crowd kicks back on silky sofas, eyes up cutting-edge art and gets down to DJ-spun jazz, electro-soul and disco funk or to live acts with a world music edge.

QUEERS & THE CITY

Rainbow flags might be thin on the ground, but Naples' modest gay scene is refreshingly unpretentious and eclectic.

    Throughout this chapter queer bars and club are included in the main listings. For info on one-off events, contact **ArciGay** (☎ 081 552 88 15; www .arcigaynapoli.org; Via San Geronimo alle Monarche 19; 🕐 5.30-8pm Wed, 5-9pm Fri; Ⓜ Dante), or pick up the free monthly *Pride* magazine from gay venues. Some clubs and saunas insist you have an ArciGay membership card (€14), which is available from those venues that require it.

    Freelovers (☎ 328 307 11 05; www.freelovers .it) organises great club nights, at locations such as amusement parks and swimming pools. Check the website for details.

    Men who are looking to sweat it out with the locals can do so at the city's only gay sauna, **Blu Angels** (Map pp278-9; ☎ 081 562 52 98; Centro Direzionale Isola A7; admission €12; 🕐 1.30pm-midnight, daily), with its two Finnish saunas, Turkish bath, gym and darkroom.

OFFICINA 99
☎ 081 552 23 99; www.officina99.org in Italian; Via Gianturco 101; Ⓜ Gianturco
No Philippe Starck lighting here, just an abandoned factory packed with hardcore lefties, punks and raw live acts ranging from radical Neapolitan rap to anti-Establishment reggae. Gigs are sporadic, so call ahead or check the website.

RISING SOUTH MAP PP280-1
☎ 081 333 653 42 73; www.risingsouth.it; Via San Sebastiano 19; 🕐 Mon-Sat mid-Oct–May; admission €10; Ⓜ Dante
This club is so popular there is a 'guest list only' policy from Thursday to Saturday; call a day in advance to get your name on the door. Inside, the pierced, the arty and the unpretentiously cool watch art-house videos and groove to a mix of house, electronica and drum 'n' bass.

VELVET ZONE MAP PP280-1
☎ 347 810 73 28; Via Cisterna dell'Olio 11; admission €10; 🕐 11pm-4am Wed, Thu & Sun, 11pm-6am Fri & Sat mid-Oct–May; Ⓜ Dante
Different nights bring different sounds here at the legendary Velvet. You can expect anything from hip-hop, rock and retro, to techno, pop and more. The occasional live gigs held at this club feature local bands and dance-music outfits.

MUSIC

Music in Naples is more than mandolins and tenors. There's a thriving jazz scene, cultured classical ensembles and home-grown political hip-hop. The city also hosts the **Neapolis Rock Festival** (www.neapolis.it), a huge international rock fest in July, billed as the largest in southern Italy, which draws A-list acts and huge crowds.

Ticket prices range from about €5 to €12 for a jazz gig in a club, to €25 for a big stadium concert. In smaller venues you can usually buy your ticket at the door; for bigger events try the box office inside **Feltrinelli** (Map pp284–5; ☎ 081 240 54 11; Piazza dei Martiri) or from an agency such as **Box Office** (Map pp280–1; ☎ 081 551 91 88; www.boxofficeclub.it in Italian; Galleria Umberto I 17).

Naples' premier classical-music organis-ation, **Associazione Scarlatti** (Map pp284–5; ☎ 081 40 60 11; www.associazionescarlatti .it in Italian; Piazza dei Martiri 58; ☒ C25 to Riviera di Chiaia), organises an annual programme of chamber music concerts.

AROUND MIDNIGHT MAP P283
☎ 081 558 28 34; www.aroundmidnight.it; Via Bonito 32A; ☒ 9pm-4am Tue-Sun, live music 11pm-1am, closed Aug; Ⓜ Vanvitelli

One of Naples' most famous jazz clubs, this tiny swinging bolthole features live music six nights out of seven. Concerts are generally mainstream, but the occasional blues band puts in a performance.

BOURBON STREET
MAP PP280-1
☎ 328 068 72 21; Via Bellini 52; ☒ 9.30pm-3am Sep-Jun; Ⓜ Dante

A red-brick slice of New Orleans in Napoli. Smooth American and Italian jazz musicians perform virtually every night to a mixed-age crowd of head-swaying jazz aficionados.

CAPPELLA DELLA PIETÀ DEI TURCHINI MAP P283
☎ 081 40 23 95; www.turchini.it; Via Santa Caterina da Siena 38; funicular Centrale to Corso Vittorio Emanuele

Home to the baroque Orchestra Cappella della Pietà dei Turchini, this deconsecrated church is an evocative venue for classical concerts of mostly 17th- and 18th-century Neapolitan works. Tickets cost about €15.

OTTO JAZZ CLUB MAP P283
☎ 081 551 37 65; Piazzetta Cariati 23; ☒ 10pm-late Fri-Sun Sep-Jun; admission €8-10; Funicular Centrale to Corso Vittorio Emanuele

Up the hill towards Vomero, Otto's is arguably the top jazz joint in town. It has hosted some of the biggest names in jazz and today still features top-quality concerts by mostly local, sometimes international artists.

PALAPARTENOPE MAP P287
☎ 081 570 00 08; www.palapartenope.it in Italian; Via Barbagallo 115, Fuorigrotta; ☒ 152

Located in suburban Fuorigrotta, west of central Naples, the architecturally uninspiring

---

MUSIC IN THE METROPOLIS

Music journalist Francesco Calazzo gives the lowdown on the city's spicy soundscape:

'As a port city, Naples has always absorbed foreign influences. Musically, the result is a fusion of styles, from classic Italian melodies to African percussion and American blues.

'The late 1970s was a defining moment for the city's music scene, with Neapolitan new-wave pioneers like Eugenio Bennato, Pino Daniele and Enzo Avitabile reviving Neapolitan folk and crossing it over with rock, roots and hypnotic African beats. Enzo Avitabile now collaborates with the legendary Bottari di Portico ensemble, named for the old *bottari* (barrels) used in their music.

'Neapolitan hip-hop is a more recent example, using instruments like the tabla and jembe for a North African flavour. The most famous acts have been 99Posse and Almamegretta. While both groups have disbanded, band members still play the occasional gig at clubs like Officina 99 (opposite), where 99Posse was formed.

'The arrival of American troops in WW2 introduced jazz and blues to Naples. Don't miss Blue Stuff, who play classic Chicago blues sung in Neapolitan. Check the band's website (www.bluestuff.it) for upcoming gigs.

'For local underground groups, try Velvet Zone (opposite) and check the daily papers – *Corriere del Mezzogiorno or Repubblica* (Naples edition) are best – as some indie gigs aren't advertised until the performance date. Otherwise, head to the music shops on Via San Sebastiano in the centro storico, where musicians will always let you in on a secret.'

Palapartenope is the biggest indoor concert venue in town. A 6000-plus seating capacity sets the scene for big-name Italian and international acts, which have included everyone from local crooner Pino Daniele to vintage icons Lou Reed and Spandau Ballet.

STADIO SAN PAOLO MAP P287
☎ 081 239 56 23; Piazzale Vincenzo Tecchio, Fuorigrotta; 🚌 152

A temple to the cult of football, this massive stadium played host to the notorious 1990 World Cup semi-final between Italy and Argentina during which Diego Maradona was jeered after asking Napoli football fans to cheer for Argentina. Pride aside, the stadium also hosts occasional pop concerts by big-name Italian acts.

THEATRE

While Naples' theatre scene is not as dynamic as it was in the days of Eduardo De Filippo, it still serves up the occasional gem. Look out for works by Roberto De Simone, Luca de Filippo and Enzo Moscato, with their revealing modern takes on Neapolitan traditions, or hit the city's smaller stages for experimental work from young local and international artists.

Theatrical opulence, Teatro San Carlo RIPANI MASSIMO / SIME / 4CORNERS IMAGES

Ticket prices range from about €8 for experimental theatres to €30 and upwards for big-budget productions. To book, contact the theatre direct, or if possible log onto its website. Alternatively, try a ticketing agency such as **Box Office** (Map pp280–1; ☎ 081 551 91 88; www.boxofficeclub.it in Italian; Galleria Umberto I 17). Many hotels can also help with reservations.

BELLINI MAP PP280-1
☎ 081 549 96 88; www.teatrobellini.it in Italian; Via Conte di Ruvo; tickets from €15; 🕐 box office 10.30am-1pm & 5-8pm Mon-Fri, 10.30am-2pm Sat; Ⓜ Museo

The gorgeous 19th-century Bellini is a classic picture in gold and red. Suitably, the repertoire tends to be fairly conservative, with big-budget musicals and classics such as Shakespeare, Manzoni and Oscar Wilde.

GALLERIA TOLEDO MAP P283
☎ 081 42 50 37; www.galleriatoledo.net in Italian; Via Concezione a Montecalvario 34; tickets €13; 🕐 box office 10am-1.30pm & 3-6pm daily; Ⓜ Montesanto

Tucked away in the Quartieri Spagnoli, this is the spot for cutting-edge and experimental new work from local and international playwrights. Occasional film screenings include offbeat international art house. Check the website for upcoming events.

MERCADANTE MAP PP280-1
☎ 081 551 33 96; www.teatrostabilenapoli.it in Italian; Piazza del Municipio 1; tickets from €13; 🕐 box office 10.30am-1pm & 5.30-7.30pm Mon-Fri, 10.30am-1pm Sat Sep-Apr; 🚌 R2 to Piazza del Municipio

Recently restored, the 18th-century Mercadante is home to Naples' major theatre company, the Teatro Stabile. A bumper season of high-standard productions includes new and classic Neapolitan, Italian and international works from the likes of Luca de Filippo, Roberto de Simone and Paul Léautaud.

TEATRO NUOVO MAP PP280-1
☎ 081 40 60 62; www.nuovoteatronuovo.it in Italian; Via Montecalvario 16; tickets around €8; 🕐 box office 10.30am-1pm & 5-7pm Tue-Fri, 10.30am-1pm Sat Oct-May; Ⓜ Montesanto

Samuel Beckett and controversial Italian director Pier Paolo Pasolini are among the more recognisable names to appear on the Nuovo's

DEATH IN NAPLES

If you like your theatre with a murder or two, check out **Il Pozzo e Il Pendolo Teatro** (☎ 081 542 20 88; www.ilpozzoeilpendolo.it in Italian; Piazza San Domenico Maggiore 3). This theatre company performs whodunnit plays in atmospheric locations, including the Orto Botanico (p96). It also hosts murder-mystery dinners and weekends, and spine-tingling night tours of Naples. While the plays and dinners are in Italian, tours can be arranged in English if booked in advance.

programme. A modern theatre, it provides a stage for emerging European writers whose works may or may not appeal.

TRIANON MAP PP280-1

☎ 081 225 82 85; www.teatrotrianon.it; Piazza Vincenzo Calenda 9; tickets €10-22; box office 10am-1.30pm & 4-8pm daily; R2 to Corso Umberto I
Deliciously kitsch, the Trianon orchestra belts out a repertoire of unashamedly sentimental Neapolitan classics while nostalgic audiences join in the chorus. Pre-concert, check out the small museum dedicated to opera star Enrico Caruso.

OPERA

Opera and Naples go together like a house on fire. After La Scala in Milan, the Teatro San Carlo is considered Italy's most important opera house and regularly stages world-class performances. Which is just as well; Neapolitan audiences are notoriously demanding.

Watching an opera at San Carlo is a magical experience, especially as tickets are not easy to come by. Most are snapped up by season ticket holders, who pay up to €800 for a year's subscription.

LA NOTTE BIANCA

For one night each September, Naples hosts La Notte Bianca (The White Night), an all-night celebration of art, culture and shopping. A huge programme of mostly free events includes theatre in piazzas, concerts in cloisters and tango lessons in train stations. Transport is free and runs all night. For details, go to www.nottebiancanapoli.it (in Italian) or check the local press the day before.

The opera season at Teatro San Carlo runs from January to December, with a mid-season break in July and August. Reckon on €40 for a place in the sixth tier and €90 for a seat in the stalls. For those who are under 30 years old, last minute tickets are available one hour before performances for €15.

For reservations contact the **Teatro San Carlo box office** (Map pp284-5; ☎ 081 797 23 31, 081 797 24 12; www.teatrosancarlo.it; Via San Carlo 98) at the theatre itself, or book online. In summer some performances are staged in the courtyard of the Castel Nuovo and at the ancient Parco Archeologico di Baia (p105). Check the local press for current opera productions.

For information about the theatre's ballet performances, see below.

TEATRO SAN CARLO MAP PP284-5

☎ 081 797 23 31; www.teatrosancarlo.it; Via San Carlo 98; box office 10am-6.30pm Tue-Sat; R2 to Via San Carlo
Italy's largest opera house, the opulent Teatro San Carlo is one of the world's premier venues. A six-tier arena in classical gold and red, it can seat up to 1000 people. The year-round programme is largely traditional; works by Wagner, Tchaikovsky and Verdi are reliable crowd pleasers. The theatre also showcases dance performances; for more information, see below.

DANCE

Based at the Teatro San Carlo, the San Carlo Ballet Company is the oldest dance academy in Italy, performing a year-round repertoire of world-class traditional and modern works.

For cutting-edge international choreography, head to Rome or Milan.

TEATRO SAN CARLO MAP PP284-5

☎ 081 797 21 11; www.teatrosancarlo.it; tickets €20-90; box office 10am-3pm Tue-Sun Oct-May, 10am-4.30pm Mon-Fri Jun-Sep; Via San Carlo 98; R2 to Via San Carlo
The in-house ballet company performs to a consistently high standard. Tickets start at €25 and rise to €60. If you're under 30 (and

can prove it) you qualify for a €15 ticket, available one hour before performances. In summer some performances are staged in the courtyard of the Castel Nuovo.

CINEMA

Catching a flick is primarily a winter activity and many smaller cinemas close in summer. Families and older viewers go to the 8pm feature, the young go to the 10.30pm showing.

Nearly all films screened in Italy are dubbed, which means that your choices are fairly limited if you don't speak Italian.

Films shown in their original language are indicated in listings by *versione originale* or VO after the title.

Cinema tickets cost between €4.50 and €8. As a rough guide, screenings begin every two hours from 4.30pm to 10.30pm. Afternoon and early-evening screenings are generally cheaper than films shown later in the evening. Check the daily papers for schedules and ticket prices.

CINEMA MODERNISSIMO MAP PP280-1
☎ 081 580 02 54; www.modernissimo.it in Italian; Via Cisterna dell'Olio; tickets €7; Ⓜ Dante

The hip and the arty head here for a mix of art house, retro and mainstream flicks. The complex includes a small cinema-themed library and is slap-bang on bar-packed Via Cisterno dell'Olio. Films are dubbed in Italian.

CINEMA PLAZA MAP P283
☎ 081 556 35 55; Via M Kerbaker 85; tickets €7; Ⓜ Vanvitelli

Featuring two screens, this cinema is popular with the district's well-heeled denizens, who come here for a film fix of the mostly blockbuster variety.

WATCHING SPORT

Naples' football team is the third-most supported in the country after Juventus and Milan. Big matches attract crowds of up to 80,000 to the San Paolo stadium, where the light-blues play on alternate Sundays.

The football season runs from September to May, with a short midseason break around Christmas. The cost of a ticket varies depending on the opposition, but as a rough guide expect to pay around €14 for a place in the curve (the stands behind the goals) and up to €40 for the *tribune* (side stands).

Buy tickets at the stadium, **Stadio San Paolo** (ticket information ☎ 081 239 56 23; Piazzale Vincenzo Tecchio; 🚌 152) or from the official outlet **Azzurro Service** (☎ 081 593 40 01; Via Galeota 17; 🚌 152), both in the Fuorigrotta district west of Mergellina.

SHOPPING

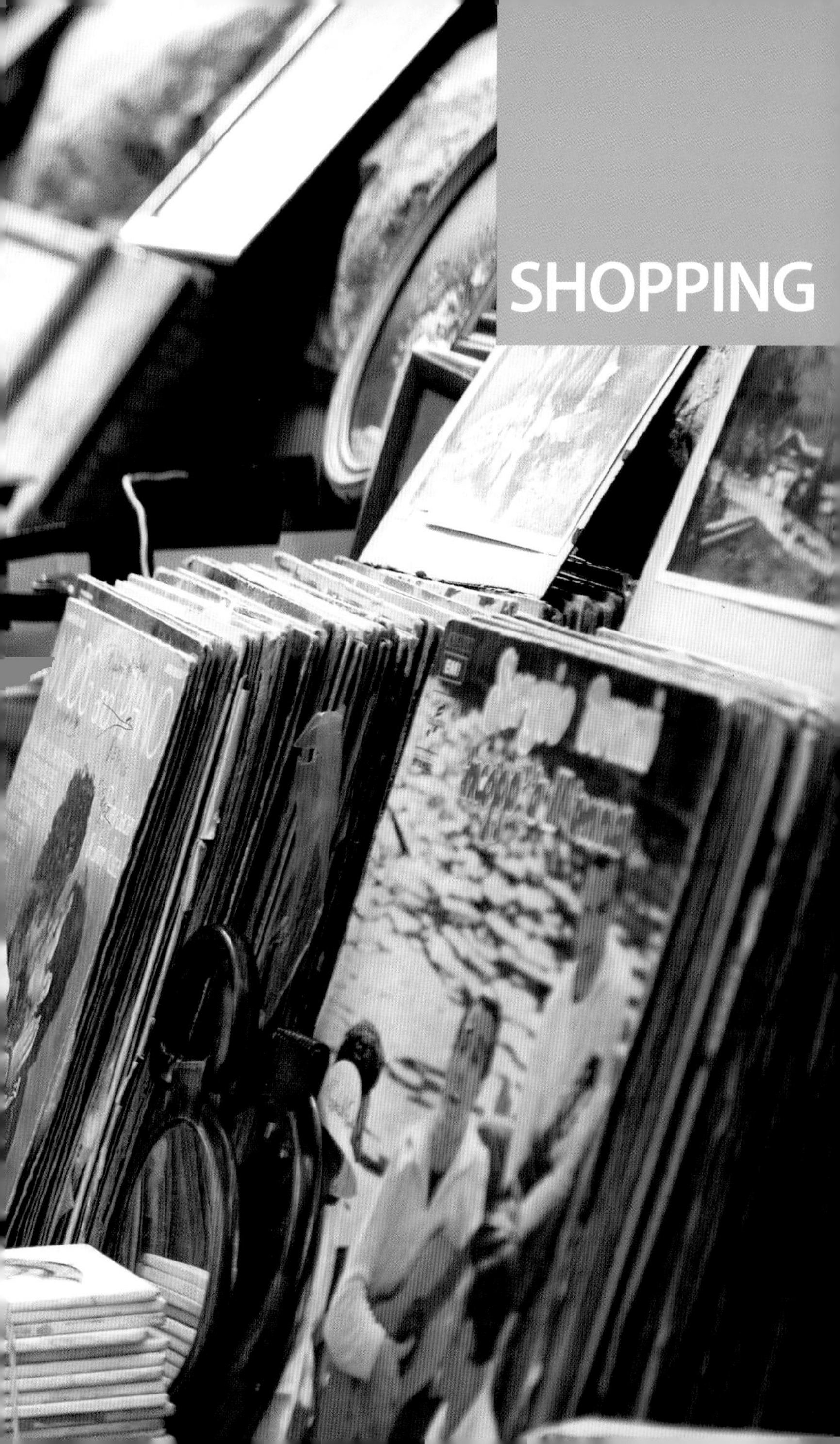

ON THE STREET

From Catholic kitsch to rings made from computer keys, Neapolitan shopping is funky and offbeat.

Forget multinational malls and homogenised high Streets. In Naples, retail therapy is as idiosyncratic as the city itself. Chain stores do exist but they play second fiddle to specialised shops owned by enterprising locals: from vintage delis crammed with local produce to artists' lounge rooms stocked with unorthodox sculpture.

Neapolitans are seasoned shoppers, and Saturday morning is their favourite time to shop. Even busier than Saturday mornings (but worth the bumps and bruises) are the sales, which take place from January to mid-March and from early July to early September. Stock is reduced at these times by up to 75% and smaller shops generally offer the best buys to shoppers.

Different neighbourhoods offer very different shopping experiences. For the hot and the haute, head to Chiaia where Via Calabritto, Via dei Mille and Via G Filangieri read like a *Vogue* directory. This is the place for Armani, Zegna and legendary local tailors like Finamore and Borrelli (see p143). Chiaia is also great for sleek homewares and cutting-edge jewellery. Just off Piazza dei Martiri, Via Domenico Morelli is the place for antiques, while Via Chiaia heaves with midprice fashion chains.

At its eastern end Via Chiaia spills onto Via Toledo, the city's buzzing high street. A prime spot to people-watch, this is where you'll find everything from upmarket department stores to chintzy *bomboniere* (christening mementos) shops.

Catch the funicular to Vomero for preppy purchases, or better still go east for trad, kooky and kitsch in the gritty centro storico (historic centre). Here, specialty streets include Via Port'Alba for secondhand bookshops, Via San Sebastiano for musical instruments and Via San Gregorio Armeno for beautifully crafted *presepi* (nativity scenes).

South of the centro storico you'll find frenetic Corso Umberto I, where cashed-up teens come for cool, cheap threads and funky trainers. Further south around Piazzetta Orefici (Goldsmiths' Sq), the Borgo degli Orefici (Goldsmiths' Quarter) is the city's traditional home of bling.

But for the ultimate Neapolitan shopping fix, hit the legendary markets. Home to one of the world's biggest counterfeit scenes, Naples will provide you with anything from bootleg CDs and kinky knickers to convincing Gucci fakes – all at dirt-cheap prices. Don't forget to haggle, and watch your wallet – pickpockets love to shop here too.

Shops are usually open from 9.30am to 1.30pm and 4.30pm to 8pm (in winter) or 4pm to 8.30pm (in summer) Monday to Saturday, closing on Monday mornings in winter and Saturday afternoons in summer. Small boutiques or speciality shops might not open until 10am, and afternoon hours

CLOTHING SIZES

Measurements approximate only, try before you buy

Women's Clothing						
Aus/UK	8	10	12	14	16	18
Europe	36	38	40	42	44	46
Japan	5	7	9	11	13	15
USA	6	8	10	12	14	16
Women's Shoes						
Aus/USA	5	6	7	8	9	10
Europe	35	36	37	38	39	40
France only	35	36	38	39	40	42
Japan	22	23	24	25	26	27
UK	3½	4½	5½	6½	7½	8½
Men's Clothing						
Aus	92	96	100	104	108	112
Europe	46	48	50	52	54	56
Japan	S		M	M		L
UK/USA	35	36	37	38	39	40
Men's Shirts (Collar Sizes)						
Aus/Japan	38	39	40	41	42	43
Europe	38	39	40	41	42	43
UK/USA	15	15½	16	16½	17	17½
Men's Shoes						
Aus/UK	7	8	9	10	11	12
Europe	41	42	43	44½	46	47
Japan	26	27	27½	28	29	30
USA	7½	8½	9½	10½	11½	12½

might be shorter. Department stores and larger chains are open from 9.30am to 8.30pm. Many shops throughout the city are closed in August. Where opening hours are listed in the reviews below, it indicates that they vary from standard opening times.

A value-added tax of 20%, known as Imposta de Valore Aggiunto (IVA), is slapped onto just about everything. If you are a non-EU resident and spend more than €180 in a single shop at once, you can claim a refund when you leave the country. See p251 for more information. Postpurchase, make sure you're given a receipt. By law, the *guardia de finanza* (finance police) can make a spot check outside the shop, and if you don't have a receipt you may be fined.

CENTRO STORICO & MERCATO

BERISIO MAP PP280-1 BOOKS
☎ 081 549 90 90; Via Port 'Alba 28-29; Ⓜ Dante
Set on a street of secondhand bookshops, this stalwart boasts floor-to-ceiling preloved titles. Pick up a Caravaggio catalogue, flick through a Neapolitan design book or adopt a dog-eared play script. Most titles are in Italian. There are also some cool puzzles for the kids.

BLUE CHIARA LUCE
MAP PP280-1 ARTISAN CRAFT
☎ 081 29 94 57; Via Tribunali 340; Ⓜ Dante
Need a frock for your *pastori* (nativity-scene figurines)? Lucia Azzurro sews up baroque costumes in silks and linens for crib-scene characters and religious statuettes, leaving

your three wise men perfectly preened for any miraculous occasion.

CARPISA MAP PP280-1 BAGS & LUGGAGE
☎ 081 563 57 77; Corso Umberto I 342; 🚍 R2 Corso Umberto I
Steal the scene with a suitcase from Carpisa. Cool, fun and cheap, colours range from eye-squinting yellow to Day-Glo green. Mix and match with tropical-print totes, or sling something over your shoulder for as little as €10.

CHARCUTERIE MAP PP280-1 FOOD
☎ 081 551 69 81; Via Benedetto Croce 43; Ⓜ Dante
Even the doors heave with gourmet grub at this jam-packed little deli. Fill your bags with pasta, macaroons, grappa (Italian pomace brandy), lemon-flavoured olive oil and chocolate-coated figs.

CRYPTON
MAP PP280-1 MENSWEAR
Corso Umberto I 105; 🚍 R2 Corso Umberto I
Perma-tanned girlfriends dress up their studs at Crypton. Two floors burst with sexy streetwear, from pec-flaunting T-shirts and cool skater jeans to a modest selection of trainers. Brands include Lee, Tiger, Asics and Lonsdale.

GAY-ODIN MAP PP280-1 CHOCOLATES
☎ 081 40 00 63; Via Toledo 427; 🕑 9.30am-8pm Mon-Sat, 10am-2pm Sun; Ⓜ Dante
No, this is not a gay bar – it's just the city's best-loved chocolate shop. Pig out on chocolate-coated coffee beans and a fiery

THE BEST OF NEAPOLITAN KITSCH

Flashing halos, Godfather bling, action-packed *pastori* (nativity-scene figurines) – Naples is a kitsch-lover's paradise. For a taste of old-school trash and tack, hit the following garish gems:

Arte in Movimento (Map pp280–1; ☎ 081 420 10 94; Via San Biagio dei Librai 33; Ⓜ Dante) Head here for motorised *pastori* and hand-painted Neapolitan clichés. Best of the bunch is a bending *pizzaiolo* (pizza maker) complete with fiery oven.

La Galleria delle Bomboniere (Map pp280–1; ☎ 081 551 80 95; Via Enrico Pessina 76; Ⓜ Dante) Southern Italian chintz at its overstated best – think Communion-themed photo frames, mock-baroque jewellery boxes, glass pumpkin carriages and chirpy ceramic squirrels.

Napolimania (Map pp280–1; ☎ 081 41 41 20; Via Toledo 312; 🚍 CS to Via Toledo) Tacky and proud of it, this offbeat shrine to local pop culture is the place for plastic Totò statues, Neapolitan 'survival kits' and cheeky jocks with bawdy local slang.

Via Francesco Caracciolo (Map pp284–5; 🚍 C25 to Riviera di Chiaia) The stalls along the sea on Via Caracciolo are the place for over-the-top seashell souvenirs and bright plastic Madonnas.

Via Mezzocannone (Map pp280–1; 🚍 E1 to Via Mezzocannone) Another great street for Catholic kitsch, here you'll find anything from the Virgin Mary with a blinking crown to a glow-in-the-dark Jesus.

MARKET TIME

Naples' legendary markets are loud, intoxicating and just a little bit edgy, so hang on to your wallet. Beware the digital/video camera scam – the result, in short, is that you buy an empty box. If you *are* tempted, then insist that you buy the particular camera being demonstrated, rather than the prepackaged one. Most designer goods are fakes (but perfect copies) and vendors are open to haggling, except where specified below. The following markets are the cream of the crop:

Bancarelle a San Pasquale (Map pp284–5; Via San Pasquale, Via Imbriani & Via Carducci; ☺ 8am-2pm Mon-Wed, Fri & Sat, closed Aug; 🚌 C25 to Riviera di Chiaia) Hit the stalls on Via Imbriani for hip threads, sarongs and avant-garde jewellery. The section between Via Carducci and Via San Pasquale is great for fish, spices, fruit and vegetables. Not a place for haggling.

Fiera Antiquaria Napoletana (Map pp284–5; Villa Comunale; ☺ 8am-2pm last Sun of month, closed Aug; 🚌 C25 to Riviera di Chiaia) Set on the waterfront, this is a cool, laid-back spot for vintage silverware, jewellery, furniture, paintings, prints and wonderful, overpriced junk.

La Duchessa (Map pp280–1; Via S G Calasanzio & surrounding streets; ☺ 8am-2pm Mon-Sat, closed Aug; 🚌 R2 to Piazza Garibaldi) Packed, gritty and obscenely cheap, this multiethnic hot spot heaves with counterfeit booty, from bootlegged blockbusters and porn to fake D&G belts and Prada bags. Stock up on African knick-knacks, soccer tops and cheap knickers.

La Pignasecca (Map pp280–1; Via Pignasecca & surrounding streets; ☺ 8am-1pm; Ⓜ Montesanto) Naples' oldest and (arguably) best market is *the* place for food. You'll find everything from fresh mozzarella and crunchy Casareccio bread to meat, fish and artichokes. It's also good for discounted perfume and linen, kitchenware, Neapolitan hip-hop CDs and cheap (fake) designer bags and threads.

Mercatino di Antignano (Map p283; Piazza degli Artisti; ☺ 8am-1pm Mon-Sat, closed Aug; Ⓜ Medaglie D'Oro) Up high in Vomero, this place is popular for bags, jewellery, linen, kitchenware, shoes, new and end-of-season clothing. And a hysterical stall owner who throws underwear in the air while screaming out *Un euro! Un euro!* (One euro! One euro!)

Mercatino di Posillipo (Map p287; Parco Virgiliano; ☺ 8am-2pm Thu, closed Aug; 🚌 140 to Viale Virgilio) Not the cheapest market, but the best for quality goods. Top buys include genuine designer labels (although the D&G and Louis Vuitton bags are fakes), women's swimwear, underwear and linen. It's only the African vendors at the bottom of the hill who don't mind a haggle.

Mercato dei Fiori (Map pp280–1; Castel Nuovo; ☺ dawn-noon; 🚌 R2 to Piazza del Municipio) Got a date? Then pick up a fresh bunch of roses at the city's flower market.

Mercato di Poggioreale (Map pp278–9; Via Nuova Poggioreale; ☺ 8am-1pm Fri-Mon, closed Aug; Ⓜ Gianturco) Set in the city's old slaughterhouse there are 40 shoe stalls alone that sell hot designer overstock and no-frills everyday brands. Equally fab are the cheap casual wear, suits, colourful rolls of fabrics and kitchenware.

Porta Nolana (Map pp280–1; Via Nolana; ☺ 8am-6pm; 🚌 R2 to Piazza Garibaldi) A heady, sprawling wonderland of bellowing fishmongers, industrious Chinese traders and contraband cigarette stalls. Grab a grilled cob of corn and hit the trestled streets for fresh fish and fruit, cheap watches, nifty gadgets and compilation CDs from the '80s.

---

peperoncino-cioccolato (chilli-chocolate) combo. Best of all, there are eight branches in Naples to lose control in; this branch is the most central and convenient.

GIUSEPPE FERRIGNO
MAP PP280-1   ARTISAN CRAFT

☎ 081 552 31 48; Via San Gregorio Armeno 8; Ⓜ Dante

King of the Christmas cribs, Ferrigno's terracotta figurines are sought by collectors worldwide. Part studio, part shop, its shelves are lined with enough doting Marys, buxom peasants and elaborate market sets to keep your *presepe* on the nativity scene A-list.

LIMONÉ MAP PP280-1   GIFTS

☎ 081 29 94 29; Piazza San Gaetano 72; Ⓜ Cavour

The organic, homemade *limoncello* has punters travelling across town for a bottle. Ask nicely and you might get a sip for free. Pucker up for lemon pasta, lemon-infused grappa and *crema di melone* (melon liqueur).

OTTICA STREVELLA MAP PP280-1   OPTICIAN

☎ 081 20 27 34; Corso Umberto I 213; 🚌 R2 to Corso Umberto I

A friendly full-service optician offering free eye tests, a basic repair service and prescription glasses from €50. A vast range of sunglasses includes Dior, DKNY, Gucci, Ralph Lauren, Cesare Paciotti, Valentino and Armani.

TATTOO MAP PP280-1 MUSIC
☎ 081 552 09 73; Piazzetta del Nilo 15; ⏱ 9am-8pm Mon-Thu, 9am-midnight Fri & Sat, 9am-2pm Sun; Ⓜ Dante

A mixed bag of pierced students, urban funksters and skivvy-clad jazz types flock here for an equally mixed bag of music. Tattoo stocks most categories, with a focus on hip-hop and soul. Vinyl is the biggest seller, and you can listen before you buy.

TOLEDO & QUARTIERI SPAGNOLI

ANTICHE DELIZIE MAP PP280-1 FOOD
☎ 081 551 30 88; Via Pasquale Scura 14; Ⓜ Montesanto

Hanging hams, succulent salami and the best mozzarella in town. This legendary deli is the perfect picnic pit stop. Stock up on *prêt-à-manger* aubergine antipasti and *caprignetti* (goat's cheese stuffed with herbs) and pick up a local wine.

ANTONIO BARBARO
MAP PP284-5 MENSWEAR & SHOES
☎ 081 42 56 07; Piazza Trieste e Trento; 🚌 CS to Trieste e Trento

Preppy guys head here for new-season shoes from TOD and Hogan and crisp shirts from Polo Ralph Lauren. Preppies-in-training can pick up toddler-sized Hogan, Rich and Baci a few doors down at Barbaro Junior (Via Toledo 231).

BERSHKA MAP PP280-1 CLOTHING & ACCESSORIES
☎ 081 552 83 62; Via Toledo 126; ⏱ 10am-8pm Mon-Sat; 🚌 CS to Via Toledo

Chic concrete floors, lurid orange walls and thumping Madonna remixes set the scene for retail rampage at this well-priced fashion hub. Bershka's two floors stock seriously cool urbanwear for guys and girls, from designer denim to retro T-shirts and look-at-me swimwear.

INTIMISSIMI MAP PP280-1 LINGERIE
☎ 081 552 55 67; Via Toledo 47-48; Ⓜ Dante

Intimissimi is a local favourite for well-priced women's and men's knickers and briefs. The look is cool and sexy, with funky prints, and ensembles such as boudoir-red-and-black satin that are guaranteed to have you – and yours – purring with pleasure.

TALARICO
MAP PP280-1 UMBRELLAS
☎ 081 40 77 23; Vico Due Porte a Toledo 4B; 🚌 CS to Via Toledo

Mario Talarico and his nephews have turned the humble umbrella into a work of art. Sought after by international heads of state, each piece is a one-off, featuring mother-of-pearl buttons, a horn tip and a handle made from a single tree branch. While top-of-the-range pieces fetch up to €300, more moderate options will keep the budget-conscious singing in the rain.

SANTA LUCIA & CHIAIA

AMARCORD 900 MODERNARIATO E COLLEZIONISMO MAP PP284-5 COLLECTABLES
☎ 081 549 82 76; Via Giacomo Piscicelli 77B; ⏱ Mon 4-7.30pm, Tue-Sat 10am-7.30pm; Ⓜ Amedeo

Can't find that limited-edition 1972 space toy? Chances are it's ready to launch at this quirky collectables bolt hole. Drop in for shagadelic lamps, retro album covers and rare vintage toys, including retro Russian ambulances and Italian tin cars. Old toys are also restored.

BOWINKEL MAP PP284-5 ANTIQUES
☎ 081 764 07 39; Via Santa Lucia 25; 🚌 C25 to Via Partenope

The city's finest vintage prints, photographs, watercolour paintings and classic frames. If you can't find what you're looking for here, check out the larger branch at Piazza dei Martiri 24 (081 764 43 44). The erudite owner speaks a smattering of English and will arrange shipments abroad.

CONTEMPORASTUDIO
MAP PP284-5 JEWELLERY
☎ 081 247 99 37; Via Francesco Crispi 50; ⏱ 10am-1.30pm & 4.30-8pm Mon-Fri, 10am-1.30pm Sat; Ⓜ Amedeo

This concrete-clad gallery stocks funky, experimental jewellery from Neapolitan Asad Ventrella: think necklaces made of solid silver *penne rigate* (penne pasta) shapes, fat double-faced rings in titanium and aluminium and sharp-looking cufflinks for style-savvy boys.

CULTI SPACAFÉ MAP PP284-5 CONCEPT STORE
☎ 081 764 46 19; Via Carlo Poerio 47; 🚌 C25 to Riviera di Chiaia

Über-chic lifestyle temple Culti Spacafé features Japanese-style homewares, signature beauty

top five

SHOPPING STRIPS

Via Toledo (Map pp280–1)
Head to the pedestrianised southern end, with its slick boutiques, *sfogliatella* (cinnamon-infused ricotta in a puff-pastry shell) stalls, street artists and dressed-to-impress strollers.

Via dei Tribunali (Map pp280–1)
It's just a few hundred metres but the stretch between Piazza San Gaetano and Via Atri is an electric combo of old-school delis, grocery shops, much-loved restaurants and a nativity-scene tailor.

Via Chiaia (Map pp278–9)
This savvy strip tempts with cute boutiques, sharp designer outfits, sassy shoes, fancy accessories and sleek, gleaming homewares.

Via San Gregorio Armeno (Map pp280–1)
Vintage artisan studios and shops burst with the best and the kitschiest of Neapolitan *presepe* (nativity scene) figurines (see p140).

Via Calabritto (Map pp284–5)
Rodeo Drive, Napoli-style. Polish that gold Amex and hit the cobbled pavement for A-list fashion from Armani to Zegna. Window-shopping doesn't get any better than this.

products, a fashionable florist, a sassy bar/restaurant and a fabulous day spa complete with glam *hammam* (communal bathhouse). Shop for silk slippers, sip a Campari, then get horizontal for a spot of shiatsu.

DELIBERTI MAP PP284-5 — SHOES
☎ 081 41 60 64; Via Chiaia 10; 🚌 C25 to Piazza dei Martiri
The place to replenish your designer trainer range. Brands include Helmut Lang, Puma, Bikkemberg and Adidas. Keep an eye out for a small, dangerous-looking range of leopard-print stilettos by Casadei. Sales are common.

EDDY MONETTI MAP PP284-5 — BOUTIQUE
☎ 081 40 32 29; Piazzetta Santa Caterina; 🚌 C25 to Piazza dei Martiri
Neapolitan style queens head here for exquisitely cut jackets, skirts and trousers, and fabulous leather handbags. Think *Vogue*-meets-*Harpers Bazaar*, with labels including Etro, Blumarine, Malo and Cucinelli. Prices start at around €250 for separates.

EDDY MONETTI MEN'S STORE
MAP PP284-5 — BOUTIQUE
☎ 081 40 70 64;Via dei Mille 45; 🚌 C25 to Piazza dei Martiri
The menswear branch of Eddy Monetti is an elegant den of Burberry blazers, Ralph Lauren shirts and irresistible cashmere sweaters. The vibe here is monied and the service suitably snooty.

FELTRINELLI MAP PP284-5 — BOOKS & MUSIC
☎ 081 240 54 11; Piazza dei Martiri; 🕒 10am-9pm Mon-Thu, 10am-10pm Fri, 10am-11pm Sat, 10am-2pm & 4-10pm Sun; 🚌 C25 to Piazza dei Martiri
Three floors of books, CDs, videos, DVDs, and a box office to boot. Locals love coming here to browse, hang out or sip espresso at the downstairs café. There's a fair-sized English-language section, including novels and the latest titles on Neapolitan culture and history.

JOSSA MAP PP284-5 — MENSWEAR & SHOES
☎ 081 39 92 23; Via Carlo Poerio 43; 🚌 C25 to Riviera di Chiaia
There's nothing restrained about the ultracool menswear collection here: paint-splashed denim, hot-pink shirts, striped pastel knitwear and sexy pinstriped suits. Match it all up with hip footwear from Pantofola d'Oro, Carshoe and Abercrombie & Fitch.

INTERFOOD MAP PP284-5 — WINE
☎ 081 764 97 92; Via Santa Lucia 6-10; 🚌 C25 to Via Partenope
This little *enoteca* (wine bar) in Santa Lucia stocks mainly Campanian vino, a rising star on the Italian wine scene. Among the better producers, look for Cantina del Taburno or Ocone or D'Ambra for reds, and Falanghina or Coda de Volpe for whites. Good deals include three bottles of reasonable wine for €15 or less.

LIVIO DE SIMONE MAP PP284-5 — BOUTIQUE
☎ 081 764 38 27; Via Domenico Morelli 15; 🚌 C25 to Piazza dei Martiri
The late Livio de Simone dressed the likes of Audrey Hepburn and Jacqui O. Today his wife and daughter keep the vision alive with bold hand-printed *robe chemisier*s (shirt dresses) and matching purses, bags, and shoes – think Capri with a Japanese twist. A second shop at Vico Satriano 3A stocks vintage Livio de Simone pieces for serious (and seriously moneyed) fashionistas.

SARTORIAL NAPLES

Milan may be the hyped-up face of Italian style, but Naples is its heart and soul. The city's bespoke tailors are legendary, and once drew the likes of early 20th-century Italian king Emmanuel III to their needles and threads. In fact, Naples' ateliers are regarded as clubs or meeting places for debonair Neapolitan gentlemen, who talk fashion, style and cut. Today, Mariano Rubinacci suits, Borrelli and Finamore shirts and Marinella ties are male fashionista must-haves from Tokyo to Turin.

The key to this success is traditional, handmade production, superlative fabrics and minute attention to detail and form. Suitwise, the look is more bratpack than powerbroker – think slim-fit flexible cut, natural and unengineered shoulders (great for gesticulating), high-set arm holes and the signature *barchetta* (little boat) breast pocket. The style itself evolved from the Savile Row suits popular in the 1920s. Local tailors began loosening the rigid Anglo cut, ditching the shoulder pads and reducing canvas and padding for a look more suitable for languid Neapolitan lounging.

A classic Neapolitan shirt will often feature fine Italian, Swiss or Irish cottons, hand-stitched collar, yolk and sleeve, hand-sewn button holes and gathered pleating at the shoulder.

While most of the boutiques offer *prêt-à-porter* threads and accessories (including ready-made suits), creating a shirt or suit from scratch will usually involve a couple of fittings and anything from three to eight weeks. Finished items can be shipped to you overseas.

Credit card at the ready, now that you're clued up hit these local legends for a Neapolitan revamp:

Mariano Rubinacci (Map pp284–5; ☎ 081 41 57 93; www.marianorubinacci.it; Via Filangieri 26) Beautiful, light-weight and precisely fitting suits from the granddaddy of Neapolitan tailoring. Former clients include Neapolitan film director Vittorio de Sica and playwright Eduardo de Filippo.

Cesare Attolini (Map pp284–5; ☎ 081 42 68 26; www.cesareattolini.it; Vico Vetriera 12) Cesare Attolini and his two stylish sons offer three lines of got-to-have suits: Cesare Attolini for fully handmade bespoke tailoring, Sartoria Attolini for fully handmade ready-to-wear suits and Sartoria for hand-finished suits for younger style-gurus.

Borrelli (Map pp284–5; ☎ 081 423 82 73; www.luigiborrelli.com; Via Filangieri 68; 🚌 C25 to Piazza dei Martiri) The look is classic preppy with a funked-up twist – think pastel blazers, chequered suits and striped blood-orange cashmere sweaters. Debonair, but always respectable.

Finamore (Map pp284–5; ☎ 081 246 18 27; www.finamore.it in Italian; Via Calabritto 16) Ready-to-wear (€160 to €250) and bespoke (€90 upwards) shirts in delectable shades such as royal blue, pastel pink and citrus green. Shirts are entirely hand sewn and there are ties and scarves to match.

Marinella (Map pp284–5; ☎ 081 245 11 82; Piazza Vittoria 287) One-time favourite of Luchino Visconti, Aristotle Onassis and Gianni Agnelli, this is *the* place for *prêt-à-porter* and made-to-measure ties. Match them with an irresistible selection of luxury accessories, including shoes, shirts, sweaters and vintage colognes.

Anna Matuozzo (Map pp284–5; ☎ 081 66 38 74; www.annamatuozzo.it; Viale Antonio Gramsci 26) The softly spoken Signora Matuozzo was once the apprentice of Mariano Rubinacci. Now the signora and her daughters are famed for their bespoke shirts, which feature mother-of-pearl buttons and vintage hand stitching. Silk ties in colour combinations such as fuchsia and baby blue complete the elegant look. Call in advance to make an appointment for a fitting.

NAPLES BEST BUYS

Books and Music Feltrinelli (p142)
Chocolate Gay-Odin (p139)
Christmas cribs Giuseppe Ferrigno (p140)
Funky homewares OK-KO Research (below)
Jewellery Contemporastudio (p141)
Mozzarella Antiche Delizie (p141)
Vintage prints Bowinkel (p141)
Shoes Antonio Barbaro (p141)
Ties Marinella (p143)

OK-KO RESEARCH MAP PP284-5   NOVELTIES
☎ 081 40 01 77; Via Cavalerizza a Chiaia 63; 🚌 C25 to Piazza dei Martiri

The ironic shop here for Andy Warhol light boxes, lurid plastic chairs, Dutch designer clocks, chill-out compilation CDs and fluoro-coloured handbags in the shape of watering cans. The counter doubles as a deck for the in-house DJ and *aperitivo* (apéritif) is served upstairs in the winter.

TABACCHERIA SISIMBRO
MAP PP284-5   CIGARS
☎ 081 40 69 83; Via San Pasquale a Chiaia 74-76; Ⓜ Amedeo

This temple to tobacco stocks hard-to-find cigarettes (including Dunhill, Dupont and Cartier varieties) as well as decadent Cuban cigars, which are maintained at optimum temperature in a special humidified walk-in room. A range of Italian pipes, cigar cutters, lighters and ashtrays complete the smoky picture.

VERDEGRANO MAP PP284-5   HOMEWARES
☎ 081 40 17 54; Via Santa Teresa a Chiaia 17; ⏱10am-1pm & 5-7pm, closed Mon morning & Sun in winter, closed Sat afternoon & Sun summer; Ⓜ Amedeo

Come here for exquisitely patterned, hand-painted porcelain pots, vases, plates and decorative items. Prices are reasonable and there are some easy-to-pack smaller pieces for the trip home. It's a small and tightly packed space so children (and the clumsy) are better off outside.

VOMERO
CS SUPERMARKET MAP P283   SUPERMARKET
Via Raffaele Morghen 26; ⏱ 8am-8.30pm Mon-Sat, 9am-1.30pm Sun Ⓜ Vanvitelli

An army of aisles stock everything from fruit and veggies to cheeses, toilet paper and blank CDs. Push it all around in some of the world's funkiest shopping trolleys.

DE PAOLA CAMEOS MAP P283   JEWELLERY
☎ 081 578 29 10; Via Annibale Caccavello 67; ⏱ 9am-8pm Mon-Sat, 9am-2pm Sun; Funicular Centrale to Fuga

A gorgeous range of finely carved cameos as well as coral necklaces, earrings, pendants and bracelets. Designs range from vintage to modern and there's no pressure to buy. There's another branch in Santa Lucia at Via Cesario Console 23.

L'ANGOLO A DUE RUOTE
MAP P283   MOTORCYCLE GEAR
☎ 081 558 43 41; Piazza Vanvitelli 19; Ⓜ Vanvitelli

You'll be stopping traffic with a helmet from this little shop – choose from lurid Hawaiian-style prints in hot pink and orange and graffiti-art styles in electric blues and lime. Brands include AGV, Suomy and Shark and there's a modest range of hot Euro riding gear to keep all (drivers') eyes on you.

PETER PAN MAP P283   CHILDRENSWEAR
☎ 081 578 39 71; Via Gianlorenzo Bernini 24; Ⓜ Vanvitelli

This boutique specialises in handmade felt *carnevale* (carnival) costumes for tots to teens. For everyday cuteness, racks stock everything from Madeleine smocked dresses to isn't-he-adorable mini-Tyrolean jackets. Bag a bargain at sale time.

CUTTING-EDGE CUTLERY

When artist Giovanni Scafuro's mother told him not to play with his food, he started playing with his fork and spoon instead. Now that he's grown up he's still toying with the stuff (and other recyclables) by twisting and melding them into avant-garde jewellery and sculpture. His ingenious body of work includes silver teaspoon bracelets and rings, twisted fork candelabras and rings made from old computer keys. Such whimsical inventiveness hasn't gone unnoticed: Giovanni's designs are stocked as far away as Fukuoka, Japan. While several shops in Naples stock his stuff, much more fun is a trip to his rooftop studio (Map p283; ☎ 081 594 52 71; www.giovanniscafuro.it; Via Matteo Renato Imbriani 191; Ⓜ Materdei), which is a treasure trove of art and design. Just remember to call first – the studio is also the artist's abode.

SLEEPING

Lush interior at Sansevero d'Angri (p151)

ROOM SERVICE

Slumber under frescoes in a 16th-century palazzo, kick back in a converted candle-lit convent or dream sweetly in an architect's style-savvy pad.

From five-star hotels to cheerful hostels, Naples isn't short on sleeping options. Particularly hot right now are the city's B&Bs – far from dowdy and constraining, many newer B&Bs are run by young professionals who'll happily give you your room key and let you come and go as you please.

Hostels are another solid budget option, with several funky privately owned newcomers hitting the scene in the last few years.

If you're after a cheap hotel, the area around Stazione Centrale is your best bet although the area is noisy, dirty and seedy at night. The places listed, however, were clean and safe at the time of research.

For maximum atmosphere, hit the centro storico (historic centre). Here, charming places lie hidden behind heavy doors and, if you're lucky, you could score yourself a baroque boudoir. Best of all, many of the city's sights are within walking distance.

Seaside Santa Lucia is home to some of the city's most prestigious hotels, Chiaia

PRICE GUIDE

Outlining prices precisely is difficult – rates can fluctuate madly depending on the time of year. Many hotels offer discounts for low-season visits, longer stays or weekend breaks; check hotel websites for special deals. Accommodation listed in the reviews below is rated € (doubles cost less than €90), €€ (€90 to €190) or €€€ (over €190). Prices listed are the maximum high-season price.

JEAN-BERNARD CARILLET

top five
SPECTACULAR SLEEPS

Hotel San Francesco Al Monte (p153)

Parteno (p153)

Costantinopoli 104 (p148)

B&B Donnaregina (p148)

Portalba 33 (p149)

is cool and chic, and Mergellina is handy for popping out to the bay islands on a hydrofoil. For lofty views, grand hotels and a chilled-out vibe, hit Vomero; for thermal-spa hotels and crater-based farmhouses, head west to Campi Flegrei.

The Stazione Centrale **tourist office** (Map pp280–1; ☎ 081 26 87 79; Stazione Centrale, Piazza Garibaldi; 🚇 Stazione Centrale) can book accommodation. Alternatively, **Rent A Bed** (Map pp280–1; ☎ 081 41 77 21; www.rentabed.com; Vico D'Afflitto 16; per night from €35; 🚌 R2 to Piazza Trieste e Trento), has an extensive selection of B&Bs and apartments covering Naples, the bay islands and the Amalfi Coast.

Check-in at the hostels listed below is 24 hours and checkout is at 10am. All hostels have mixed dorms and can be booked online at www.hostelspoint.com. There are no hard-and-fast rules with hotel check-in times, but if you plan on arriving in the late afternoon or evening it's best to mention this when booking. Hotel checkout is usually between 10am and noon – if you leave later than this you risk being charged an extra night.

Book ahead if you're coming in May as **Maggio dei Monumenti** (p18) draws huge crowds. Other peak seasons are April to mid-June, Christmas and New Year. Many hotels request a faxed confirmation of your reservation and a credit-card number as a deposit. This doesn't guarantee that the hotel accepts credit-card payment, so check ahead. Without a credit card, you may need to send a money order to cover the first night's stay. Increasingly, hotels encourage booking online to save you this hassle.

Ask for a *camera matrimoniale* if you want a double bed; ask for a *camera doppia* (double room) and you'll get twin beds.

For further information on accommodation, see p249.

CENTRO STORICO & MERCATO

For a high-voltage shot of pure Naples, you can't beat the centro storico, with its wealth of historical sites, buzzing squares and grinding street-life. This is the place for secret B&Bs, homely hostels and art-crammed converted palazzi.

Mercato is the place for budget hotels; the options we've listed were clean and reliable at the time of writing, but be warned that the area is bedlam by day and dodgy by night.

6 SMALL ROOMS MAP PP280-1   HOSTEL €
☎ 081 790 13 78; www.6smallrooms.com; Via Diodata Lioy 18; dm/d incl breakfast €18/45; Ⓜ Dante
On the top floor of a dusty old building, this happy little hostel features bright, spacious dorms, two private rooms, funky wall murals, shabby but chic furnishings and a huge communal kitchen. The little room downstairs has aircon and private bathroom. BYO lock for the lockers.

ALBERGO DUOMO MAP PP280-1   HOTEL €
☎ 081 26 59 88; hotelduomo@libero.it; Via Duomo 228; s/d €50/65; Ⓡ R2 to Piazza Nicola Amore; 🖵
Close to the cathedral, this former pink pad is now a cooler shade of cream. Brightly coloured bedspreads add a little spice, and rooms are comfy and airy, if a little anonymous. But the price is right so book ahead as rooms go quickly.

B&B COSTANTINOPOLI
MAP PP280-1   B&B €€
☎ 081 44 49 62, 333 613 59 27; lauramazzella@hot mail.com; Via Santa Maria di Costantinopoli 27; s/d incl breakfast €65/93; Ⓜ Museo; 💢
Don't let the dingy staircase scare you off; B&B Costantinopoli is a fabulous place to stay. The family of artists who own this large and exuberantly decorated 3rd-floor pad are warm, engaging and a mine of local knowledge. The two rooms are bright, comfy and clean.

B&B DONNAREGINA MAP P286   B&B €€
☎ 081 44 67 99; Via Settembrini 80; d/tr/q incl breakfast €93/120/150; Ⓜ Cavour; 💢
Part gallery, part family home, this place is a heaving treasure trove of art, books and anecdotes. Four spacious bedrooms boast individual designs, original artwork, ensuite bathrooms and satellite TVs. The garrulous artist-owner cooks breakfast, which is served at a huge old wooden table. Pride of place is given to his organic pancetta.

BELLA CAPRI HOSTEL & HOTEL
MAP PP280-1   HOSTEL & HOTEL €
☎ 081 552 92 65; www.bellacapri.it; Via G Melisurgo 4; dm €20, s/d €70/80, with shared bathroom €50/60, all incl breakfast; Ⓡ R2 to Via Agostino Depretis; 💢 🖵
This central, friendly spot offers hotel and hostel options on two separate floors. Hotel rooms are a little dowdy but clean and comfy. The much funkier hostel boasts bright citrus tones, more beds than bunks, and a bathroom in each dorm. Laundry service costs €5 and there's no curfew.

CARAVAGGIO HOTEL MAP PP280-1   HOTEL €€
☎ 081 211 00 66; www.caravaggiohotel.it; Piazza Riario Sforza 157; s/d/ste incl breakfast €125/190/240; Ⓡ CS to Via Duomo; 🖵
Bold abstract paintings hang opposite stone arches, yellow sofas line 300-year-old brick walls and original wood-beamed ceilings cap the comfortable, four-star bedrooms at this hotel. Friendly staff top it all off.

COSTANTINOPOLI 104
MAP PP280-1   HOTEL €€€
☎ 081 557 10 35; www.constantinopoli104.it; Via Santa Maria di Costantinopoli 104; s/d incl breakfast €160/200; Ⓜ Museo; Ⓟ 💢 🖵 🏊
Chic and tranquil, Costantinopoli 104 is set in a neoclassical villa. Rooms are understatedly elegant – those on the 1st floor open onto a sun terrace, while ground-floor rooms face the palm-fringed pool. Antique furniture and stained-glass windows add a dash of vintage glam.

DIMORA DEI GIGANTI MAP PP280-1   B&B €
☎ 081 44 90 53, 338 926 44 53; www.dimora deigiganti.it; Vico Giganti 55; s/d/tr/q incl breakfast €60/80/95/110; Ⓡ CS to Via Duomo; Ⓟ
Skilfully renovated by its architect owners, this urbane B&B features four colour-coordinated bedrooms with specially commissioned sculptural lamps, ethnic-inspired furnishings and designer bathrooms. There is a modern kitchen, cosy lounge and majolica-tiled terrace for late-night lounging.

HOSTEL OF THE SUN MAP PP280-1 HOSTEL €

☎ 081 420 63 93; www.hostelnapoli.com; Via G Melisurgo 15; dm/d €18/70, s/d with shared bathroom €45/50, all incl breakfast; 🚌 R2 to Via Depretis; 🖴
Handy for the ferry terminal, this cosy private hostel is a backpacker favourite thanks to its ultrahelpful young staff. There's a kitchen, no curfew, free internet access, and free laundry service for stays of more than four days. The lift costs €0.05. Wheelchair accessible.

HOTEL CASANOVA MAP PP278-9 HOTEL €

☎ 081 26 82 87; www.hotelcasanova.com; Corso G Garibaldi 333; s/d €35/56, with shared bathroom €28/46; Ⓜ Garibaldi; 🖴
This isn't a brothel, just a charming family hotel with a flower-fringed roof terrace and excellent-value rooms with modern, functional furniture and gleaming bathrooms. Use the safer Corso G Garibaldi entrance rather than the main one located on Via Venezia. Breakfast is an optional €4.

HOTEL LUNA ROSSA MAP PP280-1 HOTEL €€

☎ 081 554 87 52; www.hotellunarossa.it; Via G Pica 20-22; s/d incl breakfast €60/95; Ⓜ Garibaldi; 🆒 🖴
The Luna Rossa is a quiet place run by the daughter of a Neapolitan musician. Each room is named after a Neapolitan song, the lyrics of which are framed and hung in the rooms. The pink-hued rooms are comfy, if plain, and the large bathrooms are perfect for towel-clad tenors.

HOTEL PIGNATELLI MAP PP280-1 HOTEL €€

☎ 081 658 49 50; www.hotelpignatellinapoli.com in Italian; Via San Giovanni Maggiore Pignatelli 16; s/d incl breakfast €50/90; 🚌 R2 to Corso Umberto I; 🖴
Cheap yet chic, Hotel Pignatelli sits pretty in a restored 15th-century house. Rooms are decorated in a rustic Renaissance style, with wrought-iron beds and bronze wall lamps; some rooms also have original wood-beamed ceilings. Wheelchair accessible.

HOTEL SUITE ESEDRA MAP PP280-1 HOTEL €€

☎ 081 553 70 87; www.sea-hotels.com; Via Cantani 12; s/d/ste incl breakfast €120/130/140; 🚌 R2 to Corso Umberto I; 🆒
The Esedra stands tall on a tiny square just off car-choked Corso Umberto I, halfway between Stazione Centrale and the centro storico. The snug rooms are decorated with Neapolitan paintings, and you might even find a porthole or two in your bathroom. Suites boast private terrace Jacuzzis.

HOTEL ZARA
MAP PP278-9   HOTEL €

☎ 081 28 71 25; www.hotelzara.it; 2nd fl, Via Firenze 81; s/d/tr €45/62/80; Ⓜ Garibaldi; 🆒 🖴
Recently renovated and run by the same family as Hotel Casanova (left), this spotless bolt hole is a world away from the grungy street below. Rooms are spartan but clean, with modern furniture, satellite TVs and double-glazed windows. There's a book exchange and breakfast is an optional €4.

PORTALBA 33 MAP PP280-1 B&B €€

☎ 081 549 32 51; www.portalba33.it; Via Port'Alba 33; s/d incl breakfast €120/140; Ⓜ Dante
This funky B&B is pure offbeat cool. Three gorgeously comfy rooms feature everything from antique rocking horses and fake-fur bedspreads to leopard-print underlays and baby blue walls. There is even a weights machine for your morning workout.

Portalba 33   JEAN-BERNARD CARILLET

SCANDALOUS SLUMBER

At Piazza San Domenico Maggiore 9 you'll find the Palazzo dei Di Sangrio, home of the Soggiorno Sansevero hotel (below) and the setting for a gruesome tale of love and betrayal. Here, on the night of 17 October 1590, the famous Neapolitan musician Carlo Gesualdo murdered his wife, Maria d'Avalos, and her lover, Don Fabrizio Carafa, in a fit of jealous rage. The suspicious Gesualdo had tricked Maria into thinking that he was away on a hunting trip, when in fact he was waiting to catch her with her lover. He did and both Maria and Don Fabrizio paid the ultimate price. According to legend, the bloodied lovers died in each others' arms. Gesualdo's jealousy was hardly surprising – so good-looking was the younger nobleman that he was nicknamed 'the Angel'. Yet the Angel's death wasn't enough for the betrayed husband, who ordered the killing of his own son, suspecting him of being the fruit of his wife's adulterous tryst. According to local lore, poor Maria's ghost still roams the streets at night, searching for her slaughtered son and sweetheart.

SOGGIORNO SANSEVERO
MAP PP280-1   HOTEL €€

☎ 081 790 10 00; www.albergosansevero.it; Piazza San Domenico Maggiore 9; s/d €90/110, with shared bathroom €70/90, all incl breakfast; Ⓜ Dante; 🟦

Hidden away on the 1st floor of a famous 18th-century palazzo (see Scandalous Slumber, above) that once belonged to the creepy prince of Sansevero, this is one of several stylish Sansevero hotels. You'll find it just around the corner from the Cappella Sansevero on the eastern side of lively – read noisy at night – Piazza San Domenico Maggiore.

UNA HOTEL NAPOLI MAP PP280-1 HOTEL €€€
☎ 081 563 69 72; www.unahotels.it; Piazza Garibaldi 9-10; s €163-291, d €181-323, ste €417-478, all incl breakfast; Ⓜ Garibaldi; Ⓟ 💻

Fit for a spread in *Wallpaper* magazine (unlike the shabby square outside), this squeaky-new hotel is a design buff's paradise – MoMA-worthy light sculptures, exposed tufa walls, a minimalist rooftop restaurant-bar and 89 soothing Zenlike rooms with clean lines and flat-screen TVs. Wheelchair accessible.

TOLEDO & QUARTIERI SPAGNOLI

Via Toledo is the city's major retail strip. To the west, the earthy Quartieri Spagnoli's reputation for crime has been somewhat exaggerated.

Expect everything from humble flats to chic converted convents. The hotels listed were friendly, comfortable and safe at the time of research.

ALBERGO NAPOLIT'AMO
MAP PP280-1   HOTEL €€

☎ 081 497 71 10; albergonapolitamo@virgilio.it; Via San Tommaso d'Aquino 15; s/d incl breakfast €75/115; 🚍 R2 to Via Medina; 🟦

On the 'right' side of Via Toledo, this laid-back three-star pad is a zesty mix of lime greens, yellows and blues. The new 5th-floor wing has the best rooms, and there's a view of the Castello dell'Ovo from the breakfast room. Don't forget €0.10 for the lift. Wheelchair accessible.

HOTEL IL CONVENTO
MAP PP280-1   HOTEL €€

☎ 081 40 39 77; www.hotelilconvento.com; Via Speranzella 137A; s €68-145, d €80-210, all incl breakfast; 🚍 R2 to Piazza Trieste e Trento; 🟦

Taking its name from the neighbouring convent, the Convento is a soothing blend of antique Tuscan furniture, erudite bookshelves and candle-lit stairs. Rooms are cosy and elegant, combining creamy tones and dark woods with patches of 16th-century brickwork. For €110 to €210 you get a room with a private roof garden. The hotel is wheelchair accessible.

HOTEL TOLEDO MAP PP280-1   HOTEL €€
☎ 081 40 68 71; www.hoteltoledo.com; Via Montecalvario 15; s/d/ste incl breakfast €85/130/180; 🚍 CS to Via Toledo; Ⓟ 🟦 💻

Snugly situated in an old three-storey building, this homely hotel has comfy, smallish rooms with terracotta tiles and mod cons; the rooms are a little on the dark side, however. Suites feature a stovetop, and breakfast is served on the rooftop terrace.

LA LOCANDA DELL'ARTE & VICTORIA HOUSE MAP PP280-1 B&B €€

☎ 081 564 46 40; www.bbnapoli.org in Italian; Via Enrico Pessina 66; s/d incl breakfast €70/90; Ⓜ Dante; Ⓟ ⌖

These two B&B options are run by the same owners in a building overlooking hip Via Bellini. Rooms come with all the requisite comforts, although those in La Locanda are more modern than the larger Victoria rooms. Breakfast is served in the trendy downstairs restaurant.

NAPOLIT'AMO MAP PP280-1 HOTEL €€

☎ 081 552 36 26; www.napolitamo.it; Via Toledo 148; s €65-75, d €80-105, all incl breakfast; ⊟ R2 to Via Toledo; ⌖ ▯

Escape the common hordes and live like nobility in the 16th-century Palazzo Tocco di Montemiletto. Although it's admittedly a little tired in places, there are still enough gilded mirrors and lofty ceilings to satisfy the snob within.

SANSEVERO D'ANGRI MAP PP280-1 HOTEL €€

☎ 081 790 10 00; www.albergosansevero.it; Piazza VII Settembre 28; s/d incl breakfast €110/150; ⊟ CS to Via Toledo; ⌖

This is a gilded wonderland of baroque salons, 17th-century parquet and palatial rooms, some with frescoed ceilings. The regal vibe is not surprising given that Vanvitelli, the original architect, also designed the royal palace at Caserta.

TOLEDO 205 MAP PP280-1 APARTMENT €

☎ 081 410 70 77; www.toledo205.it; Via Toledo 205; apt €100; ⊟ R2 to Piazza Trieste e Trento; ▯

Right on the city's major shopping strip, these two miniapartments each accommodate five people. Although they're not luxurious or particularly smart, they're clean and the communal sundeck has awesome rooftop views. It's ideal for a group of friends who want somewhere cheap and central. You'll need €0.10 for the lift.

SANTA LUCIA & CHIAIA

With lavish seaside hotels and sparkling island vistas, Santa Lucia is where presidents and pop stars say goodnight. However, there are still affordable options, some with stunning bay and castle vistas. As a general rule, rooms with water views cost a little more.

A-list Chiaia is *the* place for trendy shopping, bar-hopping and chichi dolce vita, so accommodation is chic rather than cheap. Your best bets for budget beds are the two funky B&Bs.

B&B CAPPELLA VECCHIA 11 MAP PP284-5 B&B €€

☎ 081 240 51 17; www.cappellavecchia11.it; Vico Santa Maria a Cappella Vecchia 11; s/d incl breakfast €70/100; ⊟ C25 to Piazza dei Martiri; ⌖ ▯

Run by a superhelpful young couple, this B&B is a first-rate choice. Six chic and witty rooms feature different Neapolitan themes, from *mal'occhio* (evil eye) to *peperoncino* (chilli). There's a spacious communal area for breakfast, and free internet available 24/7.

B&B I 34 TURCHI MAP PP284-5 B&B €€

☎ 081 764 71 36; www.i34turchi.it; Via Marino Turchi 34; s/d/tr incl breakfast €60/100/220; ⊟ C25 to Via Partenope

This gay-friendly B&B offers guests their own self-contained apartment, with a small double room on a mezzanine floor and a sofa bed in the living area. Divided from the family home, you get your own key to come and go as you please, although you'll probably end up reclining on the rooftop terrace. Bring €0.20 for the lift.

top five

CHEAP SLEEPS

151

Style and comfort at Grand Hotel Vesuvio (both images)

GREG ELMS

B&B MORELLI MAP PP284-5 B&B €€
☎ 081 245 22 91; www.bbmorelli49.it; Via Domenico Morelli 49; s/d incl breakfast €65/95; 🚌 C25 to Riviera di Chiaia; ✸
Get in bed with Madonna at this kitschy shrine to pop, where a dedicated Madonna room is decorated with albums by the Kabbalist. Another three rooms mix Almódovar film posters, Florentine floor tiles and retro lamps in one cosy, quirky whole.

B&B SANTA LUCIA MAP PP284-5 B&B €€
☎ 081 245 74 83; www.borgosantalucia.net; Via Santa Lucia 90; s €80-110, d €90-140, all incl breakfast; 🚌 C25 to Via Partenope; ✸
What this place lacks in character – the reception area resembles an upmarket health clinic – it makes up with six sparkling white-tiled rooms, exuberant Italian-Brazilian owners and a location just a samba step away from the lapping sea.

CHIAJA HOTEL DE CHARME
MAP PP284-5 HOTEL €€
☎ 081 41 55 55; www.hotelchiaia.it; Via Chiaia 216; s €95, d €145-165 incl breakfast; 🚌 CS to Piazza Trieste e Trento
Posh yet personable, this renovated marquis' residence is a soothing blend of pale lemon walls, gilt-framed portraits, restored original furnishings and elegantly draped curtains. Each room is unique, and those facing boutique-flanked Via Chiaia come with a bubbling Jacuzzi.

GRAND HOTEL SANTA LUCIA
MAP PP284-5 HOTEL €€€
☎ 081 764 06 66; www.summithotels.com; Via Partenope 46; s/d incl breakfast €235/390; 🚌 C25 to Via Partenope; ✸
All decked out in powder blues and creams, this five-star pad owes much of its Liberty look to celebrated architect Giovan Battista Comencini. Expect impeccable service, chichi rooms with Guatemalan-marble bathrooms, and an entire nonsmoking floor – a rarity in Italy.

GRAND HOTEL VESUVIO
MAP PP284-5 HOTEL €€€
☎ 081 764 00 44; www.vesuvio.it; Via Partenope 45; s/d incl breakfast €370/410; 🚌 C25 to Via Partenope; 🅿 ✸ 💻
Known for bedding legends – past guests include Rita Hayworth and Humphrey Bogart – this five-star heavyweight is a decadent wonderland of dripping chandeliers, period antiques and opulent rooms. Count your lucky stars while drinking a martini at the rooftop restaurant. Wheelchair accessible.

silver-screen view of sea, sky and Capri. Hi-tech touches include wireless internet, satellite TV (two rooms boast plasma screens to boot), and free land-line calls to Europe, USA and Canada.

VOMERO

Middle-class Vomero is a world apart from the seething sprawl below. It's not exactly bursting with sights, but the views are divine, the streets are leafy and the heady Neapolitan chaos is just a funicular ride away.

Slumberwise, expect old-school glamour at new-school prices, with a touch of cheap chic further down the hill.

GRAND HOTEL PARKER'S
MAP PP284-5   HOTEL €€€

☎ 081 761 24 74; www.grandhotelparkers.com; Corso Vittorio Emanuele I 35; s/d incl breakfast €290/360; 🚌 C28 to Via Tasso; 🅿 ⊠

Darling of the Grand Tour set, this stately old pile once hosted the likes of Oscar Wilde, Virginia Wolfe and Robert Louis Stevenson. Today, Prada-clad guests lounge on Louis XVI armchairs, take *aperitivo* (apéritifs) on the sea-view terrace and unwind at the in-house spa centre.

HOTEL SAN FRANCESCO AL MONTE
MAP P283   HOTEL €€€

☎ 081 423 91 11; www.hotelsanfrancesco.it; Corso Vittorio Emanuele I 328; d incl breakfast €190; Funicular Centrale to Corso Vittorio Emanuele I; ⊠ 🖳 ⊠

Housed in a 16th-century monastery, this hotel is magnificent. The monks' cells are stylish rooms, the ancient cloisters house an open-air bar, and the barrel-vaulted corridors are cool and atmospheric. To top it all off there's a swimming pool on the 7th floor.

LA CASA DI LEO MAP P283   B&B €

☎ 081 544 78 43; www.bedandbreakfastnapoli.it; Via Girolamo Santacroce 5A; s/d with shared bathroom incl breakfast €50/70; Ⓜ Salvator Rosa

Bold colours, art books and the odd abstract painting define this erudite pad, home of a heritage architect. Two airy bedrooms offer simple, stylish décor and leafy courtyard views. The shared bathroom is spacious, the kitchen is yours to use, and there's a metro stop down the street.

Courtyard at Hotel San Francesco al Monte   JEAN-BERNARD CARILLET

HOTEL EXCELSIOR MAP PP284-5   HOTEL €€€
☎ 081 764 01 11; www.excelsior.it; Via Partenope 48; s/d €270/330; 🚌 C25 to Via Partenope; ⊠

Facing yacht-packed Borgo Marinaro, Hotel Excelsior sets the scene for your own *Pretty Woman* moment – think marble columns, dark limousines and giant fin-de-siècle rooms. Jaw-dropping water views provide a suitable love-scene backdrop. Wheelchair accessible.

HOTEL RUGGIERO MAP PP284-5   HOTEL €€
☎ 081 66 35 36; hotelrug@libero.it; 3rd fl, Via Campiglione Martucci 72; s/d incl breakfast €70/90; Ⓜ Amedeo; ⊠

As you enter the grand art nouveau building off Piazza Amedeo, you'll need sharp eyes to spot the lift hidden in the corner. The hotel itself is quiet, friendly and speckled with replicas of Chinese antiques. Rooms are clean, uncluttered and inviting, with those on the lower floor kept air-con cool.

PARTENO MAP PP284-5   HOTEL €€
☎ 081 245 20 95; www.parteno.it; Via Partenope 1; s €110, d €144-160, all incl breakfast; 🚌 C25 to Via Partenope; 🖳 ⊠

Six chic rooms, each named after a flower, are exquisitely decorated with period furniture, vintage Neapolitan prints and silk bedding. The azalea room (€160) steals the show with its

top five

VIEWS

Grand Hotel Parker's (p153)
Grand Hotel Vesuvio (p152)
Hotel Paradiso (below)
Hotel Excelsior (p153)
Il Casolare di Tobia (right)

LA CONTRORA MAP P283   HOSTEL €

☎ 081 549 40 14; www.lacontrora.com; Piazzetta Trinità alla Cesarea 231; dm/s/d incl breakfast €20/27.50/55; Ⓜ Salvator Rosa; ❌ ▯

In the words of Paris Hilton, this hostel looks *hot*. Think stainless-steel lamps, sleek bar, blonde-wood bunks, spearmint bathrooms, and a communal kitchen that's very Jamie Oliver. Snooze in a courtyard hammock, or surf the net for €1 per 30 minutes.

MERGELLINA & POSILLIPO

With Liberty *palazzi*, anchored yachts and a buzzing seafront scene, Mergellina is well connected to the city centre and ideal for an early-morning hydrofoil out to the bay islands.

HOTEL AUSONIA MAP PP284-5   HOTEL €€

☎ 081 68 22 78; www.hotelausonianapoli.com; Via Francesco Caracciolo 11; s/d/tr incl breakfast €90/120/140; ☒ 140 to Via Francesco Caracciolo; ❌

This modest and friendly hotel sits opposite the Mergellina marina, a fact not played down in the décor – think portholes, barometers and bed heads in the shape of ships' steering wheels. Corny? Yes, but rooms are clean and comfy, and the few that face the sea don't cost extra.

HOTEL PARADISO MAP PP278-9   HOTEL €€

☎ 081 247 51 11; www.hotelparadisonapoli.it; Via Catullo 11; s/d incl breakfast €118/170; Funicular Mergellina to S Gioacchino; ❌

Located some way above the city centre, your efforts in getting up here are rewarded with jaw-dropping views over the Bay of Naples to

Mt Vesuvius. Most of the well-furnished rooms come with a balcony, and staff are courteous and efficient. Expect to pay slightly less for a room without a view.

ELSEWHERE

To the west of Naples, the Campi Flegrei offers a somewhat slower pace than the central-city neighbourhoods, and Pozzuoli has a number of reasonably priced hotels and *pensioni* (guesthouses). Ask at a tourist office (p259) for details.

HOTEL TERME PUTEOLANE
MAP P287   HOTEL €

☎ 081 526 22 62; termeputeolane@tiscalinet.it; Corso Umberto I 195, Pozzuoli; s/d €55/75; ☒ Cumana to Pozzuoli; Ⓟ ❌ ▯

This grand old hotel in Pozzuoli is frequented as much for its sulphurous airs and thermal treatments as for its large and airy rooms. Between April and December you can complete a course of 12 thermal baths for €103, or for €155 you get 12 thermal baths and the opportunity to wallow in glorious gloopy mud.

IL CASOLARE DI TOBIA
MAP P287   AGRITURISMO €

☎ 081 523 51 93; www.datobia.it in Italian; Contrada Coste di Baia, Via Selvatico 12, Bacoli; r with/without kitchenette incl breakfast €65/55; ☒ SEPSA to Bacoli; Ⓟ ❌

Set in an extinct volcanic crater, this atmospheric 19th-century farmhouse is surrounded by lush vineyards and vegetable gardens, which are used to supply its legendary on-site restaurant. Four bright rooms feature local antiques; there's also a communal rustic-style kitchen, plus one very fabulous outdoor Jacuzzi. Il Casolare di Tobia is closed for one week in late August and one week in late December or early January.

VULCANO SOLFATARA MAP P287   CAMP SITE €

☎ 081 526 74 13; www.solfatara.it; Via Solfatara 161, Pozzuoli; per tent/person €6/€9, 2-person bungalow €43, 4-person bungalow €100; Ⓜ Pozzuoli; ☒

The nearest camp site to Naples, Vulcano Solfatara features a swimming pool and one disabled-friendly bathroom. It's located very close to the Solfatara Crater.

Mosaic detail from Pompeii, displayed in the Museo Archeologico Nazionale (p80)

ANCIENT SITES
Buried for centuries beneath metres of volcanic debris, Naples' archaeological sites are among the best-preserved and most-spectacular Roman ruins in existence.

The views across the Bay of Naples are stunning. From the westernmost tip of Posillipo in Naples you can look east over the entire bay, round to Mt Vesuvius and the Sorrentine Peninsula. And it's here, among the most densely populated towns in Europe, that you'll find Italy's great archaeological sites: Pompeii, Herculaneum and a host of lesser-known jewels.

Two thousand years ago it would all have looked very different. Farmland and forests covered Vesuvius' lower slopes, Herculaneum was a small fishing town and Pompeii an important trading centre; Nero's second wife had a villa in upmarket Oplontis (now decidedly downmarket Torre Annunziata) and aristocrats holidayed in Stabiae (Castellammare di Stabia). It was an area with a lot going for it. That is, until a double whammy of natural disasters struck in the 1st century AD: first an earthquake in AD 62 and then, on 24 August AD 79, Vesuvius erupted.

Much of what we know about the eruption comes from Pliny the Younger's unique eyewitness account. In a letter to the historian Tacitus, he wrote: 'A black and terrible cloud, rent by snaking bursts of fire, gaped open in huge flashes of flames; it was like lightening, but far more extensive.' But it wasn't the lava or the rain of pumice that killed the cowering people of Pompeii; it was a scorching blast of gaseous air off the volcano that killed everything in its path.

Following the eruption the area was largely left to its own devices until the 18th century when it experienced a glorious, if short-lived, resurrection. The Bourbon king Charles VII had a palace built in Portici in 1738 and aristocrats rushed to follow suit by constructing more than 120 villas, the Ville Vesuviane (Vesuvian Villas; see p216), along the so-called Miglio d'Oro (Golden Mile) between San Giovanni a Teduccio and Torre del Greco. To decorate his new palace, Charles had his archaeologists strip Pompeii (discovered in 1748) of its finest murals, mosaics and statues. Thankfully, most were subsequently moved up to Naples where they are now on view at the Museo Archeologico Nazionale (p80).

Of the five major archaeological sites in the Bay of Naples area, Pompeii is the obvious draw card; its majestic remains are a compelling testimony to what was once a tough trading town of 20,000 souls. Herculaneum might be smaller but it is better preserved than its more illustrious neighbour. The 16m of mud that set over the town from the eruption of Vesuvius fossilised everything from fruit and furniture to a library of ancient scrolls and a number of stunning mosaics. Further around the coast, villas unearthed at Torre Annunziata and Castellammare di Stabia stand out among the urban sprawl that stretches almost uninterrupted from Naples to Castellammare.

Sculpture from Casa di Nettuno e Anfitrite (p166)   GREG ELMS

Pompeii, Herculaneum and Oplontis are within easy walking distance of stations on the Naples–Sorrento Circumvesuviana train line. Stabiae and Boscoreale require a bit more searching out (see the boxed text, below).

Further south, 36km beyond Salerno, the ancient Greek city of Paestum is absolutely worth the effort of getting there. Without any help from Vesuvius, its imperious Greek temples have survived for almost 2750 years.

VINTAGE VILLAS

Buried beneath the distinctly unlovely streets of Torre Annunziata, Oplontis was once an upmarket seafront suburb under the administrative control of Pompeii. First discovered in the 18th century, it's been left largely untouched; only two of its houses have been unearthed, and only one, Villa Poppaea, is open to the public. This villa is a magnificent example of an *otium* villa (a residential building used for rest and recreation), thought to have belonged to Sabina Poppaea, Nero's second wife. Particularly outstanding are the 1st-century wall paintings in the *triclinium* (dining room) and *calidarium* (hot bathroom) in the west wing. Marking the eastern border of the villa is a garden with a huge swimming pool (17m by 61m). The villa is a straightforward 300m walk from Torre Annunziate Circumvesuviana train station.

South of Oplontis, Stabiae stood on the slopes of the Varano hill overlooking what was then the sea and is now modern Castellammare di Stabia. Here at Stabiae you can visit two villas: the 1st-century-BC Villa Arianna and the larger Villa San Marco, said to measure more than 11,000 sq metres. Neither is in mint condition, but the frescoes in Villa Arianna suggest that it must have once been quite something. Both are accessible by bus from Via Nocera Circumvesuviana station.

Some 3km north of Pompeii, the Antiquarium di Boscoreale is a museum dedicated to Pompeii and its ancient environs. Historical artefacts are combined with life-sized photos and reconstructions to show what the area was like 2000 years ago. To get there, take a bus for Villa Regina from Boscotrecase Circumvesuviana station.

All three sites are covered by a single ticket (adult/EU 18yr-25yr/EU under 18yr & over 65yr €5.50/2.75/free), and opening times are standard (⏰ 8.30am-7.30pm Apr-Oct, last entry 6pm, & 8.30am-5pm Nov-Mar, last entry 3.30pm).

A VOLCANIC LANDSCAPE

Brooding darkly over Naples, Mt Vesuvius (Vesuvio) is not just a monument to past horrors; it's as dangerous today as it was nearly 2000 years ago.

Since the mountain exploded into history in AD 79, burying Pompeii, Herculaneum and much of the surrounding countryside, Vesuvius has erupted more than 30 times. The most devastating of these was in 1631, and the most recent in 1944. And while there's little evidence to suggest any imminent activity, observers continue to worry, noting that the current lull is the longest in the past 500 years.

A full-scale eruption would be catastrophic. Almost three million people currently live in Vesuvius's shadow, 600,000 of these within 7km of the crater. Attempts are being made to relocate those most at risk (see p27), but even with a €30,000 grant on offer few are willing to go. Farmers in particular are reluctant to give up the area's rich volcanic soil, a source of considerable local income.

The area has always been fertile. In ancient times, before the eruption of 79 AD, the slopes of Mt Vesuvius (or Mt Somma as it then was) were planted with cereal crops and fruit orchards, boar flourished in oak woods and thick beech forests covered the mountainside. Aristocratic villas peppered the coastline below.

The mountain itself was once higher than it currently stands, rising to about 3000m rather than the 1281m of today, and had a single summit rather than the current two.

The volcano's massive eruption not only drowned Pompeii in pumice and pushed the coastline back several kilometres, but also destroyed much of the mountain top, creating a huge caldera and a new summit.

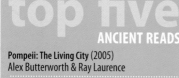

top five

ANCIENT READS

Pompeii: The Living City (2005)
Alex Butterworth & Ray Laurence

Ghosts of Vesuvius: A New Look at the Last Days of Pompeii, How Towers Fell, and Other Strange Connections (2004)
Charles Pellegrino

Pompeii (2004)
Robert Harris

The Lost World of Pompeii (2002)
Colin Amery, Brian Curran, Brian Curran Jr and Chris Caldicott

Houses and Society in Pompeii and Herculaneum (1996)
Andrew Wallace-Hadrill

Descending the crater of Mt Vesuvius   MARTIN MOOS

Today, Vesuvius itself is rather better protected than many of the towns beneath it. The **Parco Nazionale del Vesuvio** (www.parco nazionaledelvesuvio.it) was established in 1995 and attracts some 600,000 visitors annually. Most make straight for the summit (see the boxed text, below), but if you've got the time (and the legs), there's some interesting walking to be done. Ask for details at the **information centre** (9am-5.30pm daily) at the summit car park.

About halfway up the hill, the **Museo dell'Osservatorio Vesuviano** (Museum of the Vesuvian Observatory; ☎ 081 610 84 83; www.ov.ingv.it in Italian; admission free; 10am-2pm Sat & Sun), tells the history of 2000 years of Vesuvius-watching.

MARTIN MOOS

VISITING VESUVIUS

The easiest way to visit Vesuvius is to get a bus from Pompeii up to the crater car park. **Vesuviani Mobilità** (☎ 081 963 44 20) operates 10 return-trip buses daily from Piazza Anfiteatro. The journey time is one hour each way and return tickets cost €8.60.

Two of these buses stop in Ercolano, departing from the bus stop on Via Panoramica (about 50m from the Ercolano–Scavi Circumvesuviana train station) at 8.23am and 12.45pm and returning at 1.55pm and 4.30pm. Return tickets are available on board and cost €7.60 for the 90-minute round-trip.

Vesuvio Express (☎ 081 739 36 66; www.vesuvioexpress.it; Piazzale Stazione Circumvesuviana 8) operates minibus-taxis to the summit from outside Ercolano–Scavi station. The ride costs €10 (or €16.50 including crater admission) and buses depart when they are full (or overfull, as is sometimes the case).

If travelling by car, exit the A3 at Ercolano Portico and follow signs for the Parco Nazionale del Vesuvio.

Whether arriving by bus or car, the end of the road is the summit car park (or just before it if you want to avoid the €2.50 parking fee). From here an 860m path leads up to the **crater** (adult/over 65yr/under 8yr €6.50/4.50/free; 9am-6pm daily Jul-Sep, to 5pm Apr-Jun, to 3pm Oct-Mar; ticket office closes 1hr before the crater). It's not a strenuous walk (allow 35 to 40 minutes), but it's more comfortable in trainers than sandals or flip-flops (thongs). You'd also do well to take sunglasses, which are useful against swirling ash, and a sweater as it can be chilly up top, even in summer.

Note that when weather conditions are bad the summit path is shut and bus departures are suspended.

Along Vicolo di Mercurio, Pompeii

POMPEII

A stark reminder of the malign forces that lie deep inside Vesuvius, Pompeii is Europe's most compelling archaeological site.

A Roman town frozen in its 2000 year-old death throes and conserved under a sea of volcanic pumice, Pompeii (Pompei in Italian) is Italy's top tourist attraction. Each year about 2.5 million visitors pour in to wander the ghostly shell of what was once a thriving commercial centre.

Pompeii's appeal goes beyond tourism; from an archaeological point of view it's priceless. Much of its value lies in the fact that it wasn't simply blown away by Vesuvius, rather it was buried under a layer of *lapilli* (burning fragments of pumice stone), as Pliny the Younger hints at in his celebrated account: 'Darkness came on again, again ashes, thick and heavy. We got up repeatedly to shake these off; otherwise we would have been buried and crushed by the weight.'

But as terrible as the eruption was, it could have been worse. Seventeen years earlier Pompeii had been devastated by an earthquake and much of the 20,000-strong population had been evacuated. Many had not returned by the time Vesuvius blew but 2000 men, women and children perished nevertheless.

INFORMATION

First aid (☎ 081 535 91 11; Via Colle San Bartolomeo 50)
Police booth Piazza Esedra
Pompeii Sites (www.pompeiisites.org) Comprehensive website covering Pompeii, Herculaneum, Oplontis, Stabiae and the Antiquarium di Boscoreale.
Post office (☎ 081 861 09 58; Piazza Esedra)
Tourist office Porta Marina (☎ 081 850 72 55; Piazza Porta Marina Inferiore 12; ⏲ 8am-3.30pm Mon-Sat Oct-Mar, 8am-7pm Mon-Fri & 8am-2pm Sat Apr-Sep); Pompeii Town (☎ 081 850 72 55; Via Sacra 1; ⏲ as above)

Plaster cast of Pompeii victim
GREG ELMS

ADMISSION

Entrance Porta Marina; Piazza Anfiteatro
Ticket office (☎ 081 857 53 47; Porta Marina) There is also a ticket office at the Piazza Anfiteatro entrance.
Admission (adult/EU 18yr-25yr/EU under 18yr & over 65yr €11/5.50/free; combined ticket incl Herculaneum, Oplontis, Stabiae & Boscoreale €20/10/free) Bring a passport or ID card to claim discounts. Take your ticket and get a free map and booklet from the booth to the left of the toilets.
Opening times (⏱ 8.30am-7.30pm Apr-Oct, last entry 6pm, & 8.30am-5pm Nov-Mar, last entry 3.30pm)
Audioguides (€6.50) There are also special audioguides for children.

The origins of Pompeii are uncertain but it seems likely that it was founded in the 7th century BC by the Campanian Oscans. Over the next seven centuries, the city fell to the Greeks and the Samnites before becoming a Roman colony in 80 BC.

After its catastrophic demise, Pompeii receded from the public eye until 1594 when the architect Domenico Fontana stumbled across the ruins while digging a canal. Exploration proper didn't begin until 1748, however. Work continues today and although new discoveries are being made – a frescoed leisure area was revealed beneath roadworks in 2000 – the emphasis is now on restoring what has already been unearthed rather than raking for new finds.

About 1km down the road from the ruins in the modern town of Pompeii the Santuario della Madonna del Rosario (Sanctuary of Our Lady of the Rosary; p164) is a popular pilgrim destination.

Orientation

The Circumvesuviana train drops you at Pompeii–Scavi–Villa dei Misteri station, beside the main entrance at Porta Marina. Signs direct those arriving by car from the A3 to the *scavi* (excavations) and car parks. Modern Pompeii is 1km away from the station down Via Plinio.

TOURS

You'll almost certainly be approached by a guide outside the ticket office. Authorised guides wear identification tags and belong to one of four cooperatives:
Cast (☎ 081 856 42 21)
Casting (☎ 081 850 07 49)
Gata (☎ 081 861 56 61)
Promo Touring (☎ 081 850 88 55)
The official price for a two-hour tour is €100, whether you're alone, in a couple or in a group of up to 25.

The Ruins

Of Pompeii's original 66 hectares, 44 have now been excavated. Of course that doesn't mean you'll have unhindered access to every inch of the Unesco-listed site. The situation is a lot better than it used to be, but you're still likely to come across areas cordoned off for no apparent reason, a noticeable lack of clear signs and the odd stray dog. Audioguides are a sensible investment and a good guidebook will also help – try the €8 *Pompeii* published by Electa Napoli.

If visiting in summer, note that there's not much shade on site, so bring a hat, sun block and plenty of water. If you've got small children, try to visit in the early morning or late afternoon when the sun's not too hot. There's not much you can do about the uneven surfaces, unfortunately, which are a nightmare for strollers.

To do justice to Pompeii you should allow at least three or four hours, longer if you want to go into detail.

At the time of writing, the Casa dei Vettii and Terme del Foro were closed for restoration, and the Terme Suburbane were visitable subject to prior booking at www .arethusa.net. It's in the Terme Suburbane, just outside the city walls, that you'll find the erotic frescoes that so outraged the Catholic Church when they were revealed in 2001. The saucy panels decorate the changing rooms of what was once a private baths complex.

The site's main entrance is at **Porta Marina**, the most impressive of the seven gates that

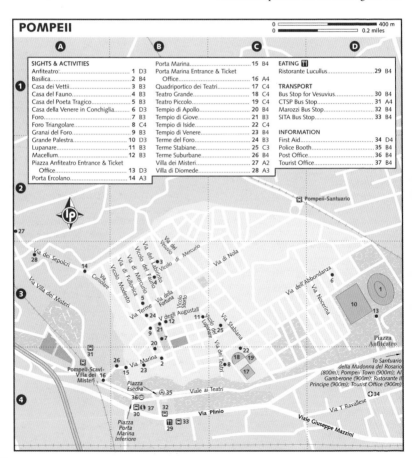

POMPEII

0 — 400 m
0 — 0.2 miles

SIGHTS & ACTIVITIES
Anfiteatro	1	D3
Basilica	2	B4
Casa dei Vettii	3	B3
Casa del Fauno	4	B3
Casa del Poeta Tragico	5	B3
Casa della Venere in Conchiglia	6	D3
Foro	7	B3
Foro Triangolare	8	C4
Granai del Foro	9	B3
Grande Palestra	10	D3
Lupanare	11	B3
Macellum	12	B3
Piazza Anfiteatro Entrance & Ticket Office	13	D3
Porta Ercolano	14	A3

Porta Marina	15	B4
Porta Marina Entrance & Ticket Office	16	A4
Quadriportico dei Teatri	17	C4
Teatro Grande	18	C4
Teatro Piccolo	19	C4
Tempio di Apollo	20	B4
Tempio di Giove	21	B3
Tempio di Iside	22	C4
Tempio di Venere	23	B4
Terme del Foro	24	B3
Terme Stabiane	25	C3
Terme Suburbane	26	B4
Villa dei Misteri	27	A2
Villa di Diomede	28	A3

EATING 🍴
Ristorante Lucullus	29	B4

TRANSPORT
Bus Stop for Vesuvius	30	B4
CTSP Bus Stop	31	A4
Marozzi Bus Stop	32	B4
SITA Bus Stop	33	B4

INFORMATION
First Aid	34	D4
Police Booth	35	B4
Post Office	36	B4
Tourist Office	37	B4

punctuated the ancient town walls. A busy passageway now as it was then, originally it connected the town with the nearby harbour. Immediately on the right as you enter the gate is the 1st-century BC **Tempio di Venere** (Temple of Venus), formerly one of the town's most opulent temples.

Continuing down Via Marina you come to the **basilica**, the 2nd-century BC seat of the city's law courts and exchange. Opposite the basilica, the **Tempio di Apollo** (Temple of Apollo) is the oldest and most important of Pompeii's religious buildings. Most of what you see today, including the striking columned portico, dates to the 2nd century BC, although fragments remain of an earlier version dating to the 6th century BC. The grassy **foro** (forum) adjacent to the temple was the ancient city's main piazza – a huge traffic-free rectangle flanked by limestone columns.

North of the forum stands the **Tempio di Giove** (Temple of Jupiter), which has one of two flanking triumphal arches remaining, and the **Granai del Foro** (Forum Granary), now used to store hundreds of amphorae and a number of body casts that were made in the late 19th century by pouring plaster into the hollows left by disintegrated bodies. The **macellum** nearby was once the city's main meat and fish market.

From the market head northeast along Via degli Augustali to Vicolo del Lupanare. Halfway down this narrow alley is the **Lupanare**, the city's only dedicated brothel. A tiny two-storey building with five rooms on each floor, it's lined with some of Pompeii's raunchiest frescoes.

At the end of Via dei Teatri, the green **Foro Triangolare** would originally have overlooked the sea and the River Sarno. The main attraction here was, and still is, the 2nd-century BC **Teatro Grande**, a 5000-seat theatre carved into the lava mass on which Pompeii was originally built. Behind the stage, the porticoed **Quadriportico dei Teatri** was initially used for the audience to stroll between acts, and later as a barracks for gladiators. Next door, the **Teatro Piccolo** (also known as the Odeion) was once an indoor theatre renowned for its acoustics, while the pre-Roman **Tempio di Iside** (Temple of Isis), was a popular place of cult worship.

Fresco detail from Casa della Venere in Conchiglia WITOLD SKRYPCZAK

Back on the main thoroughfare of Via dell'Abbondanza, the **Terme Stabiane** is a typical 2nd-century BC bath complex. Entering from the vestibule, bathers would stop off in the vaulted *apodyterium* (changing room) before passing through to the *tepidarium* (warm room) and *caldarium* (hot room).

Towards the northeastern end of Via dell'Abbondanza, **Casa della Venere in Conchiglia** (House of the Venus Marina) has recovered well from the WWII bomb that damaged it in 1943. Although unexceptional from the outside, it houses a lovely peristyle that looks onto a small, manicured garden. It's here in the garden that you'll find the striking Venus fresco after which the house is named.

The grassy **anfiteatro** nearby is the oldest known Roman amphitheatre in existence. Built in 70 BC, it was at one time capable of holding up to 20,000 bloodthirsty spectators. Over the way, the **Grande Palestra** is an athletics field with an impressive portico and, at its centre, the remains of a swimming pool.

From here, double back along Via dell'Abbondanza and turn right into Via Stabiana to see some of Pompeii's grandest houses. Turn left into Via della Fortuna and then right down Vicolo del Labirinto to get to Vicolo di Mercurio and the entrance to **Casa del Fauno** (House of the Faun), Pompeii's largest private house. Named after the small bronze statue in the *impluvium* (rain tank), it was here that early excavators found Pompeii's greatest mosaics, most of which are now in Naples' Museo Archeologico Nazionale (p78). A couple of blocks away, the **Casa del Poeta Tragico** (House of the Tragic

SANTUARIO DELLA MADONNA DEL ROSARIO

Dominating modern Pompeii's centre, the **Sanctuary of Our Lady of the Rosary** (☎ 081 857 71 11; Piazza Bartolo Longo; ⏰ 6.15am-7.30pm Mon-Sat, 5.45am-8.30pm Sun) was consecrated in 1891, some 15 years after the miracle that guaranteed its fame. In 1876 a young girl was cured of epilepsy after praying in front of the painting, *Virgin of the Rosary with Child*, which hangs above the main altar. News spread rapidly and to this day the painting is the subject of popular devotion.

The Santuario is flanked by a freestanding 80m **campanile** (bell tower; ☎ 081 850 70 00; ⏰ 9am-1pm & 3-6pm Sat-Thu).

Poet) features one of the world's first 'Beware of the Dog' – *Cave Canem* – warnings. To the north, the **Casa dei Vettii** on Vicolo di Mercurio is home to a famous depiction of Priapus whose oversized phallus balances on a pair of scales (see image on p45).

From here follow the road west and turn right into Via Consolare, which takes you out of the town through **Porta Ercolano**. Continue past **Villa di Diomede** and you'll come to **Villa dei Misteri**, one of the most complete structures left standing in Pompeii. The *Dionysiac Frieze*, the most important fresco still on site, spans the walls of the large dining room. One of the largest paintings from the ancient world, it depicts the initiation of a bride-to-be into the cult of Dionysus, the Greek god of wine.

Sleeping & Eating

There's really no great need to stay over night in Pompeii. It's easily visited on a day trip from Naples, Sorrento or Salerno, and once the excavations close, the area around the site becomes decidedly seedy.

Most of the restaurants near the ruins are large, characterless affairs set up for feeding coach-loads of tourists. Wander down to the modern town and it's a little better, with a couple of decent restaurants serving excellent local food.

If you need a bite on site, there is a perfectly good **canteen** (Via di Mercurio; meals around €18) near the Tempio di Giove (see p162).

AL GAMBERONE   TRATTORIA €
☎ 081 850 68 14; Via Piave 36; meals about €17; ⏰ Wed-Mon

Not far from Pompeii's landmark Santuario, this modest trattoria serves great food at honest prices. There's nothing particularly elaborate on the menu, just old favourites such as roast chicken and veg or *risotto pescatore* (seafood risotto).

RISTORANTE IL PRINCIPE   RISTORANTE €€€
☎ 081 850 55 66; Piazza B Longo 8; meals around €70; ⏰ daily Apr-Oct, Tue-Sat & lunch only Mon Nov-Mar

One of the top restaurants in the area, the Michelin-starred Prince specialises in historical local food. On your plate this translates to dishes such as spaghetti with *garum* (a strong Roman fish seasoning) or the restaurant's signature cassata cake, a rich ricotta affair inspired by a fresco in Oplontis (see p157).

RISTORANTE LUCULLUS   RISTORANTE €€
☎ 081 861 30 55; Via Plinio 129; pizzas from €6, meals around €22; ⏰ Wed-Mon

One of the better restaurants near the ruins, Lucullus is a good choice for pizza (count on all the usual toppings), pasta and meat classics such as *tagliatelle alla bolognese*, and risotto ai funghi porcini (risotto with mush-rooms). Vegetarians can go mad at the vast choice of mix-and-match contorni (vegetables).

Getting There & Away

The easiest way to get to Pompeii is by Circumvesuviana train. There are regular trains to Pompeii–Scavi–Villa dei Misteri station from Naples (€2.30, 40 minutes, about 30 daily) and Sorrento (€1.80, 30 minutes, about 30 daily). To get to Herculaneum from Pompeii, take the train for Naples and get off at Ercolano–Scavi station (€1.30).

SITA (☎ 199 73 07 49; www.sita-on-line.it in Italian) operates half-hourly buses to and from Naples (€2.30, 35 minutes), while **CSTP** (☎ 089 48 70 01; www.cstp.it in Italian) bus 50 runs to and from Salerno (€1.80, one hour, 15 daily). **Marozzi** (☎ 089 87 10 09; www.marozzivt.it in Italian) has a daily bus to and from Rome (€16, three hours).

Travelling by car, your best bet is to take the A3 from Naples. Look for the Pompeii exit and follow the signs to Pompeii Scavi. Car parks (approximately €4 per hour) are clearly marked and vigorously touted.

HERCULANEUM

Overshadowed by Pompeii, Herculaneum would elsewhere be the star of the show.

Buried under 16m of mud, Herculaneum is a minefield of archaeological treasures, from papyrus scrolls to mosaics, boats and skeletons. A superbly conserved Roman fishing town, it's smaller and less daunting than Pompeii (4.5 hectares as compared to Pompeii's 44), allowing you to visit without that nagging thought that you're bound to miss something important.

In contrast to modern Ercolano, an uninspiring Neapolitan suburb 12km south-east of Naples proper, classical Herculaneum was a peaceful fishing and port town of about 4000 inhabitants, and something of a resort for wealthy Romans and Campanians.

Its fate runs parallel to that of Pompeii. Destroyed by an earthquake in AD 62, it was completely submerged in the AD 79 eruption of Mt Vesuvius. Herculaneum is much closer to the volcano than Pompeii, so it drowned in a 16m-thick sea of mud that essentially fossilised the city. This meant that even delicate items, such as furniture and clothing, were discovered remarkably well preserved. Tragically, the inhabitants didn't fare so well; thousands of people tried to escape by boat but were suffocated by the volcano's poisonous gases.

The town was rediscovered in 1709 and amateur excavations were carried out intermittently until 1874, with many finds being carted off to Naples to decorate the houses of the well-to-do or to end up in museums. Serious archaeological work began again in 1927 and continues to this day, although with much of the ancient site buried beneath modern Ercolano it's slow going.

Orientation & Information

From the Circumvesuviana Ercolano–Scavi station, it's a simple 500m downhill walk to the ruins – follow the signs for the *scavi* (excavations) down the main street,

Via IV Novembre. En route you'll pass the **tourist office** on your right.

Herculaneum is much easier to navigate than Pompeii and can be done so with a map and audioguide. Pick up a free map and guide booklet from the **site information office** next to the **ticket office** before heading down the wide boulevard to the ruin's actual entrance, which is on the right shortly after the road curves.

On sale at the bookshop beside the exit, you'll find *Herculaneum, The Excavations, Local History & Surroundings* (€7), published by Electra, which provides a good historical insight into the town.

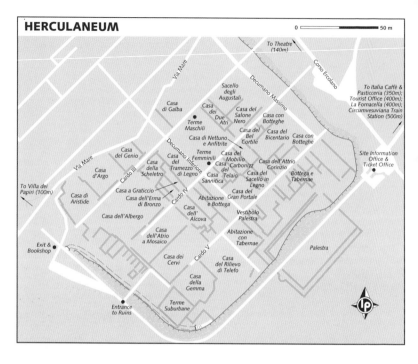

HERCULANEUM

0 ——— 50 m

To Theatre (140m)

Via Mare

Corso Ercolano

Sacello degli Augustali

To Italia Caffè & Pasticceria (350m); Tourist Office (400m); La Fornacella (400m); Circumvesuviana Train Station (500m)

Casa di Galba

Casa dei Due Atri

Casa del Salone Nero

Casa con Botteghe

Decumano Massimo

Terme Maschili

Casa del Bel Cortile

Casa del Bicentario

Casa con Botteghe

Casa di Nettuno e Anfitrite

Site Information Office & Ticket Office

Via Mare

Casa del Genio

Casa del Femminili

Terme Femminili

Casa del Mobilio Carbonizz

Casa dell'Attrio Corinzio

Decumano Inferiore

Casa d'Argo

Casa della Scheletro

Casa del Tramezzo di Legno

Casa del Telaio

Casa del Sacello in Legno

Bottega e Tabernae

Cardo III

Casa Sannitica

Casa a Graticcio

Cardo IV

Casa del Gran Portale

To Villa dei Papiri (100m)

Casa di Aristide

Casa dell'Erma di Bronzo

Abitazione e Bottega

Casa dell'Albergo

Casa dell' Alcova

Vestibolo Palestra

Casa dell'Atrio a Mosaico

Abitazione con Tabernae

Cardo V

Palestra

Exit & Bookshop

Casa dei Cervi

Casa del Rilievo di Telefo

Casa della Gemma

Entrance to Ruins

Terme Suburbane

The Ruins

The ruins are easily visited in a leisurely morning. Navigation is easy: the site is divided into 11 *insulae* (islands) carved up in a classic Roman grid pattern with Decumano Massimo and Decumano Inferiore running horizontally and Cardos III, IV and V vertically.

Note that at any given time some houses will invariably be shut for restoration; at the time of writing these included the Terme Suburbane and the Casa dell'Atrio a Mosaico.

To enter the ruins you pass through what appears to be a moat around the town but is in fact the ancient shoreline. It was here in 1980 that archaeologists discovered some 300 skeletons, the remains of a crowd that had fled to the beach only to be overcome by the terrible heat of surge clouds sweeping down from Vesuvius.

Marking the sites' southernmost tip the 1st-century AD **Terme Suburbane** (Suburban Baths) is one of the best preserved bath complexes in existence, with deep pools,

stucco friezes and bas-reliefs looking down upon marble seats and floors.

Nearby, and accessible from Cardo V, **Casa dei Cervi** (House of the Deers) is an imposing example of a Roman noble family's house. The two-storey villa, built around a central courtyard, contains murals and some beautiful still-life paintings. In the courtyard is a diminutive pair of marble deer assailed by dogs, and an engaging statue of a peeing Hercules.

Continuing up Cardo V, turn left into Decumano Inferiore for the **Casa del Gran Portale** (House of the Large Portal), named after the elegant brick Corinthian columns that flank its main entrance. Inside you'll find some well-preserved wall paintings.

To the southwest the **Casa dell'Atrio a Mosaico** (House of the Mosaic Atrium) on Cardo IV is an impressive mansion with extensive floor mosaics, although time and nature have left the floor buckled and uneven. Particularly noteworthy is the black-and-white chessboard mosiac in the atrium.

For even more impressive mosaics head up Cardo IV to the **Casa di Nettuno e Anfitrite**

VILLA DEI PAPIRI

The Villa dei Papiri (Villa of the Papyri) was the most luxurious villa in Herculaneum. Owned by Lucius Calpurnius Piso Caesoninus, Julius Caesar's father-in-law, it was a vast four-storey, 245m-long complex stretching down to the sea; there were swimming pools, fountains and a collection of up to 80 sculptures. There was also an important library and it is the 1800 papyrus scrolls found there that gave the villa its name.

Most of the carbonised scrolls, now in Naples' Museo Archeologico Nazionale (p78) contain works by the minor Epicurean philosopher Philodemus (multispectral imaging has enabled scholars to decipher the writing on the blackened papyri), although researchers still hope to find writings by Aristotle, Livy and Sappho among the thousands still to be recovered.

Excavation work on the villa has been continuing on and off since 1765 – in the 1990s two new floors were revealed – yet up to 2800 sq m remain to be explored. At the time of writing, work was at a halt subject to the outcome of a feasibility report, even though financing has already been secured – the American millionaire David W Packard (of Hewlett-Packard fame) has promised to pay for any further excavations.

To visit the villa, of which only the atrium and parts of the upper floors are open to the public, you need to book ahead. The easiest way to do so is to go online at www.arethusa.net. Visits are limited to groups of 25 people on Saturdays and Sundays between 9am and 5pm.

(House of Neptune & Amphitrite). This aristocratic house takes its name from the extraordinary mosaic in the *nymphaeum* (fountain and bath), depicting Neptune and Amphitrite. The warm colours in which the two deities are depicted hint at how lavish the original interior must once have been.

Over the road, the **Terme Femminili** was the women's section of the Terme del Foro (Forum Baths) – the male half, the **Terme Maschili**, is accessible from Cardo III. While women passed from the *apodyterium* (note the finely executed naked figure of Triton adorning the mosaic floor) through the *tepidarium* to the *caldarium*, men had the added bracing option of the *frigidarium* (cold bath). You can still see the benches where bathers sat and the wall shelves for their clothing.

At the northeastern end of Cardo IV, along Decumano Massimo, a crucifix found in an upstairs room of the **Casa del Bicentenario** (Bicentenary House) provides possible evidence of a Christian presence in pre-Vesuvius Herculaneum.

Virtually the last house on Cardo III before the exit, the noble **Casa d'Argo** (Argus House) would originally have opened onto Cardo II (as yet unearthed). Onto its porticoed, palm-treed garden open a *triclinium* and other residential rooms.

North of the ruins along Corso Ercolano are the remains of a **theatre**, dating from the Augustan period, and the **Villa dei Papiri** are to the northwest (see above).

Sleeping & Eating

As with Pompeii, you're unlikely to want to stay over night at Ercolano – there's not much to see other than the ruins, and it's an easy rail journey from Naples or Sorrento. There are a couple of places to grab a bite.

ITALIA CAFFÈ & PASTICCERIA   CAFÉ €
☎ 081 732 14 99; Corso Italia 17; snacks from €3
Just off Via IV Novembre, this run-of-the-mill café serves refreshing *granite* (flavoured ice drinks), decent coffee and great cakes. Pick up a snack for your journey or sit and munch on the pavement seats.

LA FORNACELLA   RISTORANTE €
☎ 081 777 48 61; Via IV Novembre 90-92; set menu €7
Touristy and not very inviting, La Fornacella nevertheless dishes up pretty good food. The lunchtime menu (pasta, main course and side dish) is good value at €7, with dishes like *pollo alla cacciatora* (chicken baked with tomatoes and paprika) and fresh grilled vegetables. If you really want to fill up fast, grab a couple of wedges of fried spaghetti with tomato.

Getting There & Away

By far the easiest way to get to Ercolano from Naples or Sorrento is by the Circumvesuviana train (get off at Ercolano–Scavi station). Trains run regularly throughout the day and single tickets cost €1.70 to and from Naples, €1.30 for Pompeii and €1.80 for Sorrento.

If you're driving from Naples, take the A3 and exit at Ercolano Portico, and following the signs to car parks near the site's entrance.

Tempio di Nettuno, Paestum

ROBERTO SONON GEROMETTA

PAESTUM

Paestum's unforgettable Unesco-listed temples are among the best-preserved monuments of Magna Graecia, the Greek colony that once covered much of southern Italy.

Paestum, or Poseidonia as the city was originally called (in honour of Poseidon, the Greek god of the sea), was founded in the 6th century BC by Greek settlers and fell under Roman control in 273 BC. Decline later set in following the demise of the Roman Empire. Savage raids by the Saracens and periodic outbreaks of malaria forced the ever-dwindling population to abandon the city altogether. Its temples were rediscovered in the late 18th century but the site as a whole wasn't unearthed until the 1950s.

The first temple you meet on entering the site from the northern end is the 6th-century-BC Tempio di Cerere (Temple of Ceres). Originally dedicated to Athena, it served as a Christian church in medieval times.

As you head south you can pick out the basic outline of the large rectangular forum, the heart of the ancient city. Among the partially standing buildings are the vast domestic housing area and, further south, the amphitheatre.

The **Tempio di Nettuno** (Temple of Neptune), dating from about 450 BC, is the largest and best preserved of the three temples at Paestum; only parts of its inside walls and roof are missing. Almost next door, the so-called **basilica** (in fact, a temple to the goddess Hera) is Paestum's oldest surviving monument. Dating from the middle of the 6th century BC, it's a magnificent sight with nine columns across and 18 along the sides.

Just east of the site, the **museum** houses a collection of much-weathered metopes (bas-relief friezes). This collection includes 33 of the original 36 metopes from **Tempio di Argiva Hera** (Temple of Argive Hera), situated 9km north of Paestum, of which virtually nothing else remains. The star exhibit, however, is the 5th-century BC frescoes *Tomba del Truffatore* (Tomb of the Diver), whose depiction of a diver in midair is thought to represent the passage from life to death.

There are various restaurants on site, of which the best is the **Ristorante Nettuno** (☎ 0828 81 10 28; Via Principe di Piemonte; meals around €25) near the southern entrance. Alternatively you can buy some mozzarella from the nearby **La Fattoria del Casaro** (☎ 0828 72 27 04; Via Licinella 5).

For a place to stay, **Hotel Villa Rita** (☎ 0828 81 10 81; www.hotelvillarita.it; s/d incl breakfast €62/88; ✖ ♋) has comfortable three-star rooms and a swimming pool in its own verdant grounds.

Winding seaside path, Capri (p172)

BAY OF NAPLES & THE AMALFI COAST

A vertical world of gleaming limestone cliffs and hidden coves, of romantic corners and blue horizons, a world where boats outnumber cars and stairs serve in place of streets.

The Amalfi Coast is the most spectacular stretch of coastline in Italy and, indeed, one of the most entrancing in Europe. The heady mix of stunning scenery, legend and romance has been seducing visitors since Roman times. The contrast couldn't be greater between coast and city: just an hour down the road from the urban mayhem of central Naples and you're in a different world.

Yet its stunning topography has not always been a blessing. For centuries after the passing of Amalfi's glory days as a maritime superpower (from the 9th to the 12th centuries), the area was poor, its isolated villages regular victims of foreign incursions, earthquakes and landslides. But it was this very isolation that first drew visitors in the early 1900s, paving the way for the advent of tourism in the latter half of the century. Today, the Amalfi Coast is one of Italy's top tourist destinations, a favourite of well-to-do jet-setters and young couples seeking romance.

There are two main entry points to the coast: to the west **Sorrento** and 50km further east **Salerno**. The former, a cliff-top resort whose charm has miraculously survived the onslaught of package tourism, is not actually on the Amalfi Coast but on the northern side of the Sorrento Peninsula (the thin strip of land that divides the Bay of Naples from the Gulf of Salerno). However, it's only a short and spectacular drive away from pastel-hued **Positano**, the Amalfi Coast's smartest and most expensive town.

It's also the nearest point to **Capri**, the most famous and fashionable of the bay's three islands. A day-trip mecca, Capri is an intriguing mix of luxury hotels, designer boutiques

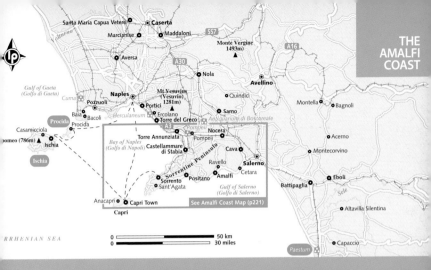

Santa Maria Capua Vetere
Caserta
Marcianise
Maddaloni
SS7
Aversa
A30
Nola
Monte Vergine 1493m
A16
Avellino
Mt Vesuvius (Vesuvio) 1281m
Quindici
Naples
Pozzuoli
Portici
Cuma
Baia
Bacoli
Herculaneum
Ercolano
Torre del Greco
Antiquarium di Boscoreale
Montella
Bagnoli
Casamicciola
Procida
Procida
Torre Annunziata
Pompeii
Nocera
Sarno
Acerno
omeo (786m)
Ischia
Bay of Naples (Golfo di Napoli)
Castellammare di Stabia
Cava
Montecorvino
Ischia
Sorrentine Peninsula
Ravello
Salerno
Sorrento
Positano
Amalfi
Cetara
Eboli
Anacapri
Sant'Agata
Gulf of Salerno (Golfo di Salerno)
Battipaglia
Capri Town
See Amalfi Coast Map (p221)
Capri
Sele
RRHENIAN SEA
0   50 km
0   30 miles
Altavilla Silentina
Paestum
Capaccio
Gulf of Gaeta (Golfo di Gaeta)

HIGHLIGHTS

- Take the chairlift to the top of **Monte Solaro** (p177), the highest point in Capri, and walk back down again
- Chill out with a seafront beer at **Marina Corricella** (p201) in Procida
- Enjoy a classical music concert in the fabulous gardens of **Villa Rufolo** (p238), in Ravello
- Sample *limoncello* in **Sorrento** (p204) while looking over the water to Mt Vesuvius
- Hike down to the **Bay of Ieranto** (p219) for the coast's best swimming

and unspoiled Mediterranean countryside. To the northwest, **Ischia** has long sold itself on its curative spa waters, lush gardens and fine beaches, while a short ferry ride away **Procida** is the smallest and least developed of the islands. Although not totally free of tourism, its colourful fishing villages retain an authenticity that's not always apparent elsewhere.

Back on the mainland, **Amalfi** is a pretty little town with a weighty history of maritime power and commerce. Today, however, its revenue comes mainly from the tourists disgorged daily from the ferries to idle around the Piazza del Duomo, wander the medieval streets and visit the extraordinary cathedral.

Perched above the coast is aloof **Ravello**, famed for its Wagnerian connection and grandiose villas. Finally, and by way of the ceramic town of **Vietri sul Mare**, there is **Salerno**, a workaday port whose appeal lies in its lack of souvenir shops and vibrant centro storico (historic centre).

Waterfront at Marina Corricella, Procida (p201)   DALLAS STRIBLEY

Capri's limestone Isole Faraglioni (p175)

HOLGER LEUE

HIGHLIGHTS

- Wash yourself in the hallucinogenic blue light of the **Grotta Azzurra** (see the boxed text, p178)
- Give your imagination a work-out in the vast ruins of Tiberius' **Villa Jovis** (p176)
- Walk the **Sentiero dei Fortini** (see Stretch Your Legs, p176), the scenic path that runs down the island's unexplored west coast
- Take the chairlift to the top of **Monte Solaro** (p177) and revel in the unbelievable views
- Treat yourself to a drink in **la Piazzetta** (p174), the centre of café life in Capri Town

CAPRI

Cliffs, cafés, villas, VIPs and vistas – Capri has charmed Roman emperors, Russian revolutionaries and a who's who of showbiz stars.

Ever since the Roman Emperor Tiberius earned Capri (pronounced *Ca*-pri, with the stress on the first syllable) a reputation as a decadent retreat, the island has fuelled the public imagination. A stark mass of limestone rock that sheers up through impossibly blue water, it's the perfect microcosm of Mediterranean appeal – a smooth cocktail of chichi piazzas and cool cafés, Roman ruins and rugged seascapes.

It's also a hugely popular day trip destination and a summer favourite of holidaying VIPs. Inevitably, the two main centres, **Capri Town** and its uphill rival **Anacapri**, are almost entirely given over to tourism and prices are high. But explore beyond the designer boutiques and pointedly traditional trattorie and you'll find that Capri's rural hinterland retains an unspoiled charm with grand villas, overgrown vegetable plots, sun-bleached peeling stucco and banks of brilliantly coloured bougainvillea. All of this overlooks deep blue water that laps unseen into secluded coves and mysterious grottoes.

There are few must-sees on the island but there's one you'd be sorry to miss. The **Grotta Azzurra** (Blue Cave) might be Capri's most visited sight but the impact of the ethereal blue light is no less powerful for the crowds and singing boat owners. On the island's other extremity, the ruins of **Villa Jovis** testify to the presence of the infamous Tiberius.

Already inhabited in the Palaeolithic age, Capri was briefly occupied by the Greeks before the Emperor Augustus made it his private playground, and Tiberius retired here in AD 27. Its modern incarnation as a tourist centre dates to the early 20th century when it was invaded by an army of European artists, writers and Russian revolutionaries.

ORIENTATION

About 5km from the mainland at its nearest point, Capri is a mere 6km long and 2.7km wide. As you approach, there's a great camera shot of Capri Town with the dramatic slopes of Monte Solaro (589m) to the west, hiding the village of Anacapri.

All hydrofoils and ferries arrive at Marina Grande, the island's transport hub. The quickest way up

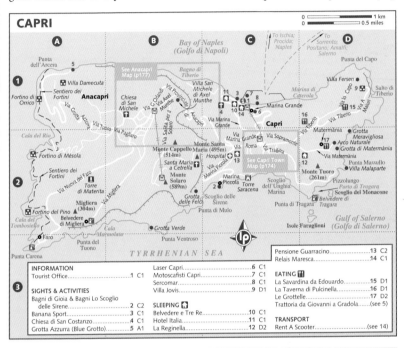

CAPRI

INFORMATION	
Tourist Office	1 C1
SIGHTS & ACTIVITIES	
Bagni di Gioia & Bagni Lo Scoglio delle Sirene	2 C2
Banana Sport	3 C1
Chiesa di San Costanzo	4 C1
Grotta Azzurra (Blue Grotto)	5 A1
Laser Capri	6 C1
Motoscafisti Capri	7 C1
Sercomar	8 C1
Vula Jovis	9 D1
SLEEPING	
Belvedere e Tre Re	10 C1
Hotel Italia	11 C1
La Reginella	12 D2
Pensione Guarracino	13 C2
Relais Maresca	14 C1
EATING	
La Savardina da Edouardo	15 D1
La Taverna di Pulcinella	16 D1
Le Grottelle	17 D2
Trattoria da Giovanni a Gradola	(see 5)
TRANSPORT	
Rent A Scooter	(see 14)

INFORMATION

- **Anacapri** (www.anacapri-life.com) News and information about Anacapri.
- **Capri Internet Point** (Map p177; ☎ 081 837 32 83; Via de Tommaso 1, Anacapri; per hr €4; ☘ 8am-9pm Mon-Sat, 8am-2pm Sun May-Oct, shorter hours Nov-Apr) Also has international newspapers and some English books for sale.
- **Capri Island** (www.capri.net) Excellent website with listings, itineraries and ferry schedules.
- **Capri Tourism** (www.capritourism.com) Official website of Capri tourist office.
- **Exchange office** (Map p177; ☎ 081 837 31 46; Piazza Vittoria 2b, Anacapri; ☘ 8.30am-6pm daily)
- **Farmacia Barile** (Map p177; ☎ 081 837 14 60; Piazza Vittoria 28, Anacapri)
- **Farmacia Internazionale** (Map p174; ☎ 081 837 04 85; Via Roma 24, Capri Town)
- **Hospital** (Map p173; ☎ 081 838 11 11; Via Provinciale di Anacapri 5, Capri Town)

- **Police station** (Map p174; ☎ 081 837 42 11; Via Roma 70, Capri Town)
- **Post office Anacapri** (Map p177; ☎ 081 837 10 15; Via de Tommaso 8, Anacapri)
- **Post office Capri Town** (Map p174; ☎ 081 978 52 11; Via Roma 50, Capri Town)
- **San Paolo Banco di Napoli** (Map p177; ☎ 081 838 21 69; Via G Orlandi 150, Anacapri) ATM.
- **Tourist office Anacapri** (Map p177; ☎ 081 837 15 24; www.capritourism.com; Via G Orlandi 59, Anacapri; ☘ 8.30am-8.30pm Jun-Sep, 9am-3pm Mon-Sat Oct-Dec & Mar-May)
- **Tourist office Capri Town** (Map p174; ☎ 081 837 06 86; www.capritourism.com; Piazza Umberto I, Capri Town; ☘ 8.30am-8.30pm Jun-Sep, 9am-1pm & 3.30-6.45pm Mon-Sat Oct-May)
- **Tourist Office Marina Grande** (Map p173; ☎ 081 837 06 34; www.capritourism.com; ☘ 9am-1pm & 3.30-6.45pm Jun-Sep, 9am-3pm Mon-Sat Oct-May)
- **Unicredit Banca** (Map p174; ☎ 081837 05 11; Via Roma 57, Capri Town) ATM.

to Capri Town from here is by funicular, but there are also buses and taxis. On foot, it's a tough 2.25km climb along Via Marina Grande. At the top, turn left (east) at the junction with Via Roma for the centre of town or right (west) for Via Provinciale di Anacapri, which eventually becomes Via G Orlandi as it leads up to Anacapri.

Pint-sized Piazza Umberto I is the focal point of Capri Town. A short hop to the east, Via Vittorio Emanuele leads down to the main shopping street, Via Camerelle.

Up the hill in Anacapri, buses and taxis drop you off in Piazza Vittoria, from where Via G Orlandi, the main strip, runs southwest and Via Capodimonte heads up to Villa San Michele di Axel Munthe.

SIGHTS & ACTIVITIES
Capri Town

With its whitewashed stone buildings and tiny, car-free streets, Capri Town seems more film set than real life. A diminutive model of upmarket Mediterranean chic, it's a pristine mix of luxury hotels, expensive bars, restaurants and designer boutiques. In summer its toy-town streets swell with crowds of curious, camera-wielding daytrippers and gangs of the glossy rich.

Central to the Capri experience is **Piazza Umberto I** (aka la Piazzetta), the showy, open-air salon beneath the town's clock tower. This is the place to sit and watch the world go by, or, more importantly, to sit and let the world watch you watch it go by. When you feel like a little exercise, pop up the stairs to the baroque 17th-century **Chiesa di Santo Stefano** (Map p174; ☎ 081 837 00 72; Piazza Umberto I; ⏱ 8am-8pm daily), with its well-preserved marble floor (taken from Villa Jovis, see p176) and statue of San Costanzo, Capri's patron saint. Note also the pair of languidly reclining patricians in the chapel to the south of the main altar, who seem to mirror some of the roués in the cafés outside. Beside the northern chapel is a reliquary with a saintly bone that reputedly saved Capri from the plague in the 19th century.

Over the road, the **Museo del Centro Caprense i Cerio** (Map p174; ☎ 081 837 66 81; Piazzetta Cerio 5; adult/under 14yr & over 65yr €2.60/1; ⏱ 10am-1pm

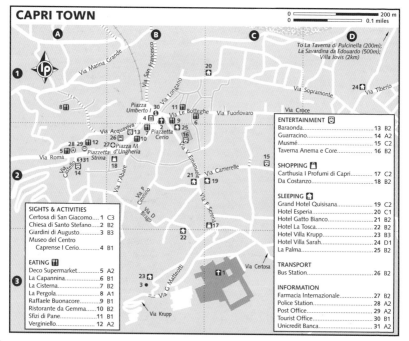

CAPRI TOWN

To La Taverna di Pulcinella (200m);
La Savardina da Edouardo (500m);
Villa Jovis (2km)

SIGHTS & ACTIVITIES
Certosa di San Giacomo.... 1 C3
Chiesa di Santo Stefano....2 B2
Giardini di Augusto...........3 B3
Museo del Centro
    Caprense I Cerio...........4 B1

EATING 🍴
Deco Supermarket...........5 A2
La Capannina.................6 B1
La Cisterna...................7 A2
La Pergola....................8 A1
Raffaele Buonacore.........9 B1
Ristorante da Gemma......10 B2
Sfizi di Pane.................11 B1
Verginiello..................12 A2

ENTERTAINMENT 🎭
Baraonda......................13 B2
Guarracino...................14 A2
Musmé........................15 C2
Taverna Anema e Core......16 B2

SHOPPING 🛍
Carthusia I Profumi di Capri...17 C2
Da Costanzo..................18 B2

SLEEPING 🛏
Grand Hotel Quisisana......19 C2
Hotel Esperia................20 C1
Hotel Gatto Bianco..........21 B2
Hotel La Tosca...............22 B2
Hotel Villa Krupp............23 B3
Hotel Villa Sarah............24 D1
La Palma.....................25 B2

TRANSPORT
Bus Station..................26 B2

INFORMATION
Farmacia Internazionale....27 B2
Police Station................28 A2
Post Office...................29 A2
Tourist Office................30 B1
Unicredit Banca..............31 A2

Port views, Capri Town   DALLAS STRIBLEY

FOR THE BEST VIEWS HEAD TO...

- Monte Solaro (p177)
- Belvedere di Tragara (see the boxed text, p176)
- Villa Jovis (p176)
- Villa San Michele di Axel Munthe (p177)
- Villa Damecuta (p178)

Tue-Sat) has a library of books and journals about the island (mostly in Italian), and a collection of locally found Neolithic and Palaeolithic fossils.

To the east of the Piazzetta, Via Vittorio Emanuele and its continuation Via F Serena lead down to the picturesque **Certosa di San Giacomo** (Map p174; ☎ 081 837 62 18; Viale Certosa 40; ☾ 9am-2pm Tue-Sun), a 14th-century monastery generally considered to be the finest remaining example of Caprese architecture. Established between 1363 and 1371 by Giacomo Arucci, a local nobleman and secretary to the Angevin Queen of Naples, Giovanna I, it became the stronghold of the island's powerful Carthusian fraternity. It was eventually closed in the early 19th century on the orders of Napoleon's occupying forces and today houses a school, library and a museum with some fairly forgettable 17th-century paintings. There are two cloisters – the smaller of which dates to the 14th century, the larger to the 16th century – and some fine 17th-century frescoes in the church.

Southwest of the monastery, at the end of Via G Matteotti, the colourful **Giardini di Augusto** (Gardens of Augustus; Map p174; ☾ dawn-dusk daily) were founded by the Emperor Augustus. The view from the gardens is breathtaking, looking over to the **Isole Faraglioni** (Map p173), three limestone pinnacles rising vertically out of the sea. Measuring 109m, 81m and 104m respectively, the stacks are home to a rare blue lizard that was once thought to be unique to the Faraglioni but has since been found on the Sicilian coast.

From the gardens, **Via Krupp** zigzags down to Marina Piccola. Named after the German steel manufacturer Alfred Krupp, the road is now closed for safety reasons. Curiously, there's a bust of Lenin overlooking the road from a nearby platform.

For further views of the Faraglioni, head for the Belvedere at the end of Via Tragara.

STRETCH YOUR LEGS

Surprisingly for such a small place, Capri offers some memorable hiking. A network of well-maintained paths weaves its way across the island, leading through areas that even in the height of summer are all but deserted. The following are the island's four best routes.

Capri to Arco Naturale, Grotta di Matermània & Belvedere di Tragara

This classic Capri walk leads from the Arco Naturale 1.2km along the coast to the Belvedere di Tragara.

From the Arco Naturale, at the end of Via Matermània, backtrack to Le Grottelle restaurant and take the nearby set of stairs. About halfway down you'll pass the Grotta di Matermània, a giant natural cave used by the Romans as a *nymphaeum* (shrine to the water nymph) and dedicated to the Mater Magna (Great Mother). At the bottom, continue down the path as it follows the rocky coastline south. The bizarre red villa you eventually see on your left, on the Punta Massullo promontory, is Villa Malaparte, the former holiday home of Tuscan writer Curzio Malaparte (1898–1957). Carrying on, the sea views become increasingly impressive as the path continues westward around the lower slopes of Monte Tuoro. A few hundred metres further along and you come to a staircase on the right, which leads up to the Belvedere di Tragara and some stunning views of the Isole Faraglioni.

To get back to the centre of Capri Town simply follow Via Tragara and its continuation Via Camerelle.

Anacapri to Monte Solaro

Rising 589m above Anacapri, Monte Solaro is Capri's highest point. To get to the top you can either take the *seggiovia* (chairlift) from Piazza Vittoria or you can walk (about 2km). To do the latter take Via Axel Munthe and turn right up Via Salita per il Solaro. Follow the steep trail until you come to the pass known as La Crocetta, marked by a difficult-to-miss iron crucifix. Here the path divides: go right for the summit and its spectacular views over the Bay of Naples and Amalfi Coast; go left for the valley of Cetrella and the picturesque hermitage of Santa Maria a Cetrella (generally open on Saturday afternoon until sunset).

If you don't fancy the walk up, do what many people do and take the chairlift up and walk down.

Anacapri to Belvedere di Migliera

A lovely, relaxing 2km walk, this leads out to the Belvedere di Migliera, a panoramic platform with spectacular sea views.

The route couldn't be simpler: from Piazza Vittoria take Via Caposcuro and continue straight along its continuation Via Migliera. Along the way you'll pass fruit orchards, vineyards and small patches of woodland. Once at the Belvedere you can return to Anacapri via the Torre di Materita or, if you've still got the legs, continue up Monte Solaro. Note, however, that this is a tough walk graded medium by the Club Alpino Italiano (CAI; Italian Alpine Club).

Carena to Punta dell'Arcera, the Sentiero dei Fortini

Snaking its way along the island's oft-overlooked western coast, the Sentiero dei Fortini (Path of the Small Forts; 5.2km) takes you from Punta Carena, the island's southwestern point, up to Punta dell'Arcera near the Grotta Azzurra in the north. Named after the three coastal forts (Pino, Mèsola and Orrico) along the way, it passes through some of Capri's most unspoiled countryside.

Villa Jovis & Around

East of the town centre, a comfortable 2km walk along Via Tiberio, is **Villa Jovis** (Jupiter's Villa; Map p173; ☎ 081 837 06 34; Via Tiberio; adult/EU citizen 18-25yr/EU citizen under 18yr & over 65yr €2/1/free; ☾ 9am until 1hr before sunset), also known as the Palazzo di Tiberio. Standing 354m above sea level, this was the largest and most sumptuous of the island's 12 Roman villas and was Tiberius' main Capri residence. It's not in great nick today but the size of the ruins gives an idea of the scale on which Tiberius liked to live. His private rooms, offering superb views over to the Punta della Campanella, were on the northern and eastern sides of the complex.

Spectacular but hardly practical, the villa's location posed major headaches for Tiberius' architects. The main problem was how to collect and store enough water to supply the villa's baths and 3000-sq-m gardens. The solution they eventually hit upon was to build a complex canal system to transport rainwater to four giant storage tanks, the remains of which are clearly visible today.

The stairway behind the villa leads to the 330m-high **Salto di Tiberio** (Tiberius' Leap; Map p173), a sheer cliff from where, says the story, Tiberius had out-of-favour subjects hurled into the sea.

Close to the villa, down Via Tiberio and Via Matermània, is the **Arco Naturale**, a huge rock arch formed by the pounding sea.

Anacapri & Around

Traditionally Capri Town's quieter and less forward sister, modern Anacapri is no stranger to tourism. But attention is largely limited to Villa San Michele di Axel Munthe and the souvenir stores on the main streets. Get off these – and it only really takes a couple of minutes' walking to do so – and you'll discover that Anacapri is still, at heart, the laid-back, rural village that it's always been.

Coming up from Capri Town, the bus (or taxi) deposits you in Piazza Vittoria, from where it's a short walk to **Villa San Michele di Axel Munthe** (Map p173; ☎ 081 837 14 01; Via Axel Munthe; admission €5; ⏱ 9am-6pm May-Sep, 10.30am-3.30pm Nov-Feb, 9.30am-4.30pm Mar, 9.30am-5pm Apr & Oct), the former home of self-aggrandising Swedish doctor Axel Munthe. The story behind the villa, built on the ruined site of a Roman villa, is told by Munthe himself in his bestselling autobiography *The Story of San Michele* (1929). Other than the collection of Roman sculpture, the villa's best feature is the beautifully preserved garden and its superb views. In summer, the **Axel Munthe Foundation** (☎ 081 837 14 01; www .sanmichele.org) organises evening concerts in the gardens.

Beyond the villa, Via Axel Munthe continues to the 800-step stairway leading down to Capri Town. Built in the early 19th century, this was the only link between Anacapri and the rest of the island until the present mountain road was constructed in the 1950s. Throughout history, the people of Capri and Anacapri have been at loggerheads and they are always ready to trot out their respective patron saints to ward off the *mal'occhio* (evil eye) of their rivals.

Anacapri's other great attraction is the **Seggiovia del Monte Solaro** (Map p177; ☎ 081 837 14 28; single/return €5/6.50; ⏱ 9.30am-5pm Mar-Oct, 10.30am-3pm Nov-Feb), a chairlift that whisks you to the top of Monte Solaro in 12 minutes. The views from the top are quite outstanding – on a clear day you can see the entire Bay of Naples, the Amalfi Coast and the islands of Ischia and Procida.

Back in Anacapri, the baroque **Chiesa di San Michele** (Map p177; ☎ 081 837 23 96; Piazza San Nicola;

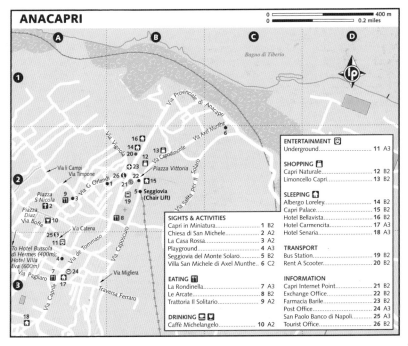

ANACAPRI

0 _____ 400 m
0 _____ 0.2 miles

Bagno di Tiberio

ENTERTAINMENT
Underground......................... 11 A3

SHOPPING
Capri Naturale...................... 12 B2
Limoncello Capri.................... 13 B2

SLEEPING
Albergo Loreley..................... 14 B2
Capri Palace........................ 15 B2
Hotel Bellavista.................... 16 B2
Hotel Carmencita.................... 17 A3
Hotel Senaria....................... 18 A3

SIGHTS & ACTIVITIES
Capri in Miniatura.................. 1 B2
Chiesa di San Michele............... 2 A2
La Casa Rossa....................... 3 A2
Playground.......................... 4 A3
Seggiovia del Monte Solaro.......... 5 B2
Villa San Michele di Axel Munthe.. 6 C2

TRANSPORT
Bus Station......................... 19 B2
Rent A Scooter...................... 20 B2

EATING
La Rondinella....................... 7 A3
Le Arcate........................... 8 B2
Trattoria Il Solitario.............. 9 A2

INFORMATION
Capri Internet Point................ 21 B2
Exchange Office..................... 22 B2
Farmacia Barile..................... 23 B2
Post Office......................... 24 A3
San Paolo Banco di Napoli........... 25 A3
Tourist Office...................... 26 B2

DRINKING
Caffè Michelangelo.................. 10 A2

GROTTA AZZURRA

Capri's single most famous attraction is the **Grotta Azzurra** (Blue Grotto; Map p173; adult/EU citizen under 18yr & over 65yr €4/free; ⏱ 9am until 1hr before sunset), a stunning sea cave illuminated by an other-worldly blue light.

Long known to local fishermen, it was rediscovered by two Germans – writer Augustus Kopisch and painter Ernst Fries – in 1826. Subsequent research, however, revealed that Emperor Tiberius had built a quay in the cave around AD 30, complete with a *nymphaeum* (shrine to the water nymph). You can still see the carved Roman landing stage towards the rear of the cave.

Measuring 54m by 30m and rising to a height of 15m, the grotto is said to have sunk by up to 20m in prehistoric times, blocking every opening except the 1.3m-high entrance. And it's this that's the key to the magical blue light. Sunlight enters through a small underwater aperture and is refracted through the water; this, combined with the reflection of the light off the white sandy seafloor, produces the vivid blue effect to which the cave owes its name.

The easiest way to visit is to take a boat tour from Marina Grande. A return trip will cost €18.50, comprising a return motorboat to the cave (€10), the rowing boat into the cave itself (€4.50) and admission fee (adult/EU citizen under 18yr & over 65yr €4/free); allow a good hour. You only save a little money and lose a lot of time by catching a bus from Anacapri or Capri since you still have to pay for the rowing boat and admission fee. The singing 'captains' are included in the price, so don't feel any obligation if they push for a tip.

The grotto is closed if the sea is too choppy, so before embarking check that it's open at the Marina Grande tourist office, about 25m from the motorboat ticket booth.

Swimming in the cave is forbidden but you can swim outside the entrance – get a bus to Grotta Azzurra, take the stairs down to the right and dive off the small concrete platform.

adult/child €1/free; ⏱ 9.30am-7pm Apr-Oct, 9.30am-3pm Nov-Mar) is memorable for its 18th-century majolica floor, representing Adam and Eve in earthly paradise. More notable than the holy duo, however, are the vivid animal depictions, which include a unicorn, bull, several goats and an elephant.

On Via G Orlandi, **Capri in Miniatura** (Map p177; ☎ 081 837 1082 101; Via G Orlandi 101; admission €3; ⏱ 9am-6pm daily) might amuse the kids for a minute or two. A scale model of the island set in a ceramic bath and festooned with bonsai trees, it took a year and a half to carve out of island rock. In the surrounding walls you can also see modelled scenes from Capri's history. If the little 'uns are still playing up there's a **playground** with swings and a climbing frame further down Via G Orlandi (turn left as you exit Capri in Miniatura and follow the road as it bears left until you see the park on your left).

Still on Via G Orlandi, **La Casa Rossa** (Map p177; ☎ 081 837 21 93; Via G Orlandi; admission €2; ⏱ 10.30am-1.30pm & 6.30-9.30pm daily), is hard to miss. The red house was built by an American colonel, JC Mackowen, in the late 19th century and today houses an odd collection of antiquities and paintings.

To the northeast of Anacapri, near the island's heliport, are the remains of **Villa Damecuta** (Map p173; admission free; ⏱ 9am until 1hr

before sunset), one of the largest of Tiberius' 12 Capri residences. There's not a lot left to see but it's a lovely tranquil spot, with views over to Ischia and the Bay of Naples. The easiest way to get here is to take the Grotta Azzurra bus from Anacapri and ask the driver to set you down nearby.

Rising above Punta Carena, Capri's rugged southwesterly point, is the **faro** (Map p173), Italy's second-tallest and most powerful lighthouse. The rocks nearby are a popular swimming spot in the summer. From Anacapri a bus runs to the *faro* every 20 minutes in summer and every 40 minutes in winter.

Marina Grande

Capri's main port is a chaotic and shabby place with little evidence of the glitz that awaits up the hill. There's little to see, although if you're desperate for a swim there's a 200m-long pebble beach to the west of the port. Capri's oldest church, the 5th-century **Chiesa di San Costanzo** (Map p173; ☎ 081 837 70 28; Via Marina Grande) is also a short walk away. The whitewashed church is dedicated to the island's patron saint, who settled on the island after escaping a vicious storm en route from Constantinople to Rome. It was originally built over an earlier Roman construction, although the Byzantine version you see today is the result of a 10th-century make-over.

The marina is the hub of Capri's thriving water sports business and it's here you should come to hire a boat or book a dive. On the eastern edge of the waterfront, **Sercomar** (Map p173; ☎ 081 837 87 81; www.caprisub .com; Via Colombo 64; ☒ closed Nov) offers various diving packages, costing from €100 for a single dive (maximum of three people) to €350 for a four-session beginners course.

Operating out of a kiosk on the private Pontile beach (to the west of the ferry ticket booths), **Banana Sport** (Map p173; ☎ 081 837 51 88; ☒ mid-Apr–Oct) hires out five-person motorised dinghies for €75 for two hours or €160 for the day (from 9.30am until 5.30pm). You can also pick up a boat to the popular swimming spot **Bagno di Tiberio**, a small inlet west of Marina Grande. It's said that Tiberius once swam here, although

he would not have had to pay €7.50 to access the private beach as you will.

Marina Piccola

Little more than a series of private bathing facilities, Marina Piccola is on the southern side of the island, directly south of Marina Grande. A short bus ride from Capri Town, or a downhill 15-minute walk, it has a 50m-long public pebble beach hemmed in by the **Scoglio delle Sirene** (Rock of the Sirens) at the western end and a **Saracen tower** at the other. The swimming's not great, although the two rocks rising out of the water about 10m offshore make excellent diving boards.

You can hire canoes at **Bagni di Gioia** (Map p173; ☎ 081 837 77 02) and **Bagni Lo Scoglio delle Sirene** (Map p173; ☎ 081 837 02 21) for around €12 per hour for a double canoe, €7 for a single.

LAST ONE IN IS A...

Come to Capri expecting beautiful sandy beaches and you'll be in for a shock. There aren't any. There are very few beaches on the island and those that do exist are almost all pebbly. That said, there's some fantastic swimming. Most of the best spots have been monopolised by private bathing clubs, entrance to which typically costs around €8 plus extra for an umbrella and sun bed. Note, also, that Capri is not a great place for inexperienced swimmers – in most places the rocky 'beaches' stand over deep water.

The island's best swimming spots:

Grotta Azzurra (opposite)
Dive off the platform into the deep blue water by the cave's entrance.

Punta Carena (opposite)
Popular with locals, the rocks by the *faro* (lighthouse) get very busy on summer weekends.

Bagno di Tiberio (above)
A private beach where Tiberius is said to have swum.

Tragara (see the boxed text, p176)
Go down the steps by the Belvedere di Tragara to rocks in front of the Isole Faraglioni.

Marina Piccola (above)
A small pebbly beach, much of which has been taken over by private clubs.

Arco Naturale (p176)   STEPHEN SAKS

Tours

Various companies offer island tours. **Motoscafisti Capri** (Map p173; ☎ 081 837 56 46; www .motoscafisticapri.com; Marina Grande pier) runs three sea tours: one to the Grotta Azzurra (€10 plus €8.50 admission to the cave, one hour); one around the island (€13, two hours), and one to the Isole Faraglioni (€10, one hour). Tickets are available from the wooden hut near the tourist office in Marina Grande.

Laser Capri (Map p173; ☎ 081 837 52 08; www .lasercapri.com; Via Don Giobbe Ruocco 45) also operates island tours (€11) and will ferry you to the Grotta Azzurra for €8 (entry to the cave costs an additional €8.50). Get your tickets from its office opposite dock 23.

FESTIVALS & EVENTS

Capri's two main religious events (**Festa di San Costanzo** on 14 May and Anacapri's **Festa di Sant'Antonio** on 13 June) are marked by colourful processions and open-air concerts.

Over the first 15 days of September Anacapri stages **Settembrata Anacaprese**, an annual celebration of the town's grape harvest, with gastronomic evenings, sports competitions and open-air markets.

To welcome the new year, local folk groups strut their stuff on Piazza Diaz in Anacapri and Capri's Piazza Umberto I on 1 and 6 January.

Try www.capri.com for further details on these festivals.

SLEEPING

Sleeping, like everything else on Capri, is an expensive pastime. The island's accommodation is very top heavy with plenty of four- and five-star hotels but few budget options; camping is forbidden and although there are a growing number of B&Bs, they rarely constitute much of a saving. Standards, however, are universally high, and wherever you stay you're likely to be met with courteous and efficient service.

Always make sure to book ahead. Hotel space is at a premium during summer and many places close in winter, typically between November and March.

Marina Grande

Convenient if you've got an early-morning ferry, Capri's port is the island's main transport hub and offers little in the way of charm.

BELVEDERE E TRE RE MAP P173   HOTEL €€

☎ 081 837 03 45; www.belvedere-tre-re.com; Via Marina Grande 264; r €90-140; ⌚ Apr-Nov; ⚡

Difficult to miss thanks to its rusty red walls, this friendly, old-fashioned hotel is an easy five-minutes walk from the port. The rooms are simple, with white walls, tiled floors and unexciting furniture, but they are all large and the best have small terraces overlooking the sea. There's also a sun-bronzing terrace on the top floor.

HOTEL ITALIA MAP P173   PENSIONE €€

☎ 081 837 06 02; www.pensioneitaliacapri.com; Via Marina Grande 204; r €80-120; ⌚ Apr-Nov

Offering old-school hospitality and few frills, Hotel Italia is a modest, homely *pensione*. The reception area is decorated with family knick-knacks and yellowing postcards, while the rooms have high ceilings and old-fashioned wardrobes and beds. The only drawback is the dining room, which looks like an institutional canteen.

RELAIS MARESCA MAP P173   HOTEL €€

☎ 081 837 96 19; www.relaismaresca.it; Via Marina Grande 284; d incl breakfast €140-220; ⊙ Mar-Dec; 🅿 💻

A delightful four-star, this is the top choice in Marina Grande. The look is classic Capri, with acres of gleaming ceramic in turquoise, blue and yellow, and stylish furniture. There is a range of rooms (and corresponding prices), the best of which have terraces and sea views – if yours doesn't you can always nip up to the 4th-floor flower-filled terrace. There's an internet station for guests and free cots for kids.

Capri Town

If you want to be right in the heart of the action, Capri Town is the place. An easy ride from the port, it's the buzzing centre of island life and correspondingly pricey.

GRAND HOTEL QUISISANA
MAP P174   HOTEL €€€

☎ 081 837 07 88; www.quisi.com; Via Camerelle 2; r/ste incl breakfast from €300/620; ⊙ mid-Mar–1st week Nov; 🅿 💻

One of only three hotels on the island to boast a five-star L (luxury) rating, the Quisisana is Capri's most famous address. A hotel since the 19th century, it's a bastion of unapologetic opulence, with two swimming pools (one inside, one out), a fitness centre and spa, subtropical gardens, restaurants and bars. Rooms are suitably elegant, with cool colour schemes and classy furniture.

HOTEL ESPERIA MAP P174   HOTEL €€

☎ 081 837 02 62; fax 081 837 09 33; Via Sopramonte 41; r incl breakfast €120-170; ⊙ Apr-Oct; 🅿

A short uphill walk from the centre of town, the Esperia exudes a fading air of debonair charm. Housed in a 19th-century villa, complete with peeling façade, handsome columns and giant urns, it offers large, airy rooms with modern furniture and a floral theme. The best (and most expensive) have good-sized terraces with sea views.

HOTEL GATTO BIANCO MAP P174   HOTEL €€

☎ 081 837 51 43; www.gattobianco-capri.com; Via V Emanuele 32; incl breakfast, s €102-158, d €153-220; ⊙ Apr-Nov; 🅿 💻

Boasting a central location and a welcoming management, this gay-friendly hotel is an excellent option. The light-filled rooms are decorated in traditional style with blue and yellow majolica tiling and there's an elegant patio with attractive wrought-iron furniture. Internet access is available to guests for €3 per 15 minutes.

HOTEL LA TOSCA MAP P174   HOTEL €

☎ 081 837 09 89; www.latoscahotel.com; Via Dalmazio Birago 5; s €45-80, d €65-125; ⊙ Apr-Oct; 🅿

A charming one-star *pensione* near the Certosa di San Giacomo, La Tosca is one of the island's top budget options. Hidden away down a quiet back lane within easy walking distance of Capri Town's bright lights, it offers 11 sparkling white rooms, some with sea views, all furnished with unfussy simplicity. The owner, a genial, hospitable guy, extends a warm welcome. Not surprisingly, it's a popular choice, so book ahead.

HOTEL VILLA KRUPP MAP P174   HOTEL €€

☎ 081 837 03 62; fax 081 837 64 89; Viale G Matteotti 12, Parco Augusto; incl breakfast, s €90, d €125-155; ⊙ Apr-Oct; 🅿

Housed in the former residence of Russian author Maxim Gorky, this historic hotel oozes old-school charm, with floral tiling, fading antiques and heavy bedsteads. It also commands some fabulous views over the Giardini di Augusto and beyond to the Isole Faraglioni. If your room doesn't have the view (and not all do), simply adjourn to the blue terrace outside reception.

HOTEL VILLA SARAH MAP P174   HOTEL €€

☎ 081 837 06 89; www.villasarah.it; Via Tiberio 3A; incl breakfast, s €80-125, d €125-195; Easter-Oct; 🅿 💻

On the road up to Villa Jovis – a 10-minute walk from the centre of Capri Town – Villa Sarah retains a rustic appeal that so many of the island's hotels have long lost. Surrounded by its own fruit-producing gardens, it has 19 airy rooms, all decorated in classical local style – ceramic tiles and old-fashioned furniture – and, outside, a small swimming pool.

LA REGINELLA MAP P173   HOTEL €€

☎ 081 837 05 00; www.lareginella.it; Via Matermània 36; s/d incl breakfast €70/140; ⊙ Apr-Sep

Rooms at this friendly, no-frills hotel are about as basic as they come on Capri. Facing onto a sunken terrace, they are ultra-simple, with a bed, the bare essentials and little else. They are, however, spotless, and all come with a table and chair on the terrace for whiling away those long, sultry evenings. The upstairs restaurant **La Palette** (meals around €25) serves decent seafood and a range of regional wines.

PENSIONE GUARRACINO
MAP P173   PENSIONE €€

☎ /fax 081837 71 40; Via Mulo 13; s €70-85, d €90-115; 🕙 year-round; ☒ 🔀

'Value for money' is a relative term when used in connection with Capri and accommodation but if you'll find it anywhere, you'll find it here, at this small, family-run *pensione*. A short walk from the centre of Capri Town and within easy striking distance of Marina Piccola, it has 13 sparkling white rooms, each decked out with a comfy bed, decent shower and independent air-con.

Anacapri

Quieter and marginally cheaper than Capri Town, Anacapri is a good base for exploring the island's less-visited western half. On the downside, it's a bit of a slog from the port.

ALBERGO LORELEY MAP P177   HOTEL €€

☎ 081 837 14 40; www.loreley.it; Via G Orlandi 16; incl breakfast, d €90-120, tr €135; 🕙 Apr-Oct

A welcoming, old-school hotel, the Loreley is the sort of place where telephones and TVs are listed as modern comforts. In other words, a fine place to get away from it all. Rooms, all of which are a decent size, are decorated in styles ranging from granny chintz to Mediterranean classic – cool tiled floors and heavy antique furniture. The location, just off

CELEBRITY ISLAND

A byword for Mediterranean chic, Capri has long enjoyed a reputation as a celebrity haunt.

The first big name to decamp here was Emperor Tiberius in AD 27. A man of sadistic sexual perversions, at least if the Roman author Suetonius is to be believed, he had 12 villas built on the island, including the vast Villa Jovis (p176). He also left deep scars and until modern times his name was equated with evil by islanders. When the Swedish doctor Axel Munthe first began picking about the Roman ruins on the island in the early 20th century and built his villa on the site of a Tiberian palace, locals would observe that it was all *'roba di Tiberio'* – Tiberius' stuff.

But more than Tiberius' capers, it was the discovery of the Grotta Azzurra in 1826 that paved the way for Capri's celebrity invasion. As news of the spectacular cave spread so artists, intellectuals, industrialists and writers began to visit, attracted by the island's isolated beauty and, in some cases, the availability of the local lads. An early habitué, Alfred Krupp, the German industrialist and arms manufacturer, was involved in a gay scandal, while author Norman Douglas and French count Jacques Fersen set all manner of tongues wagging.

The island also proved an escape for Russian revolutionaries. In 1905 the author Maxim Gorky moved to Capri after failing to topple the Russian tsar and five years later Lenin stopped by for a visit.

In the course of the early 20th century the Chilean poet Pablo Neruda and German author Thomas Mann visited regularly; British writers Compton Mackenzie and Graham Greene lived here for extended periods; and Britain's wartime singer Gracie Fields retired here.

Today it's the Hollywood stars and international models who keep Capri's reputation alive and its overworked paparazzi in business.

the main road into Anacapri, is convenient and surprisingly quiet.

CAPRI PALACE MAP P174 — HOTEL €€€

☎ 081 978 01 11; www.capripalace.com; Via Capodimonte 2B; s/d/ste incl breakfast from €190/295/620; Apr-Oct;

A VIP favourite (Harrison Ford, Liz Hurley and Naomi Campbell have all stayed here), the super-slick Capri Palace is the hotel of the moment. Its stylish Mediterranean interior is enlivened with eye-catching contemporary art and its guest rooms are never less than lavish – some even have their own terraced garden and private pool. For stressed guests, the health spa is said to be the island's best. Note that there's a three-night minimum stay in high season.

HOTEL BELLAVISTA MAP P174 — HOTEL €€

☎ 081 837 14 63; www.bellavistacapri.com; Via G Orlandi 10; s €80-105, d €120-200; Apr-Oct;

One of Capri's oldest hotels, the Bellavista is more than a hundred years old. And although you can't say the same for the décor, a make-over wouldn't do the place any harm. The large rooms have 1960s-style tile floors with enormous floral motifs, and ad hoc furniture. On the plus side, it's conveniently positioned near the entrance to Anacapri, and boasts a tennis court, a restaurant with wonderful views and discounted access to a nearby swimming pool.

HOTEL BUSSOLA DI HERMES — HOTEL €€

☎ 081 838 20 10; www.bussolahermes.com; Trav La Vigna 14; dm €27-32, s €40-70, d €75-120, q €120-180; year-round;

There's something for everyone at this great hotel-cum-hostel. There's a dorm-style room for students, quads for families and eight recently renovated doubles on the 2nd floor. These sun-filled rooms are modern and comfortable with flat-screen TVs, white walls and blue marble floors. For a sea view you'll pay an extra €10. To get here take the bus up to Piazza Vittoria and call for the hotel shuttle service.

HOTEL CARMENCITA MAP P177 — HOTEL €€

☎ 081 837 13 60; www.hotelcarmencita-capri.com; Via de Tommaso 4; s €69-95, d €110-145; mid-Mar–mid-Nov;

Near the town bus station, the Carmencita is run by a chatty couple who extend a warm welcome. They'll even come and pick you up from the ferry terminal at Marina Grande if you

phone ahead with your arrival details. Rooms are bright – think mustard-yellow walls and majolica ceramic tiling – big and comfortable. At the time of writing the hotel had just attained permission to start building a swimming pool, so don't forget the costume.

HOTEL SENARIA — HOTEL €€

☎ 081 837 12 23; www.senaria.it; Via Follicara 6; r incl breakfast €120-160; Apr-Nov;

It's quite a trek to this delightful family-run hotel in Anacapri's original town centre, but once you've found it you'll be glad of the effort. Housed in a discreet whitewashed villa, the rooms are a picture of elegant understatement, with polished tiled floors, cooling cream tones and the tasteful water-colours of local artist Giovanni Tessitore. It's a very quiet spot and except for Sunday-morning church bells you're unlikely to be disturbed by anything other than the breeze.

HOTEL VILLA EVA — HOTEL €€

☎ 081 837 15 49; www.villaeva.com; Via La Fabbrica 8; s €50-80, d €90-120; Mar-Oct,

A veritable rural retreat, Villa Eva is an absolute gem. Hidden among fruit and olive trees (on-to which hammocks have been hung), rooms feature an extensive list of original trappings including a tiled fireplace, a model ship, a brick well, domed ceilings and a waist-height boxed radio (room 6). Ideal for families, the hotel also has a swimming pool, snack bar and treetop views down to the sea. The only drawback is that it's not an easy place to get to: take the Grotta Azzurra bus from Anacapri and ask the driver where to get off, or cough up €20 for a portside pick-up.

EATING

Traditional Italian food served in traditional Italian trattorie is what you'll find on Capri. And it's what they do very well, particularly in the restaurants peppered around the island's interior. Prices are high but drop noticeably the further you get from Capri Town.

The island's culinary gift to the world is *insalata caprese*, a salad of fresh tomato, basil and mozzarella bathed in olive oil. Look out for *caprese* cheese, a cross between mozzarella and ricotta, and *ravioli caprese*, ravioli stuffed with ricotta and herbs.

Many restaurants, like the hotels, close over winter.

Next to the police station in Capri Town, the **Deco supermarket** (Map p174; Via Roma; ☻ 8am-8.30pm Mon-Sat, 8am-1pm Sun) is a good place to load up with picnic provisions.

Capri Town & Around

LA CAPANNINA MAP P174   TRATTORIA €€€
☎ 081 837 07 32; Via Le Botteghe 12; meals around €50; ☻ mid-Mar–Oct
There's rarely a shortage of celebrity visitors on Capri and most sooner or later will eat here, at the island's most famous traditional trattoria. Set up to look like a Hollywood version of a rustic eatery – pink tablecloths, hanging copper pots and carved wooden chairs – it serves a classic island menu with high-quality seafood pasta, *ravioli caprese*, grilled meat and fresh fish.

LA CISTERNA MAP P174   TRATTORIA €€
☎ 081 837 56 20; Via M Serafina 5; meals around €25; ☻ closed Feb
Named after and housed in a 2000-year-old Roman cistern, this bustling, unpretentious trattoria is a perennial favourite. Owned by the larger-than-life Salvatore, whose memorable picture adorns the bottles of house wine, it's good for traditional dishes such as pasta with beans, veal cutlets and wood-fired pizzas. Rumbling tummies won't go hungry, as the portions are huge.

LA PERGOLA MAP P174   TRATTORIA €€€
☎ 081 837 74 12; Via Traversa Lo Palazzo 2; meals around €30; ☻ Thu-Tue Nov-Sep
A step up from the average island trattoria, La Pergola is a lovely place to eat. Its vine-shaded terrace and sea views provide a wonderful setting for the delicious, innovative food. The menu comprises all the Capri classics plus a number of more modern dishes such as *paccheri con cozze, patate e peperoncino* (large pasta rings with mussels, potatoes and chilli). It's hard to find; persevere and follow the signs.

LA SAVARDINA DA EDOUARDO
MAP P173   RISTORANTE €€€
☎ 081 837 63 00; Via Lo Capo 8; meals around €30; ☻ daily Jul & Aug, closed Tue Mar-Jun & Sep-Oct, closed Nov-Feb
You will build up an appetite as you stroll up to this laid-back restaurant in the Capri coun-tryside. But as you sit down on the open-air terrace and look out to Ischia in the hazy distance you'll appreciate the effort. The food is great too. Dishes are made with local pro-duce and are unapologetically simple. For proof try the *papardelle con ragùdi coniglio* (pasta with rabbit sauce) followed by succulent lamb chops.

LA TAVERNA DI PULCINELLA
MAP P173   TRATTORIA €€
☎ 081 837 64 85; Via Tiberio 7; meals around €20, pizzas around €7; ☻ Apr-Oct
Thousands of tourists walk past this down-to-earth trattoria-cum-pizzeria every day on their way up to Villa Jovis. Very few stop off to eat – perhaps put off by the sight of waiters in Punchinello (Pulcinella) costumes. Islanders know better and come here for their takeaway pizzas. And with good reason – they're the best on the island. If you're really hungry go for the Vesuvio, a stomach-challenging combo of ricotta cheese, ham, mushroom and peppers.

LE GROTTELLE MAP P173   RISTORANTE €€
☎ 081 837 57 19; Via Arco Naturale 13; meals around €28; ☻ Apr-Oct
A great place to impress your partner. Not so much for the food, which is decent enough – think simple pasta dishes followed by grilled fish, chicken or rabbit – but for its atmospheric setting. About 150m from the **Arco Naturale** (p176), it's got two dining areas, one set in a cave, the other, more appealing, on a terrace perched above a wooded hillside falling down to the sea.

RAFFAELE BUONACORE MAP P174 SNACKS €
☎ 081 837 78 26; Via Vittorio Emanuele 35; ☻ 8am-midnight Mar-Oct
Ideal for a quick fill-up, this popular snack bar does a roaring trade in takeaway pizzas, frittatas, *panini* (bread rolls; from about €4), pastries, waffles and ice cream. Hard to beat, though, are the delicious *sfogliatelle* (cinnamon-infused ricotta in a puff pastry shell) for €1.50.

RISTORANTE DA MAP P174   RISTORANTE €€€
☎ 081 837 04 61; Via M Serafina 6; meals around €30; ☻ Tue-Sun Mar-Dec
While there's nothing exceptional about the food here, there's something undeniably appealing about eating in a restaurant where John Lennon once dined. The Beatle's face is one of many featured in the fading photo

collage papered inside the restaurant's entrance. And what would the great man have ordered? *Inslata caprese*? Pizza Margherita? Nonvegetarians might be tempted by the grilled scampi or steak with green pepper.

SFIZI DI PANE MAP P174   BAKERY €
☎ 081 837 61 80; Via Le Botteghe 15; ☺ 7am-1.25pm & 4.45pm-8.45pm Tue-Sun

Let the warm, yeasty odours tempt you and step inside this *panificio* (bakery) for a *pizza al taglio* (pizza slice; about €3) or a delicious savoury tart. Bread rolls are made fresh every day, ideal for picnics.

VERGINIELLO MAP P174   RISTORANTE €€
☎ 081 837 09 44; Via Lo Palazzo 25; meals around €20; ☺ daily Apr-Oct, closed Tue Dec-Mar, closed Nov

As near to a budget diner as you'll find in Capri Town, Verginiellio caters to an impressive number of hungry visitors. Offering safe, reliable food and grandstand views over Marina Grande, it's a big, bustling restaurant staffed by a hard-working team of harried waiters. Of the pasta dishes, the *ravioli caprese* and *spaghetti alle cozze* (spaghetti with mussels) are worth trying; of the main courses, the grilled steaks are a dependable choice.

ROCCO FASANO

Anacapri & Around

LA RONDINELLA
MAP P177   RISTORANTE €€
☎ 081 837 12 23; Via G Orlandi 295; meals around €28; ☺ year-round

One of Anacapri's most consistently good restaurants – apparently Graham Greene was a fan – La Rondinella has a relaxed, rural feel. The menu features a number of Italian classics such as *saltimbocca alla Romana* (veal slices with ham and sage), *cotoletta alla Milanese* (bread-crumbed veal cutlet) and *gnocchi alla sorrentina* (potato gnocchi baked in tomato sauce with mozzarella). For something different try chef Michele's *linguine alla ciammura,* a delicious pasta dish with a creamy white sauce of anchovies, garlic and parsley.

LE ARCATE MAP P177   RISTORANTE €€
☎ 081 837 33 25; Via de Tommaso 24; meals around €28; ☺ year-round

Take your cue from the reception folk at the nearby Capri Palace Hotel and grab a table here. An unpretentious place with hanging baskets of ivy, sunny yellow tablecloths and terracotta tiles, it specialises in delicious *primi* (first courses) and pizzas. A real show stopper is the *risotto con polpa di granchio, rughetta e scaglie di parmigiano* (risotto with crab meat, rocket and shavings of parmesan cheese).

TRATTORIA DA GIOVANNI A GRADOLA MAP P173   TRATTORIA €€
Grotta Azzurra; meals around €18; ☺ Apr-Oct

Beyond the swish bathing facilities at the Grotta Azzurra, you'll find this laid-back, lunch-in-a-costume trattoria. The setting is lovely – basic wooden tables on a thin terrace overlooking the deep blue sea – and the food straightforward. Menu stalwarts include *parmigiana di melanzane* (baked aubergine with tomato and cheese), fried fish and *pasta e fagioli* (pasta and beans stew). Better suited to summer lunches than formal dinners.

TRATTORIA IL SOLITARIO
MAP P177   TRATTORIA €€
☎ 081 837 13 82; Via G Orlandi 96; meals around €20, pizzas from €4.50; ☺ Apr-Oct

One of the better trattoria in the heart of Anacapri's touristy centre, Il Solitario serves excellent food at honest prices. There's nothing remarkable about the menu, which lists the usual island fare – pasta and seafood,

RUSSELL MOUNTFORD

grilled meat and pizzas – but the helpings are large and the quality high. It's a relaxed place with a young staff, and tables are laid out in an inviting green backyard. Book ahead on summer weekends.

DRINKING & ENTERTAINMENT

Capri's nightlife is a showy business. The main activity is dressing up and hanging out, ideally at one of the four cafés on la Piazzetta (Piazza Umberto I). Be warned, however, that the moment you sit down for a drink (and the slick waiters stationed on the piazza can be very persuasive), you're going to pay handsomely for the privilege (around €15 for a couple of white wines).

Cafés apart, Capri's nightlife is fairly staid, with few nightclubs to speak of and only several upmarket taverns. Most places open around 10pm, closing late, typically about 4am, and charge anywhere between €20 and €30 for admission.

In Capri Town, celebs like to be seen singing classical Neapolitan songs at **Taverna Anema e Core** (Map p174; ☎ 081 837 64 61; Via Sella Orta 39E; 🕔 closed Nov-Mar), one of the island's most famous nightspots. **Guarracino** (Map p174; ☎ 081 837 05 14; Via Castello 7; 🕔 closed Nov-Mar) offers more of the same, with guitar-strumming crooners and a well-to-do crowd of TV presenters, models and moneyed tourists.

For something a bit more racy, run the gauntlet of bouncers outside **Musmè** (Map p174; ☎ 081 837 60 11; Via Camerelle 61B; 🕔 closed Nov-Mar), a flash disco on Capri Town's elite shopping strip, or join the younger crowd dancing to hip-hop, house and revival at **Baraonda** (Map p174; ☎ 081 837 25 23; Via Roma 6; 🕔 year-round).

Up in Anacapri, **Underground** (Map p177; ☎ 081 837 25 23; Via G Orlandi 259; 🕔 year-round) attracts a mixed foreign and Italian crowd with its funk and house nights and its festive beach parties. Nearby, **Caffè Michelangelo** (Map p177; Via G Orlandi 138; 🕔 year-round) is a relaxing place to people-watch while sipping on something cool and listening to Village People on the stereo.

SHOPPING

Boasting more designer boutiques per square metre than almost anywhere else on earth, Capri's shopping scene is conservative and expensive. Along the two main strips, Via Vittorio Emanuele and Via Camarelle, you'll find most of the fashion big guns as well as a number of jewellery and shoe shops. If you're not in the market for a new Rolex or Prada bag, look out for the ceramic work and anything lemony, in particular, lemon-scented perfume and *limoncello*, a sweet lemon liqueur.

CAPRI NATURALE
MAP P177   WOMEN'S FASHIONS & SHOES
☎ 081 837 47 19; Via Capodimonte 15, Anacapri;
🕔 Apr-Oct

One of the better shops along touristy Via Capodimonte, Capri Naturale sells a limited range of women's fashions. Expect whisper-thin linen frocks in delphinium blue or dip-dyed lavender and a small selection of handmade sandals. Everything is made locally and prices are reasonable.

CARTHUSIA I PROFUMI DI CAPRI
MAP P174   PERFUMES
☎ 081 837 03 68; Viale Parco Augusto 2C, Capri;
🕔 year-round

Legend has it that Capri's famous floral perfume was discovered in 1380 by the prior of the Certosa di San Giacomo. Caught unawares by a royal visit, he arranged a floral display of the island's most beautiful flowers for the queen. Three days later he went to change the water in the vase only to discover that it had acquired a mysterious floral odour. This became the base of the perfume that's now sold at this smart laboratory outlet.

DA COSTANZO   MAP P174   SHOES
☎ 081 837 80 77; Via Roma 49; 🕔 Mar-Nov

In 1959 Clarke Gable stopped off at this tiny, unpretentious shoe shop to get himself a pair of handmade leather sandals. The shop's still going, selling a bewildering range of colourful styles to a mixed crowd of passers-by and shoe aficionados. Prices start at around €90.

LIMONCELLO CAPRI MAP P177 GIFTS

☎ 081 837 29 27; Via Capodimonte 27, Anacapri;
🕑 9am-7pm May- Sep, 9am-5pm Oct-Apr

Don't be put off by the gaudy yellow display; this historic shop stocks some of the island's best *limoncello*. In fact, it was here that the drink was first concocted. Apparently, the grandmother of current owner Vivica made the tot as an after-dinner treat for the guests in her hotel. Nowadays, the shop produces some 70,000 bottles each year, as well as lemon chocolate, lemon marmalade and lemon honey. You can also buy lemon-motifed ceramics.

GETTING THERE & AWAY

Unless you are prepared to pay **Sam Helicopters** (☎ 0828 35 41 55; www.capri-helicopters.com) €1650 for a helicopter transfer from Naples' Capodichino Airport, you'll arrive in Capri by boat. The two major ferry routes to Capri are from Sorrento and Naples, although there are also connections with Ischia and the Amalfi Coast (Amalfi, Positano and Salerno).

The information listed here refers to high-season crossings; if you're travelling in low season check timetables with tourist offices or direct with ferry companies.

All ferries arrive and depart from Marina Grande.

To/from Naples, **Caremar** (☎ 081 837 07 00; www .caremar.it) operates ferries/hydrofoils (€7.60/ 12.50, 75/50 minutes, five daily), while **Snav** (☎ 081 837 75 77; www.snav.com), **Neapolis** (☎ 081 837 08 19) and **Navigazione Libera del Golfo** (NLG; ☎ 081 552 07 63; www.navlib.it, in Italian) ensure 25 hydrofoil runs a day. The standard cost of the 45-minute journey is adult/child €14/10.

To/from Sorrento, Caremar operates four daily ferry crossings (adult/child €7.80/4.90, 25 minutes) while **LMP** (Linee Marittime Partenope; ☎ 081 704 19 11; www.consorziolmp.it, in Italian) runs 20 hydrofoil crossings (adult/child €12/ 7.50, 25 minutes).

To/from the Amalfi Coast, LMP runs services to Positano (ferry/hydrofoil €13/ 15.50, six daily), Amalfi (€13.50/16, seven daily) and Salerno (€14.50/16, five daily).

LMP and **Alilauro** (☎ 081 837 69 95; www .alilauro.it) operate hydrofoils between Capri and Ischia. With the former you will pay €13, with the latter adult/child €15.50/8.

Note that some companies require you to pay a small supplement for luggage, typically around €1.50.

GETTING AROUND

The first challenge facing visitors is how to get from Marina Grande to Capri Town. The easiest, quickest and most popular solution is to take the **funicular** (🕑 6.30am-12.30am Jun-Sep, to 9.30pm Apr-May, to 9pm Oct-Mar). Tickets (€1.30) are available from the booths to the west of the port or, at the top, from the funicular station.

Once up the hill the best way to get around the island is by bus. Operating from the bus station on Via Roma, **Sippic** (☎ 081 837 04 20) runs regular buses to/from Marina Grande (5.45am to 12.30am), Anacapri (5am to 4.30am) and Marina Piccola (6am to 2am). It also operates buses from Marina Grande to Anacapri (5.45am to 10.10pm) and from Marina Piccola to Anacapri (12.30pm to 7.30pm).

From the bus station on Via de Tommaso in Anacapri, regular **Staiano Autotrasporti** (☎ 081 837 24 22; www.staiano-capri.com) buses serve the Grotta Azzurra and Faro di Punta Carena.

Single bus tickets cost €1.30 on all routes. All-day tickets, valid from 6am to 4am May to September, 6am to midnight October to April, are also available, for €6.70, but unless you're planning a lot of bus travel you're better off sticking to singles.

There is no vehicle-hire service on the island and few roads are wide enough for a car. Between March and October you can only bring a vehicle to the island if it's either registered outside Italy or hired at an international airport – but there's really no need, as buses are regular and taxis plentiful. You can, however, hire a scooter from **Rent a Scooter** Marina Grande (Map p173; ☎ 081 837 79 41; Via Marina Grande 280, Marina Grande; per hr/day €15/65); Anacapri (Map p177; ☎ 081 837 38 88; Piazza Barile 20, Anacapri; per hr/day €15/65).

From Marina Grande, a taxi ride costs around €20 to Capri and around €25 to Anacapri; from Capri to Anacapri costs around €15. For a taxi in and around Capri call ☎ 081 837 05 43 or if you are in Anacapri ☎ 081 837 11 75.

GREG ELMS

ISCHIA

Weary muscles ache for Ischia. Rugged, lush and steamy, its mineral springs and fumaroles have seduced the stressed since antiquity.

The biggest and busiest island in the bay, Ischia is a bubbling concoction of sprawling spa towns, mud-wrapped Germans, subtropical gardens and ancient booty. Spa resorts flank buried necropoli, hillsides are sprinkled with hermitages and jasmine-scented gardens hide restored artists' villas.

While most day-trippers head to more chic Capri from Naples, Ischia pulls a solid summer crowd. Most head for the touristy north-coast towns of Ischia Porto, Ischia Ponte, Casamicciola Terme, Forio and Lacco Ameno. Of these, Ischia Porto boasts the best bars, Casamicciola the worst traffic and Ischia Ponte and Lacco Ameno the most appeal.

On the calmer south coast, the car-free perfection of Sant'Angelo is a blissful blend of twisting laneways, cosy harbour, sunning cats and nearby bubbling beaches. In between the coasts lies a less-trodden landscape of chestnut forests, dusty farms and earthy hillside towns.

The island was one of the first Greek colonies in the 8th century BC, named Pithekoussai after the *pithos* (pottery clay) found there. An important stop on the trade route from Greece to northern Italy, it was renamed Aenaria by the Romans, who followed Pliny's and Strabo's advice and soaked in its salubrious springs.

But this island gem has also seen its fair share of disaster. The 1301 eruption of the now-extinct (and unfortunately named) Monte Arso forced the locals to flee to the mainland, where they remained for four years. Five centuries later, in 1883, an earthquake killed more than 1700 people and razed the burgeoning spa town of Casamicciola to the ground. To this day, the town's name signifies 'total destruction' in the Italian vernacular.

ORIENTATION

Ischia sits 19km southeast of Pozzuoli and 33km from Naples. Ferries and hydrofoils from both ports reach Casamicciola Terme and Ischia Porto. The latter is Ischia's major gateway and tourist hub. The island's main bus terminus is a one-minute walk west of the pier, with buses servicing all other parts of the island. East of the pier, shopping strip Via Roma eventually becomes Corso Vittoria Colonna and heads southeast to Ischia Porto.

SIGHTS

Ischia Porto & Ischia Ponte

Although technically two separate towns, Ischia Porto and Ischia Ponte are bookends to one long, sinuous sprawl of candy-coloured buildings, frappé-sipping beach babes, card-playing old-timers, and palm-fringed shops and hotels.

The ferry port itself was a crater lake, opened up to sea at the request of Spanish King Ferdinand II in 1854. While the story goes that he couldn't stand the stench of the lake, his request was more likely inspired by the prospect of increased shipping tax revenue. The harbour is fringed by a string of restaurants serving fresh seafood with harbour views. Opposite the ferry pier stands the 19th-century **Chiesa di Santa Maria di Portosalvo** (Via Iasolino, Ischia Porto; ☽ 8am-12.30pm & 4-8pm daily). Just to the east is the former Royal Palace, now a military spa off limits to mere civilians.

While cadets soothe their muscles, armies of bronzed shoppers raid the racks along Via Roma and the more chic Corso Vittoria Colonna. Offering a spot of spiritual respite is the 18th-century **Chiesa di San Pietro** (cnr Corso Vittoria Colonna & Via Gigante, Ischia; ☽ 8am-12.30pm & 4-7.30pm daily), with its fetching convex façade, semicircular chapels and elevated terrace sprinkled with flirty teens and gossipy *signore* (women).

Further down Corso Vittoria Colonna, past Via F D'Avalos, emerald-green gates on the left lead into the lush **Giardini Pubblici** (Public Gardens; Corso Vittoria Colonna, Ischia; ☽ 7am-8pm daily). Head further to the east and you will hit the heart-stealing **Spiaggia dei Pescatori** (Fishermen's Beach), a technicolour spectacle of brightly painted fishing boats, bronzed flesh, lurid beach umbrellas and mothers on balconies calling in their chubby kids for lunch.

From here, Corso Vittoria Colonna becomes Via Pontano, ending at Via Seminario. Recently pedestrianised, Via Seminario is Ischia Ponte's prime *passeggiata* (stroll) strip, attracting the occasional film shoot. Detour left into Via Marina. The sombre grey building at the water's edge is the 16th-century **Palazzo Malcoviti**, featured in *The Talented Mr Ripley* and French film *Plein Soleil*. Originally built as a watchtower, it patiently waits for the next film crew to give it a fresh lick of paint. Further east along the shore stands the 15th-century watchtower Torre del Mare, now bell tower to Ischia's cathedral **Santa Maria della Scala** (Via Mazzella, Ischia Ponte; ☽ 8am-12.30pm & 4.30-8pm daily). The current church, designed by Antonio Massinetti and completed in 1751, stands on the site of two older churches, one built in the 13th century and the other in the 17th century. Inside its peeling interior you will find the original 14th-century baptismal font, Romanesque wooden crucifix and an 18th-century canvas by Giacinto Diano.

INFORMATION

- **Bay Watch** (☎ 081 333 10 96; Via Iasolino 37, Ischia Porto) Accommodation and tour bookings.
- **Pharmacy** (☎ 081 99 40 60; Piazza Marina, Casamicciola Terme)
- **Hospital** (☎ 081 507 91 11; Via Fundera 2, Lacco Ameno)
- **Ischia** (www.ischiaonline.it) Lists hotels, sights, activities and events.
- **Internet Point** (☎ 081 98 15 89; Corso Vittoria Colonna 123, Ischia; per hr €5; ☽ 9am-1pm & 4pm-3am Oct-Mar, 10am-1pm & 5pm-4am Apr-Sep)
- **Launderette** (☎ 081 99 18 86; Via Alfredo De Luca 91, Ischia; ☽ 8:30am-1pm & 3-8pm Mon-Fri, 8:30am-1pm Sat, closed Sun)
- **Tourist office** (☎ 081 507 42 31; Via Iasolino, Banchina Porto Salvo; ☽ 9am-2pm & 3-8pm Mon-Sat)

ISCHIA

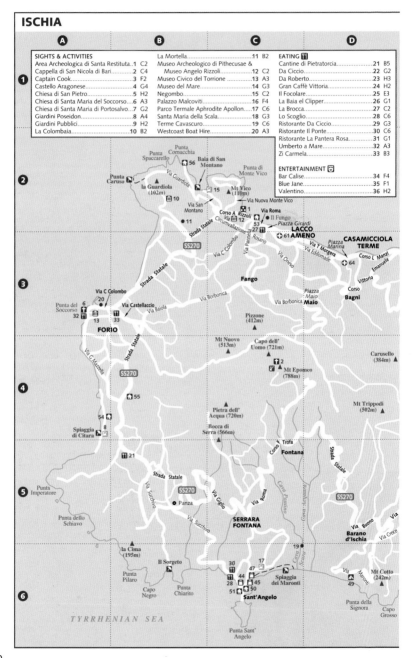

A   **B**   **C**   **D**

SIGHTS & ACTIVITIES
Area Archeologica di Santa Restituta..1 C2
Cappella di San Nicola di Bari..........2 C4
Captain Cook...................................3 F2
Castello Aragonese..........................4 G4
Chiesa di San Pietro..........................5 H2
Chiesa di Santa Maria del Soccorso...6 A3
Chiesa di Santa Maria di Portosalvo...7 G2
Giardini Poseidon.............................8 A4
Giardini Pubblici..............................9 H2
La Colombaia.................................10 B2

La Mortella.....................................11 B2
Museo Archeologico di Pithecusae &
  Museo Angelo Rizzoli....................12 C2
Museo Civico del Torrione...............13 A3
Museo del Mare.............................14 G3
Negombo......................................15 C2
Palazzo Malcoviti...........................16 F4
Parco Termale Aphrodite Apollon....17 C6
Santa Maria alla Scala.....................18 G3
Terme Cavascuro...........................19 C6
Westcoast Boat Hire........................20 A3

EATING 🍴
Cantine di Pietratorcia....................21 B5
Da Ciccio......................................22 G2
Da Roberto....................................23 H3
Gran Caffè Vittoria..........................24 H2
Il Focolare.....................................25 E3
La Baia el Clipper............................26 G1
La Brocca.......................................27 C2
Lo Scoglio.....................................28 C6
Ristorante Da Ciccio........................29 G3
Ristorante Il Ponte..........................30 C6
Ristorante La Pantera Rosa..............31 G1
Umberto a Mare.............................32 A3
Zi Carmela....................................33 B3

ENTERTAINMENT 🎭
Bar Calise......................................34 F4
Blue Jane.......................................35 F1
Valentino.......................................36 H2

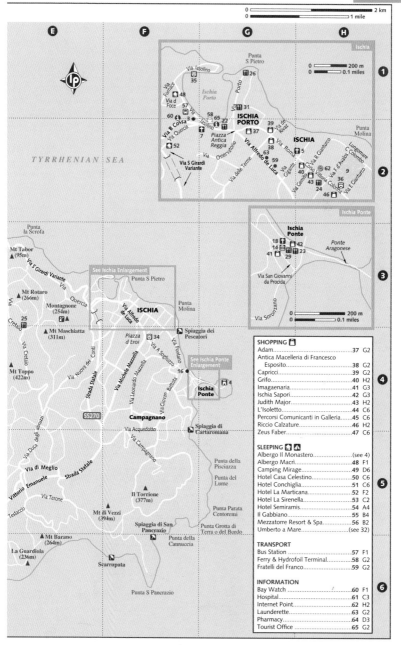

Ischia's maritime history is lovingly documented at the modest **Museo del Mare** (☎ 081 98 11 24; Via Giovanni da Procida 2, Ischia Ponte; admission €2.58; ☷ 10.30am-12.30pm Nov-Jan & Mar, 10.30am-12.30pm & 3-7pm Apr-Jun & Sep-Oct, 10.30am-12.30pm & 6.30-10pm Jul-Aug, closed Feb). Objects include cult ex-votos from sailors to saints, ancient urns, beautifully crafted model ships and revealing photographs of island life in the 20th century, including the arrival of Ischia's first American car in 1958.

From here, Via Mazzella leads down to the elegant 15th-century **Ponte Aragonese**, which connects the town to the sprawling **Castello Aragonese** (☎ 081 99 28 34; Rocca del Castello; admission €10; ☷ 9am-7pm Apr-Oct, 10am-5pm Nov-Mar), perched high and mighty on a rocky islet. While Syracusan tyrant Gerone I built the site's first fortress in 474 BC, the bulk of the current structure dates from the 1400s, when King Alfonso of Aragon gave the older Angevin fortress a thorough make-over, building the fortified bastions, current causeway and access ramp cut into the rock.

Pick up the free English-language itinerary at the ticket booth before making your way up the ramp. Channel your inner masochist at the **Museo delle Armi** (Weaponry Museum), with its small but curious collection of medieval skull clamp, feet-crushing vice, his and her chastity belts, and kinky illustrations. More substantial is the collection of medieval Italian and German armoury.

Further along inside the complex lie the sunbaked, stuccoed ruins of the 14th-century **Cattedrale dell'Assunta**. Built to replace the cathedral destroyed in the eruption of Monte Arso in 1301, it was restyled in the 18th century before collapsing under British cannonfire in 1809. The 11th-century **crypt** below features snippets of 14th-century frescoes inspired by Giotto. Better preserved is the 18th-century **Chiesa dell'Immocolata** with its Greek-cross plan and look-at-me dome studded with curved tympanum windows. Commissioned by the adjoining **Convento delle Clarisse** (Convent for Clarisse nuns), it was left in its minimalist state after building funds ran out. When the nuns' own lives expired, they were left to decompose sitting upright on stone chairs in the macabre **Cimitero delle Monache Clarisse**. Heading back into daylight and further up the islet you will find the elegant, hexagonal **Chiesa di San Pietro a Pantaniello** and sombre **Carcere Borbonico**, one-time prison pad for leading figures of the Risorgimento (the 19th-century Italian unification movement), such as Poerio, Pironti, Nusco and Settembrini. Finally, check out the **Casa del Sole** with its sharp collection of contemporary art, including luscious paintings by local artists Clementina and Michele Petroni.

Lacco Ameno

In the 1950s and 1960s, French starlets and European royalty came to play at the legendary Terme Regina Isabella spa resort. The stars may have gone but one local icon remains, sprouting out of the sea: the iconic **Il Fungo** (The Mushroom) is a 10m volcanic rock formation spat out by Monte Epomeo thousands of years ago.

top five

ISCHIA BEACHES

Spiaggia dei Maronti (p194) Long, sandy and very popular, this strip was a favourite landing spot for pirates, who would bury their loot beneath the sand. Reach it by bus from Barano, by water taxi from Sant'Angelo or on foot along the path leading east from Sant'Angelo.

Il Sorgeto (p194) Catch a water taxi from Sant'Angelo or reach it on foot from the town of Panza. Waiting at the bottom is an intimate cove complete with bubbling thermal spring. Perfect for a winter dip.

Spiaggia dei Pescatori (p189) Wedged in between Ischia Porto and Ischia Ponte is the island's most atmospheric seaside strip – think colourful vintage fishing boats, soccer matches on the sand and a looming castle perched high above in the distance.

Baia di San Montano Just outside Lacco Ameno, this gorgeous bay is the place for warm, shallow, crystal-clear waters. Here you'll also find the **Negombo spa park** (opposite).

Punta Caruso Located on Ischia's northwestern tip, this secluded rocky spot is perfect for a solitary swim in clear, deep water. To get here, follow the walking path that leads off Via Guardiola down to the beach. Not suitable for children or when seas are rough.

In **Piazza Restituta** you'll find the **Terme Regina Isabella** and pretty-in-pink **Chiesa di Santa Restituta**, rebuilt after the 1883 earthquake. According to legend, the martyred Restituta was washed ashore on nearby San Montano Beach in the 4th century on a boat steered from Tunisia by a seaworthy angel. Every May, residents re-enact her arrival on the beach.

Beneath the church is the must-see **Area Archeologica di Santa Restituta** (☎ 081 98 05 38; Piazza Restituta; admission €3; ☼ 9.30am-12.30pm & 5-7pm Mon-Sat, 9.30am-12.30pm Sun, closed Nov-Mar). Excavations undertaken between 1951 and 1974 have uncovered parts of an ancient Greek kiln, Roman temple and street, 4th-century burial amphorae and an early Christian basilica. Rows of cabinets display other ancient objects, from Roman bracelets and votive gifts to a 3300-year-old stove from Procida. The ground-floor collection goes back to the future, with exquisite 17th-century *pastori* (nativity scene figurines), colourful 18th-century ceramics, high camp clerical garb and the 18th-century wooden statue of Santa Restituta still used in the annual procession in the Bay of San Montano. You can borrow a informative, handwritten guide to the excavations from the ticket desk.

The town's other cultural heavyweight is the **Museo Archeologico di Pithecusae** (☎ 081 99 61 83; www.pithecusae.it; Corso Angelo Rizzoli 210, Lacco Ameno; admission €5; ☼ 9.30am-1pm & 3-7pm Oct-May, 9.30am-1pm & 4-8pm Jun-Sep, closed Mon), housed in the elegant Villa Arbusto, former pad of Angelo Rizzoli. The villa overlooks Monte Vico, site of the ancient settlement and acropolis of Pithecusae, and its collection features important finds from the island's Hellenic settlement, from imported earthenware to parts of the acropolis itself. Older still are the fragments of Mycenaean pottery and Bronze Age vases from Casamicciola. The collection spans Ischia's development from Neolithic to Roman times. A highlight is the legendary 7th-century Nestor's Cup in Sala (Room) II. The three Homeric verses scratched onto its side read: 'I am Nestor's Cup, good to drink from. Whoever drinks from this cup, straightaway desire for beautiful-crowned Aphrodite will seize him'. The drinking ballad is one of the oldest examples of early Greek writing in existence. The museum also houses the

Museo Angelo Rizzoli, which pays homage to the man who turned humble little Lacco into a celebrity hot spot in the 1950s. Cool paparazzi shots and clippings of a Hitchcock-esque Rizzoli and his famous pals decorate rooms once host to the likes of Gina Lollabrigida, Grace Kelly and Federico Fellini. Equally striking are the villa's gardens, complete with lemon trees, fountain, a children's playground and star-worthy views towards the Campi Flegrei.

Recover from museum fatigue at the nearby **Negombo** (☎ 081 98 61 52; www.negombo.it; Baia di San Montano, Lacco Ameno; admission €25 all day, €20 from 1pm, €13 from 4.30pm, €5 from 5pm; ☼ 8.30am-7pm daily Apr-Oct). Part spa resort, part botanical wonderland, its combination of Zen-like thermal pools, hammam, contemporary sculpture and private beach on San Montano Bay draws a younger crowd than many other Ischia spa spots. There's a Japanese labyrinth pool for weary feet, a decent *tavola calda* (snack bar) for growling stomachs and enough massage and beauty treatments to keep you *oooh*-ing all day long. Those arriving by car or scooter can park on site (car €3.60, scooter €2, all day).

For a free dip in the bay, follow the signs to the *spiaggia* (beach) out the front of Negombo.

Forio & the West Coast

Long before the invasion of sarongs and sunscreen, Forio was the hapless target of medieval pirate raids. One of the 12 watchtowers built to defend its frazzled citizens houses the **Museo Civico del Torrione** (☎ 081 333 29 34; Via Torrione, Forio; admission €2; ☼ 9.30am-12.30pm & 6pm-9pm Tue-Sun). Dating from 1480, this former Bourbon prison now exhibits the works of painter and sculptor Giovanni Maltese, who once lived in the tower.

On the western edge of town, perched high above the sea, the **Chiesa di Santa Maria del Soccorso** (Via Soccorso 1, Forio; ☼ 10am-sunset daily) is a Tex-Mex vision in white. The church was originally part of a 14th-century Augustinian monastery; its side chapel and dome were added in 1791 and 1854 respectively, the latter rebuilt after the 1883 earthquake. Most beautiful are the 18th-century mismatched majolica tiles adorning the semicircular staircase out the front. From here, the views are heavenly.

Ischia's own Garden of Eden can be found at **La Mortella** (☎ 081 98 62 20; Via F Calese 39, www.lamortella.it; Forio; admission €10; 🕑 9am-7pm Tue, Thu, Sat & Sun Apr-Nov). Designed by Russell Page and inspired by the Moorish gardens of Granada's Alhambra in Spain, this garden is one of Italy's finest. More than 1000 rare and exotic plants from all over the world thrive here, from luscious lotus flowers to the rare Amazonian water lily. This veritable Eden was established by the late British composer Sir William Walton and his Argentinian wife, Susana, who made it their home in 1949. Ever so civilised, the grounds host classical music concerts in the spring and autumn.

A soothing 10-minute walk down the road takes you to the neo-Renaissance villa **La Colombaia** (☎ 081 333 21 47; www.colombaia.org; Via F Calise 130, Forio; admission €6; 🕑 10am-2pm & 3-7pm daily Aug-Dec), former pad of Italian film director Luchino Visconti. Born into one of Milan's wealthiest families in 1906, his 1969 film *The Damned,* about a wealthy German family that turns fascist, received an Academy Award nomination for best screenplay. His recently restored whitewashed bachelor pad now houses an arts foundation, including a documentary library focussing on Visconti and cinema history, as well as costumes, set pieces and stills from his films. It's also a venue for the Ischia Film Festival (opposite).

South of Forio, spa lovers can soak and splash at the sprawling **Giardini Poseidon** (Poseidon Gardens; ☎ 081 908 71 11; www.giardiniposeidon.it; Via Mazzella, Spiaggia di Citara; day pass €28; 🕑 9am-6.30pm daily Apr, 8.30am-7pm daily May-Oct, closed Nov-mid-Apr). Breathe in as you ponder a mind-boggling choice of treatments and facilities, which include saunas, Jacuzzis and baby-blue pools filled with salubrious mineral waters. If it's all too stressful, settle for the dazzling private beach below.

Sant'Angelo & the South Coast

A world away from north-coast crowds, tiny Sant'Angelo is the most chic spot on the island. Quiet laneways spill down the hill, flanked by chic boutiques, galleries, frangipani and sunning cats. At the bottom on Piazzetta Ottorino Troia, tanned Italians

sip Campari soda and take in late-night summer music concerts. Keeping an eye on it all is the great hulking *scoglio* (rock), joined to the village by a long sandbar sprinkled with fishing boats, beach umbrellas and lithe-limbed *bagnini* (lifeguards).

From the pier, brightly painted water taxis reach some of the island's best beaches, including the sandy **Spiaggia dei Maronti** (one way €3) and the intimate cove of **Il Sorgeto** (one way €5), with its steamy thermal spring. Sorgeto can also be reached on foot down a poorly signposted path from the village of Panza.

For a fabulously atmospheric spa experience, catch a water taxi to Cavascura (one way €2.50) and follow the signs 300 metres down a rocky gorge to **Terme Cavascuro** (☎ 081 99 92 42; www.cavascura.it; Via Cavascura 1, Spiaggia dei Maronti, Sant'Angelo; basic thermal bath €10; 🕑 8.30am-1.30pm & 2.30-6pm mid-Apr–mid-Oct, closed mid-Oct–mid-Apr). Wedged between soaring cliffs, this historic frills-free outdoor spa is Ischia's oldest. Soak in old Roman baths hewn into the cliff, sweat it out in a grotto, then (for an extra fee) top it all off with a mud wrap (€20), manicure (€13) or massage (€26). The sulphurous waters are reputedly beneficial for rheumatic, bronchial and skin conditions.

A spectacular, if partly strenuous, 2km walk above the coast from Sant'Angelo also reaches the spa, passing on its way the faded luxury of **Parco Termale Aphrodite Apollon** (☎ 081 99 92 19; www.aphrodite.it; Via Petrelle, Sant'Angelo; admission €23; 🕑 8am-6pm mid-Apr–Oct, closed Nov–mid-Apr). Beyond its ivy-clad entrance is a rambling complex of gyms, saunas, lush terraced gardens and 12 differently heated pools, including one for hydro-cycling. Beauty treatments include tailored kinesiology therapies (€60), wine facials (€60) and soothing mud showers (€20). Buffed and balanced, flaunt that new bod at the beach bar below.

Monte Epomeo

A roughly 2.5km (50 min) calf-building uphill walk from the village of Fontana brings you to the top of **Monte Epomeo** (788m). Formed by an underwater eruption, it boasts superlative views of the Bay of Naples. The little church near the top is the 15th-century **Cappella di San Nicola di Bari**, which features a pretty majolica floor. The adjoining hermitage was built in the 18th century by an island governor who, after narrowly escaping death, swapped politics for poverty and spent the rest of his days here in saintly solitude.

ACTIVITIES

If diving takes your fancy, **Captain Cook** (☎ 335 636 26 30; www.captaincook.it; Via Iasolino 106, Ischia Porto) has equipment for hire and runs courses. A single dive will typically cost from €35. **Westcoast** (☎ 081 90 86 04; www.westcoastischia.it; Porto di Forio) provides full- and half-day hire of motorised boats and dinghies (with or without a sailor).

FESTIVALS & EVENTS

Ischian festivals are all about the good life – food, wine, film and a little laid-back jazz to while away those summer evenings.

Ischia Film Festival (www.ischiafilmfestival.it) Serves up free flicks and exhibitions in star locations around the island, including Castello Aragonese, Villa Arbusto and La Colombaia, usually in June.

Vinischia (www.vinischia.it in Italian) Foodies flock to this four-day celebration of regional food and wine, with free tastings and concerts along the Lungomare Aragonese, usually in June and early July.

Festa di Sant'Anna The allegorical 'burning of the Castello Aragonese' takes place on the feast day of St Anne on 26 July, with a hypnotic procession of boats and fireworks.

Ischia Jazz Festival (www.ischiajazzfestival.com in Italian) Ischia's annual jazz festival pumps out five days of smooth Italian sax with a dash of foreign acts, usually in September.

SLEEPING

Most hotels close in winter and prices normally drop considerably at those that stay open. Prices quoted here are for high season. In addition to the hotels listed here, there are the spa hotels, most of which only take half- or full-board bookings. The tourist office can supply you with a list.

ALBERGO IL MONASTERO   HOTEL €€
☎ 081 99 24 35; www.albergoilmonastero.it; Castello Aragonese, Rocca del Castello, Ischia Ponte; s/d/ste incl breakfast €75/110/125; Easter-Oct
Freshly revamped, this ex-convent mixes vaulted ceilings, crisp white walls and vintage

cotto tiles with chic plush sofas, a sprinkle of antiques and bold contemporary art by the late owner and artist Gabriele Mattera. Rooms are simple but stylish, and sans TV. Not that they're needed – the sea and island views are prime-time.

ALBERGO MACRÌ   HOTEL €
☎ /fax 081 99 26 03; Via Iasolino 96, Ischia Porto; s/d/t incl breakfast €46/76/101; year-round; P
Down a blind alley near the main port, this place has an affable owner and a friendly low-key vibe. While the pine and bamboo furnishings won't snag any design awards, rooms are clean, bright and comfy. All 1st-floor rooms have terraces and the small downstairs bar serves a mean espresso.

CAMPING MIRAGE   CAMP SITE €
☎ 081 99 05 51; www.campingmirage.it; Via Maronti 37, Spiaggia dei Maronti, Barano d'Ischia; per tent/car/person €5.50/9.50/10.50; year-round; P
On one of Ischia's best beaches, this shady camp site offers 50 places, showers, laundry facilities, bar and a restaurant serving lip-smacking plates of pasta.

IL GABBIANO   HOSTEL €
☎ /fax 081 90 94 22; SS Forio-Panza 182, Forio; r incl breakfast €16; Apr-Oct;
This hostel is one of the best around. Near the beach, it has bedrooms sleeping two, four or six. Monastically basic, the rooms are, nevertheless, spotlessly clean and all have small balconies with five-star sea views.

HOTEL CASA CELESTINO   HOTEL €€
☎ 081 99 92 13; www.casacelestino.it; Via Chiaia di Rose 20, Sant'Angelo; s €90-110, d €75-100, ste €110-125 incl breakfast; Jan-Oct;
On the pedestrian walkway down to the headland, this chic little number is a soothing blend of creamy furnishings, whitewashed walls, contemporary art and terracotta highlights. The uncluttered bedrooms boast majolica-tiled floors, modern bathrooms and enviable balconies overlooking the sea. There is a good, unfussy restaurant across the way.

HOTEL CONCHIGLIA   HOTEL €
☎ 081 99 92 70; Via Chiaia di Rose, Sant'Angelo; s/d incl breakfast €40/80; year-round
Charming, clean and centrally located behind Sant'Angelo's people-watching piazza, this

humble beachside hotel is excellent value. Rooms are cosy and the kitsch art and plastic flowers add to its raffish charm. The buffet breakfast is generous and is served on the restaurant's waterfront terrace. Ask about special seasonal rates, which can be a steal.

HOTEL LA MARTICANA   HOTEL €
☎ 081 333 44 31; www.lamarticana.it; Via Quercia 48-50, Ischia Porto; s/d incl breakfast €88/68; ☺ year-round; ⓟ ✇

A short suitcase trundle from the ferry, this small hotel has a friendly homey feel and there's a well-established garden with grapevines, tomato plants and a barbecue (available for guests). Rooms are small but well equipped with fridges, TVs and hairdryers. The breakfast buffet is more generous than most.

HOTEL LA SIRENELLA   HOTEL €€
☎ 081 99 47 43; www.lasirenella.net; Corso Angelo Rizzoli 41, Lacco Ameno; s/d incl breakfast €70/140; ☺ Apr-Oct; ✇

Run by a young smiling team of siblings, this affable address sits right on the beach. Terraced rooms boast sand-and-sea views, freshly tiled bathrooms and a cool, breezy vibe. When the sea air piques your hunger, succumb to pizza at the downstairs restaurant.

HOTEL SEMIRAMIS   HOTEL €
☎ 081 90 75 11; www.hotelsemiramisischia.it; Spiaggia di Citara, Forio; s/d incl breakfast €75/51; ☺ Apr-Oct; ⓟ ✇ ⚐

A few minutes' walk from the Poseidon spa complex, this newish hotel, run by friendly Giovanni and his German wife, has a tropical oasis feel with its central pool surrounded by palms. Rooms are large and beautifully tiled in the traditional yellow-and-turquoise pattern. The garden is glorious, with fig trees, vineyards and distant sea views.

MEZZATORRE RESORT & SPA   RESORT €€€
☎ 081 98 61 11; www.mezzatorre.it; Via Mezzatorre 23, Forio; s €200-300, d €250-380, ste €500-700 incl breakfast; ☺ mid-Apr–Oct; ✇ 🖳 ⚐ ⓟ

Perched on a bluff above the sea, this luxurious resort is surrounded by a 7-acre pine wood. An in-house spa centre and tennis courts crank up the spoil factor. The sitting rooms and some guest rooms are located in a 15th-century defensive tower. Rooms are decorated in earthy colours, some have private garden and Jacuzzi. Check out the infinity pool above the beach for the ultimate film-star setting. If funds are short, just have a long, slow drink in the adjacent bar.

UMBERTO A MARE   HOTEL €
☎ 081 99 71 71; www.umbertoamare.it; Via Soccorso 2, Forio; s €75-110, d €110-170 incl breakfast; ☺ Apr-Oct

Tucked under one of Ischia's finest restaurants, with crystal sea below, these 12 quiet rooms ooze understated chic, with cool ceramic tiles, modern bathrooms and a terracotta terrace boasting killer views and sun beds.

EATING

Seafood aside, Ischia is famed for its rabbit, which is bred on inland farms. Another local speciality is *rucolino*, a green, liquorice-flavoured liqueur made from *rucola* (rocket) leaves.

CANTINE DI PIETRATORCIA   WINERY €€€
☎ 081 90 72 32; www.pietratorcia.it; Via Provinciale Panza 267, Forio; meals €30; ☺ 10am-1pm & 4-8pm Mon-Thu & til late Fri-Sun Apr–mid-Jun & mid-Sep–mid-Nov, 5.30pm-late mid-Jun–mid-Sep, closed mid-Nov–Mar

Set among vines, figs and rosemary bushes, this A-list winery is a foodie's nirvana. Tour the old stone cellars, sip a local drop and eye up the delectable degustation menu. Offerings include fragrant bruschetta and cheeses, hearty Campanian sausages and spicy *salumi* (cold meats). Full dinners are also available if booked in advanced.

DA CICCIO   SNACKS €
☎ 081 99 13 14; Via Porto 1, Ischia Porto, snacks from €1; ☺ year-round

Just the spot for ferry-weary arrivals, this much-loved bar does cheap, light meals, luscious pastries and dangerously good gelato. Eat in or take away, the *calzone* (pizza folded over to form a pie) stuffed with spinach, pinenuts and raisins (€1) is divine.

DA ROBERTO   GELATERIA €
☎ 081 98 23 13; Via Luigi Mazzella 28, Ischia Ponte; cones from €1.50; ☺ year-round

Owners Roberto and Eugenia made the move here from Belluno in the Veneto, an area famed for its skilled gelato makers. The proof is in the cone. Utterly superlative are the *gran biscotti*, *crema della nonna* and the Mozart chocolate and hazelnut combo. The *semi-freddi* (partially frozen desserts) are made fresh on the premises and legitimise any gluttonous impulse.

THE AMALFI COAST

GRAN CAFFÈ VITTORIA
CAFÉ €

☎ 081 199 16 49; Corso Vittorio Colonna 110, Ischia; pastries €2; ⌚ year-round

At the chic end of the port, this elegant, wood-panelled café has been spoiling customers and waistlines for more than a hundred years with its irresistible cakes, pastries, coffees and cocktails, all served by old-school, bow-tied waiters.

LA BAIA EL CLIPPER
RISTORANTE €€€

☎ 081 333 42 09; Via Porto 116, Ischia Porto; meals €40; ⌚ year-round

Located at the entrance to the port and now run by the second generation, this place sets the scene for romance. Dress up, order cocktails, clink glasses and fall in love. No chemistry? There's always the view and seafood. And the waiters are friendly, the service slick.

LA BROCCA
TRATTORIA €€

☎ 081 90 00 51; Via Roma 24, Lacco Ameno; meals €17; ⌚ Jan-Oct

Across the road from the beach, this unadorned trattoria serves simple, superlative seafood to in-the-know locals. Mamma cooks out the back, *nonna* polishes the cutlery and the spunky sun-kissed son serves salubrious seafood straight off the boat. Do not miss the spaghetti with mussels, but tuck a napkin into your collar!

LO SCOGLIO
RISTORANTE €€

☎ 081 99 95 29; Via Cava Ruffano 58, Sant'Angelo; meals €28; ⌚ closed Jan-Mar & mid-Nov–mid-Dec

Dramatically located jutting out over the sea beside a picture-perfect beach cove, this is a great place for sunsets and seafood. Mussel soup, grilled bass and butterfly noodles with salmon are examples of the fishy fare on offer. The service is brisk and efficient. Sunday lunchtime is a popular weekly event.

RISTORANTE DA CICCIO
RISTORANTE €€

☎ 081 99 16 86; Via Luigi Mazzella 32, Ischia Ponte; meals €25; ⌚ closed Nov & Tue Dec-May & Oct

Sublime local seafood and a charming host make this a heart-stealer. Highlights are *tubettoni* pasta with clams and pecorino cheese, and a zesty mussel soup topped with bread and chilli. The wizened man sitting out front was once the chef. These days he spends his evenings with cigarette in one hand, wine in the other, happily muttering to himself.

RISTORANTE IL PONTE
RISTORANTE €

☎ 081 90 42 55; Via Chiaia delle Rose 89, Sant'Angelo; pizzas from €3.50; ⌚ Apr-Oct

Inexpensive, no-frills grub just up from the car park. The pizzas are good, if unexceptional, the seafood satisfyingly fresh and the salads large and varied. Order a margherita, a jug of icy beer and laze away the afternoon under the palm-thatched terrace. Popular with the sun-bronzed boys and babes from the beach across the street.

RISTORANTE LA PANTERA ROSA
RISTORANTE €€

☎ 081 99 24 83; Riva Destra, Ischia Porto; meals €28; ⌚ Apr-Nov

There are some good choices and good prices for those suffering from black-tie burnout at this laid-back restaurant on the port's savvy suppertime strip. The menu has all the traditional pasta and pizza choices, plus meat dishes such as veal with wine (€9), which comes warmly recommended.

UMBERTO A MARE
RISTORANTE €€€

☎ 081 99 71 71; Via Soccorso 2, Forio; meals €46; ⌚ Mar-Dec

In the shadow of the Spanish mission–style Soccorso church, this sassy waterside number has the choice of low-key café-bar for light snacks, or more formal restaurant for Med-chic dining. Highlights include *ziti* (long thick tubes of pasta) with tuna, fresh tomato and *peperoncino* (chilli) and the decadent penne with lobster and asparagus.

ZI CARMELA
RISTORANTE €€

☎ 081 99 84 23; Via Schioppa 27, Forio; meals €20; ⌚ Apr-Oct

Frequented by locals, here for seafood dishes such as the *fritturina e pezzogne* (a local white fish baked with potatoes and herbs in the wood-fired pizza oven). Dining space is gaily decorated with copper pans, ceramic mugs and strings of garlic and chillies. Undecided taste buds can go for the €25 four-course set menu.

ENTERTAINMENT

Ischia is not Ibiza. That said, the area around Ischia Porto has the best buzz, with a handful of bars and clubs to keep night owls hooting.

Bar Calise (☎ 081 99 12 70; Piazza degli Eroi 69, Ischia; admission €15, incl 1 drink; ⌚ 7pm-3am Thu-Sun) draws young and old with its languid mix of palms, cocktails, waistcoated waiters and live Latin, swing and folk.

Clubbing types bump and grind to house and techno at the hyperactive (and hyper-expensive) **Valentino** (☎ 081 99 26 53; Corso Vittoria Colonna 97; admission €30 Jul & Aug, €10 Sep-Jun; ☽ midnight-late daily).

In the 1960s, docked boat **Blue Jane** (☎ 081 99 32 96; Viale Pagoda 1, Ischia Porto; admission €20, incl 1 drink; ☽ midnight-late Fri-Sun) was the famous *A Lampara*, floating playground for the likes of Mick and Bianca Jagger, Kirk Douglas and cult Italian singer Fabrizio de Andre. Today it pumps out mainly commercial and house tunes to a friendly, chilled-out crowd.

SHOPPING

Those with the S-word on their mind head to Ischia's Via Roma and the web of narrow streets leading to Ischia Ponte. From floss-thin bikinis to decadent jars of *babà* (sponge soaked in rum), there's enough shopping on these cobbled stones to burn up the plastic fantastic. Done? Explore the tiny boutiques and art galleries in Sant'Angelo and Forio.

ADAM   ANTIQUES
☎ 081 98 22 05; Via Roma 102, Ischia

Looking for a Renaissance pistol? Pick one up at this offbeat ode to all things vintage Italian. It's all here, from antique Ischian urns

and handmade Punchinello dolls to shining armour (knight not included). Take a detour through the leafy back garden, complete with giant lemons, sleepy turtles and one very determined pussycat.

ANTICA MACELLERIA DI
FRANCESCO ESPOSITO   FOOD
☎ 081 98 10 11; Via delle Terme 2, Ischia; ☽ year-round, closed Sun winter

For a perfect picnic hamper head to this century-old deli. Drop in from 8am for fresh mozzarella and wood-fired *casareccio* bread. Fill the latter with a lip-smacking choice of cheeses, *prosciutti*, homemade *peperoncino* salami and marinated peppers. Then wash it all down with a bottle of *falanghina* (dry white wine). *Meraviglioso!* (Marvellous!).

CAPRICCI   LINGERIE & BEACHWEAR
☎ 081 98 20 63; Via Roma 37, Ischia

Fabulous lingerie and men's and women's beachwear by Versace, Moschino, La Perla and Roberto Cavalli. Expect high quality and matching prices for looking this good on the beach and in bed.

GRIFO   CLOTHING
☎ 081 98 37 25; Corso Vittoria Colonna 210, Ischia

Cool threads for fashion-literate guys. Stock up on Burberry, Richmond, and St Tropez

ISCHIA ON A FORK

Ischian restaurateur Carlo Buono gives the low-down on classic island grub:

'Fresh, seasonal ingredients are the cornerstone of Ischian cooking, from silky olive oil to plump *pomodorini* (cherry tomatoes). Like Neapolitan cooking, the emphasis is on simple, uncomplicated home cooking using premium produce. Traditionally, there are two types of Ischian cuisine: coastal and mountain. For centuries, the fishermen of Lacco Ameno and Sant'Angelo would barter with the farmers of Barano and Serrara Fontana, who'd offer wine, vegetables, pork and rabbit in exchange for the fishermen's catch.

'Indeed, rabbit is a typical Ischian meat and we're seeing a revival of the traditional *fossa* (pit) breeding method, where rabbits are bred naturally in deep *fosse* instead of in cages. The result is a more tender, flavoursome meat. Leading this renaissance is local Slow Food advocate Riccardo D'Ambra, whose famous trattoria **Il Focolare** (☎ 081 90 29 44; Via Cretaio 3, Barano d'Ischia; meals €25; ☽ 8-11pm Mon-Fri, 12-3pm & 8-11pm Sat & Sun, closed Wed Nov-Mar, open New Year's Eve) is well known for its rabbit and rustic mountain dishes. Definitely worth eating on the island is a popular Sunday dish called *coniglio all'ischitana* (Ischia-style rabbit), which is prepared with olive oil, unpeeled garlic, chilli, tomato, basil, thyme and white wine.

'Like the land, the sea is seasonal, so the seafood that we cook depends on the time of year. Typical local fish include *pesce bandiera* (sailfish), the flat *castagna*, *lampuga* and *palamide* (a small tuna). A popular way of cooking it is in *acqua pazza* (crazy water). Traditionally prepared on the fishing boats, it's a delicate sauce made with *pomodorini*, garlic and parsley. Fried fish is also very typical; a fresh serve of *frittura di mare* (mixed fried seafood) drizzled in lemon juice is just superb. May to September is *totano* (squid) season and a great time to try *totani imbotti* (squid stuffed with olives, capers and breadcrumbs, and stewed in wine).

'Equally wonderful is fresh, wood-fired *casareccio* bread. Soft and dense on the inside and crunchy on the out, it's perfect for doing the *scarpetta* (wiping your plate clean) or for filling with salami or *parmigiano* cheese. If you have any room left, track down a slice of *torta caprese*, a moist chocolate and almond cake. *Buon appetito.*'

label Vilebrequin. The pastel-striped Borrelli sweaters are sublime. Across the street at no. 162 is the women's store.

IMAGAENARIA — BOOKS

☎ 081 98 56 32; Via Giovanni da Procida, Ischia Ponte

Charming and erudite, this little bookshop is also a local publishing house that prints a fetching series of minibooks dedicated to Ischian folklore, culture, history and nature in Italian. The shop also sells rare prints and lithographs of Ischia and Naples at a range of prices. The most expensive date back to the 1600s. Open until 9pm in winter and 1am in summer for some serious late-night shopping.

ISCHIA SAPORI — FOOD & GIFTS

☎ 337 97 24 65; Via Luigi Mazzella 5, Ischia Ponte

This savvy little produce shop is the home of *rucolino*, a local, liquorice-flavoured digestive made with *rucola* (rocket). The recipe is a guarded secret, but the liquid is yours for the taking. The shop also sells its own wines, gourmet food stuffs, *limoncello*-soaked *babà*, olive-oil soaps, and fragrances, all reasonably priced and gorgeously packaged with trademark Italian flair.

JUDITH MAJOR — CLOTHING & SHOES

☎ 081 98 32 95; Corso Vittoria Colonna 174, Ischia

Exclusive stockist of Italian label Brunello Cucinelli, the look here is Polo Ralph Lauren with a sexy Italian twist. Cashmere sweaters, suave shirts, blazers and chic womenswear. Shoes include Prada, Barrett and Alberto Guardiani for men and Stuart Weitzman and Pedro Garcia for women. Everything you'll need for a jaunt on the yacht.

L'ISOLETTO — GIFTS & SOUVENIRS

☎ 081 99 93 74; Via Chiaia delle Rose 36, Sant'Angelo

Stock up on a mouthwatering selection of local produce, from spicy *peperoncino*, rum-soaked *babà* and *cannoncelli* (pastry filled with lemon cream) to Ischian vino and the ubiquitous *limoncello*. Less tasteful – but equally delicious – is a collection of kitsch tourist tack, from seashell placemats to 3-D souvenir wall plates.

PERCORSI COMUNICANTI IN GALLERIA — CERAMICS

☎ 081 90 42 27; Via Sant'Angelo 93, Sant'Angelo

Contemporary ceramic respite from smiling sun platters. This slick little gallery features bold, contemporary ceramics from Neapolitan artist Massimiliano Santoro. A modest selection of Murano glass jewellery and designer silk kaftans further loosen the purse strings.

RICCIO CALZATURE — SHOES

☎ 081 98 41 99; Corso Vittoria Colonna 216, Ischia

Italian footwear sans the designer price tag. Men's, women's, formal and sporty, last season's stock is slashed by up to 50%. Fashion victims needn't fret. New-season stock is also available, at new-season prices. The choice isn't huge but definitely worth a browse, with names such as Diesel, Richmond, Miss Sixty and Cesare Paciotti in the mix.

ZEUS FABER — CLOTHING & ACCESSORIES

☎ 333 760 33 02; Via Sant'Angelo 81, Sant'Angelo

A dimly lit mix of boho chic and local art. Indian pashminas, embroidered sandals, jewellery and handbags sit beside vintage prints, one-off gauche re-creations and owner Rosario De Paola's original paintings of a fiery Vesuvius.

GETTING THERE & AROUND

You can catch hydrofoils direct to Capri (€10.40) and Procida (€4, 20 minutes) from Ischia, as well as to Naples and the Amalfi Coast. See p262 for details of year-round ferries and hydrofoils.

The island's main bus station is in Ischia Porto. There are two principal lines: the CS (Circolo Sinistro; Left Circle), which circles the island anticlockwise, and the CD line (Circolo Destro; Right Circle), which travels in a clockwise direction, passing through each town and leaving every 30 minutes. Buses pass near all hotels and camp sites. A single ticket, valid for 90 minutes, costs €1.20, an all-day, multiuse ticket is €4, while a two-day ticket is €6. Taxis and microtaxis (scooter-engined three-wheelers) are also available.

You can do this small island a favour by not bringing your car. If you want to hire a car or scooter for a day, there are plenty of rental firms, although razor-thin roads and holiday traffic make driving a car here stressful. In addition to hiring out cars (from €32 per day) and mopeds (€25 to €35), **Fratelli del Franco** (☎ 081 99 13 34; Via A De Luca 127, Ischia Ponte) also has mountain bikes (around €10 per day). You can't take a rented vehicle off the island.

GREG ELMS

PROCIDA

The Bay of Naples' smallest island is also its best-kept secret: a soulful blend of hidden lemon groves, weathered fishermen and pastel arabesque abodes.

Mercifully off the mass-tourist radar, Procida feels refreshingly real. August aside – when beach-bound mainlanders flock to its shores – its skinny sun-bleached streets are the domain of the locals: wiry young boys clutch fishing rods, weary mothers clutch wiry young boys and wizened old seamen swap tales of malaise on **Piazza dei Martiri** (Martyrs' Square). Here, the hotels are smaller, fewer waiters speak broken German and the islanders' welcome lacks that seasoned smarminess.

On **Marina Grande**, colourful cubic houses crowd the waterfront like a row of bright, blunt crayons. Under strung wet washing, fishermen mend their nets while waiters serve their catch in well-worn restaurants. Further exploration does little to detract from this image. Over the hill, sleepy **Corricella** tumbles down to the sea in a riot of yellows, pinks and whites. External staircases adorn stark, wide-arched houses, adding a spicy Arabian touch.

High above the village, the abandoned **Castello d'Avalos** was a prison until 1985. So spectacular are its views that prisoners required a recommendation to serve time here. Procida is also a seasoned film set; the international hit *Il Postino* was partly filmed here, as were parts of *The Talented Mr Ripley*. To this day, Procida is the preferred island retreat of Naples' creative set, who come here seeking solitude, inspiration and the best lemon *granita* (crushed ice flavoured with lemon juice) this side of Sorrento.

ORIENTATION & INFORMATION

Marina Grande is the hop-off point for ferries and hydrofoils, and forms most of the tourist showcase. Here, **Graziella Travel Agency** (☎ 081 896 95 94; www.isoladiprocida.it; Via Roma 117), is your best bet for organising accommodation, boat trips and bicycle hire. It also has a good free map of the island.

ETP (☎ 081 896 90 67; www.casavacanza.net, in Italian; Via Principe Umberto I, Marina Grande) can also organise accommodation as well as tickets to the Il Vento del Cinema film festival (right).

Surf the internet at nearby **Call Me** (☎ 081 896 80 33; Via Vittorio Emanuele 3, Marina Grande; per hr €3).

SIGHTS & ACTIVITIES

The best way to explore the island – a mere 4 sq km – is on foot or by bike.

Clinging onto Procida's highest point is the crumbling 16th-century **Castello d'Avalos**, former Bourbon hunting lodge and ex-prison. Soak in the dizzying bay views before exploring the adjoining **Abbazia di San Michele Arcangelo** (☎ 081 896 76 12; Via Terra Murata 89; admission €2; ✆ 10am-12.45pm year-round, plus 3.30-6pm May-Oct). Built in the 11th century and remodelled between the 17th and 19th centuries, this one-time Benedictine abbey contains a church, a small museum with some arresting paintings, and a honeycomb of catacombs.

From panoramic Piazza dei Martiri, the village of **Marina Corricella** tumbles down to its marina in a riot of pinks, yellows and whites. The bright colours made it easier for fishermen to play 'spot your house' while out at sea.

Further south, off Via Pizzaco, a steep flight of steps leads down to sand-brushed **Spiaggia di Chiaia**, one of the island's most beautiful beaches and home to **La Conchiglia** (p203).

All pink, white and blue, little **Marina di Chiaiolella** features a yacht-stocked marina, old-school eateries and a languid disposition. From here, head to the heaving **Lido di Procida** beach, where hyperactive water babies, flirting church-group teens and wandering-eyed husbands make for a voyeuristic feast.

The small satellite island of **Vivara** is protected by WWF; it contains rare native fauna and is an important archaeological site. It is currently closed to visitors indefinitely.

The **Procida Diving Centre** (☎ 081 896 83 85; www .vacanzeaprocida.it/framediving01-uk.htm; Via Cristoforo Colombo 6) runs diving courses and hires out equipment. Budget €32 for a single dive, €60 for a full day.

On the harbour at Marina Corricella, ask for Cesare, who runs **boat trips** (per 2½ hrs €20) and half-day trips in a galleon for €90 (minimum 25 people). **Ippocampo** (☎ 081 810 14 37, 333 720 01 93; www.ippocamposas.it; Marina Chiaiolella) hires out *gommoni* and *gozzi* (wooden boats) from €80 per day.

You can charter a yacht from **Blue Dream** (☎ 081 896 05 79, 339 572 08 74; www.bluedreamcharter .com; Via Ottimo 3) from €60 per person, per day.

FESTIVALS & EVENTS

Good Friday sees a colourful **Procession of the Misteri**. A wooden statue of Christ and the Madonna Addolorata, along with life-sized tableaux of plaster and papier-mâché illustrating events leading to Christ's crucifixion, are carted across the island. Men dress in blue tunics with white hoods, while many of the young girls dress as the Madonna.

Il Vento del Cinema (www.ilventodelcinema.it) is an annual five-day festival of art-house cinema and English-language workshops run by prolific film-makers. See the website for festival dates.

SLEEPING

Accommodation tends to be of the small-scale variety – think converted farmhouses and family-run hotels. A good choice of self-contained bungalows and apartments can work out quite cheap if you're in a group. Many places close over the winter and book out in August – so check ahead during these periods.

Camp sites are dotted around the island and are open from April to October. Typical prices are €10 per site plus €10 per person. Reliable sites include **Vivara** (☎ 081 896 92 42; Via IV Novembre) or, on the same road, **La Caravella** (☎ 081 810 18 38; Via IV Novembre).

Spiaggia di Chiaia (p201)   DALLAS STRIBLEY

CASA GIOVANNI DA PROCIDA   B&B €
☎ 081 896 03 58; www.casagiovannidaprocida.it;
Via Giovanni da Procida 3; s €50-80, d €65-100 incl
breakfast; ☕ closed Feb; Ⓟ ✂
This chic converted-farmhouse B&B features
split-level, minimalist rooms with low-rise
beds and contemporary furniture. Bathrooms
are small but slick, with bronze and aqua tiling,
cool cube basins, huge showerheads and the
odd vaulted ceiling. In the lush garden, chilled-
out guests read and eat peaches.

HOTEL CRESCENZO   HOTEL €€
☎ 081 896 72 55; www.hotelcrescenzo.it; Via Marina
di Chiaiolella 33; s €60-120, €d 70-120 incl breakfast;
☕ year-round; ✂
Just 10 smallish rooms; choose between a
bay view or balcony. The décor is a suitably
nautical blue and white. This hotel is fronted
by a restaurant, generally bursting with an
affable local crowd.

HOTEL LA CORRICELLA   HOTEL €€
☎ 081 896 75 75; Via Marina Corricella 88; s €70-100,
d €90-120 incl breakfast; ☕ Apr-Oct
One bookend to Marina Corricella, it's hard
to miss this shocking-pink number. Low-fuss
rooms feature modular-style furniture with
fans and TVs. The large shared terrace boasts
top-notch harbour views, the restaurant
serves decent seafood and a boat service
reaches the nearby beach.

HOTEL RIVIERA   HOTEL €
☎ 081 896 71 97; Via Giovanni da Procida 36, Marina
di Chiaiolella; s/d incl breakfast €35/70; ☕ Apr-Oct;
Ⓟ ✂
The downside? It's an uphill hike from the
marina, the interiors look a little tired and the
vibe is somewhat anonymous. On the upside,
there's birdsong, air-con, clean comfy beds
and it's fabulously cheap.

LA ROSA DEI VENTI   BUNGALOW €
☎ /fax 081 896 83 85; www.vacanzeaprocida.it; Via
Vincenzo Rinaldi 34; s per week €320-490, d €390-690,
tr €450-750 incl breakfast; ☕ Mar-Oct; Ⓟ 🖥
Perched on a tranquil cliff top, these 18 self-
contained bungalows feature private cooking
facilities, patios and clean, no-frills interiors.
There's a private beach and vineyard, and
matriarch Titta cooks up a weekly Procidan
feast, eaten under a lemon-clad pergola.

LE GRAND BLEU
GUESTHOUSE   APARTMENT €€
☎ 081 896 95 94; www.isoladiprocida.it; Via Flavio
Gioia 37; apt per week €250-950; ☕ closed mid-
Dec–Jan; ✂ 🖥
Close to Chiaia beach, these fresh apartments
feature bright functional furniture, funky
bathrooms, stovetops, internet access and
a cool rooftop terrace with wood-fired
oven, barbecue and views of Ischia. Wheelchair access.

EATING
Prime waterfront dining here needn't
equal an overpriced disappointment, with
portside trattorie serving fresh classic fare.
Several inland trattorie use home-grown
produce and game in their cooking. Try
the zesty *insalata al limone*, a lemon salad
infused with chilli oil.

BAR CAVALIERE   PASTICCERIA €
☎ 081 810 10 74; Via Roma 76, Marina Grande;
pastries from €1; ☕ year-round
Procida's prime pastry peddler will leave you a
drooling mess. All the rage is the *lingua di bue*
(ox tongue), flaky pastry shaped like a tongue
and filled with *crema pasticcera* (custard).

FAMMIVENTO   TRATTORIA €€
☎ 081 896 90 20; Via Roma 39, Marina Grande; meals
€25; ☕ closed Sun night, Mon & Nov-Mar
Get things going with the *alici ripiene* (stuffed
anchovies), then try the *fusilli carciofi e calamari*
(pasta with artichokes and calamari). For a
splurge, go for the *zuppa di crostaci e moluschi*
(crustacean and mollusc soup). It ain't the
house speciality for nada.

GRAZIELLA   TRATTORIA €

☎ 081 896 74 79; Via Marina Corricella 14; meals €12; ⏰ Mar-Oct

Along this unpretentious marina, with its old fishing boats, piles of fishing nets and sleek, lazy cats, any restaurant will provide you with a memorable dining experience. Choices include sandwiches and burgers, spicy *penne alla siciliana* (pasta with a spicy tomato and chilli sauce) and juicy grilled chicken with sweet-chilli sauce.

LA CONCHIGLIA   TRATTORIA €€

☎ 081 896 76 02; Via Pizzaco 10; meals €25; ⏰ Mar-Oct

No, you're not hallucinating, the view is real. Topaz waves at your feet, pastel Corricella in the distance. On the terrace, boisterous fishermen and sun-kissed lovers tuck into gems such as *antipasto al mare* (seafood antipasto) and a knockout *spaghetti alla povera* (spaghetti with *peperoncino*, green peppers, cherry tomatoes and anchovies). To get here, take the steep steps down from Via Pizzaco or book a boat from Corricella.

RISTORANTE L'APPRODO   TRATTORIA €

☎ 081 896 99 30; Via Roma 76, Marina Grande; meals €12; ⏰ Mar-Oct

Preened navy cadets flock here for home-style cooking. Dive into a spicy bowl of *penne alla siciliana* or slurp your way through the *zuppa di pesce* (fish stew). When you're done, sit back and watch the boats dock.

RISTORANTE SCARABEO   RISTORANTE €€

☎ 081 896 99 18; Via Salette 10; meals €27; ⏰ daily Dec-Oct, weekends only Dec-Feb

Behind a veritable jungle of lemon trees lies the venerable kitchen of Signora Battinelli. With husband Francesco, she whips up classics such as *fritelle di basilico* (fried patties of bread, egg, parmesan and basil) and homemade aubergine and *provola* ravioli (€9). They breed their own rabbits, make their own *falanghina* and it's all yours to devour under a pergola of bulbous lemons.

ENTERTAINMENT

People flock to Procida for peace and quiet, so don't come expecting a wild time. Marina Grande has a few low-key options. **GM Bar** (☎ 081 896 75 60; Via Roma 117; ⏰ 24hrs Jul-Aug, 5am-2am Sep-Jun, closed Tue Oct-May) features live jazz, latin or local pop acts on Friday night, and DJ-spun commercial/house and commercial/Latin on Saturday and Sunday night respectively.

Further up the street, wood decking, potted palms and chill-out tunes set the scene for languid people-watching at **Bar Roma** (☎ 081 896 74 60; Via Roma 163, Marina Grande; ⏰ closed Tue Oct-Apr).

SHOPPING

Low-key Procida isn't a shopping heavy-weight. Good buys include ceramics, wine and local art.

ENOTECA PECCATI DI GOLA   WINE

☎ 081 810 19 99; Via Vittorio Emanuele 13, Marina Grande

Provocatively called 'Sins of the Throat', this slick little bottle shop stocks the best of Campanian vino and a smattering of other Italian drops.

LUIGI NAPPA GALLERY   ART & JEWELLERY

☎ 081 896 05 61, Via Roma 50, Marina Grande

Nappa's paintings are fresh and contemporary with a Procidan theme; his sculpture and jewellery are offbeat and original.

SISTERS   CERAMICS & SOUVENIRS

☎ 081 896 03 33; Via Roma 154, Marina Grande

Go Med with the hand-painted ceramic jugs, platters, coasters, lemon squeezers and serious-ly dishy coffee cups. The vintage island photo-graphs make for soulful souvenirs.

GETTING THERE & AROUND

Procida is linked by ferry and hydrofoil to Ischia (€4, 20 minutes), Pozzuoli and Naples (see p262). There is a limited bus service (€0.80), with four lines radiating from Marina Grande. Bus L1 connects the port and Via Marina di Chiaiolella.

Small, open micro-taxis can be hired for two to three hours for around €35, depending on your bargaining prowess. Contact **Graziella Travel Agency** (☎ 081 896 95 94; www.isoladiprocida.it; Via Roma 117) for bicycle hire (€5 half day, €8 full day).

HIGHLIGHTS

- Ponder the dark forces that rage in Mt Vesuvius from the **Villa Comunale park** (p208)
- Dive into the limpid waters off the **Bay of Ieranto** (p219)
- Sit down to seafood with the VIPs at **Marina del Cantone** (p219)
- Immerse yourself in the silence of the hills while **walking** (see the boxed text, p218) the peninsula's network of ancient paths
- Take in a concert in the 14th-century cloisters of the **Chiesa di San Francesco** (p207)

SORRENTO

Gateway to the silent land of the sirens, Sorrento is a resort town with a southern-Italian soul.

On paper Sorrento is a place to avoid – a package holiday centre with few must-see sights, no beach to speak of and a glut of brassy English-style pubs. In reality, it's a strangely appealing place, its laid-back southern Italian charm resisting all attempts to swamp it in souvenir tat and graceless development.

Dating to Greek times and known to Romans as Surrentum, its main selling point is its fabulous location. Straddling cliffs that look directly over the Bay of Naples to Mt Vesuvius, it's ideally situated for exploring the surrounding area: to the south, the best of the peninsula's unspoiled countryside and, beyond that, the Amalfi Coast; to the north, Pompeii and the archaeological sites; offshore, the fabled island of Capri.

In town, the action focuses on the medieval **centro storico**. An attractive quarter of shops, restaurants, churches and piazzas, it gets very busy in high summer, although even in July and August you don't have to walk far to avoid the worst of the crowds.

For an altogether more tranquil scene, head to the green hills around Sorrento. Known as the land of the sirens, in honour of the mythical maiden-monsters who were said to live on Li Galli (a tiny archipelago off the peninsula's southern coast), the area to the west of **Massa Lubrense** is among the least developed and most beautiful in the country. The best way to appreciate it is to walk the ancient footpaths that connect the sleepy villages and the coast's hidden coves. For the more adventurous, there's some great diving in the **Punta Campanella Marine Reserve**.

Views of the Bay of Naples from Sorrento's Museo Correale (p208)   GREG ELMS

ORIENTATION

Piazza Tasso, bisected by Sorrento's main street, Corso Italia, is the centre of town. It's about a 300m walk northwest of the Circumvesuviana train station, along Corso Italia. From Marina Piccola, where ferries and hydrofoils dock, walk south along Via Marina Piccola then climb about 200 steps to reach the piazza. Corso Italia becomes the SS145 on its way east to Naples and, heading west, changes its name to Via Capo.

SIGHTS & ACTIVITIES
Centro storico

The town centre is compact and all the main sights (of which there are surprisingly few) are within walking distance of **Piazza Tasso**, the town's focal square. Spearing off to the west, Corso Italia (closed to traffic in the centre between 10am and 1pm and 7pm to 7am) cuts through the centro storico, whose narrow streets throng with tourists on summer evenings. In the middle of the loud souvenir stores, pubs, cafés and trattorie, the 15th-century **Sedile Dominava** on Via San Cesareo looks uncomfortably out of place. A domed enclave used by the town's medieval aristocracy as a meeting point, it now houses a working men's club.

Walking in Piazza Tasso   GREG ELMS

INFORMATION

- **Deutsche Bank** (Piazza Angelina Lauro 22-29) One of several banks in and around Piazza Angelina Lauro with an ATM; there are others along Corso Italia.
- **Farmacia Farfalla** (☎ 081 878 13 49; Via De Maio 19; ☷ 8.30am-1.30pm & 4-11pm daily)
- **Hospital** (☎ 081 533 11 11; Corso Italia 1)
- **Info Sorrento** (www.infosorrento.it) Extensive website with tourist information on Sorrento and environs.
- **Internet Train** (☎ 081 878 57 42; Via degli Aranci 49; per 30 mins/1hr €1.50/3; ☷ 9.30am-1.30pm & 3.30-10.30pm Mon-Sat, 9.30am-1.30pm & 6-10pm Sun)
- **Police station** (☎ 081 807 53 11; Via Capasso 11)

- **Post office** (☎ 081 878 14 95; Corso Italia 210)
- **Sorrento Info** (☎ 081 807 40 00; www.sorrento info.eu; Via Tasso 19; per 30 mins €2.50; ☷ 10am-1.30pm & 4-8pm Mon-Sat Nov-Apr, 10am-1.30pm & 5-10.30pm Mon-Sat May-Oct) Office providing tourist information and internet access.
- **Telephone office** (☎ 081 807 33 17; Piazza Tasso 37; ☷ 9am-1pm & 4-10pm daily)
- **Tourist office** (☎ 081 807 40 33; www.sorrento tourism.com; Via Luigi De Maio 35; ☷ 8.45am-6.15pm Mon-Sat, plus 8.45am-12.45pm Sun Aug) In the Circolo dei Forestieri (Foreigners' Club), it has plenty of useful printed material and provides the free monthly information magazine, *Surrentum*.

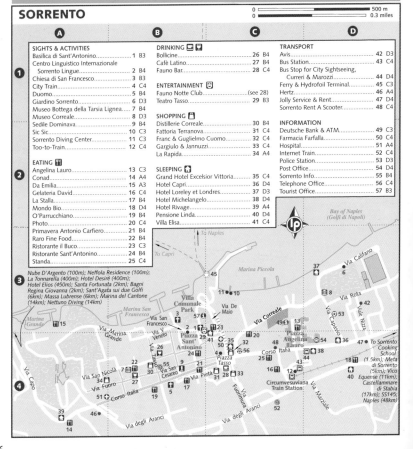

SORRENTO

| 0 | 500 m |
| 0 | 0.3 miles |

	A	B	C	D
SIGHTS & ACTIVITIES		**DRINKING**		**TRANSPORT**	
Basilica di Sant'Antonino	1 B3	Bollicine	26 B4	Avis	42 D3
Centro Linguistico Internazionale		Café Latino	27 B4	Bus Station	43 C4
Sorrento Lingue	2 B4	Fauno Bar	28 C4	Bus Stop for City Sightseeing,	
Chiesa di San Francesco	3 B3			Curreri & Marozzi	44 D4
City Train	4 C4	**ENTERTAINMENT**		Ferry & Hydrofoil Terminal	45 C3
Duomo	5 B4	Fauno Notte Club	(see 28)	Hertz	46 A4
Giardino Sorrento	6 D3	Teatro Tasso	29 B3	Jolly Service & Rent	47 D4
Museo Bottega della Tarsia Lignea	7 B4			Sorrento Rent A Scooter	48 C4
Museo Correale	8 D3	**SHOPPING**			
Sedile Dominava	9 B4	Distillerie Correale	30 B4	**INFORMATION**	
Sic Sic	10 C3	Fattoria Terranova	31 C4	Deutsche Bank & ATM	49 C3
Sorrento Diving Center	11 C3	Franc & Guglielmo Cuomo	32 C4	Farmacia Farfalla	50 C4
Too-to-Train	12 C4	Gargiulo & Jannuzzi	33 C4	Hospital	51 A4
		La Rapida	34 A4	Internet Train	52 C4
EATING				Police Station	53 D3
Angelina Lauro	13 C3	**SLEEPING**		Post Office	54 D4
Conad	14 A4	Grand Hotel Excelsior Vittoria	35 C4	Sorrento Info	55 B4
Da Emilia	15 A3	Hotel Capri	36 D4	Telephone Office	56 C4
Gelateria David	16 C4	Hotel Loreley et Londres	37 D3	Tourist Office	57 B3
La Stalla	17 B4	Hotel Michelangelo	38 D4		
Mondo Bio	18 D4	Hotel Rivage	39 A4		
O'Parrucchiano	19 B4	Pensione Linda	40 C4		
Photo	20 C4	Villa Elisa	41 C4		
Primavera Antonio Carfiero	21 B4				
Raro Fine Food	22 B4				
Ristorante il Buco	23 C4				
Ristorante Sant'Antonino	24 B4				
Standa	25 C4				

Nube D'Argento (100m); Neffola Residence (100m);
La Tonnarella (400m); Hotel Desiré (400m);
Hotel Elios (450m); Santa Fortunata (2km); Bagni
Regina Giovanna (2km); Sant'Agata sui due Golfi
(6km); Massa Lubrense (6km); Marina del Cantone
(14km); Nettuno Diving (14km)

Cathedral & Churches

On Corso Italia, the gleaming white façade of Sorrento's **Duomo** (☎ 081 878 22 48; Corso Italia; 7.30am-noon & 5-8pm daily) gives no hint of the exuberance housed within. Of particular note is the marble bishop's throne (1573) and the beautiful wooden choir stalls decorated in the local *intarsio* (marquetry) style. The cathedral's original structure dates to the 15th century but it has been rebuilt several times, most recently in the early 20th century when the current façade was added. The side door, however, is an original, dating to 1474. A short way to the east, the triple-tiered bell tower rests on an archway into which three classical columns and a number of other fragments have been set.

One of Sorrento's most beautiful spaces, the cloisters of the **Chiesa di San Francesco** (☎ 081 878 12 69; Via San Francesco; 8am-1pm & 2-8pm daily) are well worth a look. A harmonious marriage of architectural styles – two sides are lined with 14th-century crossed arches, the other two with round arches supported by octagonal pillars – they are often used to host exhibitions and summer concerts.

Nearby and of note mainly because it houses the bones of Sorrento's patron saint is the **Basilica di Sant'Antonino** (☎ 081 878 14 37; Piazza Sant'Antonino; 9am-noon & 5-7pm daily). The much-loved saint is said to have performed numerous miracles, including one in which he rescued a child from a whale's stomach.

THE AMALFI COAST

Arched cloister of Chiesa di San Francesco   GREG ELMS

This explains the presence of two whale bones in the basilica. The saint's bones lie beneath the baroque interior in an 18th-century crypt.

Museums

Since the 18th century Sorrento has been famous for its *intarsio* furniture, some wonderful examples of which are to be

Mural inside Sorrento's Duomo   EMILY RIDDELL

8am-midnight mid-Apr–mid-Oct) directly across the Bay of Naples from Mt Vesuvius. A popular place to while away the sunset hours, it's a lively spot, with benches, operatic buskers and a small bar.

For parents with toddlers, there's a pleasant park a short walk east of Piazza Tasso, the **Giardino Sorrento** (Via Califano; ☺ 9am-1pm & 4.30-11pm daily summer, 9am-5pm winter), with climbing frames and games.

Beaches

Sorrento does not have great beaches. In town the two main swimming spots are **Marina Piccola** and, to the east, **Marina Grande**, although neither is especially appealing. Marina Grande, a 700m walk west of Piazza Tasso, has a pleasant seafront lined with trattorie and ramshackle houses and a small strip of dark sand. The jetties nearby sport ubiquitous umbrellas and deck chairs, which cost up to €17 a day. Nearer the centre, Marina Piccola is popular with young Italians, who crowd the stamp-sized beach like hyperactive sardines. If you want to swim here it's worth paying to access one of the private bathing clubs.

Nicer by far is **Bagni Regina Giovanna**, a rocky beach about 2km west of town. Set among the ruins of the Roman Villa Pollio Felix, it's a picturesque spot with clear, clean water. It is possible to walk here (follow Via Capo) but you'll save your strength if you get the SITA bus headed for Massa Lubrense.

The best swimming, however, is to be had in the tiny coves that dent the craggy coast to the west and south of Sorrento. To search out the top spots, hire a boat. **Sic Sic** (☎ 081 807 22 83; www.nauticasicsic.com; Marina Piccola; ☺ May-Oct) rents out a variety of boats, starting at around €30 per hour or €90 per day (excluding petrol).

Operating out of Marina Piccola, the **Sorrento Diving Center** (☎ 081 877 48 12; www.sorrento divingcenter.it; Via Marina Piccola 63) organises daily dives (weather permitting) and a series of courses. For eight- to 11-year-olds, a half-day course costs €75, for adults €90. For qualified divers a single dive (up to 45 minutes) will set you back €35, including equipment hire.

found in the **Museo Bottega della Tarsia Lignea** (☎ 081 877 19 42; Via San Nicolà 28; admission €8; ☺ 10am-1pm & 3pm-6pm Mon-Sat). There is also an interesting collection of paintings, prints and photographs depicting the town and surrounding area in the 19th century.

Sorrento's main museum, however, is the **Museo Correale** (☎ 081 878 18 46; Via Correale 50; admission €6; ☺ 9.30am-1.30pm Wed-Mon) to the east of the city centre. Here you'll find a rich assortment of 17th- and 19th-century Neapolitan art; Japanese, Chinese and European porcelains; clocks, furniture, and, on the ground floor, Greek and Roman artefacts. The bulk of the collection, along with the 18th-century villa in which it's housed, was donated to the city in the 1920s by Alfredo and Pompeo Correale, the last descendants of the aristocratic Correale family. Outside, the gardens offer great views of the bay.

Parks

Another great viewpoint is the small **Villa Comunale park** (☺ 8am-8pm daily mid-Oct–mid-Apr,

HOLGER LEUE

Courses

In the nearby suburb of Sant'Agnello, the **Sorrento Cooking School** (☎ 081 878 32 55; www.sorrento cookingschool.com; Viale Dei Pini 52, Sant'Agnello) offers two-hour cooking classes followed by lunch or dinner for €140 per person. Hotel pickups are available at 9am for the morning session and 2pm for the afternoon lesson. The school also runs courses on pizza making, wine tasting and *limoncello*. For further information check out the English-language website.

Less appetising but no less challenging are the Italian language courses taught at the **Centro Linguistico Internazionale Sorrento Lingue** (☎ 081 807 55 99; www.sorrentolingue.com; Via San Francesco 8). Group courses typically comprise four hours of lessons five days a week in classes of up to 12 students. Prices start at €206 for a basic one-week group course, rising to €760 for a four-week package. Residential courses are also available, with accommodation provided in local homes.

Tours

A big hit with both adults and children alike, the **City Train** (tours €5) is a popular way of touring town. The dinky minitrain departs from Piazza Tasso every 45 minutes between 9am and midnight. Tours, complete with English-language commentary, last about 35 minutes.

City Sightseeing Sorrento (☎ 081 877 47 07; www .sorrento.city-sightseeing.it; adult/6-15yrs €15/7.50) runs a hop-on, hop-off bus tour of Sorrento and surrounding area. Departing daily from Piazza Angelina Lauro at half past the hour, every hour between 9.30am and 4.30pm, the open-top double-decker buses stop in Rione Cappuccini and Cocumella (both northeast of Sorrento), before heading, via Piazza Tasso, to Massa Lubrense, Termini and Sant'Agata sui due Golfi. English-language commentaries are provided and tickets, available onboard, are valid for six hours.

Operating out of a converted train carriage outside the Circumvesuviana train station, **Too-To-Train** (☎ 081 734 17 55; www.too-to-train.com) offers a range of tours, including trips to the Sorrento Peninsula (€28.50), Pompeii and Vesuvius (€45) and Herculaneum (€27).

FESTIVALS & EVENTS

The city's patron saint, Sant'Antonino, is remembered on 14 February each year with processions and huge markets. The saint, whose bones lie in the Basilica di Sant'Antonino (see p207) is credited with having saved Sorrento during WWII when Salerno and Naples were heavily bombed.

The Settimana Santa (Holy Week; see p18) Easter processions are famous throughout Italy. There are two main processions: the first takes place at midnight on the Thursday preceding Good Friday, with robed and hooded penitents in white; the second occurs on Good Friday itself, when those taking part wear black robes and hoods to commemorate the death of Christ.

Between July and September, concerts are held in the cloisters of the Chiesa di San Francesco (see p207) as part of the **Sorrento Festival** (☎ 081 807 40 33). Performances, generally of classical music, usually begin at 9pm. For specific details and ticket information ask at the tourist office.

Until recently, the town's November Film Festival was regarded as the most important in the country for Italian-produced cinema. However, it wasn't held in 2005 and its future remains uncertain.

SLEEPING

You shouldn't have any problems finding accommodation in Sorrento, although if you're coming in high summer (July and August) you'll need to book ahead. Most of the big city-centre hotels are geared towards package tourism and prices are correspondingly high. There are, however, some excellent choices, particularly on Via Capo, the coastal road west of the centre. This area is within walking distance of the centre but if you've got luggage it's easier to catch a SITA bus for Sant'Agata or Massa Lubrense.

GRAND HOTEL EXCELSIOR VITTORIA   HOTEL €€€
☎ 081 807 10 44; www.exvitt.it; Piazza Tasso 34; incl breakfast, s/d €340/390, ste from €690; ☺ year-round; ⚙ ⚑

A hotel for more than 170 years, the grand old dame of Sorrento oozes old-world elegance. Huge potted palms adorn public rooms awash with sunlight and antique furniture. Guest rooms vary in size and style, ranging from tasteful simplicity to extravagant, frescoed opulence. All, however, have views, either of the hotel's lush, colourful gardens or over the sea to Mt Vesuvius. Past guests have included Pavarotti, Wagner, Goethe, Sophia Loren and British royalty.

HOTEL CAPRI   HOTEL €€
☎ 081 878 12 51; www.albergocapri.it; Corso Italia 212; s/d incl breakfast €100/150; ☺ Mar-Oct; ⚙ ⚑

A decent three-star near the train station, the Capri has comfortable, modern rooms decorated with lemon-and-blue majolica tiles and functional furniture. They're not the biggest in the world but they come with satellite TV and sound-proofing, something not to be sniffed at given the hotel's roadside location. Breakfast, served in the hotel restaurant, is a buffet of fruit juice, croissants, ham and cheese.

HOTEL DÉSIRÉ   HOTEL €
☎ 081 878 15 63; www.desireehotelsorrento.com; Via Capo 31B; s/d incl breakfast €60/90; ☺ Mar-Dec; Ⓟ

One of a cluster of hotels along Via Capo, the Désiré is a top budget choice. It's not so much the simple, sunny rooms (although they're fine) or the facilities (a TV lounge and panoramic roof terrace) as the relaxed atmosphere, friendly owner and beautiful views. The lift down to the rocky beach below is a further plus, even if you still have to pay for the umbrellas and deck chairs.

HOTEL ELIOS   HOTEL €
☎ 081 878 18 12; Via Capo 33; s €40, d €70-60; ☺ Easter-Nov

Offering views that many city centre hotels would charge the earth for, the Elios is a great little *pensione*. Run by a charming old dear, it boasts no frills (unless you count the views), just impeccable old-fashioned hospitality and light, airy rooms. If your room doesn't have a balcony, and few do, enjoy the views from the downstairs terrace.

HOTEL LORELEY ET LONDRES   HOTEL €€
☎ 081 807 31 87; fax 081 532 90 01; Via Califano 12; r incl breakfast €95; ☺ Mar-Nov

The elegance has long since faded but the charm remains. This defiantly old-fashioned hotel boasts one of the best sites in town – on the cliff tops looking over to Mt Vesuvius. And it's for this, more than the pleasantly ramshackle, floral interior, that you're paying for. Some rooms have *the* view, although those that do have no air-con; conversely (or perversely), rooms without the view have air-con. Outside there's a shaded terrace bar/restaurant overlooking the sea – perfect for an apéritif (€4) at sunset.

HOTEL MICHELANGELO HOTEL €€€

☎ 081 878 12 51; www.michelangelohotel.it; Corso Italia 275; s/d incl breakfast €125/210; ⊗ year-round; P ☒ ☒

Convenience and comfort are the hallmarks of this modern four-star hotel. Situated on the main road into town and near the train station, it's well placed for most things. The marble and terracotta floors, inoffensive artwork and courteous service leave a pleasant impression. Rooms are unpretentious, if a little anonymous, and the swimming pool is a major plus.

HOTEL RIVAGE HOTEL €€

☎ 081 878 18 73; www.hotelrivage.com; Via Capo 11; s/d €88/110; ⊗ Mar-Oct; P ☐ ☒

More often booked by tour groups than walk-ins, this low-rise hotel stands at the western edge of town. Within easy walking distance of the centre, it offers 53 bland, white rooms, all with private terrace. Wi-fi internet access is available, as is parking (€10 per day). There's a reasonable restaurant and rooftop sun terrace.

LA TONNARELLA HOTEL €€

☎ 081 878 11 53; www.latonnarella.it; Via Capo 31; incl breakfast, d €150-165, ste €255-270; ⊗ Apr-Oct & Christmas; ☒ ☐

No place for modernists, La Tonnarella is a picture of blue and yellow majolica tiles, antiques, chandeliers and statues. Rooms, most of which have their own balcony or small terrace, continue the classical theme with traditional furniture and discreet mod cons. The hotel also has a private beach, accessible by lift, and a highly regarded terrace restaurant.

NEFFOLA RESIDENCE FLAT €€

☎ 081 878 13 44; www.neffolaresidence.com; Via Capo 21; prices on request only; ☒

The 10 self-contained flats in this stone farmhouse are ideal for self-caterers and families. Sleeping from two to four people, they all have their own kitchen area and bathroom and most have private balconies. If not, there's a communal sun terrace with views over the surrounding tree tops and, beyond that, to the sea. Guests have free access to the swimming pool in the adjacent Nube d'Argento camp site.

NUBE D'ARGENTO CAMP SITE €

☎ 081 878 13 44; www.nubedargento.com; Via Capo 21; per car/person/tent €5/10/10, 2-person bungalows €50-80, 4-person bungalows €65-110; ⊗ Mar-Dec; ☐ ☒

This inviting camp site is an easy 1km drive west of the Sorrento town centre. Pitches and wooden chalet-style bungalows are spread out beneath a panoply of olive trees – a source of much-needed summer shade – and the facilities are excellent. Youngsters in particular will enjoy the open-air swimming pool, table-tennis table, slides and swings.

PENSIONE LINDA PENSIONE €

☎ /fax 081 878 29 16; Via degli Aranci 125; s/d €50/75; ⊗ year-round

Don't be put off by the decidedly unpicturesque suburban setting or the dark, un-appealing entrance – Pensione Linda is a pearl. A homely 2nd-floor *pensione* run by a hospitable family, it offers spotless, modern rooms with good-sized bathrooms and inoffensive décor. There's no air-con but fans are provided in summer and the showers work a treat. Noise from the surrounding buildings can sometimes be a nuisance.

SANTA FORTUNATA CAMP SITE €

☎ 081 807 35 74; www.santafortunata.com; Via Capo 39; per car/tent/person/tent/car €5/6.50/9, 2-person bungalows €50-60, 4-person bungalows €80-110; ⊗ Mar-Oct; ☐ ☒

A large, well-equipped camp site with a range of sleeping options. As well as tent pitches, there are 35 wooden bungalows and 25 mobile homes dotted around the verdant site. Four-person bungalows comprise a double bedroom, second room with bunk bed and small kitchen corner, and bathroom. Unnecessary and annoying is the €2.50 charge to use the swimming pool in July and August. Credit cards are not accepted.

VILLA ELISA HOTEL €

☎ 081 878 27 92; www.villaelisasorrento.com; Piazza Sant'Antonino 19; d/tr/ste €80/100/120; ⊗ year-round; ☒

You can't really get much more central than this small, friendly set-up. The simple rooms, all of which come with cooking facilities, look over a central courtyard where you can sit and eat. Up a steep staircase, the self-contained suite (unavailable between March and June) has a pint-sized living room, bathroom, bedroom and kitchen. It's not a big place and rooms are smallish, but the washing machine's a definite plus and the owner's a very welcoming lady.

EATING

The centre of town is full of bars, cafés, trattorie, restaurants and even the odd kebab takeaway. Many of these, particularly those with waistcoated waiters stationed outside, are unashamed tourist traps serving bland food at inflated prices. But not all are and it is perfectly possible to eat well. If you've got your own wheels there are some superb restaurants dotted around the nearby countryside, including one of Italy's top restaurants, in Sant'Agata sui due Golfi.

A local speciality to look out for is *gnocchi alla sorrentina* (potato gnocchi baked in tomato sauce with mozzarella).

Self-caterers can stock up at one of the various supermarkets around town: there's a **Standa** (Corso Italia 225; 8.30am-1.20pm & 5-8.55pm Mon-Sat, 9.30am-1pm & 5-8.30pm Sun) in the centre and a **Conad** (Via Capo 10; 8.30am-9pm Mon-Sat & 9am-1pm Sun) on the western edge of town.

ANGELINA LAURO
BAR €

081 807 40 97; Piazza Angelina Lauro 39-40; self-service meal around €12; daily Jul-Aug, Wed-Mon Sep-Jun

Resembling a college canteen with its metal chairs and bright lights, this unexceptional bar is great for a filling, inexpensive self-service lunch. Simply grab a tray (at the far end of the bar) and choose from the daily selection of pastas, meats and vegetable side dishes. You can sit down and order from a menu but you'll end up paying much more if you do, typically around €6 for pasta and from €10 for meat dishes.

DA EMILIA
TRATTORIA €€

081 807 27 20; Via Marina Grande 62; meals around €20; year-round, closed Tue mid-Sep–Apr

One of a clutter of eateries along the Marina Grande seafront, Da Emilia is the archetypal family-run trattoria. It's welcoming and laid-back with an uncomplicated menu of seafood classics – pasta with mussels or clams, fried squid and grilled fish. Needless to say, the food is delicious and the portions are huge. Order an *antipasto della casa* (house starter) and you'll be tucking into slices of ham, marinated and grilled aubergines, local *treccia* cheese, marinated salmon, anchovies, olives and salami.

GELATERIA DAVID
GELATERIA €

338 365 06 99; Via Marziale 19; cones around €2.50; 9-2am daily Mar-Oct

A small, brightly lit gelateria near the train station, David's has up to 30 different flavours. Speciality of the house is the spaghetti ice cream, but if that doesn't appeal there are all the traditional flavours – *straciatelle*, pistachio, chocolate, strawberry and so on – plus *granite* (ice drinks) and crêpes. Outside there are a few tables on the pavement.

LA STALLA
TRATTORIA €€

081 807 41 45; Via Pietà 30; meals around €25, pizzas from €4.50; closed Wed

Go up the grand staircase to the large, open-air terrace covered by bamboo awnings and flanked by an orchard of lemon and orange trees. Here a small army of black-clad waiters work tirelessly, serving pastas and pizzas, meats and fish. The pastas are fine but it's the pizzas that stand out. Prepared in a wood-fired oven, they arrive bubbling hot, the cheese melted to perfection and the base just beginning to char. Delicious.

MONDO BIO
VEGETARIAN €

081 807 56 94; Via Degli Aranci 146; snacks/pasta €3/6.50; 10am-3pm Mon-Sat year-round

Flying the banner for organic vegetarian food, this bright shop-cum-restaurant serves a limited range of meat-free pastas and tofu dishes. The menu, chalked up outside, changes daily but typical dishes include *pasta con melanzane* (pasta with aubergines) and *polpette di tofu* (tofu balls). Seating is limited but you can always peruse the shop's shelves if you have to wait.

O'PARRUCCHIANO
TRATTORIA €€

081 878 13 21; Corso Italia 67; meals around €22; Thu-Tue year-round

Presumably the TV screen transmitting direct from the kitchen has been placed by the entrance to try to lure customers in. They'd do just as well to beam out pictures of diners tucking into bowls of cannelloni (said to have been invented here) or *gnocchi alla sorrentina*, the ubiquitous Sorrentine speciality. As memorable as the food is the luxurious foliage that adorns the greenhouse-style interior.

PHOTO
BAR/RISTORANTE €€€

081 877 36 86; Via Correale 19-21; meals around €40; year-round

With its modish look (which changes every couple of weeks) and regular photo projections, Photo is a far cry from Sorrento's traditional trattorie. Part bar and part restaurant, it serves several menus with dishes ranging from sushi-style raw fish to new takes on Italian classics –

think Angus beef carpaccio with rocket salad and parmesan shavings. The wine list is also interesting, with a limited selection of local labels. In winter a DJ adds to the trendy vibe.

PRIMAVERA ANTONIO CARFIERO
GELATERIA €

☎ 081 807 32 52; Corso Italia 142; cones from €2.50; ☽ 8am-11pm daily, to 3am summer

Stop off at Sorrento's most famous gelateria for the best ice cream you'll ever have. With tons of flavours to choose from, including vegan-friendly jasmine and the full range of Italian classics, you'll be spoiled for choice. While you eat, admire the photos of Italian celebs who have dropped by for a quick cone.

RARO FINE FOOD
DELI €

☎ 081 878 39 20; www.rarofinefood.com; Vico I Fuoro 18; panini/salads €6/7; ☽ 10am-4pm & 5.30pm-midnight daily Apr-Oct, shorter hrs winter

A trendy re-take on the traditional Italian *salumeria*, this modern deli serves light meals (pastas and salads) and some of the best *panini* in Sorrento. Made with fresh bread rolls and traditional fillers (cheese, ham, tomatoes), it makes an excellent lunch, to eat in or take away. You can also order packed lunches and buy a whole range of foodie treats, from marmalades to wine glasses.

RISTORANTE IL BUCO
RISTORANTE €€€

☎ 081 878 23 54; Rampa Marina Piccola 5; meals around €55; ☽ Feb-Dec, closed Wed

Even the most disgruntled critic would be hard pushed to describe this Michelin-starred restaurant as a hole, as the name translates. Housed in a monks' former wine cellar, it is a refined restaurant offering far from monastic cuisine. The onus is on innovative regional cooking, so expect modern combos such as pasta with rock fish sauce or *treccia* (local cheese) and prawns served on a bed of caper, tomato and olive sauce. In summer, there's outdoor seating near one of the city's ancient gates. Reservations recommended.

RISTORANTE SANT'ANTONINO
RISTORANTE €€

☎ 081 877 12 00; Via Santa Maria delle Grazie 6; meals around €23, pizzas around €6; ☽ Dec-Oct

If you can't find anything you like here you're going to have trouble eating in Italy. Running the gamut from pizzas, through pastas and risottos to meats, fish, salads and crêpes, the menu is surely the longest in town. If you don't fancy scrolling through the whole thing, there are also four set menus (€18/22/26/32). Seating is on a terrace surrounded by greenery and lemon trees.

DRINKING

You can do the whole drinking trip in Sorrento – you can down pints of lager while watching Sky sport on a big screen; you can try local wines in wood-panelled wine bars or sip cocktails in swish cafés; you can people-watch over an apéritif at squareside bars or linger over wine while pondering Vesuvius over the water.

BOLLICINE

☎ 081 878 46 16; Via dell' Accademia 9; ☽ 6pm-1am daily Jul & Aug, Tue-Sun Sep-Jun

An unpretentious wine bar with a dark wooden interior and boxes of bottles littered around the place. The wine list includes all the big Italian names and a selection of interesting local labels – if you can't decide what to go for, the amiable barman will happily advise you. There's also a small menu of *panini*, bruschetta and one or two pasta dishes.

CAFÉ LATINO

☎ 081 878 37 18; Vico I Fuoro 4A; ☽ 10am-1am daily Apr-Sep

The place to impress your partner with cocktails (from €7) on the terrace. Sit among the orange and lemon trees and gaze into each other's eyes over a Mary Pickford (rum, pineapple, grenadino and maraschina) or a glass of chilled white wine. If you can't drag yourselves away, you can also eat here (meals around €30).

FAUNO BAR

☎ 081 878 11 35; Piazza Tasso; ☽ Dec-Oct

On Piazza Tasso, this high-profile café covers half the square and offers the best people-watching in town. It's not, however, the cheapest place to drink or eat – cocktails start at around €8.50, sandwiches at €7.

ENTERTAINMENT

For such a busy resort Sorrento's entertainment is fairly low-key. In summer, concerts are held in the cloisters of Chiesa di San Francesco; otherwise it's the theatre for a good old-fashioned sing-along.

FAUNO NOTTE CLUB

☎ 081 878 10 21; www.faunonotte.it; Piazza Tasso 1

A direct competitor of the more established Teatro Tasso, the Fauno offers 'a fantastic journey through history, legends and folklore'. In other words, 500 years of Neapolitan history set to music. Sing along to the Masaniello Revolt (see p29) and other folkloristic episodes.

TEATRO TASSO

☎ 081 807 55 25; www.teatrotasso.com; Piazza San Antonino

The southern Italian equivalent of a cockney music hall, Teatro Tasso is home to the Sorrento Musical (€25), a sentimental revue of Neapolitan classics such as 'O Sole Mio' and 'Trona a Sorrent'. The 75-minute performances start at 9.30pm Monday to Saturday from March to October.

SHOPPING

The pedestrianised centro storico is the place to shop. Ignore the replica football shirts and souvenir tat and look out for inlaid wood and *limoncello*.

Unless otherwise stated, the following shops open all day until late in summer and close for lunch in winter.

DISTILLERIE CORREALE   FOOD & GIFTS

☎ 081 877 46 22; Via Tasso 20

One of many shops selling *limoncello* in the historic centre. Sample a free slug before choosing from the ample assortment of pretty bottles. You can also top up on larder favourites such as pickled mushrooms and artichokes, fancy olive oils and classy jams.

FATTORIA TERRANOVA   FOOD

☎ 081 878 12 63; Piazza Tasso 16

Fattoria Terranova is an agriturismo (farm stay; p218) near the village of Sant'Agata sui due Golfi in the hills to the south of Sorrento. It produces everything that you'll find for sale in this, its in-town shop – wine, olive oil, preserves and marmalades, vegetables in olive oil, dried herbs. An ideal place for a foodie gift.

FRANC & GUGLIELMO CUOMO   GIFTS

☎ 081 878 11 37; Piazza Tasso 32

Inlaid wood is the speciality of the house at this intriguing shop on central Piazza Tasso. Alongside a selection of exquisite music boxes you'll find a bewildering collection of chess

sets (costing up to €150) and a veritable zoo of porcelain animals, including a magnificently kitsch tiger.

GARGIULO & JANNUZZI   GIFTS

☎ 081 878 10 41; Viale Enrico Caruso 1

Dating from 1863, this old-fashioned shop-cum-warehouse is a classic. Elderly shop assistants will guide you through three-floors of locally made goods ranging from ceramic crockery to inlaid cabinets, embroidered lace and pottery. Shipping can be arranged.

LA RAPIDA   SHOES

☎ 338 877 77 05; Via Fuoro 67; ⏱ 9am-1pm & 5-9pm Apr-Oct, 9am-1pm & 3.30-8pm rest of year

Walk through the centro storico and you'll find numerous stores selling leather sandals; head to the far end of Via Fuoro and you'll find this tiny cobbler's shop. A bit old-fashioned, it doesn't have the range of sandals offered by bigger places, but the quality's as good and the prices (from €25) are generally better. It also does repairs, so if your bag's broken or you need a button sewn on, this is your place.

GETTING THERE & AWAY
Boat

From Naples' Molo Beverello, **Alilauro** (☎ 081 878 14 30; www.alilauro.it) and **Linee Marrittime Partenope** (LMP; ☎ 081 807 18 12; www.consorziolmp .it) runs up to 15 daily hydrofoils to Sorrento. The 35-minute journey costs €9. In August, the **Metrò del Mare** (☎ 199 60 07 00; www .metrodelmare.com) covers the same route. Journey time varies from 50 minutes to an hour and a half depending on the number of intervening stops. Tickets, available on the boat, cost €4.50.

Sorrento is the main jumping-off point for Capri, and ferries/hydrofoils run year-round; in summer every hour, in winter less frequently. Information listed here refers to high season schedules. **LMP** runs up to 20 hydrofoils daily (€12, 20 minutes), while **Caremar** (☎ 081 807 30 77; www.caremar.it) has four daily fast ferries (€7.80, 25 minutes). All depart from the port at Marina Piccola, where you can buy your tickets.

For the Amalfi Coast, **TraVelMar** (☎ /fax 089 87 29 50; Largo Scario 5, Amalfi) ferries sail to Amalfi (€8, three daily) and **Metrò del Mare** (☎ 199 44 66 44; www.metrodelmare.com) runs three daily services for Amalfi (€7).

Bus

To get to Sorrento from Naples Capodi-chino airport, **Curreri** (☎ 081 801 54 20; www.curreri viaggi.it) runs six daily services, departing from outside the Arrivals hall and arriving in Piazza Angelina Lauro. Buy tickets (€7) for the 75-minute journey on the bus. There are also plenty of private agencies that will arrange airport transfers for around €60.

Marozzi (☎ 080 579 01 11; www.marozzivt.it) operates two weekday buses to/from Rome. Leaving Rome's Stazione Tiburtina at 7am and 3pm, they arrive in Sorrento at 10.45pm and 7pm respectively. Tickets cost €17. The return bus for Rome departs from Piazza Angelina Lauro at 6am and 5pm, arriving at 9.45am and 9pm.

SITA (☎ 199 73 07 49; www.sita-on-line.it, in Italian) buses serve Naples (€3.20, one hour 20 minutes, twice daily), the Amalfi Coast and Sant'Agata, leaving from outside the Circumvesuviana train station. Buy tickets at the station bar or from shops bearing the blue SITA sign. At least 12 buses a day run between Sorrento and Amalfi (€2.40, 1½ hours), looping around Positano (€1.30, 40 minutes). Change at Amalfi for Ravello.

Car & Motorcycle

If you are coming from Naples and the north, take the A3 autostrada until Castellammare di Stabia; exit there and follow the SS145 southeast.

Train

Sorrento is the last stop on the **Circumvesuviana** (☎ 081 772 24 44; wwww.vesuviana.it) train line from Naples. From the station, just off Corso Italia, trains run every half-hour for Naples (€3.20, one hour 10 minutes), via Pompeii (€1.80, 30 minutes) and Ercolano (€1.80, 50 minutes).

GETTING AROUND

The best way to get around Sorrento is to walk – distances are not great and traffic restrictions mean that the city centre is closed to cars for much of the day. There are, however, local buses to the port at Marina Piccola (Line B, every 20 minutes between 7am and 11.30pm), to Sant'Agnello (Line C, 7am to 11.30pm) and Marina Grande

(Line D, 7.20am to 12.20am). Tickets (€1 for 90 minutes) are available at tobacconists, newsagents and bars.

If you want to hire a scooter or car you will be spoiled for choice. The big international operators are here – **Avis** (☎ 081 878 24 59; www.avisautonoleggio.it; Via Nizza 53), **Hertz** (☎ 081 807 16 46; www.hertz.it; Via degli Aranci 9) – as well as a host of local out-fits. At **Sorrento Rent a Scooter** (☎ 081 878 13 86; www.sorrento.it; Corso Italia 210A) you can pick up a scooter for €45 for 24 hours and cars from €55 per day. **Jolly Service & Rent** (☎ 081 877 34 50; www.sorrentorent.com; Via degli Aranci 180) has smart cars from €60 a day and 50cc scooters from €30.

For a taxi call ☎ 081 878 22 04.

EAST OF SORRENTO

More developed and less appealing than the coast west of Sorrento, the area to the east of town is not totally without interest. There's the district's longest sandy beach, **Spiaggia di Alimuri**, at **Meta di Sorrento** and, 12km beyond that, the Roman villas at **Castel-lammare di Stabia** (see the boxed text, p157). Rising above Castellammare and accessible by **cable car** (adult/19-26yr/under 18yr return trip €6.71/3.10/2.58; 8 minutes, about 30 daily Apr-Oct) from the town's Circumvesuviana train station is Monte Faito (1055m), one of the highest peaks in the Lattari mount-ains. Covered in thick beech forests, the summit offers some lovely walking and sensational views.

VICO EQUENSE

Known to the Romans as Aequa, Vico Equense (Vico) is a small cliff-top town about 10km east of Sorrento. Largely by-passed by international tourists, it's a laid-back, authentic place worth a quick stopover. Information on the area's attrac-tions is available from the helpful **tourist office** (☎ 081 801 57 52; www.vicoturismo.it; Piazza Umberto I; ✆ 9am-2pm & 3-8pm Mon-Sat, 9.30am-1.30pm Sun Mar-Oct, 9am-2pm & 3-5pm Mon-Sat Nov-Feb) in the main square.

Vico is on the main SS145 coastal road and is five stops from Sorrento by Cir-cumvesuviana train.

Sights & Activities

From Piazza Umberto I, the town's 19th-century focal point, take Corso Filangieri along to the small centro storico. Here, on a small balcony overlooking the village of Marina di Equa, you'll find the **Chiesa dell'Annunziata** (☎ 081 879 80 04; Via Vescovado; ⏰ 10am-noon Sun), Vico's former cathedral and the only Gothic church on the Sorrento Peninsula. Little remains of the original 14th-century structure other than the lateral windows near the main altar and a few arches in the aisles. In fact, most of what you see today, including the chipped pink and white façade, is 17th-century baroque. In the sacristy, check out the portraits of Vico's bishops, all of whom are represented here except for the last one, Michele Natale, who was executed for supporting the ill-fated 1799 Parthenopean Republic (see p30). His place is taken by an angel with its finger to its lips, an admonishment to the bishop to keep his liberal thoughts to himself.

Heading back along Corso Filangieri, the **Antiquarium 'Silio Italico'** (☎ 081 801 92 50; Palazo Municipale; Corso Filangieri 98; admission free; ⏰ 9am-1pm Mon-Fri & 3.30-6.30pm Tue & Thu), boasts a collection of 5th- to 7th-century BC archaeological artefacts found in a series of local tombs. Although the museum is officially open at the times given above, it's rarely staffed, so you'll probably have to go to the council's Ufficio Anagrafico (in the same building – follow the directions on the door) to get someone to open it for you.

Nearby, the **Museo Mineralogico** (☎ 081 801 56 68; www.museomineralogicocampano.it; Via San Ciro 2; admission €2; ⏰ 9am-1pm & 5-8pm Tue-Sat, 9am-1pm Sun Mar-Sep, 9am-1pm & 4-7pm Tue-Sat, 9am-1pm Sun Oct-Feb) has a 5000-strong collection of rock specimens, fossils and meteorites.

Dotted around Vico's surrounding hills are a number of ancient hamlets, known as *casali*. Untouched by mass tourism, they offer a glimpse into a rural way of life that has changed little over the centuries. You will, however, need wheels to get to them. From Vico, take Via Roma and follow Via Rafaelle Bosco, which passes through the *casali* before circling back to town. Highlights include **Massaquano** and the **Cappella di Santa Lucia** (open on request), famous for its 14th-century frescoes; **Moiano**, from where an ancient path leads to the summit of **Monte Faito**; and **Santa Maria del Castello**, with its fabulous views towards Positano.

Three kilometres to the west of Vico, **Marina di Equa** stands on the site of the original Roman settlement, Aequa. Among the bars and restaurants lining the popular pebble beaches are the remains of 1st-century AD Villa Pezzolo, as well as a defensive tower, the Torre di Caporivo, and the Gothic ruins of a medieval limestone quarry.

Eating

Vico Equense is worth the stop, if only to do nothing else but eat some of the town's famous *pizza a metro* (pizza by the metre).

RISTORANTE & PIZZERIA DA GIGINO   PIZZERIA €€
☎ 081 879 83 09; Via Nicotera 15; pizza per metre €12-26; ⏰ midday-1am

Run by the five sons of Gigino Dell'Amura, the inventor of pizza by the metre, this barn-like pizzeria (aka the University of the Pizza) produces kilometres of pizza each day in three huge ovens to the right of the entrance. There's a large selection of toppings and the quality is superlative.

WEST OF SORRENTO

The countryside west of Sorrento is what you come to this part of the world for. Tortuous roads wind their way through hills covered in olive trees and lemon groves passing through sleepy villages and tiny fishing ports. There are magnificent views at every turn, the best from the high points overlooking **Punta della Campanella**, the westernmost point of the Sorrento Peninsula. Offshore, Capri seems no more than a leap away.

MASSA LUBRENSE

The first town you come to as you follow the coast west from Sorrento is Massa Lubrense. Situated 120m above sea level, it's a disjointed place, comprising a small town centre and 17 *frazioni* (fractions or hamlets) joined by an intricate network of paths and mule tracks. For those without a donkey, there are good road connections and SITA buses regularly run between them. Bus timetables and maps are available at the **tourist office** (☎ 081 533 90 21; www .massalubrense.it; Viale Filangieri 11; ⏰ 9.30am-1pm daily & 4.30-8pm Mon, Tue & Thu-Sat).

Forming the heart of the town centre, Largo Vescovado commands good views over to Capri. On its northern flank stands the town's former cathedral, the 16th-century **Chiesa di Santa Maria della Grazia** (Largo Vescovado; ⏰ 7am-noon, 4.30-8pm daily), worth a quick look for the bright majolica floor. From the square it's a 2km descent to **Marina della Lobra** (a 20-minute downhill walk, a wheezing 40-minute ascent), a pretty little marina backed by ramshackle houses and verdant slopes. On the way down you'll pass the **Chiesa di Santa Maria della Lobra** (⏰ 6.30-8am & 5-8pm daily), a 16th-century church topped by a tiled dome.

The marina is a good place to rent a boat, the best way of reaching the otherwise difficult to get to bays and inlets along the coast. Of the hire companies, **Coop Marina della**

Lobra (☎ 081 808 93 80; www.marina lobra.com) is a reliable operator.

Sleeping & Eating

AGRITURISMO AGRIMAR   FARM STAY €

☎ 081 808 96 82; Via Maggio 9; B&B per person €40; ⏰ Easter–mid-Oct; **P**

In a terraced olive grove off the road between Massa Lubrense and Marina della Lobra, this back-to-basics agriturismo is ideal for those who want to escape telephones and TVs. Nestled among the trees are six spotless chalets, big enough for a double bed, tiny bathroom and not a lot else. Hammocks have been thoughtfully hung about the place and deck chairs laid out on a platform overlooking the sea. Dinner is available on request.

FUNICULÌ FUNICULÀ   BAR/RISTORANTE €€

Via Fontanelle 16, Marina dell Lobra; meals around €23; ⏰ Apr-Oct

A great bar/restaurant on the seafront at Marina dell Lobra. Unsurprisingly, the menu is dominated by seafood, but there are also meal-in-one salads and the usual array of grilled meat dishes. Less predictably, the helpings are huge and the food is delicious. For proof try the *tubettoni con cozze, rucola e parmigiano* (pasta tubes with mussels, rocket and parmesan).

HOTEL RISTORANTE
PRIMAVERA   HOTEL/RISTORANTE €€

☎ 081 878 91 25; www.laprimavera.biz; Via IV Novembre 3G; s/d incl breakfast €70/100; ⏰ year-round; 🖳

A welcoming family-run two-star with cool, airy rooms and a bright terrace-restaurant. The décor is Mediterranean standard – white walls, floral ceramic tiling and functional furniture – but the bathtubs (in most, not all, rooms) are an unexpected treat. Expect to pay around €30 for a full dinner.

Getting There & Away

By car, Massa Lubrense is an easy 20-minute drive from Sorrento – follow Via Capo and keep on going until you reach Piazza Vescovardo, some five minutes or so beyond the Massa Lubrense town sign.

From the Circumvesuviana train station in Sorrento, SITA (☎ 199 73 07 49; www.sita -on-line.it, in Italian) buses depart every hour throughout the day. The 20-minute journey costs €1.

HIKING THE PENINSULA

Forming a giant horseshoe between **Punta della Campanella** and **Punta Penna**, the beautiful **Bay of Ieranto** is generally regarded as the top swimming spot on the Sorrento Peninsula. To get there you have two alternatives: you can either get a boat or you can walk from the village of Nerano, the steep descent forming part of a longer 6.5km hike from nearby Termini.

This picturesque path is just one of 20 (for a total of 110km) that cover the area. These range from tough all-day treks such as the 14.1km **Alta Via dei Monti Lattari** from the Fontanelle hills near Positano down to the Punta della Campanella, to shorter walks suitable for all the family.

Tourist offices throughout the area can provide maps detailing the colour-coded routes. With the exception of the Alta Via dei Monti Lattari, which is marked in red and white, long routes are shown in red on the map; coast-to-coast trails in blue; paths connecting villages in green; and circular routes in yellow. On the ground, trails are fairly well marked, although you might find some signs have faded to near-indecipherable levels.

SANT'AGATA SUI DUE GOLFI

Perched high in the hills above Sorrento, Sant'Agata sui due Golfi is the most famous of Massa Lubrense' 17 *frazioni*. Boasting spectacular views of the Bay of Naples on one side and the Bay of Salerno on the other (hence its name, St Agatha on the two Gulfs), it's a tranquil place that manages to retain its rustic charm despite a fairly heavy hotel presence. Information on the village and surrounding countryside is available at the small **tourist office** (☎ 081 533 01 35; www .santagatasuiduegolfi.it; Corso Sant'Agata 25; 9am-1pm, 5.30-9pm Apr-Oct) near Piazza Sant'Agata, the main square.

The best place to enjoy the views is the Carmelite convent of **Deserto** (☎ 081 878 01 99; Via Deserto; 8.30am-12.30pm & 2.30-4.30pm Oct-Mar, 8.30am-12.30pm & 4-9pm Apr-Sep), 1.5km uphill from the village centre. Founded in the 17th century, the convent is still home to a closed community of Benedictine nuns.

Back in the centre, the village's 17th-century parish church, the **Chiesa di Sant'Agata** (Piazza Sant'Agata; 8am-1pm & 5-7pm daily) is famous for its polychrome marble altar. Designed by the Florentine artist Dionisio Lazzari in 1654, it's an exquisite work of inlaid marble, mother-of-pearl, lapis lazuli and malachite.

Sleeping & Eating

It is possible to walk to the two agriturismi (farm stays) listed here, but a car is highly recommended.

AGRITURISMO FATTORIA TERRANOVA   FARM STAY €
☎ 081 533 02 34; www.fattoriaterranova.it; Via Pontone 10; d incl breakfast €80; Mar-Dec; P
A picture of rural chic – stone floors, dried flowers hanging from heavy wooden beams and big wine barrels artfully positioned – this great agriturismo has accommodation in small apartments spread over the extensively cultivated grounds. They're fairly simple but the setting is delightful and the swimming pool is a lovely luxury. See p214 for details of the farm shop in Sorrento.

AGRITURISMO LA TORE   FARM STAY €
☎ 081 808 06 37; www.letore.com; Via Pontone 43; s/d incl breakfast €55/90, half-board per person €60; Easter-end Oct; P
A working organic farm, La Tore is a wonderful place to stay. Decidedly off the beaten track, it offers eight barnlike rooms and a five-person apartment, all in a lovely rustic farmhouse hidden among fruit trees. Terracotta tiles and heavy wooden furniture add to the rural appeal. Children between two and six years old get a 50% discount (30% for seven- to 10-year-olds) if they sleep in their parents' room. During winter, a self-contained apartment is available.

LO STUZZICHINO   RISTORANTE €€
☎ 081 533 00 10; Via Deserto 1A; meals around €18; closed Jan
Just down the road from the village church, this laid-back restaurant/pizzeria serves good hearty food at pleasant prices. Using locally grown produce, dishes include pasta with aubergine, mozzarella and tomato and mixed grill. There's outdoor summer seating or a simple interior with wine racks and a TV in the corner.

RIOSTORANTE DON ALFONSO 1890   RISTORANTE €€€
☎ 081533 02 26; Corso Sant'Agata 11; meals €115-125; closed Mon & Tue, except Tue night Jun-Sep, closed Jan–early Mar & Nov-Dec; P
This Michelin two-star restaurant is generally regarded as one of Italy's best. Dishes are prepared with produce from the chef's own 6-hectare farm in nearby Punta Campanella; the

dining hall is a picture of refined taste, and the international wine list is one of the country's finest. The menu changes seasonally but hallmark dishes include lightly seared tuna in red pepper sauce and pasta with clams and courgettes. Booking is essential.

Getting There & Away

If you enjoy a walk, there's a pretty 3km (approximately one hour) trail between Sorrento and Sant'Agata. From Piazza Tasso head south along Viale Caruso and Via Fuorimura to pick up the Circumpiso footpath, marked in green on the walking maps available from tourist offices.

Hourly SITA (☎ 199 73 07 49; www.sita-on-line .it, in Italian) buses leave from the Circum-vesuviana train station in Sorrento.

By car, follow the SS145 west from Sorrento for about 7km until you see signs off to the right.

MARINA DEL CANTONE

From Massa Lubrense, follow the coastal road round to **Termini**. Stop a moment to admire the views before continuing on to **Nerano**, from where a beautiful hiking trail leads down to the stunning **Bay of Ieranto**, and **Marina del Cantone**. This unassuming village with its small pebble beach is not only a lovely, tranquil place to stay but also one of the area's prime dining spots, a magnet for VIPs who regularly boat over from Capri to eat here – Bill Gates, Roman Abramovich, Michael Douglas and Catherine Zeta-Jones have visited in the past year alone.

It is also a popular diving destination. The rich waters, protected as part of the 11-sq-km **Punta Campanella Marine Reserve**, support a healthy marine ecosystem with flora and fauna flourishing among under-water grottoes and ancient ruins. To see for yourself, the PADI-certified **Nettuno Diving** (☎ 081 808 10 51; www.sorrentodiving.com; Via A Vespucci 39) runs various underwater act-ivities for all ages and abilities, including snorkelling excursions, beginner courses, cave dives and immersions off Capri and Li Galli, the islands where the sirens are said to have lived. Costs start at €18 (children €10) for a day-long outing to the Bay of Ieranto.

Sleeping & Eating

LO SCOGLIO   RISTORANTE €€€

☎ 081 808 10 26; Marina del Cantone; meals around €50; ☼ year-round

The only of Marina's restaurants directly accessible from the sea, this is a favourite of visiting celebs. The setting is certainly mem-orable – a glass pavilion built around a kitsch fountain on a wooden jetty – and the food is top-notch. Although you can eat *fettucine al bolognese* and steak, you'd be sorry to miss the superb seafood. Menu tempters include a €20 antipasto of raw seafood and *spaghetti al riccio* (spaghetti with sea urchins).

PENSIONE LA CERTOSA   HOTEL €

☎ 081 808 12 09; www.hotelcertosa.com; Marina del Cantone; r incl breakfast €85-95, half-/full board per person €75/85/; ☼ year-round; ❑

A rambling seafront hotel with a good terrace restaurant (meals around €30) and unspectacular modern rooms. The low wooden ceilings and concrete box-balconies are a curious feature but the rooms are clean and so close to the beach that you can virtually step directly onto the pebbles below. Half-board is compulsory in August.

VILLAGGIO RESIDENCE
NETTUNO   CAMP SITE €

☎ 081 808 10 51; www.villaggionettuno.it; Via A Vespucci 39; per person/tent €9/13, apt €110-215; ☼ Mar-Nov

Marina's camp site – in the terraced olive groves by the entrance to the village – offers an array of accommodation options (tent pitches, apartments for two to six people, mobile homes for two to four people) priced according to a complex seasonal scale. It's a friendly, environmentally sound place (all rubbish is recycled) with excellent facilities and a comprehensive list of activities. If you feel the call of Sorrento's bright lights, a private shuttle bus runs to and from town, departing from the camp site at 8.30pm and returning at 11.30pm.

Getting There & Away

SITA (☎ 199 73 07 49; www.sita-on-line.it, in Italian) buses run 10 times daily between Sorrento and Marina del Cantone (marked on timetables as Nerano Cantone; €1, one hour).

Spiaggia Grande, Positano (p222)

DALLAS STRIBLEY

AMALFI TOWNS

The quintessential Mediterranean coastline, the Amalfi Coast is nature at its most alluring.

Whitewashed villas on improbable slopes, fishing huts squeezed into tiny coves and smart hotels perched above spectacular cliffs – the Amalfi towns are like no other. Cliffs terraced with scented lemon groves sheer down into sparkling blue seas; huge *fichi d'India* (prickly pears) guard silent mountain paths while bougainvillea explodes between stacks of whitewashed houses.

Amalfi, the most famous of the coast's towns, is also the most visited. Once the capital of a powerful maritime republic, it is today a hugely popular day trip destination, its pretty centre an appealing ensemble of gaudy ceramic shops, hidden alleyways and beachside restaurants. Up above, **Ravello** strikes a more sophisticated chord, with its lush gardens and sensational views. More than anywhere though, it's **Positano** that fulfils visitors' visual expectations. Viewed from the sea, its mountainside townscape is unique, a multicoloured mass of precarious pastel-tinted houses clinging for dear life to the unforgiving slopes.

Beyond the big names there are a wealth of lesser-known gems: the tumbledown fishing village of **Cetara**, famous for its tuna fleet and fabulous fish restaurants; **Vietri sul Mare**, home of the area's historic ceramic industry and the best place to pick up a souvenir; **Conca dei Marini** with its haunting sea cave, the **Grotta dello Smeraldo**, and **Marina di Praia** with its fine swimming.

The best time to visit the coast is in spring and early autumn. In summer the coast's single road (SS163) is bumper to bumper with coaches, convertibles and SUVs and prices are inflated; in winter much of the coast simply shuts down as hotels and restaurants lower the shutters until the next season.

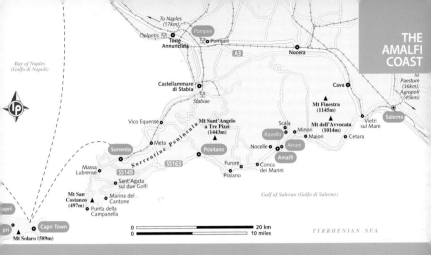

HIGHLIGHTS

- Gape open-mouthed at the views from the **Belvedere of Infinity** (p238) in Ravello's Villa Cimbrone
- Sit down to superfresh seafood at the tiny harbour of **Cetara** (p242)
- Mix with the beautiful people on the designer-clad streets of vertiginous **Positano** (below)
- Soothe your soul in the harmonious **Chiostro del Paradiso** (p232), adjacent to Amalfi's landmark cathedral
- Hire a boat at **Amalfi** (p232) and pootle down the coast in search of the perfect swimming spot

POSITANO

The pearl in the pack, Positano is the coast's most picturesque and photogenic town. With its steeply stacked houses banked up like spectators on a stadium terrace and its pretty peach, pink and terracotta colours, it presents a memorable façade. No less colourful are its near-vertical streets (many of which are, in fact, staircases) lined with flamboyant shop displays, jewellery stalls, elegant hotels and smart restaurants.

Look closely though and you will find reassuring signs of everyday reality – crumbling stucco, streaked paintwork and even, on occasion, a faint whiff of drains. John Steinbeck visited Positano in 1953 and wrote in an article for *Harper's Bazaar*: 'Positano bites deep. It is a dream place that isn't quite real when you are there and becomes beckoningly real after you have gone.' There certainly is something special about the place and this is reflected, predictably, in the prices, which tend to be higher here than elsewhere on the coast.

ORIENTATION

Positano is split in two by a cliff bearing the Torre Trasita (tower). West of this is the smaller, less-crowded Spiaggia del Fornillo beach area and the less expensive side of town; east is Spiaggia Grande, backing up to the town centre.

Navigating is easy, if steep. Via G Marconi, part of the main SS163 coastal road, forms a huge horseshoe around and above the town, which cascades down to the sea. From it, one-way Viale Pasitea makes a second, lower loop, ribboning off Via G Marconi from the west towards the town centre then climbing back up as Via Cristoforo Colombo to rejoin Via G Marconi and the SS163. Branching off the bottom of Viale Pasitea, Via dei Mulini leads down to Spiaggia Grande.

SIGHTS & ACTIVITIES

Positano's most memorable sight is its townscape – a vertiginous stack of multi-coloured houses clinging precariously to the steep mountainside. Rising above the rooftops, the ceramic-tiled dome of the **Chiesa**

221

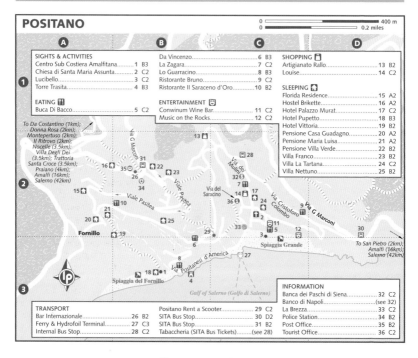

POSITANO

0 — 400 m
0 — 0.2 miles

SIGHTS & ACTIVITIES
Centro Sub Costiera Amalfitana..........1 B3
Chiesa di Santa Maria Assunta..........2 C2
Lucibello..........3 C2
Torre Trasita..........4 B3

EATING
Buca Di Bacco..........5 C2

Da Vincenzo..........6 B3
La Zagara..........7 C2
Lo Guarracino..........8 B3
Ristorante Bruno..........9 C2
Ristorante Il Saraceno d'Oro..........10 B2

ENTERTAINMENT
Conwium Wine Bar..........11 C2
Music on the Rocks..........12 C2

SHOPPING
Artigianato Rallo..........13 B2
Louise..........14 C2

SLEEPING
Florida Residence..........15 A2
Hostel Brikette..........16 A2
Hotel Palazzo Murat..........17 C2
Hotel Pupetto..........18 B3
Hotel Vittoria..........19 B2
Pensione Casa Guadagno..........20 A2
Pensione Maria Luisa..........21 A2
Pensione Villa Verde..........22 B2
Villa Franco..........23 B2
Villa La Tartana..........24 C2
Villa Nettuno..........25 B2

To Da Costantino (1km);
Donna Rosa (2km);
Montepertuso (2km);
Il Ritrovo (2km);
Nocelle (3.5km);
Villa Degli Dei
(3.5km); Trattoria
Santa Croce (3.5km);
Praiano (4km);
Amalfi (16km);
Salerno (42km)

Via del Saracino

Fornillo

Spiaggia Grande

Gulf of Salerno (Golfo di Salerno)

Spiaggia del Fornillo

To San Pietro (2km);
Amalfi (16km);
Salerno (42km)

INFORMATION
Banca dei Paschi di Siena..........32 C2
Banco di Napoli..........(see 32)
La Brezza..........33 C2
Police Station..........34 B2
Post Office..........35 B2
Tourist Office..........36 B2

TRANSPORT
Bar Internazionale..........26 B2
Ferry & Hydrofoil Terminal..........27 C3
Internal Bus Stop..........28 C2

Positano Rent a Scooter..........29 C2
SITA Bus Stop..........30 D2
SITA Bus Stop..........31 B2
Tabaccheria (SITA Bus Tickets)..........(see 28)

---

di Santa Maria Assunta (Piazza Flavio Gioia; 8am-noon & 3.30-7pm daily) is the town's most famous sight. Inside the church, regular classical lines are broken by pillars topped with gilded Ionic capitals, while winged cherubs peek above every arch. Above the main altar is a 13th-century Byzantine Black Madonna and Child.

It's a short hop to the nearby beach, Spiaggia Grande. Although no-one's dream beach, with greyish sand covered by legions of brightly coloured umbrellas, the water's clean and the setting is memorable. Hiring a chair and umbrella on the fenced-off areas costs around €15 per person per day but the crowded public areas are free. Boating

isn't cheap, either. Operating out of a kiosk on Spiaggia Grande, **Lucibello** (☎ 089 875 50 32; www.lucibello.it; Spiaggia Grande; 9am-8pm daily Easter-Nov) hires out small motorboats for €30 per hour. It also organises boat excursions to Capri and the Grotta dello Smeraldo (see p229). Over on Spiaggia del Fornillo, **Centro Sub Costiera Amalfitana** (☎ 089 81 21 48; www .centrosub.it) runs dives (€60 for two hours) and lessons for adults and children.

SLEEPING

Accommodation is plentiful in Positano, although if you're on a budget you'll find your choices limited. Most hotels are three-star and above and prices are universally

BLUE RIBBON

Stretching about 50km from Vietri sul Mare to Piano di Sorrento, the SS163 (nicknamed the Nastro Azzurro or Blue Ribbon) is one of Italy's most dramatic roads. Commissioned by the Bourbon king Ferdinand II and completed in 1853, it tortuously wends its way along the Amalfi Coast's entire length, snaking round impossibly tight curves, over deep ravines and through tunnels gouged out of sheer rock. It's a magnificent feat of civil engineering. It's also a severe test of driving skill and courage, a white-knuckle ride that will pit you against the extraordinary ability of the local bus drivers. Originally designed for horse-drawn carriages, it can get very narrow in parts, particularly on hairpin bends. To avoid blocking oncoming buses get used to checking the circular mirrors on the roadside and listening for the sound of klaxons – if you hear one slow right down as it will invariably be followed by a coach. The trick to driving the Amalfi Coast is to stay calm, even when your toddler throws up all over the back seat or your partner tells you to look at the view while you're inching around a blind corner.

high. Like everywhere on the Amalfi Coast it gets very busy in summer, so book ahead, particularly at weekends and in July and August. Ask at the tourist office about rooms or apartments in private houses.

FLORIDA RESIDENCE   HOTEL €€

☎ 089 87 58 01; www.floridaresidence.net Viale Pasitea 171; d €85-105, apt €115; ☼ Apr-Oct; P ✂

A friendly place up from the town centre, the Florida Residence packs a lot of perks for the price – free parking, air-con (in most but not all of the rooms) and even a small (very small) freestanding swimming pool. The clean, basic rooms are fairly forgettable but the

terrace views are not, and the apartments are a superb deal – with cooker and fridge they could save you serious euros on dining out.

HOSTEL BRIKETTE   HOSTEL €

☎ 089 87 58 57; www.brikette.com; Via G Marconi 358; dm €22-25, d €60, apt €115-180; ☼ late Mar-Nov; ▣

Not far from the Bar Internazionale bus stop on the SS163 coastal road, this bright and cheerful hostel offers the cheapest accommodation in town. There are various options: six-to-eight person dorms (single sex and mixed), double rooms, a suite with a big private terrace, and apartments for between two and five people. There's also an extended list of extras, including laundry, CD burning, free wi-fi, left luggage, Italian and cooking lessons and massage (one hour €30). Curfew at 3am.

HOTEL PALAZZO MURAT   HOTEL €€€

☎ 089 87 51 77; www.palazzomurat.it; Via dei Mulini 23; s incl breakfast €120-250, d €150-375; ☼ May–mid-Jan; ✂

Of the upmarket hotels in the town centre, the Palazzo Murat has the most character. Housed in the 18th-century palazzo that Gioacchino Murat, Napoleon's brother-in-law and one-time King of Naples, used as his summer residence, it's quite a sight. Through the palatial arched entrance, lush gardens overflow with banana trees, bottlebrush, Japanese maple and pine trees. Rooms, five in the original part of the building (more expensive), 25 in the newer section, are decorated in traditional style with antiques, original oil paintings and plenty of glossy marble. Wi-fi is available in the central courtyard at €5 for 30 minutes.

WALK WITH THE GODS

Probably the best-known walk on the Amalfi Coast, the 12km **Sentiero degli Dei** (Path of the Gods; 5½ to six hours) follows the steep, often rocky paths linking Positano to Praiano. It's a spectacular walk, passing through some of the area's least developed countryside and offering breathtaking views. The route is marked by red and white stripes daubed on rocks and trees, although some of these have become worn in places and might be difficult to make out.

A second, more demanding route, the 14km **Capo Muro** (6½ to seven hours) follows a similar route, passing beneath soaring limestone cliffs as it climbs to a height of 1039m. You can walk it either way, but you'll get the best views by walking east to west, starting in Praiano and finishing in Positano.

If you're intent on trying either hike make sure you've got a decent map – the most reliable is the CAI's (Club Alpino Italiano; Italian Alpine Club) *Monti Lattari, Penisola Sorrentina, Costiera Amalfitana: Carta dei Sentieri* (€8) at 1:30,000 scale. Route details are also available in Lonely Planet's *Walking in Italy* guide.

For great views with much less effort, stroll the **Via Positanesi d'America**, the cliff-side path that links Spiaggia Grande with the Spiaggia del Fornillo. Reward yourself with a cold drink on the terrace of **Hotel Pupetto** (p224).

HOTEL PUPETTO HOTEL €€

☎ 089 87 50 87; www.hotelpupetto.it; Via Fornillo 37; s incl breakfast €80-90, d €130-160; ☼ Apr–mid-Nov; Ⓟ

Overlooking Spiaggia del Fornillo, this is as close to the beach as you can get without sleeping on a sun-lounger. A bustling, cheerful place, the hotel forms part of a large, rambling beach complex, with a popular terraced restaurant (meals around €25; the food pretty good), a nautical-themed bar (check out the great wall motifs) and, upstairs, the airy guest rooms. These are simple affairs with dizzily tiled floors, a blue-and-white colour scheme and lovely sea views.

HOTEL VITTORIA HOTEL €€

☎ 089 87 50 49; www.hotelvittoriapositano.it; Via Fornillo 19; s incl breakfast €75-90, d €120-140; Ⓟ ⚹

In the western part of town, above Spiaggia del Fornillo, the Vittoria is a laid-back, friendly three-star with simple all-white rooms. Spread over four floors, they are fairly anonymous – white walls, floral ceramic floors and the bare minimum of furniture – but they do all come with their own private terrace. A private lift carries you down to the beach and car parking is available at €13 per day.

PENSIONE CASA GUADAGNO PENSIONE €

☎ 089 87 50 42; www.pensionecasaguadagno.it; Via Fornillo 36; incl breakfast, s €50-75, d €65-90; ☼ year-round

In the tangled upper town, this modest *pensione* offers basic accommodation at honest rates. There are six white rooms all decorated in regional style with ceramic floors, floral bedspreads and small balconies (all but one of which boast sea views). Frills are few and far between but everywhere is clean, sunny and perfectly comfortable.

PENSIONE MARIA LUISA HOTEL €

☎ 089 87 50 23; www.pensionemarialuisa.com; Via Fornillo 42; s €50, d €70-80; ☼ year-round

A perennial budget favourite, the Maria Luisa is a lovely little hotel. There's nothing remotely flashy about the place, but the quirky old-fashioned rooms, the sunny communal area (with a fridge and coffee machine) and the jovial owner make for a memorable stay. It's well worth paying the €10 extra for a room with a private terrace as there are magnificent views of the bay.

PENSIONE VILLA VERDE HOTEL €

☎ 089 87 55 06; www.pensionevillaverde.it; Viale Pasitea 338; incl breakfast, s €50, d €60-90, tr €80-123; Ⓟ ⚹

One of only three one-star hotels in Positano, this homely, old-fashioned *pensione* is good value for money. Its 12 good-sized rooms, all of which come with a small terrace, sport a shocking blue and yellow colour scheme and a relaxing lack of mod cons. Televisions are available on request, although unless you speak Italian you'll probably be happier admiring the views from your terrace. Parking costs an extra €10 per day.

SAN PIETRO HOTEL €€€

☎ 089 87 54 55; www.ilsanpietro.it; Via Laurito 2; r incl breakfast from €420; ☼ Apr-Oct; Ⓟ ⚹ ⚹

For such a talked-about hotel, the San Pietro is remarkably discreet. Built into a rocky headland 2km east of Positano, it's almost entirely below road level – if driving, look for an ivy-clad chapel and a red British telephone box by the side of the road. Once safely ensconced, you probably won't want to leave. All of the individually decorated rooms have spectacular sea views, a private terrace and Jacuzzi; there's a tennis court, semi-circular swimming pool, Michelin-starred restaurant and, 88m below reception, a private beach (accessible by lift).

VILLA FRANCO HOTEL €€€

☎ 089 87 56 55; www.villafrancahotel.it; Viale Pasitea 318; r incl breakfast €190-340; ☼ Apr–mid-Oct; Ⓟ ⚹

An immaculate boutique hotel with a sparkling blue-and-white Mediterranean feel. Unashamedly classical in style, the sun-drenched public rooms are awash with *objets d'art*, impressively potted plants and ornate lamps. The small but sweet guest rooms feature tiled frescoes, balconies and great panoramas. The best views, however, are from the rooftop swimming pool, one of the best in Positano. Downstairs, there's a small bar, plus a gym with high-tech machinery and a Turkish bath. Parking costs €20 per day.

VILLA LA TARTANA HOTEL €€

☎ 089 81 21 93; www.villalatartana.it; Via Vicolo Vito Savino 6-8; d incl breakfast €140-150; ☼ Apr-Oct; ⚹

Only a few metres from Spiaggia Grande, this is one of the more affordable options in Positano's pricey centre. Rooms are spread over three floors and although they are all pretty much of a muchness, with blue floors, white walls and pretty floral bedsteads, those on the 3rd floor offer private balconies and the best views. To get to them, however, you'll have to lug your bags up the stairs, as there is no lift. There's also no dining room, which means that breakfast is served in your room.

VILLA NETTUNO   HOTEL €
☎ 089 87 54 01; www.villanettunopositano.it; Viale Pasitea 208; s/d €70/85; ⌚ year-round
Hidden behind a barrage of perfumed foliage, Villa Nettuno oozes charm. Go for one of the original rooms in the 300-year-old part of the building with their heavy rustic décor, frescoed wardrobes and communal terrace. Rooms in the renovated part of the villa are still good value but lack the character of the originals, their lime-green bathroom tiling and cheap furniture something of a letdown. That said, you probably won't be thinking of the furniture as you lie in bed looking out to the sea directly in front of you.

EATING
You're unlikely to have the meal of your trip in Positano. Most restaurants, bars and trattorie are unashamedly touristy, geared to turning over numbers rather than producing quality food. Which isn't to say that you can't eat well here, just that you'll pay more to do so than you would elsewhere. Needless to say, the nearer you get to the seafront, especially to Spiaggia Grande, the more expensive everything becomes. Many places close over winter, making a brief reappearance for Christmas and New Year.

BUCA DI BACCO   SNACKS €
☎ 089 81 14 61; Viale del Brigantino 35-37; snacks around €5
This is the most convenient snack bar for sunbathers on Spiaggia Grande. You'll find the usual range of nibbles including well-stuffed *panini* and tasty sweet pastries. Sit down at the upstairs **La Pergola** restaurant, though, and you're into a whole different price league. So unless you fancy paying from €15 for pasta standards and main courses, stick to the downstairs snack bar.

DA COSTANTINO   TRATTORIA €€
☎ 089 87 57 38; Via Montepertuso; meals around €20, pizzas from €4; ⌚ closed Wed
If you haven't got wheels of your own you'll be real hungry by the time you make it up to Costantino's, about ˌ300m north of Hostel Brikette. One of the few authentic trattorie in Positano (OK, technically it's in Montepertuso), it serves honest, down-to-earth Italian grub. The house speciality, apart from the quite amazing views, is *scialatielli* (ribboned pasta) served with aubergines, tomato and mozzarella. There are also excellent pizzas and a selection of fail-safe grilled meats.

DA VINCENZO   RISTORANTE €€€
☎ 089 87 51 28; Viale Pasitea 172-178; meals around €35; ⌚ Mar-Oct, closed Tue lunch Jul & Aug
If you don't usually eat dessert this is the place to push out the boat and go for it – they are, according to at least one local, the best in town. There are all the usual suspects – *babà*, tiramisu, and *crème brûlée* – plus originals such as strawberry and pistachio mousse. If you don't find any of these – the seasonal

DALLAS STRIBLEY

menu changes regularly – go for whatever sounds good. For the rest, seafood features heavily, service is friendly and the atmosphere is elegant without being pretentious. Dinner reservations are preferred.

DONNA ROSA   RISTORANTE €€€
☎ 089 81 18 06; Via Montepertuso 97-99; meals around €38; ✆ Wed-Mon Apr-Dec
Locals have long known that if you really want to eat well without paying an arm and a leg, head to Montepertuso. Up in the village, Donna Rosa, once a family-run trattoria, now an elegant family-run restaurant, serves some of the best food on the coast. Particularly sought after are her handmade pastas such as *fusilli al ragù con salsiccia e mozzarella* (pasta twists with meat sauce, sausage and mozzarella) or *ravioli alle melanzane* (aubergine ravioli). The mains and desserts are also excellent and the wine list is long enough to confuse most amateurs. Book ahead.

LA ZAGARA   CAFFÈ/PASTICCERIA €
☎ 089 87 59 64; Via dei Mulini 6; ✆ Apr–mid-Nov
Everybody passes this unapologetic tourist trap at least once during their time in Positano. And although not everyone stops off, a whole lot do, drawn by its tempting display of overpriced sweet treats (take the €2.50 giant *babà* and cream) and savoury snacks (pizza slices and *panini* from about €3). The service is predatory, as waiters skilfully manoeuvre you onto their tables, but the food is pretty good and the outdoor terrace, with its red floors and encroaching lemon trees, is redolent of Mediterranean summers.

LO GUARRACINO   RISTORANTE €€€
☎ 089 87 57 94; Via Positanesi d'America; meals around €35, pizzas from €8.50; ✆ Mar-Dec
It's difficult to beat the location of this cliffside restaurant. On the scenic path connecting Positano's two beaches, it's a memorable place to eat even if you are more likely to remember the unfettered sea views than the straightforward food. The menu is seafood heavy, with dishes such as grilled swordfish (€16) and *tubetti al ragù di mare* (small pasta tubes with fish sauce; €16). If those don't appeal there are also pizzas and steaks. It's a popular spot, so if possible book ahead.

RISTORANTE BRUNO   RISTORANTE €€€
☎ 089 87 53 92; Via Cristoforo Colombo 157; meals around €30; ✆ closed Thu lunch & Feb-Oct
It doesn't look like much with its unassuming décor and unspectacular venue, but the food here is really very good, a cut above the Positano average. Speciality of the house is seafood, which appears in various guises: as an antipasto there's marinated fish with vegetables, orange and parmesan; as a primo you can try linguine with clams, courgettes and pecorino cheese; while for a main course keep it simple with grilled fish and a wedge of local lemon. The wine list offers an ample choice of Italian labels.

RISTORANTE IL SARACENO D'ORO   RISTORANTE €€€
☎ 089 81 20 50; Viale Pasitea 254; meals around €25, pizzas from €5; ✆ Mar-Oct
On the main road into town, the Golden Saracen continues to win plaudits. A busy, bustling place, its blend of cheery service, uncomplicated food and reasonable prices (in Positano terms, of course) continues to attract the punters. The pizzas are excellent, the pasta's tasty and the profiteroles superb – either in chocolate or lemon sauce. The complimentary end-of-meal glass of *limoncello* is a nice touch.

ENTERTAINMENT

Unless the idea of parading up and down with a cashmere sweater draped over your shoulders turns you on, Positano's nightlife is not going to do much for you. More piano bar than warehouse, it's genteel, sophisticated and safe.

CONWINUM WINE BAR
☎ 089 81 16 87; Via Rampa Teglia 12; ✆ 9am-1am Mar-Dec
A favourite of trendy, well-dressed Italians, Conwinum is part wine bar, part internet café (€3 for 30 minutes) and part art gallery. Just off Spiaggia Grande, it's a snazzy, softly lit place with tangerine walls, a vaulted ceiling and swinging lounge music. There's live jazz on Friday and Saturday night (summer only) and wine buffs will enjoy the daily wine tasting (€10 with appetisers). If you miss that you can always choose from the 900-label wine list.

MUSIC ON THE ROCKS

☎ 089 87 58 74; www.musicontherocks.it; Via Grotte dell'Incanto 51; admission €10-25; ⏱ Easter-Oct

Positano's only genuine disco is dramatically carved into the tower at the eastern end of Spiaggia Grande. One of the best nightspots on the coast, it attracts a good-looking, up-for-it crowd and some of the region's top DJs. The sounds are largely mainstream house and reliable disco. Upstairs, diners sit down to €60 dinners at **La Terrazze** restaurant.

SHOPPING

Whether you're a shopaholic or an only-if-I-have-to shopper, you can't miss Positano's colourful boutiques – everywhere you look, shop displays scream out at you in a riot of exuberant colour. After a while, though, you may glaze over at the sameness of the fashions on sale. The humble lemon also enjoys star status; not just in *limoncello* and lemon-infused candles, but blazoned across tea towels, aprons and pottery.

ARTIGIANATO RALLO   SHOES

☎ 089 81 17 11; Viale Pasitea 96; ⏱ 10am-9.30pm daily Apr-Oct, to 6pm Nov-Mar

Run by the third generation of a Sorrentine shoemakers family, this small shop sells an attractive range of handmade leather sandals. If you don't see anything you fancy you can always have a pair made to order. Prices start at around €33.

LOUIS   CLOTHING & ACCESSORIES

☎ 089 87 51 92; Via Dei Mulini 22; ⏱ 9am-10pm daily Jun-Sep, 9am-1pm & 3-7pm Oct-May

Positano's most famous shop is a riot of brilliant floral-patterned dresses, shirts, skirts and scarves. These distinctive fashions have been designed and made here for 40 years under the watchful eye of Louis, the doyen of Positano fashion. You should be able to pick up a dress for around €40.

GETTING THERE & AWAY

Boat

Ferries all sail from/into the quay to the west of Spiaggia Grande. Between Easter and October, various ferry companies link Positano with towns along the coast and Capri:

Alicost (☎ 089 87 14 83; Largo Scario 5, Amalfi) Operates services to/from Salerno (€7, five daily), Ischia (€19, one daily) and Capri (€15.50, five daily).

LMP (Linee Marittime Partenope; ☎ 081 704 19 11; www.consorziolmp.it; Via Guglielmo Melisurgo 4, Naples) Has three daily ferries to/from Sorrento (€7).

Metrò del Mare (☎ 199 44 66 44; www.metrodelmare.com) In spring and summer sails to/from Naples (€9, four daily), Sorrento (€6, five daily), Amalfi (€6, six daily) and Salerno (€7, three daily).

TraVelMar (☎ /fax 089 87 29 50; Largo Scario 5, Amalfi) Runs to Salerno (ferry/hydrofoil €6.50/7, seven daily), Amalfi (ferry/hydrofoil €5.50/6, seven daily) and Sorrento (€7, three daily).

Bus

Sixteen kilometres west of Amalfi and 18km from Sorrento, Positano is on the main SS163 coastal road. In fact, it's just beneath the road, so if you arrive by bus you might have to ask the driver where to get off. There are two main bus stops: coming from Sorrento and the west, it's opposite Bar Internazionale; arriving from Amalfi and the east, it's at the top of Via Cristoforo Colombo. To get into town from the former, follow Viale Pasitea; from the latter take Via Cristoforo Colombo. When departing, buy bus tickets at Bar Internazionale or, if headed eastwards, from the tobacconist at the bottom of Via Cristoforo Colombo.

ROCCO FASANO

SITA (☎ 199 73 07 49; www.sita-on-line.it, in Italian) runs frequent buses to and from Amalfi (€1.30, 40 minutes, more than 12 daily) and Sorrento (€1.30, 40 minutes, at least 12 daily).

Car & Motorcycle

By car, take the A3 autostrada to Vietri sul Mare and then follow the SS163 coastal road. The problem, however, is not how to get to Positano by car but what to do with it when you arrive. Unless your hotel offers parking you could end up paying between €3 and €8 per hour in a private car park, such as the one at Piazza dei Mulini 4.

GETTING AROUND

Getting Around Positano is largely a matter of walking. If your knees can take the slopes, there are dozens of narrow alleys and stairways that make walking relatively easy and joyously traffic-free. Otherwise, orange **Flavia Gioia** (☎ 089 81 30 77; Via Cristoforo Colombo 49) buses follow the lower ring road every half-hour, passing along

Viale Pasitea, Via Cristoforo Colombo and Via G Marconi. Stops are clearly marked and you buy your ticket (€1) on board. The Flavia Gioia buses pass by both SITA bus stops. There are also 17 daily buses up to Montepertuso and Nocelle.

To hire a scooter, try **Positano Rent a Scooter** (☎ 089 812 20 77; Viale Pasitea 99; per day from €50).

FROM POSITANO TO AMALFI

PRAIANO

An ancient fishing village, Praiano is the archetypal coastal community. With no centre as such, its whitewashed houses pepper the verdant ridge of Monte Sant'Angelo as it slopes towards Capo Sottile. Formerly an important silk production centre, it was a favourite of the Amalfi Dogi, who made it their summer residence.

In the upper village the 16th-century **Chiesa di San Luca** (☎ 089 87 41 65; Via Oratorio 1) features an impressive majolica floor and paintings attributed to the 16th-century artist Giovanni Bernardo Lama. But it's the small beach at **Marina di Praia** that most people stop off here. From the SS163 (next to the Hotel Continentale) a steep path leads down the side of the cliffs to a tiny inlet with a small stretch of coarse sand and very tempting sea water; the best is actually off the rocks just before you get to the bottom. In what were once fishermen's houses, you'll now find a couple of bars and a very decent fish restaurant.

Sleeping & Eating

DA ARMANDINO   RISTORANTE €€€

☎ 089 87 40 87; Via Praia 1; meals around €35; ✕ Apr-Oct

On the beach in Marina di Praia, this laid-back restaurant is great for fish fresh off the boat. There is a menu but you'd do as well just to agree to whatever the waiter suggests as the dish of the day – it's all excellent. The holiday atmosphere and appealing setting – at the foot of sheer cliffs towering up to the main road – round things off nicely.

HOTEL CONTINENTALE & LA TRANQUILITA   HOTEL €

☎ 089 87 40 84; www.continental.praiano.it; Via Roma 21; s €40-60, d€60-85, apt per week €850-1,250, mini-apt €400-800, tent €30; ☼ r Apr-Oct, apt year-round

On the main road just to the east of Praiano, this gay-friendly hotel offers the full gamut of accommodation. There are cool, white rooms with sea views; there are two large self-contained apartments and three mini-apartments (sleeping up to four people); and there's even space for 15 tents on a series of grassy terraces. From the lowest of the camping terraces a private staircase leads down to a rocky platform on the sea. Transport is no problem either, as there's a bus stop just outside the hotel.

Entertainment

AFRICANA

☎ 089 87 40 42; Marina di Praia; ☼ Jun-Sep

Locals say that the Africana nightclub is not what it was since the death of its previous owner. But it's still worth an evening of anybody's time, if nothing else for the unique setting – in a series of caves round the corner from Marina di Praia beach. The glass-panelled dance floor looks down into sea water illuminated by multicoloured lights – a potentially hallucinogenic sight after a glass or two too many.

FURORE

It's difficult to imagine that Marina di Furore, a recently restored fishing village, was once a busy little commercial centre. And yet that's just what it was in medieval times, its unique natural position freeing it from the threat of foreign raids and providing a ready source of water for its flour and paper mills.

Originally founded by Romans fleeing barbarian incursions, it sits at the bottom of what's known as the fjord of Furore, a giant cleft that cuts through the Lattari mountains. The main village, however, stands 300m above, in the upper Vallone del Furore. A one-horse place that sees few tourists at any time of the year, it breathes a

distinctly rural air despite the colourful murals and unlikely modern sculpture. It also boasts a fantastic agriturismo.

To get to upper Furore by car follow the SS163 and then the SS366 signposted to Agerola; from Positano, it's 15km. Otherwise, regular SITA buses depart from the bus terminus in Amalfi (€1, 30 minutes, 17 daily).

Sleeping

AGRITURISMO SERAFINA   FARM STAY €

☎ 089 83 03 47; www.agriturismoserafina.it; Via Picola 3, Loc. Vigne; r incl breakfast €30-35, half-board €45-50; ☼ year-round; ✇

It's difficult to get more off the beaten track than this superb agriturismo. But make it up here and you'll find one of the best deals on the coast. Accommodation is in seven spruce, air-conditioned rooms in the main farmhouse, each with its own small terrace and views over the lush green terraces below. Meals are served on the central terrace or, in winter, in the light-filled dining room. The food, needless to say, is quite special, virtually everything made with the farm's own produce (which includes salami, pancetta, wine, olive oil, fruit and veg).

CONCA DEI MARINI

Four kilometres west of Amalfi, Conca dei Marini is home to one of the coast's most popular sights, the **Grotta dello Smeraldo** (admission €5; ☼ 9am-4pm Mar-Oct, 9am-3pm Nov-Feb), a haunting cave named after the eerie emerald colour that emanates from the sea water. Stalactites hang down from the 24m-high ceiling while stalagmites grow up to 10m in height. Each year, on 24 December and 6 January, skin-divers from all over Italy make their traditional pilgrimage to the ceramic *presepe* (nativity scene) submerged beneath the sea water.

SITA buses regularly pass the car park above the cave entrance (from where you take a lift or stairs down to the rowing boats). Alternatively, **Coop Sant'Andrea** (☎ 089 87 31 90; www.coopsantandrea.it; Lungomare dei Cavalieri 1) runs two daily boats from Amalfi (€10 return) at 9am and 3.30pm. Allow 1½ hours for the round trip.

CRAIG PERSHOUSE

AMALFI

Fetching as it is with its sun-filled piazzas and small beach, there's very little to suggest that Amalfi was once the capital of a powerful maritime republic boasting a population of more than 70,000. For one thing, Amalfi's not a big place – you can easily walk from one end to the other in about 20 minutes. For another thing, there are very few historical buildings of note. The explanation for this is quite chilling – most of the old city, and its populace, simply slid into the sea during an earthquake in 1343.

Today, although the resident population is no more than around 5000, the numbers swell significantly during the summer months when day-trippers pour in by the coachload. Most visitors stick to the standard tourist programme: a quick stop-off in **Piazza del Duomo** and the landmark **cathedral**, a bit of window shopping along Via Lorenzo d'Amalfi, and then a bite to eat at a streetside trattoria. Which is, in fact, pretty much all there is to do in Amalfi. But more than its sights, Amalfi is all about its beautiful seaside setting, which is the perfect spot for aimless wandering and long, lingering lunches.

Just around the headland, neighbouring **Atrani** is a picturesque tangle of whitewashed alleys and arches centred on a lively, lived-in piazza and popular beach.

ORIENTATION

Buses and boats drop you off at Amalfi's main transport hub, Piazza Flavio Gioia. From here cross the road and duck through to Piazza del Duomo, the town's focal square. Most of the hotels and restaurants are in the tangled lanes either side of the main strip, Via Lorenzo d'Amalfi and its continuation, Via Capuano, which snake north from the cathedral. On the seafront, Corso delle Repubbliche Marinare follows the coast eastwards, becoming Via Pantaleone Comite as it bends round to the Saracen tower on the headland. Continue down the other side, through the tunnel and off to the right for Atrani.

SIGHTS & ACTIVITIES
Cathedral

Dominating Piazza del Duomo, the iconic **Cattedrale di Sant'Andrea** (☎ 089 87 10 59; Piazza del Duomo; ☼ 9am-7pm Apr-Jun, 9am-9pm Jul-Sep, 9.30am-5.15pm Oct & Mar, 10am-1pm & 2.30-4.30pm Nov-Feb), makes an imposing sight at the top of its sweeping flight of stairs. The cathedral dates in part from the early 10th century and its striking stripy façade has been rebuilt twice, most recently at the end of the 19th century. Although the building is a hybrid, the Sicilian Arabic-Norman style predominates, particularly in the two-tone masonry and the 13th-century bell

INFORMATION

- **Altra Costiera** (☎ 089 873 60 82; www
  .altracostiera.com; Via Lorenzo D'Amalfi 34;
  ⏰ 9am-9pm daily May-mid-Sep, closed Sun
  rest of year) Provides internet access (per 15 mins
  €2) and accommodation referral, plus arranges
  walking and other tours. Also hires out scooters
  (from €45 per day excluding petrol).
- **Deutsche Bank** (Corso Repubbliche Marinare)
  Next door to the tourist office; has an ATM.
- **Farmacia del Cervo** (☎ 089 87 10 45; Piazza
  del Duomo; ⏰ 8.30am-1pm & 5-9pm Mon-Fri)
  Pharmacist.
- **Post office** (☎ 089 87 29 96; Corso Repubbliche
  Marinare) Next door to the tourist office.

- **Toilets** (€0.50) Just outside the
  tourist office.
- **Tourist Office** (☎ 089 87 11 07; www
  .amalfitouristoffice.it; Piazza Flavio Gioia 3;
  ⏰ 8.30am-1.30pm & 3-5.15pm Mon-Fri,
  8.30am-midday Sat, afternoon opening to
  7.15pm Mon-Fri Jul & Aug) Has bus and
  boat timetables and a few maps, but precious
  little else.
- **Travel Tourist Office Divina Costiera** (☎ 089
  87 24 67; Piazza Flavio Gioia 3; ⏰ 8am-1pm &
  2-8pm daily) Sells bus and boat tickets, organises
  excursions, books hotels (€3 fee) and provides left
  luggage (€3 per bag).

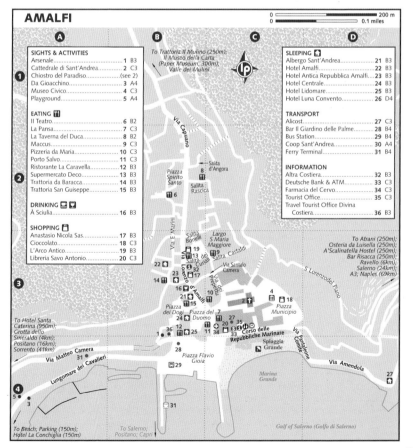

AMALFI

SIGHTS & ACTIVITIES	
Arsenale	1 B3
Cattedrale di Sant'Andrea	2 C3
Chiostro del Paradiso	(see 2)
Da Gioacchino	3 A4
Museo Civico	4 C3
Playground	5 A4

EATING	
Il Teatro	6 B2
La Pansa	7 C3
La Taverna del Duca	8 B2
Maccus	9 C3
Pizzeria da Maria	10 C3
Porto Salvo	11 C3
Ristorante La Caravella	12 B3
Supermercato Deco	13 B3
Trattoria da Baracca	14 B3
Trattoria San Guiseppe	15 B3

DRINKING	
À Sciulia	16 B3

SHOPPING	
Anastasio Nicola Sas	17 B3
Cioccolato	18 C3
L'Arco Antico	19 C3
Libreria Savo Antonio	20 C3

SLEEPING	
Albergo Sant'Andrea	21 B3
Hotel Amalfi	22 B3
Hotel Antica Repubblica Amalfi	23 B3
Hotel Centrale	24 B3
Hotel Lidomare	25 B3
Hotel Luna Convento	26 D4

TRANSPORT	
Alicost	27 C3
Bar Il Giardino delle Palme	28 B4
Bus Station	29 B4
Coop Sant'Andrea	30 A4
Ferry Terminal	31 B4

INFORMATION	
Altra Costiera	32 B3
Deutsche Bank & ATM	33 C3
Farmacia del Cervo	34 C3
Tourist Office	35 C3
Travel Tourist Office Divina	
Costiera	36 B3

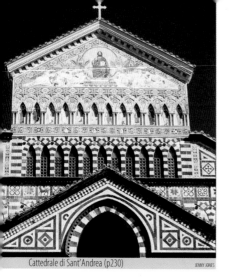
Cattedrale di Sant'Andrea (p230)   JENNY JONES

tower. The huge bronze doors also merit a look – the first of their type in Italy, they were commissioned by a local noble and made in Syria before being shipped over to Amalfi. Less impressive is the baroque interior, although the altar features some fine statues and there are some interesting 12th- and 13th-century mosaics. In high season, entrance to the cathedral between 10am and 5pm is through the adjacent Chiostro del Paradiso, meaning that you have to pay an entrance fee of €2.50.

To the left of the cathedral's porch, the **Chiostro del Paradiso** (☎ 089 87 13 24; adult/child €2.50/1; 🕒 9am-7pm Jun-Oct, 9am-1pm & 2.30-4.30pm Nov-May) is well worth the small admission charge. Built in 1266 to house the tombs of Amalfi's prominent citizens, it's a model of architectural elegance: 120 marble columns support a series of tall, slender Arabic arches around a central garden. From the cloisters go through to the Basilica del Crocefisso, where you'll find various religious artefacts displayed in glass cabinets, and some fading 14th-century frescoes. Beneath lies the 1206 crypt containing the remains of Sant'Andrea.

Museums
In the town hall building, the one-room **Museo Civico** (☎ 089 87 10 66; Piazza Municipio; admission free; 🕒 8.30am-1pm Mon-Fri) contains the Tavole Amalfitane, an ancient manuscript

draft of Amalfi's maritime code, and other historical documents. Ask at the window halfway up the entry stairs for a guide sheet in English.

Amalfi's other museum of note is the fascinating **Museo della Carta** (Paper Museum; ☎ 089 830 45 61; www.museodellacarta.it; Via delle Cartiere; admission €3.70; 🕒 10am-6.30pm Apr–mid-Nov, 10am-3pm Tue, Wed & Fri-Sun rest of year). Housed in a 13th-century paper mill (the oldest in Europe), it lovingly preserves the original paper presses, which are still in full working order as you'll see during the 15-minute guided tour (in English). The stationery sold in the gift shop makes for ideal gifts.

Harking back to Amalfi's days as a great maritime republic, the cavernous **Arsenale** (Via Matteo Camera; admission free; 🕒 9am-1.30pm Easter-Sep) was once the town's main shipbuilding depot. Today it's used to host temporary exhibitions.

Beaches & Boats
For all it's seafaring history, Amalfi is not a great place to swim. The town's beach, **Spiaggia Grande**, about 150m of coarse sand, is not very appealing even if it's highly popular with visitors, who throng to the private bathing facilities off Corso delle Repubbliche Marinare. About a 15-minute walk away, **Atrani** also has a small, black-sanded beach.

If you're really intent on a swim, you're better off hiring a boat. You'll find a number of operators along Lungomare dei Cavalieri, including **da Gioacchino** (☎ 328 649 41 92; www.amalfiboats.it; Spiaggia del Porto, Lungomare dei Cavalieri), which hires out boats and organises excursions along the coast. Prices start at €50 for two hours' boat hire.

If you've got kids, the nearby **merry-go-round** and **trampoline** might provide some welcome distraction. A few metres away, on the other side of the road, there's a rather sorry-looking **playground** with a slide and climbing frame.

FESTIVALS & EVENTS
The **Regatta of the Four Ancient Maritime Republics**, which rotates between Amalfi, Venice, Pisa and Genoa, is held on the first Sunday in June. Amalfi's turn comes around again in 2009.

SLEEPING

Despite its reputation as a day trip destination, Amalfi has plenty of accommodation. It's not especially cheap, though, and most hotels are in the midrange to upper price brackets. Always try to book ahead, as the summer months are very busy and many places close over winter. Note that if you're coming by car, consider a hotel with parking, as on-street parking is horribly difficult to find.

ALBERGO SANT'ANDREA   HOTEL €
☎ 089 87 11 45; Via Santolo Camera; s/d €50/80; ☾ Mar-Oct; ✵
Enjoy the atmosphere of busy Piazza del Duomo from the comfort of your own room. Bang opposite the cathedral, this modest two-star has basic rooms that while unspectacular provide little cause for complaint – they're clean, the TV and air-con work, there's hot water and the rates are reasonable. What is a nuisance, however, is the noise from the piazza outside. The same family also runs the Ristorante Pizzeria Sant'Andrea on the other side of the square.

A'SCALINATELLA HOSTEL   HOSTEL €
☎ 089 87 14 92; www.hostelscalinatella.com; Piazza Umberto I; incl breakfast, dm €21-25, d €73-83, d with shared bathroom €50-60; ▣
Just around the headland in Atrani, this rough-and-ready budget operation has 10-bed dorms, rooms and apartments scattered across the village. It's strictly no frills, so don't expect much more than a bed and running water, but it has the usual hostel extras – internet, laundry and a kitchen – and there's an upbeat traveller atmosphere. Doors are locked at 2am.

HOTEL AMALFI   HOTEL €€
☎ 089 87 24 40; www.starnet.it/hamalfi; Vico dei Pastai 3; incl breakfast, s €60-120, d €80-160; ℗ ✵
In the backstreets just off Amalfi's main pedestrian thoroughfare, this family-run three-star is comfortable and central. Rooms, some of which have their own balconies, sport pale-yellow walls and majolica-tiled flooring, while bathrooms are modern and clean. Upstairs, the roof garden is a relaxing place to idle over a drink. Parking costs between €18 and €20 per day.

HOTEL ANTICA REPUBBLICA AMALFI   HOTEL €€
☎ 089 873 63 10; www.antica reppublica.it; Vico dei Pastai 2; r €90-160; ☾ year-round; ✵
A smart hotel snugly housed in a whitewashed 11th-century palazzo. Inside it's all warm terracotta floors and earthenware vases, floral ceramic tiling and wrought-iron lamps. Upstairs, rooms are tastefully decorated, if not the biggest in town. Breakfast is served on the panoramic rooftop terrace.

HOTEL CENTRALE   HOTEL €€
☎ 089 87 26 08; www.hotelcentraleamalfi.it; Largo Piccolomini 1; incl breakfast, s €70-100, d €85-135, tr €125-165, q €140; ☾ year-round; ℗ ✵
For the money, this is one of the best-value hotels in Amalfi. The entrance is on a tiny little piazza in the centro storico but many rooms actually overlook Piazza del Duomo. And fine, fresh rooms they are too, with vibrant blue and yellow tiles, white walls and pristine bathrooms; some even have their own balconies. Additional bonuses include breakfast on the top-floor terrace, and parking, albeit for an extra €16 per day.

HOTEL LA CONCHIGLIA   HOTEL €
☎ /fax 089 87 18 56; Lungomare dei Cavalieri; d €100, half-board per person €80; ☾ Easter-Oct; ℗
One of the few budget options in Amalfi, this characterful place is a five-minute walk west of the centre on the seafront beyond the marina. It's not in a particularly scenic spot but the airy rooms are comfortable enough, with their cool white walls and old-fashioned furniture. The parking is a definite plus in a town where space is a much sought-after commodity. Between July and mid-September half-board is compulsory.

HOTEL LIDOMARE   HOTEL €€
☎ 089 87 13 32; www.lidomare.it; Largo Duchi Piccolomini 9; s/d incl breakfast €50/110; ☾ year-round; ✵
Oozing character, this friendly, family-run hotel is a gem. The spacious rooms have a real air of gentility, with their appealingly haphazard décor, old-fashioned tiles and fine old antiques. Surprisingly, some, such as room 31, even have Jacuzzi bathtubs; others, room 57 among them, have sea views. Among the

general bric-a-brac, look out for the king-sized *presepe* in the hallway.

HOTEL LUNA CONVENTO HOTEL €€€
☎ 089 87 10 02; www.lunahotel.it; Via Pantaleone Comite 33; s incl breakfast €160-200, d €180-220; ✤ year-round; P ✕ ≋

Surely one of the most captivating hotel courtyards anywhere in Italy, the 13th-century cloister at the heart of this historic hotel is quite something. The centrepiece of St Francis' 1226 convent, it's now a delightful spot for a drink. Rooms, many of which are in the former monks' cells, are far from monastic, with bright tiles, balconies and seamless sea views. Some, rather disturbingly, also boast religious frescoes over the beds. Over the road in the Saracen tower, there's a restaurant and saltwater swimming pool. Parking, at €20 per day, is available on request.

HOTEL SANTA CATERINA HOTEL €€€
☎ 089 87 10 12; www.hotelsantacaterina.it; Strada Amalfitana 9; d €250-700, ste from €500; ✤ Mar-Oct; P ✕ ≋

An Amalfi landmark, the Santa Caterina is one of Italy's most famous hotels. Everything about the place screams luxury, from the discreet service to the fabulous gardens, the private beach (actually, more a platform than a beach) to opulent rooms. And if that weren't enough, the views are among the best on the coast. For honeymooners, the Romeo and Juliet suite is the one to go for, a private chalet in the colourful grounds, it's a snip at anywhere between €650 and €1300 per night.

EATING & DRINKING

Inevitably most of the restaurants in and around Amalfi's centre cater to the tourist trade. But that shouldn't put you off, as standards are generally high and it's rare (although not impossible) to eat badly. Most places serve pizzas, the best cooked in traditional wood-ovens (look for signs advertising *forno a legna*), and a range of pastas, grilled meats and seafood. The Amalfi drinking scene is fairly subdued, revolving round streetside cafés and bars rather than pubs. It gets a bit more boisterous in Atrani but it's hardly hard-core.

Picnickers and self-caterers can stock up at the **Supermercato Deco** (Salita dei Curiali; ✤ 8am-1.30pm daily & 5-8.30pm Mon-Sat).

À SCIULIA SNACKS €
☎ 339 589 36 08; Via Fra Gerardo Sasso 2; granitas €5; ✤ 10-2am daily Mar–mid-Nov

For the best lemon *granita* in town, head for this brightly coloured hole in the wall. You'll also find sorbets, smoothies, yoghurts and fruit salads, all made on the premises and all truly delicious. Yoghurts cost around €4.50.

BAR RISACCA BAR €
☎ 089 87 28 66; Piazza Umberto I 16, Atrani; pizza/bruschetta from €4/3

Popular with travellers staying at the nearby A'Scalinatella Hostel, this boisterous Atrani bar is about as lively as it gets. Music pumps out over squareside tables as tanned students sip on garish cocktails and bottled beer. Save yourself a euro or two by stocking up during happy hour (between 6pm and 8pm). Pizza and bruschetta are available to ward off hunger pangs.

IL TEATRO TRATTORIA €€
☎ 089 87 24 73; Via Herculano Marini 19; meals around €25; ✤ Thu-Tue Feb-Dec

One of the better trattorie tucked away in the whitewashed centro storico. Tables are set outside on the narrow lane or in the cavernous interior decorated with black-and-white photos and assorted bric-a-brac. Seafood features heavily in dishes such as *spaghetti e cozze* (spaghetti with mussels) or *farfalle con gamberi e rucola* (butterfly-shaped pasta with prawns and rocket). But there's also plenty of meat and some good vegetarian options, including ribbon-style *scialatielli* with tomatoes and aubergines.

LA PANSA CAFÉ €
☎ 089 87 10 65; Piazza del Duomo 40; cornettos & pastries from €1.50; ✤ Wed-Mon year-round

A swish café on Piazza del Duomo, this place serves a great Italian breakfast – freshly made cornettos and deliciously frothy cappuccino. If you don't fancy a cornetto, there are any number of cakes and pastries to choose from, all made in-house and all absolutely irresistible.

LA TAVERNA DEL DUCA RISTORANTE €€€
☎ 089 87 27 55; Piazza Spirito Santo 26; meals around €35, pizzas from €6; ✤ Fri-Wed year-round

A popular restaurant with a fishy reputation. Specials vary according to the catch of the day but might include *carpaccio di baccalà* (thin strips of raw salted cod) or linguine with scampi. Steak in balsamic vinegar is a meaty alternative or there are pretty good pizzas. Tucked into the corner of a small piazza away from the centre, the dark woody interior of this restaurant is lined with dusty wine bottles and paintings. There are a few tables out on the square.

MACCUS RISTORANTE €€€

☎ 089 873 63 85; Largo S Maria Maggiore 1-3; meals around €38; ☁ 7.30-10.30pm Wed-Sun

An elegant, intimate setting and better-than-average food set Maccus apart. The menu, which changes according to the chef's morning shop, features plenty of seafood, such as meaty swordfish served with tomato and olive oil or *paccheri* (big tubes of pasta) with scorpion fish. Desserts, for which there's a separate menu, are original and tasty – try the Coppa Maccus, a rich mix of sponge, mascarpone, rum, torrone and amaretto. Sit outside on the petite piazza or inside in the refined, softly lit interior.

OSTERIA DA LUISELLA TRATTORIA €€€

☎ 089 87 10 87; Piazza Umberto, Atrani; meals around €30; ☁ Thu-Tue year-round

Great food, great people-watching, and an atmospheric setting. These are the three ingredients that make Luisella such an attractive choice. Situated under the arches in Atrani's Piazza Umberto I, it serves excellent regional food with an emphasis on seafood. The menu often changes but if it's on, the fish ravioli is delicious and the *cassuola* (octopus stew) very filling. Vegetarians might go for the *caporalessa*, a tasty baked concoction of aubergines, tomatoes and cheese. The wine's excellent and the service laid-back but efficient.

PIZZERIA DA MARIA PIZZERIA €€

☎ 089 87 18 80; Via Lorenzo D'Amalfi 16; pizzas from €5, meals around €28; ☁ Dec-Oct; ☒

Just off Piazza del Duomo, at the beginning of the main pedestrian thoroughfare, this cavernous place inevitably attracts hordes of tourists. But that shouldn't necessarily put you off, particularly in the evening when the day-trippers have gone home, as the wood-fired pizzas are excellent. The pastas and main courses are not bad either but are pretty expensive for what they are. Service is fast and English is spoken.

PORTO SALVO SNACKS €

☎ 338 906 01 69; Via Supportico Marina Piccola 8; ice cream/panini from €2/3.50; ☁ year-round

The place for a quick snack. Choose from sliced pizza, *panini*, fried rice balls, croquettes – they are all pretty good. Next door, the ice cream served in the gelateria of the same name makes for a simple pud. Take it away or sit at one of the few outside tables.

RISTORANTE LA CARAVELLA RISTORANTE €€€

☎ 089 87 10 29; Via Matteo Camera 12; meals around €60, tasting menu €75; ☁ Wed-Mon Jan–mid-Nov

One of the few places in Amalfi where you pay for the food rather than the location. Which in this case is far from spectacular – by the road tunnel on the main coastal road. But that doesn't worry the discreet, knowledgeable crowd who eat here. The food is regional with a nouvelle zap, meaning mussels stuffed with mozzarella and prawns on a bed of creamed tomato and capers, or black ravioli with cuttlefish ink, scampi and ricotta. Wine aficionados are likely to find something to try on the 15,000-label list.

TRATTORIA DA BARACCA TRATTORIA €€

☎ 089 87 12 85; Piazza dei Dogi; meals around €25, tourist menu €17; ☁ Thu-Tue Feb-Oct

With its stripy blue awnings and maritime paraphernalia, its genial waiters and mealtime crooner, this cheerful seafood trattoria makes quite an impression. There are no great surprises on the menu, which includes lasagne and *gnocchi alla sorrentina* alongside pastas with mussels, clams and a variety of fishy sauces. Best of all is the really very good fish soup.

TRATTORIA IL MULINO TRATTORIA €€

☎ 089 87 22 23; Via delle Cartiere 36; meals around €20, pizzas around €6; ☁ year-round

Near the Museo della Carta, this is about as authentic a trattoria/pizzeria as you will find in Amalfi. A TV-in-the-corner, kids-running-between-the-tables sort of place, it's not the restaurant to impress your partner. But if you just want to eat some good, hearty pasta and simple grilled meat/fish, it'll do just fine. The *scialatiella alla pescatore* (ribbons of pasta with prawns, mussels, tomato and parsley) is much recommended, as is the calamari in the *cassuola* (octopus stew). Service is pretty slow but the prices are fair.

TRATTORIA SAN GIUSEPPE TRATTORIA €€

☎ 089 87 26 40; Salita Ruggiero II 4; meals around €22, pizzas from €5; ☁ Fri-Wed year-round

Some say the pizzas here are the best in town. Certainly they are good (although not exceptional) with toppings ranging from the traditional margherita (tomato, mozzarella and basil) to marine combos such as clams, prawns and anchovies. Pastas are also served, usually in huge helpings. The back-alley location is atmospheric even if the occasional whiff of antique drains might be a bit too atmospheric for people dining outside. If so, head into the fan-cooled interior.

SHOPPING

You'll have no difficulty loading up on souvenirs here – Via Lorenzo d'Amalfi is lined with garish shops selling local ceramic work, paper-made gifts and the local lemon liqueur, *limoncello*. Prices are set for tourists so don't expect many bargains.

ANASTASIO NICOLA SAS   FOOD
☎ 089 87 10 07; Via Lorenzo D'Amalfi 32; ☺ year-round

Unless you're flying to Australia, gourmet goodies can make excellent gifts. Here, among the hanging hams, you'll find a full selection, ranging from local cheese and preserves to coffee, chocolate, *limoncello* and pasta. There's also a collection of fruit-scented soaps.

CIOCCOLATO   CHOCOLATE
☎ 089 87 32 91; Piazza Municipio 12; ☺ Wed-Mon year-round

Wafting out of the door, the enticing scent of chocolate is hard to resist. So why fight it? Treat yourself to a box of delicious chocs, all of which have been made on the premises. You'll not regret it.

L'ARCO ANTICO   PAPER
☎ 089 873 63 54; Via Capuano 4; ☺ closed Jan & Feb

Amalfi's connection with paper-making dates back to the 12th century when the first mills were set up to supply the republic's small army of bureaucrats. Now little is made here but you can still buy it and the quality is still good. This attractive shop sells a range of paper products including beautiful writing paper, leather-bound notebooks and huge photo albums.

LIBRERIA SAVO ANTONIO   BOOKS & MAPS
☎ 089 87 11 80; Via Repubblica Marinare 17; ☺ 7am-11pm

Among the piles of dusty books, comics and international newspapers that crowd this gloomy newsagent-cum-bookshop, you will find a good selection of local maps, necessary reading for anyone touring the region.

GETTING THERE & AWAY
Boat

The easiest way to get to Amalfi is by bus or, between Easter and mid-September, by boat. The following companies all serve Amalfi:

Alicost (☎ 089 87 14 83; Largo Scario 5) Operates ferries to/from Salerno (€5.50, six daily) and Ischia (€19, one daily)

Alilauro (☎ 081 497 22 67; www.alilauro.it; Stazione Marittima, Naples) Has services to/from Capri (€13.50, two daily)

Coop Sant'Andrea (☎ 089 87 31 90; www.coopsant andrea.it; Lungomare dei Cavalieri 1) Runs boats to/from Maiori (€2, eight daily) and Minori (€2, eight daily)

Metrò del Mare (☎ 199 44 66 44; www.metrodelmare .com) Lines MM2 and MM3 stop at Amalfi. Using either of these there are sailings to Positano (€6, five daily), Sorrento (€7 four daily), Naples (€10, four daily) and Salerno (€6, two daily).

TraVelMar (☎ /fax 089 87 29 50; Largo Scario 5) Connects with Salerno (ferry/hydrofoil €4.50/5, seven daily), Positano (ferry/hydrofoil €5.50/6, seven daily) and Sorrento (€8, three daily).

Bus

SITA (☎ 199 73 07 49; www.sita-on-line.it, in Italian) runs buses from Piazza Flavio Gioia to Sorrento (€2.40, 1½ hours, more than 12 daily) via Positano (€1.30, 40 minutes), and also to Ravello (€1, 25 minutes, every 40 minutes), Salerno (€1.80, 1¼ hours, at least hourly) and Naples (€3.10, seven daily, two to three hours depending on the route). You can buy tickets and check current schedules at **Bar Il Giardino delle Palme** (Piazza Flavio Gioia) opposite the bus stop.

Car & Motorcycle

If driving from the north, exit the A3 autostrada at Vietri sul Mare and follow the SS163. From the south leave the A3 at Salerno and head for Vietri sul Mare and the SS163.

RAVELLO

Sitting high in the hills above Amalfi, Ravello is a refined, polished town almost entirely dedicated to tourism. Boasting impeccable bohemian credentials – Wagner, DH Lawrence and Virginia Woolf all spent time here – it's today known for its ravishing gardens and stupendous views, the best in the world according to former resident Gore Vidal, and certainly the best on the coast.

Most people visit on a day trip from Amalfi – a nerve-tingling 7km drive up the Valle del Dragone – although to best enjoy its romantic other-worldly atmosphere you'll need to stay overnight here.

SIGHTS & ACTIVITIES
Cathedral

Forming the eastern flank of Piazza Duomo, the **cathedral** (Piazza Duomo; ☉ 8.30-1pm & 4.30-8pm) was originally built in 1086 but has since undergone various make-overs. The façade is 16th-century, even if the central bronze door, one of only about two dozen in the country, is an 1179 original; the interior is a late-20th-century interpretation of what the original must once have looked like. Of particular interest is the striking pulpit, supported by six twisting columns set on marble lions and decorated with

flamboyant mosaics of peacocks, birds and dancing lions. Note also how the floor is tilted towards the square – a deliberate measure to enhance the perspective effect. To the right of the central nave, stairs lead down to the cathedral **museum** (admission €2) and its small collection of religious artefacts.

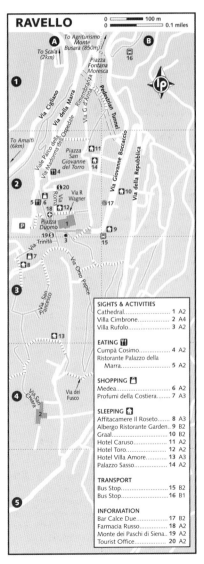

The beautiful gardens of Villa Cimbrone   GREG ELMS

Villas & Gardens

To the south of the cathedral, the 14th-century tower marks the entrance to **Villa Rufolo** (☎ 089 85 76 57; adult/under 12yr & over 65yr €5/3; ⏰ 9am-sunset), famous for its spectacular **gardens**. Created by a Scotsman, Scott Neville Reid, in 1853, they are indeed magnificent, commanding superb views and packed with exotic colours, artistically crumbling towers and luxurious blooms. On seeing them on 26 May 1880, Wagner was moved to write: 'The enchanted garden of Klingsor (setting for the second act of the opera *Parsifal*) has been found'. Today the gardens are used to stage concerts during the town's classical music festival. The villa itself was built in the 13th century for the wealthy Rufolo dynasty and was home to several popes as well as King Robert of Anjou.

Some way east of Piazza Duomo the early-20th-century **Villa Cimbrone** (☎ 089 85 80 72; adult/under 12yr & over 65yr €5/3; ⏰ 9am-sunset) is well worth seeking out. If not for the villa itself, now an upmarket hotel, then for the fabulous views from the delightfully ramshackle gardens. Deemed the most beautiful in the world by former Ravello resident Gore Vidal, they are best admired from the **Belvedere of Infinity**, an awe-inspiring terrace lined with fake classical busts. Something of a bohemian retreat in its early days, Villa Cimbrone was used by Greta Garbo and her lover Leopold Stokowski as a secret hideaway.

Walking

Ravello is the starting point for numerous walks – some of which follow ancient paths through the surrounding Lattari mountains. If you've got the legs for it you can walk down to **Minori**, or, heading the other way, to Amalfi, via the ancient village of **Scala**. Once a flourishing religious centre with more than a hundred churches, Scala is now a sleepy place where the wind whistles through empty streets and gnarled locals go patiently about their daily chores. In the central square, the Romanesque **Duomo** (Piazza Municipio; ⏰ 8am-noon & 5-7pm daily) retains some of its 12th-century solemnity. Ask at the Ravello tourist office for further walking information.

FESTIVALS & EVENTS

Between June and mid-September the **Ravello Festival** (☎ 089 85 83 60; www.ravellofestival.com) turns much of the town centre into a stage. Events ranging from orchestral concerts and chamber music to ballet performances, film screenings and exhibitions are held in atmospheric outdoor venues, most notably the famous overhanging terrace in the Villa Rufolo gardens.

However, you don't have to come in high summer to catch a concert. Ravello's programme of classical music begins in March and continues until late October. It reaches its crescendo in June and September with the International Piano Festival and Chamber Music Weeks. Performances by top Italian and international musicians are world-class and the two venues (Villa Rufolo and the Convento di Santa Rosa in Conca dei Marini – see p229) are unforgettable. Tickets, bookable by phone, fax or online, start at €20. For further information and reservations, contact the **Ravello Concert Society** (☎ 089 85 81 49; www.ravelloarts.org).

Ravello's patron saint, San Pantaleon, is recalled with fun and fireworks in late July.

SLEEPING

Ravello is an upmarket town and its accommodation reflects this, both in style and price. There are some superb top-end hotels and several lovely midrange places. But all's not lost if you're on a budget – there's a fine agriturismo nearby and one or two cheapish options in town. Book well ahead for summer – especially if you're planning to visit during the music festival.

AFFITACAMERE IL ROSETO
RENTED ROOMS €

☎ 089 858 64 92; Via Trinità 37; www.ilroseto.it; d €80; ☺ year-round

If you're after a no-frills, clean room within easy walking distance of everything, you'll do OK here. There are only two rooms, both of which have been decorated in medical white, with white walls, white sheets and white floors. But what they lack in charm they make up for in value, and, if you want colour, you can always sit outside and admire the pretty rose garden.

AGRITURISMO MONTE BUSARA
FARM STAY €

☎ 089 85 74 67; www.montebrusara.com; Via Monte Brusara 32; per person incl breakfast €35, half-board €50

An authentic working farm, this mountainside agriturismo is the real McCoy. Located a tough half-hour walk of about 1.5km from Ravello centre (a car is not essential but it's highly recommended), it's ideal for families with kids – they can feed the pony while you sit back and admire the views – or for those who simply want to escape the crowds. The three rooms are comfy but basic, the food is fabulous and the owner is a charming, garrulous host. Campers can also pitch tents here (€12 per person).

ALBERGO RISTORANTE GARDEN
HOTEL €€

☎ 089 85 72 26; www.hotelgardenravello.it; Via Boccaccio 4; r €110; ☺ mid-Mar–late Oct

No longer the celebrity magnet that it once was – Jackie Kennedy passed by with her young family and Gore Vidal was a regular at the terrace restaurant (meals from around €25) – this family-run three-star is still a good bet. The smallish rooms leave little impression (clean with nondescript décor) but the private terraces most certainly do. With some of the finest views on and of the coastline they're well worth the money. If you arrive by bus, you'll save on lugging your bags around, as the hotel's right by the stop.

GRAAL
HOTEL €€

☎ 089 85 72 22; www.hotelgraal.it; Via della Repubblica 8; incl breakfast, s €75-95, d €130-170; ☺ year-round; 🛂 ✕ 🖦

Nicer in than out (which is lucky because the exterior looks more like a car park than a hotel), the Graal is a decent three-star with tasteful rooms and an excellent panoramic restaurant (fixed menu €30). The public areas are fairly charmless but the sun-and-sea-coloured rooms, the balcony views and the open-air swimming pool make for a very relaxing stay.

HOTEL CARUSO
HOTEL €€€

☎ 089 85 88 01; www.hotelcaruso.com; Piazza San Giovanni del Toro 2; s incl breakfast €446, d €608-743; ☺ mid-Mar-Nov; 🅿 ✕ 🖦

There can be no better place to swim than the Caruso's sensational infinity pool. Seemingly set on the edge of a precipice (in fact the hotel gardens are a few metres below), its blue waters merge with sea and sky to magical effect. Inside the sublimely restored 11th-century palazzo, it's no less impressive, with Moorish arches doubling as window frames, 15th-century vaulted ceilings and high-class ceramics. Rooms are suitably mod-conned with English, German and US plug sockets and a TV/DVD system that slides sexily out of a wooden cabinet at the foot of the bed. Free wi-fi.

HOTEL TORO
HOTEL €€

☎ /fax 089 85 72 11; www.hoteltoro.it; Via Wagner 3; s/d incl breakfast €78/109; ☺ Easter-Nov

By Ravello standards excellent value for money, the Toro offers comfort, location and history. A hotel since the late 19th century, it's just off Piazza Duomo within easy range of the clanging cathedral bells (a potential sleep hazard). The not-huge rooms are decked out in traditional Amalfi Coast style with terracotta or light marble tiles and soothing cream furnishings. Outside, the grassy, walled garden is a delightful place in which to sip your sundowner. Former guests have included Norwegian composer Grieg and the Dutch artist Escher.

HOTEL VILLA AMORE
HOTEL €

☎ /fax 089 85 71 35; Via dei Fusco 5; incl breakfast, s €50-56, d €75-95; ☺ year-round

A welcoming pensione, this is the best budget choice in town. Tucked away down a quiet lane, it has modest, homely rooms furnished with whatever the owner had to hand at the time, and clean bathrooms. Some, like room 3, have their own balcony looking towards the distant sea; others have bathtubs; a few have both. The garden restaurant is a further plus: the food's good, the views are memorable and the prices are right (around €20 for a meal).

PALAZZO SASSO
HOTEL €€€

☎ 089 81 81 81; www.palazzosasso.com; Via San Giovanni del Toro 28; d incl breakfast €192-320, with sea view €312-520; ⌚ Mar-Oct; ⊞ ⊞

One of three luxury hotels on Ravello's millionaires row, Palazzo Sasso has been a hotel since 1880, providing refuge for many 20th-century luminaries – General Eisenhower planned the Allied attack on Monte Cassino here while later Roberto Rossellini and Ingrid Bergman giggled over dinner in the hotel restaurant. A stunning pale-pink 12th-century palace, its décor couples tasteful antiques with Moorish colours and modern sculpture. The 20m swimming pool commands great views and its Michelin-starred restaurant, **Rossellinis**, is one of the best in town.

EATING

Surprisingly, Ravello does not offer many good eating options. It's easy enough to find a bar or café selling overpriced *panini* and pizza but not so simple to find a decent restaurant or trattoria. There are a few good hotel restaurants, most of which are open to non-guests, and a couple of excellent restaurants (listed below) but not much else. These places get very busy in summer, particularly at lunchtime, and prices are universally high.

CUMPÀ COSIMO
TRATTORIA €€€

☎ 089 85 71 56; Via Roma 44-6; meals around €30; ⌚ closed Mon Nov-Feb, daily Mar-Oct

If you're looking for some honest down-to-earth Italian grub, you can't do much better than this popular trattoria. An informal family affair – meat comes from the family butcher, vegetables and fruit are homegrown, and the house wine is homebrew – it serves excellent handmade pasta, tasty gnocchi and some fine main courses. House favourites include rabbit with tomatoes and grilled crayfish.

RISTORANTE PALAZZO DELLA MARRA
RISTORANTE €€€

☎ 089 85 83 02; Via della Marra 7; meals around €40, tourist lunch menu €17; ⌚ Wed-Mon, closed Nov & Jan-Feb

Sit down to innovative regional cuisine under the vaulted ceiling of this tastefully restored 12th-century palazzo. The menu strikes a good balance between seafood and meat with dishes ranging from *paccheri* with sword

fish and prawns to smoked duck with fennel cream and beef fillet in thyme. Desserts are also given a creative touch, as in tiramisu with cream of pistachio. The lunchtime menu, comprising a pasta, main course and side dish, is good value.

SHOPPING

Limoncello and ceramics are the mainstays of the Amalfi Coast souvenir trade and you will find both sold here.

MEDEA
CERAMICS

☎ 089 858 62 83; www.medeaceramiche.com; Via della Marra 14; ⌚ 9am-11pm daily May-Oct, 9am-5pm Mon-Fri Nov-Apr

If you're after something ceramic but are fed up with the ubiquitous range of gaudy yellow fruit bowls, then look no further. At this gallery-cum-laboratory-cum-shop, you'll find an interesting selection of original handmade vases, lamps, animals, figurines, plates and tiles. Particularly outstanding are the huge red and black vases by ceramic artist Ugo Marano. And if you're wondering, yes, they cost a bomb – for a life-sized vase expect to fork out in the region of €12,000.

PROFUMI DELLA COSTIERA
LIMONCELLO

☎ 089 85 81 67; www.profumidellacostiera.it; Via Trinità 37; ⌚ 8.30am-7pm Apr-Oct, to 5.30pm Nov-Apr

The *limoncello* produced and sold here is made with local lemons (known to experts as *sfusato amalfitano*) according to traditional recipes, so no preservatives and no colouring. And it's not just the owners who say so – all bottles carry the IGP (Indicazione Geografica Proteta; Protected Geographical Indication) quality mark.

GETTING THERE & AWAY

SITA operates hourly buses from Amalfi (€1, 25 minutes) departing from the bus stop on the eastern side of Piazza Flavio Gioia. From the bus stop in Ravello walk through the short tunnel to Piazza Duomo. Many, but not all, buses stop en route at Scala.

By car, turn north about 2km east of Amalfi. Vehicles are not permitted in Ravello's town centre but there's plenty of space in supervised car parks on the perimeter.

FROM AMALFI TO SALERNO

MINORI

Three and a half kilometres east of Amalfi, or a steep kilometre-long walk down from Ravello (tough on the knees going down, murder going up), Minori is a small, workaday town, popular with holidaying Italians. Scruffier than its refined coastal cousins Amalfi and Positano, it's no less dependant on tourism yet seems more genuine, with its festive seafront and noisy traffic jams. There's a small **tourist office** (☎ 089 87 70 87; www.proloco-minori.sa.it; Via Roma 30; 🕐 9am-noon & 5-8pm Mon-Sat, 9-11am Sun) on the seafront.

The town's one monument of note is the **Villa Roma Antiquarium** (☎ 089 85 28 93; Via Capodipiazza 28; admission free; 🕐 9am-7pm daily Jun-Aug, to 6.30pm May & Sep, to 6pm Apr & Oct, to 5.30pm Mar & Nov, to 5pm Feb & Dec, to 4.30pm Jan), the finest Roman ruins on the coast. Overshadowed by modern housing blocks, the first-century-AD villa is a typical example of the sort that Roman nobles built as holiday homes in the period prior to Mt Vesuvius' AD 79 eruption. The best-preserved rooms are those surrounding the garden on the lower level. By the entrance, there's a two-room museum exhibiting various artefacts including a collection of 6th-century BC to 6th-century AD amphorae.

Before leaving town it's worth stopping off for a quick bite at the **Bar de Riso** (☎ 089 85 36 18; Piazza Cantilena 1) on the main seafront. The outside tables next to the petrol pumps are not the most inviting in the area, but the bar's cakes certainly are (the coffee's very good too). Speciality of the house are the *babà* drenched in *limoncello* (€2) or rum (€1.50).

MAIORI

Continuing east along the coast, you come to Maiori, one of the coast's largest and most modern resorts. Founded in the 9th century and later the seat of the Amalfi Republic's powerful Admiralty, it was almost entirely destroyed by a flood in 1954. Rebuilt and reborn as a resort town, it's now a brassy place full of large seafront hotels, bars, restaurants and beach clubs.

Information on the town and its environs is available from the **tourist office** (☎ 089 87 74 52; www.aziendaturismo-maiori.it; Corso Reginna 73; 🕐 9am-1pm & 4-8pm Mon-Sat, 9am-1pm Sun Apr-Oct, 9am-1pm & 3-5pm Mon-Sat, 9am-1pm Sun Nov-Mar), next to a delightful courtyard garden on Corso Reginna, the town's main thoroughfare.

Steps by the side of the courtyard lead up to the 12th-century **Chiesa Santa Maria a Mare** (☎ 089 87 70 90; 🕐 8.30am-12.30pm & 6-8pm Mon-Sat, 8am-noon & 6-8pm Sun), one of the few buildings to survive the 1954 flood. Inside, in the small **Museo di Arte Sacra** (admission €2; 🕐 10am-noon daily), the 14th-century alabaster *paliotto* (altar covering) is said to be the oldest of its type in Italy.

About 3km east of town the **Abbazia di Santa Maria de Olearia** (☎ 339 580 34 86, 089 87 74 52; 🕐 by appointment only) is an unusual 10th-century monastery gouged into the rocks above the coastal road. Consisting of three chapels built one on top of another, it's worth a quick look for its fading 11th-century frescoes, the best of which are in the *cripta* on the lowest level.

CASA RAFFAELE CONFORTI   HOTEL €€

☎ 089 85 35 47; www.casaraffaeleconforti.it; Via Casa Mannini 10; r incl breakfast €86-136; 🅿 ; 🕐 Mar-Nov, also open Christmas

This unique hotel defies definition, or indeed description. Housed on the 2nd floor of a 19th-century palazzo, it's an extraordinary monument to the elegance of a bygone age. The nine rooms are all individually decorated but the overall style is the same – frescoes, antiques and gilt-framed mirrors, ceramic tiles and heavy silk fabrics. Curiosities abound: in the Maria Sica suite, there's a stone fireplace and a hidden door through to the bathroom; in the Camera delle Muse the bathroom's actually in a wardrobe (apparently, to protect the frescoes). The welcome is warm and the central position convenient.

LOCANDA AMALPHITANA   RISTORANTE €€

☎ 089 87 74 39; Via Nuova Chiunzi 9; meals around €25, pizza from €5; 🕐 closed mid-Jan–mid-Feb

Just off the seafront, this is one of the better of Maiori's touristy restaurants. With a comprehensive menu, it's pretty much got

Maiori at sunset (p241)

most tastes covered. You can order from a full range of pizzas or go for a local staple such as pasta with aubergines, tomato and mozzarella. There's also decent seafood and simple, tasty meat dishes. Sit in the bustling blue interior or on one of the few roadside tables.

RESIDENCE HOTEL
PANORAMIC   HOTEL €€

☎ 089 854 23 01; www.residencehotelpanoramic.com; Via Santa Tecla 12; s €45-75, d €80-130, 2-/4-/5-person apt per week €1050/1500/1600; ⌚ year-round; P ⌘ Good for self-caterers or families, this is one of the few hotels in the area to remain open year-round. A block back from the seafront, it's a friendly place, with 26 one- or two-room apartments, all decked out in marine blue and white. Each comes with a fully equipped modern kitchenette, satellite TV and, in summer, air-con. The weekly apartment rates quoted above are full-whack August prices; in winter they fall by more than 50%.

CETARA

Just beyond **Erchie** and its beautiful beach (look for the mass of scooters parked by the side of the road), Cetara is a picturesque tumbledown fishing village with a reputation as a gastronomic hot spot. Since medieval times it has been an important fishing centre and still today its deep-sea tuna fleet is considered one of the Mediterranean's most important. At night, fishermen set out in small boats (known as *lampare*) armed with powerful lamps to fish for anchovies. Recently, locals have resurrected the production of what is known as *colatura di alici*, a strong anchovy essence believed to be the descendant of *garum*, the Roman fish-seasoning. Each year, in late July or early August, the village pays homage to its main meal tickets in the *sagra del tonno*, a festival dedicated to tuna and anchovies. Further details are available from the tiny **tourist office** (☎ 328 015 63 47; Piazza San Francesco 15; ⌚ 9am-1pm & 5pm-midnight).

To take a taste of Cetara home with you, there's a fine selection of preserved goodies at **Sapori Cetaresi** (☎ 089 26 20 10; Corso Garibaldi 44; ⌚ 10am-1pm & 4-10pm daily May-Sep, closes 8pm & Mon Oct-Apr) by the small beach.

AL CONVENTO   TRATTORIA €€

☎ 089 26 10 39; Piazza San Francesco 16; meal around €20, taster menu €26; ⌚ daily mid-May–Sep, closed Wed Oct–mid-May
For the money, you probably won't eat better anywhere else on the coast. With tables set on a lovely shaded terrace above Cetara's main street, this is an excellent spot to tuck

into local fish specialities. You can eat tuna as an antipasto, served smoked with sword-fish, or lightly grilled as a main course, and anchovies prepared in various ways. Particularly delicious is the *spaghetti con alici e finocchietto selavatrico* (spaghetti with anchovies and wild fennel). Fish, fortunately, doesn't feature among the desserts. Instead, you could try classic chocolate cake with ricotta and cream.

VIETRI SUL MARE

The end of the coastal road, or the beginning if approaching from Salerno, Vietri sul Mare (Vietri) is the ceramic capital of Campania. Production dates back to Roman times but it took off on an industrial scale in the 16th and 17th centuries with the development of high, three-level furnaces. The unmistakeable local style – bold brush strokes and strong Mediterranean colours – found favour in the royal court of Naples, which became one of Vietri's major clients. Later, in the 1920s and '30s, an influx of international artists (mainly Germans) led to a shake-up of traditional designs. For more on Vietri's

ceramic past head to the **Museo della Ceramica** (☎ 089 21 18 35; Villa Guerriglia; admission free; ☒ 8am-1.15pm & 2-3pm Tue-Sat, 9am-1pm Sun) in the nearby village of Raito.

Vietri's small and not unattractive historic centre is packed to the gills with shops selling ceramic ware of every description. The most famous is **Ceramica Artistica Solimene** (☎ 089 21 02 43; www.solimene.com; Via Madonna degli Angeli 7; ☒ 8am-7pm Mon-Fri, 8am-1.30pm & 4-7pm Sat), a vast factory outlet selling everything from egg cups to ornamental mermaids, mugs to lamps. Even if you don't go in it's worth having a look at the shop's extraordinary glass and ceramic façade. For something more modern try **Klaus** (☎ 089 21 04 67; Corso Umberto I 94; ☒ 9am-8.30pm daily summer, 9am-1pm & 2.30-8.30pm daily winter), whose original red and orange designs recall Picasso's surreal patterns. Prices range from €25 to around €500.

For information on accommodation in Vietri inquire at the **tourist office** (☎ 089 21 12 85; Piazza Matteotti; ☒ 10am-1pm Mon-Sat & 5-8pm Mon-Fri) near the entrance to the centro storico.

FESTIVE FUN WITH FOOD

Food has always played an important role in local traditions. Over the years, towns have developed their own speciali-ties, many of which are celebrated in annual *sagre* (food-based festivals). These traditional jamborees are usually very well supported, drawing large crowds from the surrounding area, and provide a great opportunity to taste something of local Amalfitana life. Major foodie events:

July
Cetara In the second half of the month, the fishing folk of Cetara celebrate their main catch in the Sagra del Tonno (Tuna Festival).

August
Conca dei Marini Celebrates its historic ricotta-filled pastry, the *sfogliatella*, on the first Sunday of the month.
Maiori The Sagra delle Melanzane al Cioccolato is the perfect occasion to try the local delicacy, chocolate aubergines.
Atrani The citizens of Atrani pay homage to the humble anchovy during the Sagra del Pesce Azzurro (Blue-Fish Festival), usually in the third week of the month.

September
Minori Food-lovers from along the coast congregate here in early September for Gustaminori, the town's annual food jamboree.

October
Scala Chestnuts appear in various guises – roasted, in jam, nutcakes and pancakes – at Scala's Agra della Castagna (Chestnut Festival).

December
Positano It's time to enjoy *zeppole* (fried doughnuts served with custard cream) during the festive Sagra delle Zeppole.

SALERNO

Marking the easternmost point of the Amalfi Coast, Salerno provides something of a reality check after the coast's glut of postcard-pretty towns. One of Campania's five regional capitals, and a major port, it's unlikely to detain you long, but it's not without a certain gritty charm. The best place to hang out is the compact centro storico, where medieval churches share space with neighbourhood trattorie, neon-lit wine bars and trendy tattoo parlours. Salerno is also a major transport hub and you might well find yourself passing through en route to Paestum (p168) and the Costriera Cilentana.

Originally an Etruscan and later a Roman colony, Salerno flourished with the arrival of the Normans in the 11th century. In 1076 Robert Guiscard made it the capital of his dukedom. Under his patronage, the Scuola Medica Salernitana was renowned as one of medieval Europe's greatest medical institutes. More recently, heavy fighting left it in tatters following the 1943 landings of the American 5th Army south of the city.

INFORMATION

- **Banca Nazionale del Lavoro** (Piazza Vittorio Veneto 1) Has an ATM at the train station. There are also several banks with ATMs along Corso Vittorio Emanuele.
- **Internet Point** (☎ 089 24 18 74; Via Roma 26; per 30 mins €2.50; ☺ 10.30am-1.30pm & 4.30-10.30pm daily) Also prints digital photos and has a fax service.
- **Mail Box** (Via Diaz 19; per 25 mins €1.50; ☺ 9am-1.30pm & 5.30-8pm Mon-Sat) Internet access.

- **Ospedale Ruggi D'Aragona** (hospital; ☎ 089 67 11 11; Via San Leonardo)
- **Police station** (☎ 089 61 31 11; Piazza Amendola 16)
- **Post office** (☎ 089 257 21 11; Corso Garibaldi 203)
- **Salerno City** (www.salernocity.com, in Italian) Website with extensive city listings, ferry times and programmes of local festivals.
- **Salerno Memo** (www.salernomemo.com, in Italian) Online version of the free listings guide *Memo*.
- **Tourist office** (☎ 089 23 14 32; Piazza Vittorio Veneto 1; ☺ 9am-2pm & 3-8pm Mon-Sat, plus 9am-12.30pm & 5-7.30pm Sun Jul & Aug)

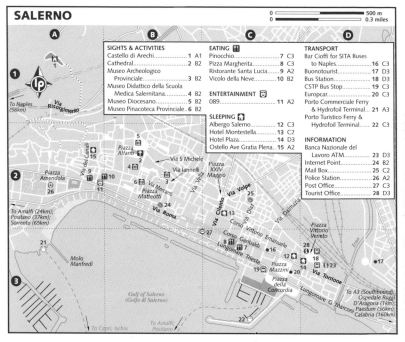

SALERNO

0 — 500 m
0 — 0.3 miles

SIGHTS & ACTIVITIES
Castello di Arechi	1 A1
Cathedral	2 B2
Museo Archeologico Provinciale	3 B2
Museo Didattico della Scuola Medica Salernitana	4 B2
Museo Diocesano	5 B2
Museo Pinacoteca Provinciale	6 B2

EATING
Pinocchio	7 C3
Pizza Margherita	8 C3
Ristorante Santa Lucia	9 A2
Vicolo della Neve	10 B2

ENTERTAINMENT
089	11 A2

SLEEPING
Albergo Salerno	12 C3
Hotel Montestella	13 C2
Hotel Plaza	14 D3
Ostello Ave Gratia Plena	15 A2

TRANSPORT
Bar Cioffi for SITA Buses to Naples	16 C3
Buonotourist	17 D3
Bus Station	18 D3
CSTP Bus Stop	19 C3
Europcar	20 C3
Porto Commerciale Ferry & Hydrofoil Terminal	21 A3
Porto Turistico Ferry & Hydrofoil Terminal	22 A3

INFORMATION
Banca Nazionale del Lavoro ATM	23 D3
Internet Point	24 B2
Mail Box	25 C2
Police Station	26 A2
Post Office	27 C3
Tourist Office	28 D3

ORIENTATION

Salerno's train station is on Piazza Vittorio Veneto, at the eastern end of town. Many intercity buses stop here and there are a number of hotels nearby. Salerno's main shopping strip, the car-free Corso Vittorio Emanuele, leads off northwest to the medieval centro storico. Running parallel is Corso Garibaldi, which becomes Via Roma as it heads out of the city towards Vietri sul Mare and the Amalfi Coast. Tree-lined Lungomare Trieste, on the waterfront, changes its name to Lungomare G Marconi at the massive Piazza della Concordia on its way out of town, southeast towards Paestum.

SIGHTS & ACTIVITIES
Cathedral

The highlight of Salerno's atmospheric centro storico is the impressive **cathedral** (☎ 089 23 13 87; Piazza Alfano; ✆ 10am-6pm). Built by the Normans under Robert Guiscard in the 11th century and remodelled in the 18th century, it sustained severe damage in the 1980 earthquake. It's dedicated to San Matteo (St Matthew), whose remains were reputedly brought to the city in 954 and now lie beneath the main altar in the vaulted crypt.

The main entrance, the 12th-century **Porta dei Leoni** – named after the marble lions at the foot of the stairway – leads through to a beautifully harmonious porticoed atrium, overlooked by a striking 12th-century bell tower. Passing through the huge bronze doors, cast in Constantinople in the 11th century, the three-aisled interior is largely baroque, with only a few traces of the original church. These include parts of the transept and choir floor and the two raised pulpits in front of the choir stalls.

In the right-hand apse, the **Cappella delle Crociate** (Chapel of the Crusades) was so named because crusaders' weapons were blessed here. Under the altar stands the tomb of the 11th-century pope Gregory VII.

Museums

To the north of the cathedral, the **Museo Diocesano** (☎ 089 23 91 26; Largo del Plebiscito 12; admission free; ✆ 9am-1.30pm daily, plus 4-7pm Sun) has a modest collection of Norman and Lombard artworks, the highlight of which is a 12th-century ivory *paliotto* decorated with 54 scenes from the Old and New Testaments.

Nearby, the **Museo Archeologico Provinciale** (☎ 089 23 11 35; Via San Benedetto 28; admission free; ✆ 9am-1.30pm & 2-3.15pm Tue-Fri, 9am-1pm

Salerno's Harbour
RUSSELL MOUNTFORD

Sun) is the province's main archaeological museum. Among the artefacts dating back to prehistoric times is a 1st-century-BC bronze head of Apollo, discovered in the Bay of Salerno in 1930.

Deep in the heart of the medieval quarter, the small **Museo Pinacoteca Provinciale** (☎ 089 258 30 73; Via Mercanti 63; admission free; ☺ 9am-1pm & 2-3.15pm Tue-Sat, 9am-1pm Sun) houses an interesting art collection dating from the Renaissance right up to the first half of the 19th century. There are some fine canvases by local boy Andrea Sabatini da Salerno and an assortment of works by foreign artists living in the area.

A visit to the **Museo Didattico della Scuola Medica Salernitana** (☎ 089 24 12 92; Via Mercanti 72; admission free; ☺ 9am-1pm & 4-7pm Tue-Sat, 9am-1pm Sun) in the ex-church of San Gregorio is rewarded with a refreshing lack of archaeological artefacts and classical sculpture. Instead, you'll find a collection of documents and illustrations recounting the fascinating history of Salerno's historic Medical School. Probably established in the 9th century, the school was the most important centre of medical knowledge in medieval Europe, reaching the height of its prestige in the 11th century. It was closed in the early 19th century.

Castle

Salerno's most famous landmark is the forbidding **Castello di Arechi** (☎ 089 22 55 78; Via Benedetto Croce; ☺ closed for restoration), spectacularly positioned 263m above the city. Originally a Byzantine fort, it was built by the Lombard duke of Benevento, Arechi II, in the 8th century and subsequently modified by the Normans and Aragonese, most recently in the 16th century. Today it houses a permanent collection of ceramics, arms and coins and is used for summer concerts.

To get here take bus 19 from Piazza XXIV Maggio in the city centre. The 20-minute ride costs €1.

SLEEPING

The little accommodation that Salerno offers is fairly uninspiring. Conveniently, though, there are several cheapish hotels near the train station and, in the centro storico, a popular youth hostel. Prices tend to be considerably lower than on the Amalfi Coast.

All of the following are open year-round.

ALBERGO SALERNO   HOTEL €
☎ 089 22 42 11; www.albergosalerno.com; 5th fl, Via G Vicinanza 42; s €45-50, d €55-60; ⊠
Don't be discouraged by the less-than-appealing entrance and rattling lift; this modest two-star is better in than out. On the 5th floor of an unexceptional palazzo, it's got large, high-ceilinged rooms and a bright communal seating area, complete with sofas and glossy mags. Air-con costs an extra €8 but in summer rooms are provided with small fans.

HOTEL MONTESTELLA   HOTEL €
☎ 089 22 51 22; www.hotelmontestella.it; Corso Vittorio Emanuele 156; s/d/t incl breakfast €70/94/104; ⊠
Within walking distance of just about everywhere worth going, the Montestella is on Salerno's main pedestrian thoroughfare, half-way between the historic centre and train station. And it's this, combined with the competitive prices, that's the hotel's forte. The 45 guest rooms are perfectly adequate – clean with air-con, TV and a dubious orange and brown colour combo – but are hardly memorable.

HOTEL PLAZA   HOTEL €
☎ 089 22 44 77; www.plazasalerno.it; Piazza Vittorio Veneto 42; s/d/t incl breakfast €65/100/115; ⊠
A short stone's throw from the train station, the Plaza is convenient, comfortable and fairly charmless. But it's not an unfriendly place and the good-sized rooms, with their brown carpet and gleaming bathrooms, are actually pretty good value for money. Those around the back have terraces overlooking the city and, beyond, the mountains.

OSTELLO AVE GRATIA PLENA   HOSTEL €
☎ 089 79 02 51; info@ostellodisalerno.it; Via dei Canali; dm incl breakfast €14, per person in a s/d/t/q €26/20/20/20; ⊡
Housed in an airy 16th-century convent, Salerno's HI hostel is right in the heart of the tight-knit centro storico. Inside, there's no shortage of space, with a charming central courtyard and a whole range of rooms, from dorms to doubles with private bathroom. Before you leave take a moment to look down into the adjacent church as once nuns did to follow mass without making eye contact with the men. Note the 2am curfew.

EATING & ENTERTAINMENT

Head to the lively medieval centre and Via Roma, where you'll find everything from traditional, family-run trattorie and gelaterie to jazzy wine bars, pubs and expensive restaurants. Stop in at **089** (☎ 089 22 18 44; Via Roma 51), a slick steel-and-neon bar popular with the hip apéritif set.

In summer, the seafront is a popular place for the evening *passeggiata* (stroll).

PINOCCHIO   TRATTORIA €€
☎ 089 22 99 64; Lungomare Trieste 56; meals around €22; 🕑 closed Fri

Ask at your hotel for somewhere to eat and chances are they'll tell you to try this place on the seafront. The food is pretty good, they'll say, excellent for the price, and the owner's a large, friendly bloke called Rodolfo. And they're right: the no-nonsense Italian food is good. Seafood is the speciality but there's also a decent selection of fail-safe meats – sausages, steak and *scaloppine* (breaded veal). In summer, tables are set out down a side street; in winter action moves into the bubbly interior with its kids'-room clutter of Pinocchio murals and mobiles.

PIZZA MARGHERITA   PIZZERIA €
☎ 089 22 88 80; Corso Garibaldi 201; pizzas/buffet from €5.50/4.50, lunchtime menu €7; 🕑 daily

It looks like a bland, modern canteen, but this is in fact one of Salerno's most popular lunch spots. Locals regularly queue for the lavish lunchtime buffet, which on any given day might include mozzarella, salami, mussels in various guises, and a range of salads. If that doesn't appeal the daily lunchtime menu (pasta, main course, salad and half a litre of water) is chalked up on a blackboard, or there's the regular menu of pizzas, pastas and main courses.

RISTORANTE SANTA LUCIA   RISTORANTE €€
☎ 089 22 56 96; Via Roma 182; meals around €22; 🕑 closed Mon

The surrounding Via Roma area may be one of the city's trendiest, but there's nothing remotely flash about the delicious seafood served up here. Dishes such as *linguine ai frutti di mare* (linguine with seafood) and char-grilled cuttlefish may not be original but, cooked here, they taste quite exceptional. As do the wonderful wood-fired pizzas. The laid-back atmosphere and friendly, efficient service add to the pleasure. Just around the corner, the hotel of the same name has nine basic one-star rooms (singles/doubles €35/55).

VICOLO DELLA NEVE   TRATTORIA €€
☎ 089 22 57 05; Vicolo della Neve 24; meals around €25; 🕑 dinner Thu-Tue

A city institution, Vicolo della Neve is the archetypal centro storico trattoria. It's got brick arches and fake frescoes, the walls are hung with works by local artists and the menu is as traditional as it comes. There are pizzas and *calzoni, pasta e fagioli, pepperoni ripieni* (stuffed peppers) and a great *parmigiana di melanzane*. It can get very busy, so be prepared to wait for a table.

GETTING THERE & AWAY

Boat

Between April and October, TraVelMar (☎ /fax 089 87 29 50; Largo Scario 5, Amalfi) runs ferries to Positano (ferry/hydrofoil €6.50/7, seven daily) and Amalfi (ferry/hydrofoil €4.50/5, seven daily), while Alicost (☎ 089 87 14 83; Largo Scario 5) operates six daily sailings to Amalfi (€5.50, six daily). Departures are from the Porto Turistico, 200m down the pier from Piazza della Concordia. You can buy tickets from the booths by the embarkation points.

From Molo Manfredi at the Porto Commerciale the Metrò del Mare (☎ 199 44 66 44; www.metrodelmare.com) runs to Positano (€7, three daily), Amalfi (€6, two daily) and Sorrento (€8, three daily). For Capri, LMP (Linee Marittime Partenope; ☎ 081 704 19 11; www.consorziolmp.it) has five daily sailings (ferry/jet €14.50/16).

Bus

SITA (☎ 199 73 07 49; www.sita-on-line.it, in Italian) buses for Amalfi (€1.80, 1¼ hours, at least hourly) depart from Piazza Vittorio Veneto, beside the train station, stopping en route at Vietri sul Mare, Cetara, Maiori and Minori. Buy your tickets from the office on the western side of the square. The Naples service, however, departs every 25 minutes from outside Bar Cioffi (☎ 089 22 75 75; Corso Garibaldi 134), where you buy your ticket (€3.20).

For Pompeii, take **CSTP** (☎ 089 48 70 01; www
.cstp.it, in Italian) bus 50 from Piazza Vittorio
Veneto. There are 15 daily departures and
the hour-long journey costs €1.80. For the
south coast and Paestum (€2.90, one hour
20 minutes, 12 daily) take bus 34 from
Piazza della Concordia.

In collaboration with SITA, **Buonotourist**
(c/o SITA; ☎ 089 40 51 45; Via Vinciprova) runs four
daily services to Naples Capodichino airport, departing from the train station.
Tickets (€7) can be bought on board;
journey time is one hour.

Car & Motorcycle

Salerno is on the A3 between Naples and
Reggio di Calabria, which is toll-free from
Salerno southwards.

Train

Salerno is a major stop on southbound
routes to Calabria and the Ionian and
Adriatic coasts. From the station in Piazza
Vittorio Veneto there are regular trains to
Naples (€3.20, 50 minutes, half-hourly),
Rome (Eurostar €25, 2½ hours, hourly), and
Reggio di Calabria (€31, 4½ hours, 15 daily).

GETTING AROUND

Walking is the most sensible option if
you're staying in the heart of Salerno; from
the train station it's a 1.2km walk along
Corso Vittorio Emanuele to the historic
centre. Local orange buses are run by CSTP.
Tickets, valid for 80 minutes, cost €1.

If you want to hire a car there's a **Europcar**
(☎ 089 258 07 75; www.europcar.com. Via G Vicinanza)
agency not far from the train station.

IF YOU'VE GOT THE TIME...

Occupying the area southeast of Salerno up to the regional border with Basilicata, the **Parco Nazionale del Cilento e
Vallo di Diana** is a little-explored area of wild highlands and empty valleys. Italy's second-largest national park, it's the
perfect antidote to the holiday mayhem along the coast. You will, however, need a car to get the best out of it.

About 40km southeast of Salerno the **Grotte di Castelcivita** (☎ 0828 77 23 97; adult/reduced/0-5yr €8/6.50/
free; ☺ tours 10am, 11.30am, 1.30pm, 3pm & 4.30pm Oct–mid-Mar, 10am, 11am, noon, 1.30pm, 2.30pm, 3.30pm,
4.30pm, 5.30pm & 6.30pm mid-Mar–Aug) cave complex is where Spartacus is said to have taken refuge following
his slave rebellion in 71 BC. Further east, the **Grotte di Pertosa** (☎ 0975 39 70 37; guided visits adult/child €10/8;
☺ 9am-7pm Mar-Oct, 9am-4pm Nov-Feb) is a 2.5km-long cave system bristling with stalactites and stalagmites.

Continuing south on the A3 autostrada, the village of **Padula** harbours one of the region's best-kept secrets, the
magnificent **Certosa di San Lorenzo** (☎ 0975 777 45; adult/18-25yr/under 18yr & over 65yr €4/2/free; ☺ 9am-7.30pm).
Also known as the Certosa di Padula, it's one of Europe's biggest monasteries, with a huge central courtyard, wood-panelled
library and frescoed chapels. Inside you can peruse the modest collection of the **Museo Archeologico Provinciale della
Lucania Occidentale** (☎ 0975 771 17; admission free; ☺ 8am-1.15pm & 2-3pm Tue-Sat, 9am-1pm Sun).

On the coast, 75km south of Salerno the Greek settlement of Elea, now called **Ascea (Velia)**, was founded in the
mid-6th century BC and later became a popular resort for wealthy Romans. The **ruins** (☎ 0974 97 23 96; adult/18-25yr/
under 18yr & over 65yr €2/1/free; ☺ 9am until 1hr before sunset Mon-Sat) are not in great nick but merit a quick look if
you're in the area. Further down the coast, the white-sand beaches beyond Palinuro are among the region's best.

A good base for exploring the area is **Agropoli**, just south of Paestum. A busy summer resort, it's an otherwise tranquil
coastal town, with plenty of accommodation. The **Ostello La Lanterna** (☎ 0974 83 83 64; lalanterna@cilento.it; Via
Lanterna 8, dm incl breakfast €11; mid-Mar–Oct) is a reliable option on the northern edge of town, while in the centre,
the **Hotel Carola** (☎ 0974 82 64 22; www.hotelcarola.it; s/d €62/80; Ⓟ ☺) provides decent three-star rooms.

CSTP (☎ 089 48 70 01; www.cstp.it, in Italian) bus 34 stops at Agropoli and other coastal towns en route from
Salerno (Piazza della Concordia) to Celso.

ACCOMMODATION

There is no shortage of accommodation in Naples and on the Amalfi Coast. As a rule, the Amalfi Coast and Bay of Naples islands are more expensive than Naples, with limited budget options and a glut of upmarket hotels.

In this book, accommodation is listed in alphabetical order within each section, and is rated € (up to €90 for a double room), €€ (€90 to €190) and €€€ (above €190).

Icons in hotel listings indicate where full air-con and internet access are available.

The bulk of the region's accommodation is made up of hotels and *pensioni* (guesthouses). Prices vary enormously but expect to pay high-season rates at Easter, in summer (from June to September) and over the Christmas–New Year period. As a rough guide reckon on forking out anywhere between €80 and €300 for a double room in a three-star hotel. Unless otherwise stated, prices quoted are high season rates.

Italian *ostelli per la gioventù* (youth hostels) are run by the **Associazione Italiana Alberghi per la Gioventù** (AIG; ☎ 06 487 11 52; www .ostellionline.org; Rome), which is affiliated with **Hostelling International** (HI; www.iyhf.org). A valid HI card is required, which you can get in your home country or at many hostels. Dorm rates are typically between €15 and €25, often with breakfast included. Many places also offer dinner for around €10.

Campers are not well catered for in the region although there are a couple of decent sites at Sorrento. Expect to pay from €5 to €12 per person and €5 to €12 to pitch a tent.

Agriturismi (farm stays) are becoming increasingly popular. Although they are ideal for those who want to escape the crowds and for parents with children – think lots of space to run around in and farm animals – they can be difficult to reach without a car. Lists of operators are available from local tourist offices or **Agriturist Campania** (Map pp278-9; ☎ 081 28 52 43; www.agriturist.it in Italian; 8th fl, Corso Arnaldo Lucci 137).

B&Bs are also taking off, particularly in Naples but also on the coast. Options include everything from restored farmhouses, city palazzi and seaside bungalows to rooms in family houses. Prices are typically between €70 and €150 for a room. For more information contact **Bed & Breakfast Italia** (☎ 06 687 86 18; www.bbitalia.it) in Rome or **Rent A Bed** (Map pp280-1; ☎ 081 41 77 21; www .rentabed.com; Vico d'Afflitto 16) in Naples.

To make a reservation, whether for a hotel or an agriturismo, you'll often be required to confirm by email or fax and give a credit-card number as security (or a money order to cover the first night's stay).

Tourist offices throughout the region carry accommodation lists and some, such as the Sorrento office, offer a booking service.

Finding rental accommodation in Naples can be difficult and time consuming, but there are rental agencies that will assist, for a fee. Rental rates are higher for short-term leases and it is usually necessary to pay a deposit (generally one month in advance).

In major resort areas, such as Capri, Amalfi and Positano, tourist offices have lists of local apartments and villas for rent. As a basic estimate, reckon on at least €1000 for a two-bedroom serviced flat in high season.

There are a few online agencies that deal in villa and/or apartment rentals on the Amalfi Coast, such as www.apartment

service.com, www.cvtravel.net, www.eurvilla.com, www.indiv-travellers.com, and www.villas-in-italy-rentals.com.

Alternatively you could try:

Cuendet & Cie Spa (Italy ☎ 0577 57 63 30; www.cuendet.com) Operating from Siena, this is a major Italian operator with villas on the Amalfi Coast. From the UK you can make reservations by calling ☎ 0800 085 77 32.

Cottages & Castles (Australia ☎ 613 9889 3350; www.cottagesandcastles.com.au) The Australian associate of Cuendet.

Parker Company (USA ☎ 781-596 82 82; www.theparkercompany.com) A leading US agency with a huge portfolio of villas.

Rentals In Italy (USA ☎ 805 987 52 78) Handles Cuendet bookings in the US.

Tuscany Now (UK ☎ 020 7684 88 84; www.tuscanynow.com) Has high-quality villas on the Amalfi Coast.

BUSINESS HOURS

Shops in Naples generally open from 9.30am to 1.30pm and 4.30pm to 8pm (in winter) or 4pm to 8.30pm (in summer) Monday to Saturday. They may close on Saturday afternoons or Monday mornings. In Naples most department stores and supermarkets now have continuous opening hours from 9am to 8.30pm Monday to Saturday. Some even open from 9am to 1pm on Sunday.

Banks open from 8.30am to 1.30pm and 2.45pm to 4.30pm Monday to Friday. They are closed at weekends but it is always possible to find a *cambio* (exchange office) open in Naples and major tourist areas.

Major post offices are open from 8.30am to 6pm Monday to Friday and also 8.30am to 1pm on Saturday. All post offices close two hours earlier than normal on the last business day of each month (not including Saturday).

Farmacie (pharmacies) are open from 9am to 1pm and 4pm to 7.30pm Monday to Friday. Most shut on Saturday afternoons and Sundays but a handful remain open on a rotation basis. All closed pharmacies are obliged to display a list of the nearest ones that are open.

Bars and cafés generally open from 7.30am to 8pm, although some stay open until the small hours, typically 1am or 2am. Clubs and discos might open around 10pm but often there'll be no-one there until midnight at least.

Restaurants open from noon to 3pm and 7.30pm to 11pm (later in summer). Restaurants and bars are required to close for one day each week although in busy tourist areas this rule is not always observed.

Opening hours for museums, galleries and archaeological sites vary enormously, although many are closed on Mondays. Increasingly, the major national museums and galleries remain open until 10pm during the summer.

Note that trading hours on the Amalfi Coast and even outer suburban Naples will vary from central Naples.

CHILDREN

Naples and the Amalfi Coast are tough destinations for children. In Naples, the breathless pace is exhausting for adults and children alike; at Pompeii, the uneven surfaces make life a nightmare for strollers; and on the Amalfi Coast the twisting coastal road is almost sure to provoke car sickness. However, all is not lost – this is Italy and kids are welcome just about everywhere.

Make a point of asking staff at tourist offices if they know of any special family activities and if they have suggestions about hotels that cater for kids. Discounts are available for children (usually for those aged under 12 years but sometimes prices are based on the child's height) for public transport and for admission to sites.

Book accommodation in advance to avoid any inconvenience, and when travelling by train make sure to reserve seats to avoid having to stand for the entire journey. Most car-hire firms have children's safety seats for hire at a nominal cost, but it's essential that you book them in advance. The same goes for highchairs and cots (cribs): they're available in most restaurants and hotels, but numbers will be limited.

You can buy baby formula in powder or liquid form, as well as sterilising solutions, such as Milton, at local *farmacie*. Disposable nappies (diapers) are widely available at supermarkets and *farmacie*; a pack of 25 costs about €10. Fresh cow's milk is sold by the carton in bars that have a 'latteria' sign and in supermarkets. If it is essential that you have milk, carry an emergency carton of UHT since bars usually close at 8pm.

Baby-Sitting

Overall, forget it! Although a few top hotels may be able to arrange baby-sitting, in Italy children are generally included in all facets of family life and are carted around just about everywhere.

Sights & Activities

The key to a successful trip is planning. A common cause of strife is to try to do too much. High summer temperatures and crowded streets can fray the nerves of even the most patient of kids (and parents!). Always remember to allow some free time for the kids to play and make sure that you balance those heavy days at the museum with a day at the beach. Where possible, include children in the trip planning – if they've helped to work out where to go, they'll be much more interested when they get there.

For a list of sites suitable for children in Naples, see the boxed text, p76. Elsewhere, the ruins of **Pompeii** (p160) might appeal to older kids, while Capri's **Grotto Azzurra** (Blue Grotto; p178) will impress all ages. In Sorrento, the dinky **City Train** (p209) is a popular way of touring the town. You'll find children's parks (often little more than a field with a swing or two but better than nothing) in **Anacapri** (p178), **Sorrento** (p208), and **Amalfi** (p232), while the seafronts in **Minori** and **Maiori** are lined with all sorts of garish kids games.

For more information, see Lonely Planet's *Travel with Children* or check out www .travelwithyourkids.com and www.family travelnetwork.com.

CLIMATE

The south of Italy has a Mediterranean climate. Summers are long, hot and dry and can easily soar to an enervating 35°C, although it is generally cooler on the Amalfi Coast and Bay of Naples islands. Winter temperatures tend to be quite moderate, averaging around 10°C. Spring and early autumn are the best seasons to visit as temperatures are mild, but still warm. From December to March, you can expect plenty of rain. See p17 for more guidelines on the best times to visit.

COURSES

Cookery and language courses are popular throughout Italy and are available in the region. In Sorrento, the **Sorrento Cooking School** (Map p206; ☎ 081 878 32 55; www.sorrentocookingschool .com; Viale Dei Pini 52, Sant'Agnello) offers various food-related courses, including day-long sessions from €140; and the **Centro Linguistico Internazionale Sorrento Lingue** (Map p206; ☎ 081 807 55 99; www.sorrentolingue.com; Via San Francesco 8) runs Italian language courses costing from €206 to €760. For more details, see p209.

In Naples, the **Istituto Italiano di Cultura** (IIC; ☎ 081 546 16 62; www.istitalianodicultura.org in Italian; Via Bernardo Cavallino 89) can provide information on a whole range of study opportunities.

Divers are well catered for with a number of outfits running courses for beginners and advanced students. These include the following:

Captain Cook (Map pp190–1; ☎ 335 636 26 30; www .captaincook.it; Ischia Porto, Ischia)

Nettuno Diving (Map p206; ☎ 081 808 10 51; www .sorrentodiving.com; Via A Vespucci 39, Marina del Cantone)

Procida Diving Centre (☎ 081 896 83 85; www.vacanzea procida.it/framediving01-uk.htm; Procida)

Sercomar (Map p173 ☎ 081 837 87 81; www.caprisub .com; Marina Grande, Capri)

Sorrento Diving Center (Map p206; ☎ 081 877 48 12; www.sorrentodivingcenter.it; Sorrento).

For further information see the relevant destination sections.

CUSTOMS

Goods bought in and exported within the EU incur no additional taxes, provided duty has been paid somewhere within the EU and the goods are intended for personal consumption.

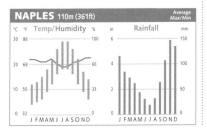

NAPLES 110m (361ft) — Average Max/Min

°C °F Temp/Humidity %   in   Rainfall   mm

Duty-free sales within the EU no longer exist. Visitors coming into Italy from non-EU countries can import the following duty free: spirits (1L), wine (2L), perfume (60mL), eau de toilette (250mL), 200 cigarettes and other goods up to a total of €175.50; anything over this limit must be declared on arrival and the appropriate duty paid. You can also bring up to €12,500 in cash into Italy.

Upon leaving the EU, non-EU citizens can reclaim any Imposta di Valore Aggiunto (IVA) value-added tax on purchases equal to or more than €180 (see p257).

DISCOUNT CARDS

At many state museums and archaeological sites EU citizens under 18 and over 65 enter free, and those aged between 18 and 25 get a 50% discount. To claim these discounts you'll need a passport or an ID card.

When sightseeing consider a *biglietto cumulativo* (cumulative ticket), a ticket that allows admission to a number of associated sights for less than the combined cost of separate admission fees.

The International Student Identity Card (ISIC), issued by the **International Student Travel Confederation** (ISTC; www.istc.org), is no longer sufficient at many tourist sites as prices are based on age, so a passport, drivers licence or **Euro<26** (www.euro26.org) card is preferable. An ISIC card will still, however, prove useful for cheap flights and theatre and cinema discounts. A similar card is also available to

---

CUMULATIVE TICKETS

Coming in various forms, the **Campania Artecard** (☎ 800 600 601; www.campaniartecard.it in Italian) is a cumulative ticket that covers museum admission and transport. In Naples a three-day ticket (adult/18-25yr €13/8) gives free admission to two participating sites, a 50% discount on others and free transport in Naples and the Campi Flegrei. Other ticket options range from €25 to €28 and cover sites as far afield as Pompeii and Paestum. The tickets can be bought at train stations, newsagents, participating museums, on the internet or through the call centre.

If you're intending to visit Pompeii and Herculaneum, you'll save by buying the combined ticket (adult/EU 18-25yr/EU under 18yr & over 65yr €20/10/free), which also covers Oplontis, Stabiae and Boscoreale.

---

teachers (the ITIC; International Teacher Identity Card).

If you're under 26, you can also apply for an International Youth Travel Card (IYTC), issued by the **Federation of International Youth Travel Organisations** (FIYTO; www.fiyto.org).

Student cards are issued by student unions, hostelling organisations and some youth travel agencies. In Naples try **CTS** (Map pp280-1; ☎ 081 552 79 60; www.cts.it in Italian; Via Mezzocannone 25).

ELECTRICITY

Most electricity wiring in Italy works on 220V. Two-pin adapter plugs can be bought at electrical shops.

EMBASSIES & CONSULATES

For foreign embassies and consulates not listed here, look under 'Ambasciate' or 'Consolati' in the telephone directory. Alternatively, tourist offices generally have a list. The following are in Naples:

France (Map pp284-5; ☎ 081 59 80 711; Via Francesco Crispi 86, 80122)
Germany (Map pp284-5; ☎ 081 61 33 93; Via Francesco Crispi 69, 80121)
Netherlands (Map pp280-1; ☎ 081 551 30 03; Via Agostino Depretis 114, 80133)
UK (Map pp284-5; ☎ 081 423 89 11; Via dei Mille 40, 80121)
USA (Map pp284-5; ☎ 081 583 81 11; Piazza della Repubblica, 80122)

EMERGENCY

At Naples' **main police station** (Map pp280-1; ☎ 081 794 11 11; Via Medina 75) there is an office for foreigners. To report a stolen car, call ☎ 081 794 14 35.

Ambulance	☎ 118
Coastguard	☎ 1530
Fire	☎ 115
Police	☎ 112/113
Road assistance	☎ 803 116

GAY & LESBIAN TRAVELLERS

Homosexuality is legal in Italy and well tolerated in Naples; however, try to avoid overt displays of affection, particularly in smaller towns on the Amalfi Coast. The legal age of consent is 16.

Naples' largest gay organisation is **Arcigay-Circola Antinoo** (Map pp280-1; ☎ 081 552 88 15; www.arcigaynapoli.org; Vico San Geronimo alle Monarche 19), which organises special events and can provide information on the city's gay scene.

Spartacus International (www.spartacusworld.com) publishes the *Spartacus International Gay Guide* (US$32.95; UK£19.95), a male-only directory of gay venues worldwide. Alternatively, log onto www.gay.it/guida (in Italian) for addresses of gay bars and hotels.

For further information see the boxed text, p132.

HOLIDAYS

Most Italians take their annual holiday in August. This means that many businesses and shops close down for at least a part of the month, particularly around Ferragosto (Feast of the Assumption) on 15 August.

Italian schools close for three months in the summer, from mid-June to mid-September, for three weeks over Christmas, and for a week at Easter. See p18 for a calendar of the region's special events and festivals.

Public holidays include the following:
Capodanno (New Year's Day) 1 January
Epifania (Epiphany) 6 January
Pasquetta (Easter Monday) March/April
Giorno della Liberazione (Liberation Day) 25 April
Festa del Lavoro (Labour Day) 1 May
Festa della Repubblica (Republic Day) 2 June
Ferragosto (Feast of the Assumption) 15 August
Ognisanti (All Saints' Day) 1 November
Immacolata Concezione (Feast of the Immaculate Conception) 8 December
Natale (Christmas Day) 25 December
Festa di Santo Stefano (Boxing Day) 26 December

INTERNET ACCESS

The easiest way to access the internet on the road is at an internet café. In Naples try the following:
Internetbar (Map pp280-1; ☎ 081 29 52 37; Piazza Bellini 74; per hr €3; ⏰ 9-2am Mon-Sat, 8pm-2am Sun)
Navig@ndo (Map pp280-1; ☎ 081 193 60 030; Via S Anna dei Lombardi 28; per hr €2; ⏰ 9.30am-8.30pm daily)
Zeudi Internet Point (Map pp284-5; ☎ 081 251 22 50; Via Chiaia 199c; per hr €3; ⏰ 9.30am-9pm Mon-Sat)

Refer to the individual town sections in the Amalfi Coast chapter for internet access in those areas.

Wi-fi hot spots are fairly thin on the ground, although some of the smarter hotels do offer them.

Most travellers use free web-based email such as **Yahoo** (www.yahoo.com), **Hotmail** (www.hotmail.com) or **Google** (www.gmail.com), which can be easily accessed from any internet-connected computer in the world.

If, however, you're bringing your own kit (laptop or PDA), you'll need to find an Internet Service Provider (ISP) with local dial-up numbers. **AOL** (www.aol.com), **AT&T** (www.att.com) and **CompuServe** (www.compuserve.com) all have dial-in nodes in Italy. Remember that if you have to plug your computer into a power socket you might need a power transformer (to convert from 110V to 220V if your notebook isn't set up for dual voltage), an RJ-11 telephone jack that works with your modem, and a plug adaptor.

LEGAL MATTERS

The most likely reason for a brush with the law is if you have to report a theft. If you do have something stolen and you want to claim it on insurance you must make a statement to the police; insurance companies won't pay up without official proof of a crime.

The Italian police is divided into three main bodies; the *polizia* who wear navy-blue jackets; the *carabinieri* (technically military police but they cover the same duties as the *polizia*) in a black uniform with a red stripe; and the grey-clad *guardia di finanza* (finance police), who are responsible for fighting tax evasion and drug smuggling. If you run into trouble you're most likely to end up dealing with the *polizia* or *carabinieri*. If, however, you land a parking ticket, you'll need to speak to the *vigili urbani* (traffic wardens).

In general, the consulate section of your embassy should be able to provide you with lists of lawyers, interpreters and translators in Naples. See p252 for police and other emergency numbers.

Drink & Drugs

Drugs are not hard to come by in Naples, but you'd do well to resist. In February 2006, the Italian parliament approved new antidrugs laws that abolished the distinction between hard and soft drugs, effectively putting cannabis on the same legal footing as cocaine, heroin and ecstasy. If caught with what the police deem to be a dealable quantity, you risk fines of up to €260,000 or prison sentences of between six and 20 years.

Regarding alcohol, the legal limit for a driver's blood-alcohol reading is 0.05% and random breath tests do occur.

Your Rights

Italy has some antiterrorism laws on its books that could make your life very difficult if you're detained. You can be held for 48 hours without a magistrate being informed and you can be interrogated without the presence of a lawyer. It is difficult to obtain bail and legally you can be held for up to three years without being brought to trial.

MAPS

The maps throughout this book, combined with tourist-office maps, are generally adequate for navigating the region's main centres. Tourist offices can also provide walking maps, although if you're intent on serious hiking you should consider a specialist map. One of the best is the CAI's (Club Alpino Italiano) *Monti Lattari, Penisola Sorrentina, Costiera Amalfitana: Carta dei Sentieri* (€8).

The best road maps and city plans are published by de Agostini, Touring Club Italiano (TCI) and Michelin, and are available at bookshops throughout the area.

MEDICAL SERVICES

Italy has a public health system that is legally bound to provide emergency care to everyone. EU nationals are entitled to reduced cost, sometimes free, medical care with a European Health Insurance Card (EHIC), available from your home health authority; non-EU citizens should take out medical insurance.

For emergency treatment, go straight to the *pronto soccorso* (casualty) section of an *ospedale* (public hospital), where it's also possible to receive emergency dental treatment. For less serious ailments call the local *guardia medica* (duty doctor); ask at your hotel or nearest tourist office for the number. Pharmacists (see p255) will fill prescriptions and can provide basic medical advice.

Ambulance (☎ 118, ☎ 081 752 06 96)
Ospedale Loreto-Mare (Loreto-Mare Hospital; Map pp280-1; ☎ 081 20 10 33; Via Amerigo Vespucci 26)

MONEY

Since 2002 Italy's currency has been the euro. The euro is divided into 100 cents. Coin denominations are one, two, five, 10, 20 and 50 cents, €1 and €2; the notes are €5, €10, €20, €50, €100, €200 and €500.

Exchange rates are given on the inside front flap of this book. For the latest rates check out www.xe.com.

The best way to manage your money is to use your debit/credit cards while keeping a fistful of travellers cheques as backup.

Credit & Debit Cards

Credit and debit cards can be used in ATMs (which are widespread and known locally as *bancomat*) displaying the appropriate sign. Visa and MasterCard are widely recognised, as are Cirrus and Maestro; Amex is accepted but is less common. If you don't have a PIN, some (but not all) banks will advance cash over the counter. Credit cards can also be used in many supermarkets, hotels and restaurants although *pensioni,* smaller trattorie and pizzerie still tend to accept cash only.

When you withdraw money from an ATM, the amounts are converted and dispensed in local currency; however, there will be fees involved. Typically, you'll be charged a withdrawal fee (usually 2% for a minimum withdrawal of €2 or more) as well as a conversion charge; if you're using a credit card you'll also be hit with interest on the cash withdrawn.

If an ATM rejects your card, don't despair. Try a few more ATMs displaying your card's logo before assuming the problem lies with your card.

If your credit card is lost, stolen or swallowed by an ATM, telephone toll-free to have an immediate stop put on it. For MasterCard call ☎ 800 87 08 66; for Visa, ☎ 800 81 90 14; and for Amex ☎ 800 86 40 46.

Changing Money

You can change money in banks, at post offices or in a *cambio* (exchange office). Banks are generally the most reliable and tend to offer the best rates. Cambio offices usually, but not always, offer worse rates or charge higher commissions. Hotels are almost always the worst places to change money.

Receipts

Under Italian law you're supposed to ask for and retain receipts for absolutely everything that you pay for. Although it rarely happens you could, in theory, be asked by the *guardia di finanza* to produce a receipt immediately after you leave a shop. If you don't have one, you risk a fine.

Travellers Cheques

Increasingly overlooked by card-wielding travellers, travellers cheques are a dying breed. They should not, however, be written off entirely as they're an excellent form of backup, especially as you can claim a refund if they're stolen (providing you've kept a separate record of their numbers).

Amex, Visa and Travelex cheques are the easiest to cash, particularly in US dollars, British pounds or euros. Increasingly banks are charging hefty commissions, though, even on cheques denominated in euros. Whatever currency they are in, cheques can be difficult to change in smaller towns. Always take your passport as identification when cashing in travellers cheques.

For lost or stolen cheques call: Amex ☎ 800 72 000; Travelex ☎ 800 33 55 11; Visa ☎ 800 874 155.

NEWSPAPERS & MAGAZINES

Italian newspapers take some getting used to. They're big on domestic politics and tend to assume the reader is well-versed in current affairs and has a working knowledge of Italian public life.

Naples' major daily newspaper is *Il Mattino,* although national dailies *La Repubblica* and *Corriere della Sera* also have Neapolitan inserts.

Foreign newspapers and magazines are available, generally one or two days after publication, at the larger city kiosks and, more commonly than in the city, at resorts along the Amalfi Coast.

PHARMACIES

Indicated by a green cross, *farmacie* are a good first port of call in case of minor illness. Pharmacies for each town along the Amalfi Coast are listed in the information boxes in the Amalfi Coast chapter. Within Naples try the following:

Farmacia Cannone (Map p283; ☎ 081 556 72 61; Via A Scarlatti 75; ⏰ 9am-midnight; Funicular Centrale to Fuga) Stocks a range of homeopathic remedies.
Officina Profumo Farmaceutica di Santa Maria Novella (Map pp284-5; ☎ 081 40 71 76; Via Santa Caterina a Chiaia 20; bus CS to Piazza dei Martiri)

If you think you'll need a prescription while in the region make sure you know the drug's generic name rather than just the brand name.

PHOTOGRAPHY

Film and video equipment are widely available everywhere in the region, but most travellers now use digital cameras. If you're shooting digitally check that you have enough memory to store your snaps. If you do run out your best bet is burn your photos onto a CD, something which many processing labs and some internet cafés will do for you.

To download your pics at an internet café you'll need a USB cable and a card reader. Some places provide a USB on request but be warned that many of the bigger chain cafés don't let you plug your gear into their computers, meaning it's back to plan A – burning onto CD.

POST

Italy's much maligned postal system, **Poste** (☎ 803 160; www.poste.it in Italian), has improved a lot in recent years but is hardly a model of efficiency.

Francobolli (stamps) are available at post offices and authorised tobacconists (look for the official *tabacchi* sign: a big 'T', usually white on black). Urgent mail can be sent by *postacelere* (also known as CAI Post), the Italian post office's courier service.

Email has rendered *poste restante (fermo posta)* services largely obsolete. However, if you want to write to a loved one in Naples you should address your letter as follows:

John SMITH,
Fermo Posta,
80100 Napoli,
Italy

Said loved one will then need to go to Naples' main post office (Map pp284–5; ☎ 081 790 47 54; Piazza Matteotti) to pick up the letter in person. They will need to present a passport or ID card to collect their mail.

RADIO

The state-owned stations RAI-I (89.3 and 94.1 MHzFM stereo and 1332 KHz AM), RAI-2 (91.3 and 96.1 MHzFM stereo and 846 KHz AM) and RAI-3 (93.3 and 98.1 MHz FM) combine current affairs programmes with classical and light music and half-hourly news bulletins. There are no English-language radio stations, unless you bring your shortwave along.

SAFETY

Naples has a certain reputation for being unsafe and recent events have done little to improve it. Most spectacularly, a turf war between Camorra gangs left up to 47 people dead in late 2004 and early 2005. And while you're unlikely to be caught in mafia crossfire you'll need to guard your valuables closely on the streets. Petty crime is rife and pickpockets and scooter snatchers are active in the main tourist areas. For tips on street safety see below) and the Naples alla Napoletana boxed text, p97.

Travellers should be careful about walking alone in the streets at night, particularly in the Quartieri Spagnoli, La Sanità and Mercato districts and around Piazza Garibaldi.

Away from Naples there are no great issues, although in Pompeii you should watch out for touts posing as legitimate guides and, in the ruins, the occasional stray dog.

Pollution

Noise and air pollution are problems in Naples, caused mainly by the heavy traffic. In summer there are periodic pollution alerts, where the elderly, children and people who have respiratory problems are warned to stay indoors. If you fit into one of these categories, keep yourself informed through the tourist office or your hotel.

Scams

The classic Piazza Garibaldi scam is the mobile-phone dodge. Basically, you buy a brand new mobile phone at a knockdown price only to get home to discover that you've bought a box with a brick in it. There's really no way to avoid this other than to ignore all dodgy offers of phones and other electrical goods.

Many cons play on people's insecurity with foreign bank notes. Short-changing is a common trick. One popular dodge goes as follows: you pay for a €4 *panino* with a €20 note. The cashier then distractedly gives you a €1 coin and a €5 note before turning away. The trick here is to wait and chances are that the €10 note you're waiting for will appear without a word being said.

Note swapping is another thing to be aware of. This con involves you paying for a taxi fare or a train ticket with a €20 note. The taxi driver or ticket seller then deftly palms your note and produces a €10 note claiming that you paid with this and not the €20 you thought you had given. In your confusion you're not quite sure what you did and so accept their word.

Theft

Pickpockets are most active in dense crowds, especially in busy train stations and on public transport. A common ploy is for one person to distract you while another whips through your pockets. Beware of gangs of dishevelled-looking kids waving newspapers and demanding attention. In the blink of an eye, a wallet or camera can go missing. Remember also that some of the best pickpockets are well-dressed.

When going out, spread your valuables, cash and cards around your body or in different bags. A moneybelt to hold your essentials (passport, cash, credit cards, airline tickets) is usually a good idea; however, to avoid delving into it in public, also carry a wallet with enough cash for the day. Don't flaunt watches, cameras and other expensive goods. Cameras and shoulder bags are an open invitation for snatch thieves, many of whom work from motorcycles or scooters. Wear cameras and bags across the body and keep under your arm. Also be very careful at cafés and bars – always loop your bag's strap around your leg while seated.

Parked cars, particularly those with foreign number plates and/or rental-agency stickers, are prime targets for petty criminals. While driving in cities, beware of thieves at traffic lights – keep doors locked and windows rolled up high. A favourite ploy of snatchers is for a scooter rider to brush past your car, knocking the side-mirror out of position; then, as you reach out to readjust it, an accomplice on a second scooter races past snatching your watch as he goes.

Car theft is a problem in Naples, so it pays to leave your car in a supervised car park. If you leave your car on the street, you will often be approached by an unofficial (that is, illegal) parking attendant asking for money. Clearly you don't have to pay them, but if you refuse you run the risk of returning to a damaged car.

In case of theft or loss, always report the incident to the police within 24 hours, and ask for a statement otherwise your travel-insurance company won't pay out.

Traffic

Neapolitan traffic requires some getting used to. Drivers are not keen to stop for pedestrians, even at pedestrian crossings, and are more likely to swerve. Locals simply step off the footpath and walk through the (swerving) traffic with determination.

It is a practice that seems to work but if you feel uncertain, wait and cross with an Italian local.

In many cities, roads that appear to be for one-way traffic have lanes for buses travelling in the opposite direction – always look both ways before stepping onto the road.

TAX & REFUNDS

A value-added tax of around 20%, known as IVA, is slapped on to just about everything in Italy. If you are a non-EU resident and you spend more than €180 on a purchase, you can claim a refund when you leave the EU. The refund only applies to purchases from affiliated retail outlets that display a 'Tax Free for Tourists' sign. You have to complete a form at the point of sale, then get it stamped by Italian customs as you leave the country. At major airports you can get an immediate cash refund; otherwise it will be refunded to your credit card. For further information, pick up a pamphlet from participating stores.

TELEPHONE
Domestic Calls

Telephone rates in Italy are among the highest in Europe, particularly for long-distance calls. Average charges range from around €0.06 per minute for local calls to €0.13 for a long-distance call and €0.40 for calls to a mobile phone. Calls from a public payphone cost more. The cheapest time to call, for all domestic and international calls, is from midnight to 8am and any time on Sundays; peak rates apply from 8am to 6.30pm Monday to Friday and until 1pm on Saturday.

Telephone area codes all begin with ☎ 0 and consist of up to four digits. Area codes, including the first zero, are an integral part of all Italian phone numbers and should be used even when calling locally. Mobile-phone numbers begin with a three-digit prefix such as ☎ 330, ☎ 339; toll-free (free-phone) numbers are known as *numeri verdi* and usually start with ☎ 800; national call rate numbers start with ☎ 848 or ☎ 199.

For directory inquiries dial ☎ 1254.

International Calls

Direct international calls can easily be made from public telephones by using a phonecard. Dial ☎ 00 to get out of Italy, then the relevant country and area codes, followed by the telephone number. Rates are €0.61 per minute to the UK, most Western European countries, the US and Canada; and €0.92 for calls to Australia and New Zealand.

To make a reverse-charge (collect) international call, dial ☎ 170. All operators speak English. Alternatively, use the direct dialling (Country Direct) service provided by your home-country phone company (such as AT&T in the USA and Telstra in Australia). You simply dial the relevant access number and request a reverse-charges call through the operator in your country. Numbers for this service include:

Australia (Telstra)	☎ 800 172 610
Canada	☎ 800 172 213
New Zealand	☎ 800 172 641
USA (AT&T)	☎ 800 172 444

For international directory inquiries, call ☎ 892412.

To call Italy from abroad, dial ☎ 39 and then the area code, including the first zero.

Mobile Phones

Italy is one of the most mobile-phone saturated countries in the world and was one of the first places to introduce video phones. Phones operate on the GSM 900/1800 network, which is compatible with the rest of Europe and Australia but not with the North American GSM 1900 or the Japanese system (although some GSM 1900/900 phones do work here).

If you have a GSM, dual- or tri-band cellular phone that you can unlock (check with your service provider), it can cost as little as €10 to activate a *prepagato* (prepaid) SIM card in Italy. TIM (Telecom Italia Mobile), Wind and Vodafone-Omnitel all offer SIM cards and all have retail outlets in Naples and Salerno. You'll need your passport to open an account.

Phonecards

You'll find Telecom Italia silver payphones on the streets, in train stations, in some stores and in Telecom offices. Most payphones accept only *schede telefoniche* (telephone cards), although some still accept credit cards and coins. Where offices are staffed, you can make international calls and pay at the desk afterwards.

Phonecards (€5, €10, €20) are available at post offices, tobacconists and newsstands. You must break the top left-hand corner off the card before you can use it. Take note also that phonecards have an expiry date.

There are cut-price call centres throughout Naples. These are run by various companies and the rates are lower than Telecom payphones for international calls. You simply place your call from a private booth inside the centre and pay for it when you've finished.

TELEVISION

There are seven main TV channels in Italy: three are operated by the state broadcaster RAI (RAI 1, RAI 2 and RAI 3), three are run by Silvio Berlusconi's Mediaset company (Rete 4, Canale 5 and Italia 1), and La7 is owned by Telecom Italia. Output is fairly dire with a glut of interminable variety shows, sitcoms and various soap operas. Midrange to top-end hotels will generally provide a satellite TV service, which, at the very minimum, will pick up CNN, BBC World and a couple of music-video channels.

TIME

Italy is one hour ahead of GMT. Daylight-savings time, when clocks are moved forward one hour, starts on the last Sunday in March. Clocks are put back an hour on the last Sunday in October. Italy operates on a 24-hour clock.

TIPPING

You are not expected to tip on top of restaurant service charges, although if you feel the service merits it feel free to leave a small amount, perhaps €1 per person. If there is no service charge, you should consider leaving a 10% to 12% tip, but this is by no means obligatory. In bars,

Italians often place a €0.10 or €0.20 coin on the bar when ordering coffee. Tipping taxi drivers is not common practice, but you are expected to tip the porter at top-end hotels.

TOILETS

Public toilets are rare in Naples. Most people use the toilets in bars and cafés, but you might need to buy a coffee first. There are public toilets at the main bus and train stations.

On the Amalfi Coast, the more popular towns have public toilets that cost €0.50 per person. There are free toilets at Pompeii and Herculaneum.

TOURIST INFORMATION

You'll find tourist offices throughout the region. Some are more helpful than others, but all can supply accommodation lists, maps, transport details and information on the major sights.

As a rule, they are open from 8.30am to 12.30pm or 1pm, and from 3pm to 7pm Monday to Friday. These hours are usually extended in summer, when some offices open on Saturday or Sunday.

English, and sometimes French or German, is spoken at tourist offices in the major tourist areas and printed information is generally provided in a variety of languages.

In Naples, Campania's **main tourist office** (Map pp284-5; ☎ 081 40 53 11; www.campaniafelix.it in Italian; Piazza dei Martiri 58; ⏲ 9am-2pm Mon-Fri) is in Chiaia.

More useful, however, are the tourist information offices at the following locations, all of which stock the essential tourist brochure *Qui Napoli:*

Piazza del Gesù Nuovo (Map pp280-1; ☎ 081 552 33 28; ⏲ 9.30am-1.30pm & 2.30-6pm Mon-Sat, 9am-1.30pm Sun)

Stazione Centrale (Map pp280-1; ☎ 081 26 87 79; ⏲ 9am-7.30pm Mon-Sat, 9am-1.30pm Sun)

Stazione Mergellina (Map pp284-5; ☎ 081 761 21 02; ⏲ 9am-7.30pm Mon-Fri, 9am-1.30pm Sat)

Via San Carlo 7 (Map pp284-5; ☎ 081 40 23 94; ⏲ 9.30am-1.30pm & 2.30-6pm Mon-Sat, 9am-1.30pm Sun)

For local tourist offices outside the city see the relevant town sections in the Amalfi Coast chapter.

TRAVELLERS WITH DISABILITIES

Naples is not an easy city for travellers with disabilities. Cobbled streets, blocked pavements and tiny lifts make life difficult for the wheelchair-bound, while the anarchic traffic can be very disorientating for partially sighted travellers or those with hearing difficulties. Elsewhere, the uneven surfaces at Pompeii virtually rule out wheelchairs and the steep slopes of many Amalfi Coast towns pose a considerable obstacle.

The excellent website www.turismoaccessibile.it gives a rundown on the disabled facilities available at Naples' museums, hotels and on transport services.

For those travelling by train, the **customer services office** (☎ 081 567 29 91; ⏲ 7am-9pm daily) at Naples' Stazione Centrale (Map pp280-1) can arrange for wheelchair-bound passengers to be helped to their trains. To use this service you'll need to phone 24 hours prior to your departure and present yourself at the office 45 minutes before your train leaves. Similarly, personnel from **Metrò del Mare** (Map pp278-9; ☎ 199 60 07 00; www.metrodelmare.com) will escort wheelchair-bound passengers on and off ferries.

Some city buses, including R2 and R3, are set up with access ramps and space for a wheelchair.

The following organisations might be of assistance:

Accessible Italy (☎ 378 94 11 11; www.acessibleitaly.com) A San Marino–based company that specialises in holiday services for the disabled.

Consorzio Cooperative Integrate (COIN; ☎ 06 712 90 11; www.coinsociale.it) Based in Rome, COIN is the best reference point for disabled travellers in Italy with contact points throughout the country.

VISAS

Italy is one of the 15 signatories of the Schengen Convention, an agreement whereby participating countries have abolished customs checks at common borders. The standard tourist visa for a Schengen country is valid for 90 days. You must apply for it in your country of residence and you can not apply for more than two in any

12-month period. They are not renewable inside Italy.

EU citizens do not need a visa to enter Italy and, with a *permesso di soggiorno* (permit to stay; see below), can stay as long as they like. Nationals of Australia, Canada, Israel, Japan, New Zealand, Switzerland and the USA do not need visas for stays of up to 90 days in Italy, or in any Schengen country. South African citizens require a visa to enter Italy.

Technically all foreign visitors to Italy are supposed to register with the local police within eight days of arrival; however, if you're staying in a hotel or hostel you don't need to bother as the hotel will do this for you.

Permesso di Soggiorno

A *permesso di soggiorno* is required by all EU citizens who stay in Italy longer than 90 days, and by all non-EU nationals. In theory, non-EU citizens should apply for one within eight days of arriving in Italy, but in practice few people do. To get one you'll need a valid passport containing a stamp with your date of entry into Italy (ask for this when you enter as it's not automatic); a study visa if necessary; four passport-style photographs; proof of your ability to support yourself financially (ideally a letter from an employer or school/university); and a €14.62 *marca da bollo* official stamp. Armed with all of this head to the **Ufficio Immigrazione** (Immigration Office; Map pp278-9; ☎ 081 606 41 11; Via G Ferraris 131; ⏲ 8.30am-1pm Mon-Fri & 2.30-5.30pm Mon & Wed, 3-5pm Tue & Thu).

Although correct at the time of writing, the documentary requirements change periodically so always check before you join the (inevitable) queue.

Study Visas

Non-EU citizens who want to study in Italy must have a study visa. These can be obtained from the nearest Italian embassy or consulate. You will normally require confirmation of your enrolment, proof of payment of fees and proof of your ability to support yourself financially. The visa covers only the period of the enrolment. This type of visa is renewable within Italy but, again, only with confirmation of ongoing enrolment and proof that you can support yourself (bank statements are preferred).

WOMEN TRAVELLERS

The most common source of discomfort for women travellers is harassment. Local men are rarely shy about staring at women and this can be disconcerting, especially if the staring is accompanied by the occasional *'ciao bella'*. The best response is to ignore unwanted approaches. If that doesn't work, politely tell them that you are waiting for your *marito* (husband) or *fidanzato* (boyfriend) and, if necessary, walk away. Avoid becoming aggressive as this may result in an unpleasant confrontation. If all else fails, approach the nearest member of the police.

Wandering hands can also be a problem, particularly on crowded public transport. If you feel someone touching you, make a fuss; molesters are no more admired in southern Italy than anywhere else, so a loud and pointed *'Che schifo!'* ('How disgusting!') should work.

In Naples, lone women should avoid the Quartieri Spagnoli, La Sanità and Mercato districts and the Piazza Garibaldi area at night. Women should also avoid hitchhiking alone. For further safety tips see p256.

The *Handbook for Women Travellers* (Piatkus Books; 1995), by Maggie and Gemma Goss, is useful for solo travellers.

AIR
Airlines

Airlines flying to Naples:

Aerlingus (code EI; ☎ 02434 58 326; www.aerlingus.com; hub Dublin airport) To/from Dublin.

Air France (code AF; ☎ 848 88 44 66; www.airfrance.com; hub Roissy Charles de Gaulle airport, Paris) To/from Paris Charles de Gaulle.

Air Malta (code KM; ☎ 06 488 46 85; www.airmalta.com; hub Malta airport) To/from Malta and Palermo.

Air Nostrum (code YW; ☎ 199 10 11 91; www.airnostrum.com; hub Madrid Barajas airport) To/from Madrid.

Airone (code AP; ☎ 199 20 70 80; www.flyairone.com; hub Leonardo da Vinci airport, Fiumicino, Rome) To/from Genoa, Bologna, Milan Linate, Turin, Trieste and Athens.

Alitalia (code AZ; ☎ 06 22 22; www.alitalia.com; hub Leonardo da Vinci airport, Fiumicino, Rome) To/from Rome Fiumicino, Milan Malpensa and Linate, Turin and Venice.

Alpieagles (code E8; ☎ 899 50 00 58; www.alpieagles.com; hub Marco Polo airport, Venice) To/from Sicily, Sardinia and Barcelona.

Austrian (code OS; ☎ 02 896 34 296; www.aua.com; hub Wien Schwechat airport, Vienna) To/from Vienna.

British Airways (code BA; ☎ 199 71 22 66; www.ba.com; hub Heathrow airport, London) To/from London Gatwick.

BMI (code WW; ☎ 199 40 00 44; www.flybmi.com; hub Nottingham East Midlands airport) To/from London Heathrow.

Easyjet (code U2; ☎ 848 88 77 66; www.easyjet.com; hub Stansted airport, London) To/from London Stansted, Basel, Berlin, Milan Malpensa and Paris Orly.

Eurofly (code GJ; ☎ 199 50 99 60; www.eurofly.it; hub Malpensa airport, Milan) To/from Moscow and New York.

Hapag Lloyd Express (code X3; ☎ 199 19 26 92; www.hlx.com; hub Cologne/Bonn airport) To/from Cologne, Hanover, Munich and Stuttgart.

Helvetic (code 2L; ☎ 02 696 82 684; www.helvetic.com; hub Zurich airport) To/from Zurich.

CLIMATE CHANGE & TRAVEL

Climate change is a serious threat to the ecosystems that humans rely upon, and air travel is the fastest-growing contributor to the problem. Lonely Planet regards travel, overall, as a global benefit, but believes we all have a responsibility to limit our personal impact on global warming.

Flying & Climate Change

Pretty much every form of motor transport generates CO_2 (the main cause of human-induced climate change) but planes are far and away the worst offenders, not just because of the sheer distances they allow us to travel, but because they release greenhouse gases high into the atmosphere. The statistics are frightening: two people taking a return flight between Europe and the US will contribute as much to climate change as an average household's gas and electricity consumption over a whole year.

Carbon Offset Schemes

Climatecare.org and other websites use 'carbon calculators' that allow travellers to offset the greenhouse gases they are responsible for with contributions to energy-saving projects and other climate-friendly initiatives in the developing world – including projects in India, Honduras, Kazakhstan and Uganda.

Lonely Planet, together with Rough Guides and other concerned partners in the travel industry, supports the carbon offset scheme run by climatecare.org. Lonely Planet offsets all of its staff and author travel.

For more information check out our website: www.lonelyplanet.com.

LTU (code LT; ☎ 02 434 58 382; www.ltu.com; hub Dusseldorf airport) To/from Dusseldorf, Frankfurt and Munich.

Lufthansa (code LH; ☎ 199 40 00 44; www.lufthansa.com; hub Frankfurt airport) To/from Munich.

Meridiana (code IG; ☎ 89 29 28; www.meridiana.it; hub Olbia airport, Sardinia) To/from Sardinia, Milan Linate, Verona and Paris Charles de Gaulle.

My Air (code 8I; ☎ 899 50 00 60; www.myair.com; hub Orio al Serio airport, Bergamo) To/from Bergamo and Bucharest.

SAS Braathens (code CNO; ☎ 02 720 00 193; www.flysas .com; hub Oslo airport) To/from Oslo.

Sky Europe (code 5P; ☎ 166 20 53 04; www.skyeurope .com; hub Bratislavia airport) To/from Bratislavia, Budapest, Krakow and Prague.

SN Brussels Airlines (code SN; ☎ 02 6968 23 64; www .flysn.com; hub Brussels National airport) To/from Brussels.

Transavia (code HV; ☎ 02 696 82 615; www.transavia.com; hub Amsterdam Schipol airport) To/from Amsterdam.

Virgin Express (code TV; ☎ 848 39 01 09; www.virgin -express.com; hub Brussels National airport) To/from Brussels.

Volareweb (code VA; ☎ 199 414 500; www.volareweb .com; hub Milan Limate airport) To/from Milan Linate.

Airports

Eight kilometres northeast of the city centre, **Capodichino airport** (NAP; ☎ 081 789 62 59; www .gesac.it) is southern Italy's main airport, linking Naples with most Italian and several major European cities, as well as New York.

To get there by public transport you can either take the regular **ANM** (☎ 800 63 95 25) bus No 3S (€1, 30 minutes, every 15 minutes) from Piazza Garibaldi, or the **Alibus** (Map pp280-1; ☎ 081 53 11 705) airport shuttle (€3, 20 minutes, half-hourly) from Piazza del Municipio or Piazza Garibaldi.

Official taxi fares to the airport are as follows: €19 from a seafront hotel or from Mergellina hydrofoil terminal; €16 from Piazza del Municipio; and €12.50 from Stazione Centrale.

Curreri (☎ 081 801 54 20; www.curreriviaggi.it) runs six services a day between the airport and Sorrento. The cost of the 75-minute journey is €7 and tickets are available on board.

BOAT

Naples, the bay islands and Amalfi Coast are served by a comprehensive ferry network. In Naples ferries and hydrofoils leave for Capri, Sorrento, Ischia, Procida and Forio from Molo Beverello in front of

Castel Nuovo; longer-distance ferries for Palermo, Cagliari, Milazzo, the Aeolian Islands (Isole Eolie) and Tunisia leave from the **Stazione Marittima** (Map pp280-1).

Tickets for shorter journeys can be bought at the ticket booths on Molo Beverello and at Mergellina. For longer journeys try the offices of the ferry companies or at a travel agent.

The monthly publication *Qui Napoli* lists timetables for Bay of Naples services. Note, however, that ferry services are pared back considerably in the winter, especially along the Amalfi Coast. Adverse sea conditions may also affect sailing schedules.

Following is a list of ferry and hydrofoil routes and the destinations they service. The fares, unless otherwise stated, are for a one-way high-season, deck-class single.

Alicost (☎ 089 87 14 83; Largo Scario 5, Amalfi) Operates normal and fast ferries from Salerno to Amalfi (€5.50, six daily) and Positano (€7, five daily); also from Amalfi to Ischia (€19, one daily), Capri (€16, eight daily) and Positano (€6, six daily); and from Positano to Ischia (€19, one daily) and Capri (€15.50, five daily).

Alilauro (Map pp280-1; ☎ 081 497 22 67; www.alilauro .it; Stazione Marittima, Naples) Operates hydrofoils from Naples to Sorrento (€9, seven daily), Ischia (€13.50, nine daily) and Forio (€15.50, five daily); also ferries between Capri and Ischia (€15.50, one daily) and Amalfi (€13.50, two daily).

Caremar (Map pp278-9 ☎ 081 551 38 82; www.care mar.it; Molo Beverello, Naples) Runs services from Naples to Capri (ferry/hydrofoil €7.60/12.50, five daily), Ischia (€5.60/12.15, 13 daily) and Procida (€4.50/9.25, 12 daily); also ferries between Sorrento and Capri (€7.80, four daily).

Coop Sant'Andrea (☎ 089 87 31 90; www.coopsant andrea.it; Lungomare dei Cavalieri 1, Amalfi) Connects Amalfi with Maiori (€2, eight daily) and Minori (€2, eight daily).

LMP (Map pp280-1; Linee Marittime Partenope; ☎ 081 704 19 11; www.consorziolmp.it; Via Guglielmo Melisurgo 4, Naples) Runs hydrofoils from Sorrento to Capri (€12, 20 daily) and Naples (€9, eight daily); also ferries from Sorrento to Positano (€7, three daily) and Amalfi (€7.50, three daily); and from Capri to Positano (€13, six daily), Amalfi (€13.50, seven daily) and Salerno (€14.50, five daily).

Medmar (Map pp280-1; ☎ 081 551 33 52; www.med margroup.com; Stazione Marittima, Naples) Operates services from Naples to Ischia (€8.50, four daily) and weekly sailings to the Aeolian Islands (€42), Sardinia (€55), Corsica (€55) and Tunis (€90).

Metrò del Mare (☎ 199 44 66 44; www.metrodelmare .com) Runs summer-only services between Naples and Sorrento (€4.50 three daily), Positano (€9, four daily), Amalfi (€10, four daily) and Salerno (€10.50, two daily) as well as between the main Amalfi Coast towns.

Navigazione Libera del Golfo (NLG; ☎ 081 552 07 63; www.navlib.it in Italian, Molo Beverello, Naples) From Naples NLG runs hydrofoils to and from Capri (€14, nine daily) year-round.

Siremar (Map pp280-1; ☎ 081 017 19 98; www.sire mar.it; Stazione Marittima, Naples) Operates boats to the Aeolian Islands and Milazzo (€44, six times weekly in summer, dropping by 50% in the low season).

SNAV (Map pp280-1 ☎ 091 428 55 55; www.snav.it; Stazione Marittima, Naples) Runs hydrofoils to Capri (€14, 11 daily), Procida (€11, four daily) and Ischia (€14, four daily); also ferries to Palermo (€16, one daily). In summer there are daily services to the Aeolian Islands (€85 to Lipari).

Tirrenia (Map pp280-1; ☎ 081 720 11 11; www.tirrenia .it; Stazione Marittima, Molo Angioino, Naples) From Naples runs a weekly boat to and from Cagliari (deck class €34.89) and Palermo (deck class €43.83). The service increases to twice weekly in summer. From Palermo and Cagliari there are connections to Tunisia, directly or via Trapani (Sicily).

TraVelMar (☎ /fax 089 87 29 50; Largo Scario 5, Amalfi) Operates from Salerno to Amalfi (ferry/hydrofoil €4.50/5, seven daily) and Positano (ferry/hydrofoil €6.50/7, seven daily); from Amalfi to Positano (ferry/hydrofoil €5.50/6, seven daily) and Sorrento (€8, three daily); and from Positano to Sorrento (€7, three daily).

BUS

In Naples, buses are operated by the city transport company ANM (☎ 800 63 95 25; www .anm.it in Italian). There's no central bus station but most busses pass through Piazza Garibaldi, the city's chaotic transport hub. To locate your bus stop you'll probably need to ask at the ANM information kiosk (Map pp280-1) in the centre of the square.

Useful bus services include:

3S From Piazza Garibaldi to the airport.

24 From Piazza del Municipio up to Piazza Dante and on to Capodimonte.

140 Santa Lucia to Posillipo via Mergellina.

152 From Piazza Garibaldi, along Corso Garibaldi, Via Nuova Marina, Via Colombo, to Molo Beverello, Via Santa Lucia, Piazza Vittoria and Via Partenope.

201 From Stazione Centrale to the Museo Archeologico Nazionale, down to Piazza del Municipio and then back to Piazza Gariboldi, via Piazza Dante.

404D A night bus operating from 11.20pm to 4am (hourly departures) from Stazione Centrale to Piazza del Municipio, on to Mergellina and Vomero, and then back down to Stazione Centrale.

C9 From Piazza Vittoria, along Riviera di Chiaia to Piazza Sannazzaro, Viale Augusto, Via Diocleziano, to Bagnoli and Via Coroglio.

C25 Piazza Amedeo to Piazza Bovio via Castel dell'Ovo and Piazza del Municipio.

C28 From Piazza Vittoria up Via dei Mille and on to Piazza Vanvitelli in Vomero.

E1 From Piazza del Gesù, along Via Constantinopoli, to Museo Archeologico Nazionale, Via Tribunali, Via Duomo, Piazza Nicola Amore, along Corso Umberto I and Via Mezzocannone.

R1 From Piazza Medaglie D'Oro to Piazza Carità, Piazza Dante and Piazza Bovio.

R2 From Stazione Centrale, along Corso Umberto I, to Piazza Bovio, Piazza del Municipio and Piazza Trento e Trieste.

R3 From Mergellina along the Riviera di Chiaia to Piazza del Municipio, Piazza Bovio, Piazza Dante and Piazza Carità.

R4 From Capodimonte down past Via Dante to Piazza Municipio and back again.

Regional bus services are operated by a number of companies, the most useful of which is SITA (☎ 199 73 07 49; www.sita-on-line.it in Italian), which runs buses from Naples to Pompeii (€2.30, 40 minutes, half-hourly), Sorrento (€3.20, one hour 20 minutes, twice daily), Positano (€3.20, two hours, twice daily), Amalfi (€3.20, two hours, six daily) and Salerno (€3.20, one hour 10 minutes, every 25 minutes). It also connects Salerno with Amalfi (€1.80, one hour 10 minutes, half-hourly) and links towns along the Amalfi Coast. Casting even wider, it runs from Salerno to Bari via Naples (€22.36, 4½ hours, twice daily) and operates a service to Germany, including Dortmund (€112) via Munich (€90), Stuttgart (€90), Frankfurt (€98) and Dusseldorf (€112). You can connect from this service to Berlin (€118)

TICKETS PLEASE

Tickets for public transport in Naples and the surrounding Campania region are managed by the Unico Campania consortium (www.unicocampania.it). For travel in Naples itself, Unico Napoli tickets are sold at stations, ANM booths and tobacconists. The standard ticket costs €1 and is valid for 90 minutes of unlimited travel by bus, tram, metro, funicular, Ferrovia Cumana or Circumflegrea; a daily ticket is good value at €3 or €2.50 on Saturdays and Sundays and a weekly ticket costs €9. These tickets are not valid to Pompeii or Ercolano on the Circumvesuviana train line. For longer distances and for travel within the region, ticket prices depend on the distance to travel – a ticket from Naples to Pompeii, for example costs €2.30, to Sorrento, Positano and Amalfi €3.20.

and Hamburg (€118). You can buy SITA tickets and catch buses either from Stazione Marittima or from Via G Ferraris, near Stazione Centrale; you can also buy tickets at **Bar Clizia** (Corso Arnaldo Lucci 173).

Most national buses depart from Piazza Garibaldi. Check destinations carefully or ask at the information kiosk in the centre of the piazza. **Marino** (☎ 080 311 23 35) has buses to Bari (€19, three hours); **Miccolis** (☎ 081 20 03 80) runs to Taranto (€16, four hours), Brindisi (€23.60, five hours) and Lecce (€26, 5½ hours), while **CLP** (☎ 081 531 17 07) serves Foggia (€9, two hours), Perugia (€27.37, 3½ hours) and Assisi (€28.92, 4½ hours).

CAR & MOTORCYCLE

There can be no greater test of courage than driving your own vehicle in Naples. As a means of locomotion, it's of limited value. The weight of the anarchic traffic means that cars rarely travel faster than walking pace and parking is an absolute nightmare. A scooter is quicker and easier to park but is even more nerve-wracking to ride. Car and bike theft is also a major problem.

If you're determined to drive, there are some simple guidelines to consider: get used to tail-gaters; worry about what's in front of you not behind; watch out for scooters; give way to pedestrians no matter where they appear from; approach all junctions and traffic lights with extreme caution, and keep cool.

Officially much of the city centre is closed to nonresident traffic for much of the day. Daily restrictions are in place in the centro storico, in the area around Piazza del Municipio and Via Toledo, and in the Chiaia district around Piazza dei Martiri. Hours vary but are typically from 8am to 6.30pm, possibly later.

Parking in Naples is no fun. If you're on a scooter you won't have too many problems, but if you're on four wheels you almost certainly will. Blue lines by the side of the road denote pay-and-display parking – buy tickets at the meters or from tobacconists – with rates ranging from €1.50 to €2 per hour. Elsewhere street parking is often overseen by illegal attendants who will expect a €1 to €2 fee for their protection of your car. It's

usually easier to bite the bullet and pay them than attempt a moral stance. To the west of the city centre there's a 24-hour car park at Via Brin (€1.10 for the first four hours, then €0.30 for every succesive hour).

Away from the city, a car becomes more practical. However, be aware that driving along the Amalfi Coast can be quite a hair-raising experience as buses career round impossibly tight hairpin bends and locals brazenly overtake anything in their path. On the bay islands – Capri, Ischia and Procida – a scooter is an excellent way of getting round.

Naples is on the north–south Autostrada del Sole, the A1 (north to Rome and Milan) and the A3 (south to Salerno and Reggio di Calabria). The A30 skirts Naples to the northeast, while the A16 heads across to Bari.

When approaching the city, the motorways meet the Tangenziale di Napoli, a major ring road around the city. The ring road hugs the city's northern fringe, meeting the A1 for Rome and the A2 to Capodichino airport in the east, and continuing towards Campi Flegrei and Pozzuoli in the west.

For Sorrento head south along the A3 autostrada until Castellammare di Stabia; from here follow the SS145 southeast. The road continues from Sorrento around the peninsula until it merges with the SS163 which runs onto Positano, Amalfi and Salerno.

Hire

The major car-hire firms are all represented in Naples.

Avis (Map pp280–1; ☎ 081 28 40 41; www.avisauto noleggio.it; Corso Novara 5 & Capodichino airport)

Europcar (☎ 081 780 56 43; www.europcar.it; Capodichino airport)**Hertz** (Map pp280–1; ☎ 081 20 62 28; www.hertz.it; Via G. Ricciardi 5, Capodichino airport & in Mergellina)

Maggiore (Map pp280–1; ☎ 081 28 78 58; www.maggiore .it; Stazione Centrale & Capodichino airport)

Rent Sprint (Map pp284–50; ☎ 081 764 13 33; Via Santa Lucia 36) Scooter hire only.

Elsewhere you'll find any number of rental agencies in Sorrento and the Amalfi Coast (see the relevant chapters for details).

An economy car will cost about €60 per day; for a scooter expect to pay about €35. If possible, try to arrange your rental in advance, as you'll get much better rates. Similarly, airport agencies tend to charge more than city centre branches.

To rent a car you'll need to be over 21 (25 for some larger cars) and have a credit card. When hiring always make sure you understand what's covered in the rental agreement (insurance, unlimited mileage, petrol etc). If the agreement doesn't cover theft and collision damage, you would be strongly advised to pay extra for it.

Road Rules

An EU driving licence is valid for driving in Italy. If you've got an old-style green UK licence or a licence issued by a non-EU country, you'll need an International Driving Permit (IDP). Valid for 12 months, these are inexpensive (about US$21 or UK£5.50) and are easily available from your national automobile association; take along a passport photo and your home driving licence. When driving you should always carry the home licence with the IDP as it's not valid on its own.

Contrary to all appearances, there are road rules in Italy. The main ones are as follows:
Drive on the right and overtake on the left.
Wear seat belts in the front and, if fitted, in the back.
Wear a helmet on all two-wheeled transport.
Carry a warning triangle and a fluorescent safety vest to be worn in the event of an emergency.
The blood alcohol limit is 0.05%.
Speed limits are 130km/h on autostrade, 110km/h on nonurban dual highways and 50km/h in built-up areas.

Italy's automobile association, the **Automobile Club d'Italia** (ACI; ☎ 081 725 38 11; www.aci.it; Piazzale Tecchio 49D) is the best source of motoring information. It also operates a 24-hour recovery service (☎ 803 116).

FUNICULAR

Three of Naples' four funicular railways connect the centre with Vomero:
Funicular Centrale (⊙ 6.30am-10pm Mon & Tue, 6.30-12.30am Wed-Sun) Ascends from Via Toledo to Piazza Fuga.

Funicular di Chiaia (⊙ 6.30am-10pm Wed & Thu, 6.30-12.30am Fri-Tue) Travels from Via del Parco Margherita to Via Domenico Cimarosa.
Funicular di Montesanto (⊙ 7am-10pm daily) From Piazza Montesanto to Via Raffaele Morghen.

The fourth, **Funicular di Mergellina** (⊙ 7am-10pm daily), connects the waterfront at Via Mergellina with Via Manzoni. Unico Napoli tickets (see the boxed text, p263) are valid for one trip only on the funiculars.

METRO

Naples' Metropolitana (☎ 800 56 88 66; www .metro.na.it) is, in fact, mostly above ground.
Line 1 (⊙ 6am-10.20pm daily) Runs north from Piazza Dante stopping at Museo (for Piazza Cavour and Line 2), Materdei, Salvator Rosa, Cilea, Piazza Vanvitelli, Piazza Medaglie D'Oro and seven stops beyond.
Line 2 (⊙ 5.30am-11pm daily) Runs from Gianturco, just east of Stazione Centrale, with stops at Piazza Garibaldi (for Stazione Centrale), Piazza Cavour, Montesanto, Piazza Amedeo, Mergellina, Piazza Leopardi, Campi Flegrei, Cavaleggeri d'Aosta, Bagnoli and Pozzuoli.

Metro journeys are covered by Unico Napoli tickets (see the boxed text p263).

TAXI

Official taxis are white, metered and bear the Naples symbol, the Pulcinella (with his distinctive white cone-shaped hat and long hooked nose), on their front doors. They generally ignore kerbside arm-wavers. There are taxi stands at most of the city's main piazzas or you can call one of the five taxi cooperatives: **Napoli** (☎ 081 556 44 44), **Consortaxi** (☎ 081 20 20 20), **Cotana** (☎ 081 570 70 70), **Free** (☎ 081 551 51 51), and **Partenope** (☎ 081 556 02 02).

The minimum fare for a ride is €4.15, of which €2.60 is the starting fare. There's also a baffling range of additional charges: €0.80 for a radio taxi call, €1.60 extra on Sundays and holidays, €2.10 more between 10pm and 7am, €2.60 for an airport run and €0.50 per piece of luggage in the boot. Guide dogs for the blind and wheelchairs are carried free of charge. See the Airports section, p261, for details of set fares to and from the airport.

Taxi drivers may tell you that the meter's kaput. However, you can (and should) insist that they switch it on.

TRAIN

Naples is southern Italy's main rail hub. Most **Trenitalia** (☎ 89 20 21; www.trenitalia .com) trains arrive at or depart from **Stazione Centrale** (Map pp280-1; ☎ 081 554 31 88) or, underneath the main station, **Stazione Garibaldi** (Map pp280-1). These include slow regional services and the faster InterCity (IC) and Eurostar (ES) trains. There are up to 30 trains daily to Rome (IC €17.53, two hours), some of which stop at Mergellina station, and some 20 to Salerno (IC €6.37, 35 minutes).

International trains departing from Naples include services to London, Paris and Madrid.

The Ferrovia Cumana and the **Circumflegrea** (☎ 800 00 16 16; www.sepsa.it), based at **Stazione Cumana di Montesanto** (Map pp280-1) on Piazza Montesanto, 500m southwest of Piazza Dante, operate services to Pozzuoli (€1, every 25 minutes) and Cuma (€1, six per day).

The **Circumvesuviana** (Map pp280-1; ☎ 081 772 24 44; wwww.vesuviana.it; Corso G Garibaldi), southwest of Stazione Centrale (follow the signs from the main concourse in Stazione Centrale), operates trains to Sorrento (€3.20, 70 minutes) via Ercolano (€1.70, 20 minutes), Pompeii (€2.30, 40 minutes) and other towns along the coast. There are approximately 40 trains daily running between 5am and 10.30pm, with reduced services on Sunday.

TRAM

The following trams may be useful:

Tram 1 Operates from east of Stazione Centrale, through Piazza Garibaldi, the city centre and along the waterfront to Piazza Vittoria.

Tram 29 Travels from Piazza Garibaldi to the city centre along Corso G Garibaldi.

It's true – anyone can speak another language. Don't worry if you haven't studied languages before or that you studied a language at school for years and can't remember any of it. It doesn't even matter if you failed English grammar. After all, that's never affected your ability to speak English! And this is the key to picking up a language in another country: you just need to start speaking. If you want to learn more Italian, pick up a copy of Lonely Planet's comprehensive but user-friendly *Italian Phrasebook*.

LANGUAGE

PRONUNCIATION

c	as the 'k' in 'kit' before a, o and u; as the 'ch' in 'choose' before e and i
ch	as the 'k' in 'kit'
g	as the 'g' in 'get' before a, o, u and h; as the 'j' in 'jet' before e and i
gli	as the 'lli' in 'million'
gn	as the 'ny' in 'canyon'
h	always silent
r	a rolled 'rr' sound
sc	as the 'sh' in 'sheep' before e and i; as 'sk' before a, o, u and h
z	as the 'ts' in 'lights', except at the beginning of a word, when it's as the 'ds' in 'suds'

SOCIAL
Meeting People

Hello.
Buon giorno. bwon *jor*·no
Goodbye.
Arrivederci. a·ree·ve·*der*·chee
Please.
Per favore. per fa·*vo*·re
Thank you (very much).
(Mille) Grazie. (*mee*·le) *gra*·tsye
Yes/No.
Sì/No. see/no
Do you speak English?
Parla inglese? *par*·la een·*gle*·ze
Do you understand?
Capisce? ka·*pee*·she
Yes, I understand.
Sì, capisco. see ka·*pee*·sko
No, I don't understand.
No, non capisco. no non ka·*pee*·sko

Could you please ...?
Potrebbe ...? po·*tre*·be ...
   repeat that
   ripeterlo ree·*pe*·ter·lo

   speak more slowly
   parlare più lentamente par·*la*·re pyoo len·ta·*men*·te
   write it down
   scriverlo *skree*·ver·lo

Going Out

What's on ...?
Che c'è in programma ...? ke che een pro·*gra*·ma ...
   locally
   in zona een *zo*·na
   this weekend
   questo finesettimana *kwe*·sto·fee·ne·se·tee·*ma*·na
   today
   oggi *o*·jee
   tonight
   stasera sta·*se*·ra

Where are the ...?
Dove sono ...? *do*·ve *so*·no ...
   clubs
   dei club *de*·yee klub
   gay venues
   dei locali gay *de*·yee lo·*ka*·lee gay
   places to eat
   posti dove mangiare *po*·stee *do*·ve man·*ja*·re
   pubs
   dei pub *de*·yee pub

Is there a local entertainment guide?
C'è una guida agli spettacoli in questa città? che oo·na *gwee*·da al·yee spe·ta·ko·lee een *kwe*·sta chee·*ta*

PRACTICAL
Question Words

Who?	Chi?	kee
What?	Che?	ke
When?	Quando?	*kwan*·do
Where?	Dove?	*do*·ve
How?	Come?	*ko*·me

Numbers & Amounts

0	zero *dze·rō*
1	uno *oo·*no
2	due *doo·*e
3	tre *tre*
4	quattro *kwa·*tro
5	cinque *cheen·*kwe
6	sei *say*
7	sette *se·*te
8	otto *o·*to
9	nove *no·*ve
10	dieci *dye·*chee
11	undici *oon·dee·*chee
12	dodici *do·dee·*chee
13	tredici *tre·dee·*chee
14	quattordici *kwa·tor·dee·dee·chee*
15	quindici *kween·dee·*chee
16	sedici *se·dee·*chee
17	diciasette *dee·cha·se·*te
18	diciotto *dee·cho·*to
19	dicianove *dee·cha·no·*ve
20	venti *ven·*tee
21	ventuno *ven·too·*no
22	ventidue *ven·tee·doo·*e
30	trenta *tren·*ta
40	quaranta *kwa·ran·*ta
50	cinquanta *cheen·kwan·*ta
60	sessanta *se·san·*ta
70	settanta *se·tan·*ta
80	ottanta *o·tan·*ta
90	novanta *no·van·*ta
100	cento *chen·*to
1000	mille *mee·*le

Days

Monday	lunedì *loo·ne·dee*
Tuesday	martedì *mar·te·dee*
Wednesday	mercoledì *mer·ko·le·dee*
Thursday	giovedì *jo·ve·dee*
Friday	venerdì *ve·ner·dee*
Saturday	sabato *sa·*ba·to
Sunday	domenica *do·me·nee·*ka

Accommodation

I'm looking for a ...
Cerco ... *cher·*ko ...
  guesthouse
  una pensione *oo·*na pen·*syo·*ne
  hotel
  un albergo *oon* al·*ber·*go
  youth hostel
  un ostello per la gioventù *oon* os·*te·*lo per la jo·ven·*too*

Do you have any rooms available?
Ha camere libere? a·*ve·*te *ka·*me·re *lee·*be·re

I'd like ...
Vorrei ... vo·*ray* ...
  a single room
  una camera singola *oo·*na *ka·*me·ra *een·*go·la
  a double room
  una camera matrimoniale *oo·*na *ka·*me·ra
    ma·tree·mo·*nya·*le
  a room with two beds
  una camera doppia *oo·*na *ka·*me·ra *do·*pya
  a room with a bathroom
  una camera con bagno *oo·*na *ka·*me·ra kon *ba·*nyo

How much is it ...?
Quanto costa ...? *kwan·*to *ko·*sta ...
  per night | per la notte per la *no·*te
  per person | per ciascuno per cha·*skoo·*no

Banking

I'd like to ...
Vorrei ... vo·*ray* ...
  cash a cheque
  riscuotere un assegno ree·*skwo·*te·re *oon* a·*sen·*yo
  change money
  cambiare denaro kam·bya·re de·na·ro
  change some travellers cheques
  cambiare degli assegni di viaggio kam·*bya·*re del·yee
    a·*se·*nyee dee vee·*a·*jo

Where's the nearest ...?
Dov'è il ... più vicino? do·*ve* ... pyoo vee·*chee·*no
  ATM | bancomat *ban·*ko·mat
  foreign exchange | cambio *kam·*byo
  office

Post

Where is the post office?
Dov'è l'ufficio postale? do·ve loo·*fee·*cho po·*sta·*le

I want to send ...
Voglio spedire ... *vo·*lyo spe·*dee·*re ...
  a letter | una lettera *oo·*na *le·*te·ra
  a parcel | un pachetto *oon* pa·*ke·*to
  a postcard | una cartolina *oo·*na kar·to·*lee·*na

I want to buy ...
Voglio comprare ... *vo·*lyo kom·*pra·*re ...
  an envelope | una busta *oo·*na *boo·*sta
  a stamp | un francobollo *oon* fran·ko·*bo·*lo

Phones & Mobiles

I want to buy a phone card.
Voglio comprare una scheda telefonica.
vo·lyo kom·*pra*·re oo·na *ske*·da te·le·*fo*·nee·ka

I want to make ...
Voglio fare ... *vo*·lyo *fa*·re ...
 a call (to ...)
 una chiamata (a ...) *oo*·na kya·*ma*·ta (a ...)
 reverse-charge/collect call
 una chiamata a carico del destinatario
 oo·na kya·*ma*·ta a *ka*·ree·ko del des·tee·na·*ta*·ryo

Where can I find a/an ...?
Dove si trova ... *do*·ve see *tro*·va ...
I'd like a/an ...
Vorrei ... vo·*ray* ...
 adaptor plug
 un addattatore oon a·da·*to*·re
 charger for my phone
 un caricabatterie oon *ka*·ree·ka ba·te·*ree*·ye
 mobile/cell phone for hire
 un cellulare da noleggiare oon *chel*·oo·*la*·re da no·le·*ja*·re
 prepaid mobile/cell phone
 un cellulare prepagato oon *chel*·oo·*la*·re pre·pa·*ga*·to
 SIM card for your network
 un SIM card per vostra rete telefonica oon *seem* kard
 per *vo*·stra *re*·te te·le·*fo*·nee·ka

Internet

Where's the local internet cafe?
Dove si trova l'internet point?
do·ve see·*tro*·va *leen*·ter·net poynt

I'd like to ...
Vorrei ... vo·*ray* ...
 check my email
 controllare le mie email kon·tro·*la*·re le *mee*·ye e·mayl
 get online
 collegarmi a internet ko·le·*gar*·mee a·*leen*·ter·net

Shopping

I'd like to buy ...
Vorrei comprare ... vo·*ray* kom·*pra*·re ...
Do you have ...?
Avete ...? a·*ve*·te ...
How much is it?
Quanto costa? *kwan*·ta *kos*·ta

more	più pyoo
less	meno *me*·no
smaller	più piccolo/a pyoo *pee*·ko·lo/la
bigger	più grande pyoo *gran*·de

Do you accept ...?
Accettate ...? a·che·*ta*·te ...
 credit cards
 carte di credito *kar*·te dee *kre*·dee·to
 travellers cheques
 assegni di viaggio a·*se*·nyee dee vee·*a*·jo

TRANSPORT

What time does the ... leave?
A che ora parte ...? a ke o·ra *par*·te ...

boat	la nave	la *na*·ve
bus	l'autobus	*low*·to·boos
train	il treno	eel *tre*·no

What time's the ... bus?
A che ora passa ... autobus? a ke o·ra pa·so ... o·to·bus

first	il primo	eel *pree*·mo
last	l'ultimo	*lool*·tee·mo
next	il prossimo	eel *pro*·see·mo

Please put the meter on.
Usa il tassametro, per favore. *oo*·sa eel ta·sa·*me*·tro per
 fa·*vo*·re
How much is it to ...?
Quant'è per ...? kwan·*te* per ...
Please take me to (this address).
Mi porti a (questo indirizzo), per favore. mee·*por*·tee a
 (*kwe*·sto een·dee·*ree*·tso) per fa·*vo*·re

EMERGENCIES

It's an emergency!
È un'emergenza! e oo·ne·mer·*jen*·tsa
Could you please help me/us?
Mi/Ci può aiutare, per favore? mee/chee pwo a·yoo·*ta*·re
 per fa·*vo*·re
Where's the police station?
Dov'è la questura? do·*ve* la kwes·*too*·ra

Call ...!
Chiami ...! *kya*·mee ...
 the police
 la polizia la po·lee·*tsee*·ya
 a doctor
 un medico oon *me*·dee·ko
 an ambulance
 un'ambulanza oo·nam·boo·*lan*·tsa

HEALTH

I need a doctor (who speaks English).
Ho bisogno di un medico (che parli inglese).
o bee·*zon*·yo doon·*me*·dee·ko (ke *par*·la een·*gle*·ze)

Where's the nearest ...?
Dov'è ... più vicino? do·ve ... pyoo vee·*chee*·no/na
  chemist (night)
  la farmacia (di turno) la far·ma·*chee*·ya (dee toor·no)

  doctor
  il medico eel *me*·dee·ko
  hospital
  l'ospedale lo·spe·*da*·le

GLOSSARY

albergo, alberghi (pl) – hotel
alimentari – grocery shop
autostrada, autostrade (pl) – motorway, highway

bagno – bathroom, also toilet
bancomat – ATM (automated teller machine)
biblioteca, biblioteche (pl) – library
biglietto – ticket

calcio – football (soccer)
cambio – currency-exchange bureau
camera – room
campanile – bell tower
carabinieri – police with military and civil duties
carta d'identità – identity card
carta telefonica – phonecard
casa – house, home
castello – castle
catacomba – underground tomb complex
centro – city centre
centro storico – historic centre, old city
chiesa, chiese (pl) – church
cimitero – cemetery
colle/collina – hill
colonna – column
commissariato – local police station
comune – equivalent to a municipality or county; town or city council; historically, a commune (self-governing town or city)
corso – main street
cupola – dome

farmacia – pharmacy
fermo posta – poste restante
ferrovia – train station
festa – feast day; holiday
fiume – river
fontana – fountain
forno – bakery
forte/fortezza – fort
forum, fora (pl) – (Latin) public square
francobolli – stamps

gabinetto – toilet, WC
gasolio – diesel
gelateria – ice-cream parlour
guglia – obelisk

isola – island

lago – lake
largo – small square
lavanderia – launderette
libreria – bookshop
lido – beach
lungomare – seafront, esplanade

mercato – market
monte – mountain
mura – city wall

orto botanico – botanical gardens
ospedale – hospital
ostello – hostel

palazzo, palazzi (pl) – mansion, palace, large building of any type (including an apartment block)
panetteria – bakery
pasticceria – cake shop
pensione – small hotel or guesthouse, often offering board
pescheria – fish shop
piazza, piazze (pl) – square
piazzale – large open square
pinacoteca – art gallery
piscina – pool
polizia – police
ponte – bridge
porta – city gate

questura – police station

reale – royal

sala – room in a museum or a gallery
salumeria – delicatessen
sedia a rotelle – wheelchair
seggiolone – child's highchair
servizio – service charge in restaurants
stazione – station

tabaccheria – tobacconist's shop
teatro – theatre
tempio – temple
terme – baths
torre – tower
treno – train

via – street, road
vicolo – alley, alleyway

THE LONELY PLANET STORY

The story begins with a classic travel adventure: Tony and Maureen Wheeler's 1972 journey across Europe and Asia to Australia. There was no useful information about the overland trail then, so Tony and Maureen published the first Lonely Planet guidebook to meet a growing need.

From a kitchen table, Lonely Planet has grown to become the largest independent travel publisher in the world, with offices in Melbourne (Australia), Oakland (USA) and London (UK). Today Lonely Planet guidebooks cover the globe. There is an ever-growing list of books and information in a variety of media. Some things haven't changed. The main aim is still to make it possible for adventurous travellers to get out there – to explore and better understand the world.

At Lonely Planet we believe travellers can make a positive contribution to the countries they visit – if they respect their host communities and spend their money wisely. Every year 5% of company profit is donated to charities around the world.

BEHIND THE SCENES

THIS BOOK

This is the 2nd edition of *Naples & the Amalfi Coast*. Duncan Garwood and Josephine Quintero wrote the previous edition. This guidebook was commissioned in Lonely Planet's London office and produced by the following:

Commissioning Editor Paula Hardy
Coordinating Editor Susan Paterson
Coordinating Cartographer Helen Rowley
Coordinating Layout Designer Tamsin Wilson
Design Development Annika Roojun
Managing Editor Liz Heynes
Managing Cartographer Mark Griffiths
Assisting Editors Gennifer Ciavarra, Kim Hutchins, Sally O'Brien, Laura Stansfeld
Assisting Cartographers Piotr Czajkowski, Amanda Sierp, Simon Tillema
Assisting Layout Designers Jim Hsu
Cover Designer Rebecca Dandens
Project Manager Rachel Imeson
Language Content Coordinator Quentin Frayne

Thanks to Sally Darmody, Eoin Dunlevy, Mark Germanchis, Trent Paton, Paul Piaia, Averil Robertson, Jessica Rose, Lyahna Spencer, Kate Whitfield, Celia Wood

Cover photograph Sorrento, Demetrio Carrasco, Alamy
Internal photographs All photos by Lonely Planet Images and Greg Elms, unless otherwise indicated or listed below: p17 Jean-Bernard Carillet; p21 Dallas Stribley; p25 Jean-Bernard Carillet; p35 Martin Moos; p43 Dallas Stribley; p63 Martin Moos; p155 Jean-Bernard Carillet; p169 Stephen Saks; p249, p261 & p277 Jean-Bernard Carillet.

All images are copyright of the photographer unless otherwise indicated. Many of the images in this guide are available for licensing from Lonely Planet Images: www.lonelyplanetimages.com.

THANKS
DUNCAN GARWOOD

A big thank you to Toby Whiting, whose map reading and company on Capri were much appreciated. Thanks also to staff at the various tourist offices who did their best to help; in particular to Lucia in Salerno and Giovanni Romano in Positano. At Lonely Planet, thank you to Paula Hardy for the assignment and her help during write-up, and to Cristian Bonetto for his enthusiasm and terrific work. On the home front, Lidia was a star, courageously looking after Ben and Nick whilst I was off gallivanting around Amalfi. Thanks also to her parents, Nello and Nicla, for their support during the hot summer months.

CRISTIAN BONETTO

First and foremost, an enormous thank you to Duilio 'Babà' Verardi for his invaluable support, insight and humour. Thanks to Paula Hardy for the commission and Duncan Garwood for his words of wisdom. *Grazie infinite* to Marcello Donnarumma, Giovanni Caccavale, all my interviewees, Leonardo Recchia, Professore Renato Ruotola, Josephine Quintero, Sally O'Brien, Carolyn Jackson and Peter Bardwell, Carolyn Court and my madcap family.

OUR READERS

Many thanks to the travellers who used the last edition and wrote to us with helpful hints, useful advice and interesting anecdotes:

Betty-Lou Ayers, Carey Baylis, Gill Branston, Brian Cleave, Marcello Donnarumma, Ian Griffin, Peder Hansen, Carol Hanson, Jim Holland, Hester Jones, David & Sarah Knight, David Mulhall, Anne Ratchford, Lisa Robinson, Amber Rowland, Leslie Rubman, Beverley Sanders, Christine Scharff, Richard Smith, Roman Steiner, Guus Stoelinga, Balazs Szanto, Chris & Carolyn Voss

SEND US YOUR FEEDBACK

We love to hear from travelers – your comments keep us on our toes and help make our books better. Our well-traveled team reads every word on what you loved or loathed about this book. Although we cannot reply individually to postal submissions, we always guarantee that your feedback goes straight to the appropriate authors, in time for the next edition. Each person who sends us information is thanked in the next edition – and the most useful submissions are rewarded with a free book.

To send us your updates – and find out about Lonely Planet events, newsletters and travel news – visit our award-winning website: www.lonelyplanet.com/contact.

Note: We may edit, reproduce and incorporate your comments in Lonely Planet products such as guidebooks, websites and digital products, so let us know if you don't want your comments reproduced or your name acknowledged. For a copy of our privacy policy visit www.lonelyplanet.com/privacy.

000 map pages
000 photographs

cultura
re

scienza
nce

scavi
eological sites

MAPS

MAP LEGEND

ROUTES

Tollway	One-Way Street
Freeway	Mall/Steps
Primary Road	Tunnel
Secondary Road	Walking Tour
Tertiary Road	Walking Tour Detour
Lane	Walking Trail
Under Construction	Walking Path
Track	Pedestrian Overpass

TRANSPORT

Ferry	Rail (Underground)
Metro	Cable Car, Funicular
Rail	

HYDROGRAPHY

River, Creek	Water

BOUNDARIES

State, Provincial	Cliff
Ancient Wall	

AREA FEATURES

Area of Interest	Forest
Beach	Land
Building, Featured	Mall
Building, Information	Park
Building, Other	Rocks
Building, Transport	Sports
Cemetery, Christian	Urban

POPULATION

CAPITAL (STATE)	Small City
Large City	Town, Village
Medium City	

SYMBOLS

Sights/Activities
- Beach
- Castle, Fortress
- Christian
- Diving, Snorkeling
- Monument
- Museum, Gallery
- Other Site
- Ruin
- Spa, Swimming

Eating
- Eating

Drinking
- Drinking
- Café

Entertainment
- Entertainment

Shopping
- Shopping

Sleeping
- Sleeping
- Camping

Transport
- Bus Station
- Parking Area

Information
- Bank, ATM
- Embassy/Consulate
- Hospital, Medical
- Information
- Internet Facilities
- Police Station
- Post Office, GPO
- Telephone
- Toilets

Geographic
- Lighthouse
- Lookout
- Mountain, Volcano
- National Park
- River Flow
- Spring, Waterfall

Materdei

Via delle Fontanelle

Piazza
Fontanelle
alla Sanità

Monte
Donzelli

Tangenziale

Materdei Ⓜ Via Ma

Via R Imbriani

Via Salita Arenella

Via B Caracciolo

Via Salvator F

Via F Verrotti

Via E Suarez

Medaglie d'Oro
Via Giotto

S Rosa

Piazza
Mazzini

Salita

See p283

Vico dei Monte

Via Vertaglien

Viale Michelangelo

Viale Raffaello

Piazza
Olivella
Montesanto

Ⓜ Cilea

Vomero

Via Luca Giordano

Stazi
Cuma
Monte

Via Solimene

Vanvitelli

Via A Scarlatti

Via F Cilea

Tangenziale di Napoli

Via Luca Giordano

Via Mattia Preti

Largo
San
Martino

Piazza
Fuga

Parco
Lamaro

Villa
Floridiana

Via Luigia Sanfelice

Via Aniello Falcone

Parco
Elena

Viale Privato Diaz

Via Filippo Palizzi

Vico

Corso Europa

6 ▯▯ 7

Parco
Ameno

Corso Vittorio Emanuele

Piazzetta
Cariati

Via Santa Citerina da Sena

Via Tasso

Ⓜ Amedeo
Piazza
Amedeo

Via Francesco Crispi

Via dei Mille

Via Michelangelo Schipa

Via Arso Mirelli

Via
Pontano

Via Campiglione Marturo

Via G Piscicelli

Via Cavalerizza a Chiaia

Via Chiaia

Via A d'Isernia

Via
Ascensione

Via G Bausan

Via G Carducci

Piazza
dei
Martiri

Mergellina

Via Carlo Poerio

Chiaia

Riviera di Chiaia

Piedigrotta

Mergellina Ⓜ

Via Piedigrotta

Largo
Torretta

Piazza
della
Repubblica

Viale Anton Dohrn

Stazione
Zoologica
(Aquario)

Vialla
Comunale

Piazza
Vittoria

Largo
Nunziatell

Via Giordano Bruno

Rotonda
Armando
Diaz

Via Francesco Caracciolo

Viale Antonio Gramsci

Via Francesco Caracciolo

Piazza
Sannazzaro

Via Mergellina

11 🏠

Porticciolo
di
Mergellina

Largo
Barbaia

Via Cabulio

Via
Orazio

Via

See p284–5

0 ——————— 1 km
0 ——————— 0.5 miles

Stella

Piazza Carlo III

Orto Botanico

Corso Amedeo di S Duca d'Aosta

Corso Malta

Via Fonia

Corso G Garibaldi

Via Nuova Poggioreale

To Mercato di Poggioreale (800m)

Via F Lavinia

Centro Direzionale

Via Arenaccia

Via Santa Teresa degli Scalzi

Vico Cristallini

Via Antonio Villari

Via Miracoli

Via Stella

Cavour

Via Cesare Rosaroli

Piazza San Francesco di Paola

Piazza Cavour

Via Carbonara

Corso Novara

Via Casanova

Via Nazionale

Piazza Salerno

Viale della Costa

Museo

Via Enrico Pessina

Via del Sole

Via Duomo

Piazza Principe Umberto

Via Firenze

Via Genova

Corso Meridionale

Via G Brombeis

Via A Pisanelli

Vico Cigante

Piazza San Gaetano

Duomo

Duomo dei Tribunali

Stazione Centrale

Garibaldi

M Dante

Piazza Dante

Via Tarsia

Piazza Bellini

Piazza Luigi Miraglia

Spaccanapoli

Via Pietro Colletta

Piazza Garibaldi

To Gian Metro St (4

Via S Anna Lombardi

Piazza San Domenico Maggiore

Via San Biagio dei Librai

Piazza Vincenzo Calenda

Piazza Nolana

Via Ranieri

Via S Cosmo Fuori Porta Nolana

Via G Pica

Via G Ferraris

To Napolijamm (400m); Officina 99 (400m); Ufficio Immigrazione (400m)

Via Benedetto Croce

Piazzetta del Nilo

Piazza Museo Filangieri

Corso Umberto I

Via Giacomo Savarese

Via Lavinaio

Via C Carmignano

Stazione Circumvesuviana

Corso Amalde Lucci

Via S Liborio

Via S Chiara

Via Nilo

Via B Capasso

Via Mezzocannone

Piazza del Gesù Nuovo

Piazza Nicola Amore

Piazza del Mercato

Via Sant'Eligio

Via E Cosenz

Mercato

Piazza G Pepe

Via Amerigo Vespucci

Via C Battisti

Piazza Masaniello

Via Nuova, Marina

Via Toledo

Via Biaco

Piazza Bovio

Via A Diaz

Via Catalana

Via Agostino Depretis

Via Alcide De Gasperi

Via Cristatoto Colombo

Via Medina

Via G Verdi

Bacino del Piliero

Darsena Bacini

See p280–1

Parco Castello

Palazzo Reale

Via A F Acton

Stazione Marittima

Piazza del Plebiscito

Santa Lucia

Via C Console

Via Santa Lucia

Via Gen F Orsini

Via Nasario Sauro

Bay of Naples (Golfo di Napoli)

Chiatamone

Partenope

Via Eldorado

Porto di Santa Lucia

SIGHTS & ACTIVITIES	(pp63–106)
Albergo dei Poveri	1 G1
Chiesa San Giovanni a Carbonara	2 F2
Chiesa Santa Caterina a Formiello	3 G2
Orto Botanico	4 F1
Porta Capuana	5 G2

DRINKING 🍷 🍸	(pp129–31)
Grooming	6 B4
St Tropez	7 B4

ENTERTAINMENT 🎭	(pp127–36)
Blu Angels	8 H2
Freezer	9 H1

SLEEPING 🛏	(pp145–54)
Hotel Casanova	10 G2
Hotel Paradiso	11 A6
Hotel Zara	12 G2

TRANSPORT	
Alibus Bus to Airport	13 G2
Alilauro	14 F4
Avis	15 G2
Caremar	16 E4
Linee Lauro	(see 14)
Maggiore	17 G2
Medmar	(see 14)
Metrò del Mare	(see 14)
Navigazione Libera del Golfo	(see 16)
SNAV	(see 14)
Tirrenia	(see 14)

INFORMATION	
Agriturist Campania	18 H3

279

CENTRAL NAPLES

VOMERO

0 ———————— 400 m
0 ———————— 0.2 miles

SIGHTS & ACTIVITIES	(pp63–106)
Castel Sant'Elmo	1 C5
Cimitero delle Fontanelle	2 D2
Museo Nazionale della Ceramica Duca di Martina	3 B6
Villa Floridiana	4 B6

EATING	(pp115–26)
Acunzo	5 B5
Angolo de Paradiso	6 B4
Antica Cantina di Sica	7 B5
Donna Teresa	8 B5
Friggitoria Vomero	9 B5

ENTERTAINMENT	(pp127–36)
Around Midnight	10 B4
Cappella della Pietà dei Turchini	11 D6
Cinema Plaza	12 B5
Galleria Toledo	13 D5
Otto Jazz Club	14 D6

SHOPPING	(pp137–44)
CS Supermarket	15 B5
De Paola Cameos	16 C5
Giovanni Scafuro Studio	17 D3
L'Angolo a due Ruote	18 B5
Mercatino di Antignano	19 A4
Peter Pan	20 B5

SLEEPING	(pp145–54)
Hotel San Francesco al Monte	21 D5
La Casa di Leo	22 C4
La Controra	23 C3

INFORMATION	
Farmacia Cannone	24 B5

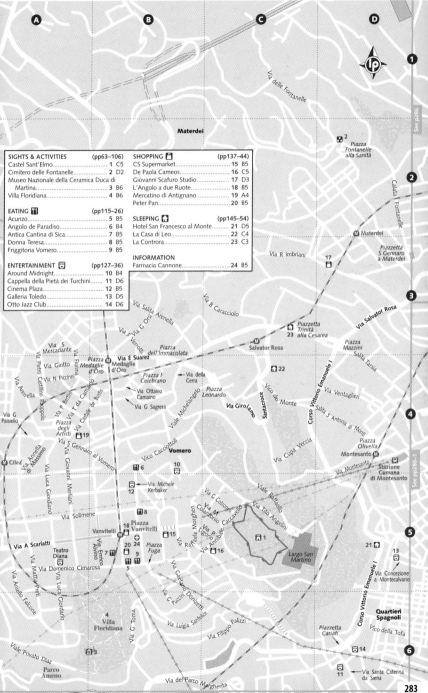

Materdei

Piazza Fontanelle alla Sanità

Matterdei

Piazzetta S Gennaro a Materdei

Via R Imbriani

Via Salvator Rosa

Piazzetta Trinità alla Cesarea

Salvator Rosa

Piazza Mazzini

Salita Tarsia

Via delle Fontanelle

Calata Fontanelle

Via Salita Arenella

Via B Caracciolo

Via F Ventotti

Via G S Oro

Piazza dell'Immacolata

Via S Mercadante

Via Pietro Castellino

Via Fiorina

Via Giotto

Via N Piccinni

Piazza Medaglie d'Oro

Via E Suarez

Medaglie d'Oro

Piazza F Celebrano

Via della Cera

Via Ottavio Camaino

Via G Sagrera

Piazza Leonardo

Viale Michelangelo

Via Girolamo

Santacroce

Vico del Monte

Corso Vittorio Emanuele I

Via Ventaglieri

Salita S Antonia ai Monti

Via Arenella

Via G Paisiello

Cilea

Via P Bernini

Via T di Camaldi

Piazza degli Artisti

Via Cataldo de Bortis

Via S Gennaro al Vomero

Via Annella di Massimo

Via Giovanni Merliani

Via Luca Giordano

Vico Cacciottoli

Vomero

Via Cupa Veccia

Piazza Olivella

Montesanto

Via Montesanto

Stazione Cumana di Montesanto

Via Solimene

Via Michele Kerbaker

Viale Raffaello

Via G Cotronei

Via M Colapionio

Via R Ugolino

Via Raffaele Morghen

Via Tito Angelini

Via A Scarlatti

Teatro Diana

Via Enrico Alvino

Piazza Vanvitelli

Vanvitelli

Piazza Fuga

Via G Carducci

Via Annibale Caccavello

Largo San Martino

Via Mattia Preti

Via Angiolo Falcone

Via Domenico Cimarosa

Via Luca Giordano

Via Gaetano Filangieri

Via G Puccini Donizetti

Via Luigia Sanfelice

Via Filippo Palizzi

Piazzetta Cariati

Via Concezione a Montecalvario

Quartieri Spagnoli

Vico della Tofa

Villa Floridiana

Via G Toma

Parco Ameno

Viale Privato Diaz

Via del Parco Margherita

Piazzetta Santa Caterina da Siena

See pp286

See pp280–1

See pp284–5

See p2

SIGHTS & ACTIVITIES	(pp63–106)
Acquedotto	1 H1
Borgo Marinaro	2 H4
Castel dell'Ovo	3 G4
Chalets	4 A5
Chiesa di San Ferdinando	5 H1
Chiesa di San Francesco di Paola	6 G2
Chiesa Santa Maria degli Angeli	7 G1
Chiesa Santa Maria del Parto	8 A4
Chiesa Santa Maria di Piedigrotta	9 A3
Chiesa Santa Maria in Portico	10 C2
Cinema di Santa Lucia	11 H2
Fontana dell'Immacolatella	12 H3
La Nunziatella	13 G2
Lungomare	14 F3
Museo di Etnopreistoria	15 G4
Museo Pignatelli	16 D2
Palazzo Calabritto	17 F2
Palazzo Cellamare	18 F1
Palazzo Partanna	(see 102)
Palazzo Reale	19 H1
PAN	20 E1
Parco Vergiliano	21 A3
Piazza Amedeo	22 D1
Piazza dei Martiri	23 F2
Piazza del Plebiscito	24 H1
Piazza Trieste e Trento	25 H1
Porticciolo	26 A4
Raccolta de Mura	27 H1
Stazione Mergellina	28 A3
Stazione Zoologica (Aquario)	29 E2
Via Chiaia	30 G1
Villa Comunale	31 E2

EATING	(pp115–26)
Antica Osteria da Tonino	32 E1
Antica Trattoria Don Peppino	33 G2
Brandi	34 G1
Caffè Gambrinus	35 H1
Castello	36 E1
Cibi Cotti	37 B3
Ciro	38 G3
Da Pietro	39 G3
Di Bruno	40 E2
Di Girolamo Giuseppe	41 A4
Dora	42 F2
Jap-One	43 F2
Kukai	44 G1
L.U.I.S.E.	45 F2
La Bersagliera	46 H3
La Caffettiera	47 F2
La Cantinella	48 H2
La Focaccia	49 F2
Maktub	50 F2
Moccia	51 E2
Salvatore	52 A5
Umberto	53 F2

DRINKING	(pp129–31)
Al Barcadero	54 G3
Chandelier	55 F2
Enoteca Belledonne	56 F2
Farinella	57 F2
Fusion Bar 66	58 F2
S'move	59 F2
White Bar	60 F2
Yachting Bar	61 A4

ENTERTAINMENT ☺ (pp127–36)
Associazione Scarlatti...................(see 102)
Feltrinelli Box Office....................(see 76)
La Mela..62 E1
Teatro San Carlo..........................63 H1
Teatro San Carlo Box Office..........(see 63)

SHOPPING (pp137–44)
Amarcord 900 Modernariato e
  Collezionismo...........................64 D1
Anna Matuozzo.............................65 A3
Antonio Barbaro...........................66 H1
Bancarelle a San Pasquale.............67 E1
Borrelli..68 F1
Bowinkel.......................................69 H2
Cesare Attolini..............................70 E1
Contemporastudio.........................71 D1
Culti Spacafè................................72 E2
Deliberti..73 F1
Eddy Monetti................................74 F2
Eddy Monetti Men's Store.............75 E1
Feltrinelli.......................................76 E2
Fiera Antiquaria Napoletana..........77 E2
Finamore.......................................78 E2
Interfood.......................................79 H2
Jossa...80 E2
Livio de Simone.............................81 E2
Mariano Rubinacci.........................82 F1
Marinella.......................................83 F2
OK-KO Research............................84 F1
Tabaccheria Sisimbro....................85 E1
Verdegrano....................................86 D1

SLEEPING (pp145–54)
B&B Cappella Vecchia 11................87 F2
B&B I 34 Turchi.............................88 H3
B&B Morelli...................................89 F2
B&B Santa Lucia............................90 H2
Chiaia Hotel de Charme.................91 G1
Grand Hotel Parker's.....................92 D1
Grand Hotel Santa Lucia................93 H3
Grand Hotel Vesuvio.....................94 H3
Hotel Ausonia................................95 B3
Hotel Excelsior..............................96 H3
Hotel Ruggiero..............................97 D1
Parteno...98 F3

TRANSPORT
Rent Sprint....................................99 H2

INFORMATION
French Consulate.........................100 D1
German Consulate........................101 D1
Main Tourist Office......................102 F2
Officina Profumo Farmaceutica di
  Santa Maria Novella..................103 F1
Post Office...................................104 H3
Tourist Information Office.............105 H1
Tourist Information Office.............106 A3
UK Consulate...............................107 E1
US Consulate...............................108 C3
Zeudi Internet Point.....................109 G1

285

CAPODIMONTE

Parco
di
Capodimonte

11

Tondo
di
Capodimonte

Stella

Via Ponti Rossi

Via Moiariello

Salita della Ricca

7

Salita Capodimonte

Via Luca Samuele

Corso Amedeo di S Duca d'Aosta

Vico San Gennaro dei Poveri

Via San Severo a Capodimonte

Via Cagnazzi Chieti

Vico dei Lammatari

Via S Maria Antesaecula

Via Carlotta

Via dei Cristallini

Via G B Alfano

Vico S Felice

Via della Sanità

Vico S Margherita

Vico della Calce

Vico della Neve

Vico San Maria della Purità

Via R Saverise

Via Materdei

Vico Lungo S Agostino degli Scalzi

salita San Raffaele

Via Salvator Rosa

Naples

Via Fonseca

Via B Celentano

Via Margherita a Fonseca

Via Antonio Villari

Vico Cimitile

Salita Stella

Via Arena della Sanità

Via Vergini

Via Mario Pagano

Via Stella

Piazza
Cavour

Via Foria

Cavour

Via Settembrini

Via Duomo

Via Miracoli

Via Maria Longo

Vico dei Cetolomini

Vico Giganti

6 Museo

See p280–1

Carb

SIGHTS & ACTIVITIES   (pp63–106)

CAMPI FLEGREI

0 ——————————— 2 km
0 ——————————— 1 mile

SIGHTS & ACTIVITIES (pp63–106)
Acropoli di Cuma 1 B2
Castello di Baia 2 C3
Città della Scienza 3 E3
Città Sommersa 4 C3
Edenlandia 5 E3
Grotta di Cocceio 6 B2
Grotta di Seiano 7 E4
Lago d'Averno 8 C2
Monte Nuovo 9 C2
Mostra d'Oltremare 10 F3
Museo Archeologico dei
  Campi Flegrei .... (see 2)
Palazzo Donn'Anna 11 F3
Parco Archeologico di Baia .. 12 B3
Parco Virgiliano 13 E4
Piscina Mirabilis 14 C4
Solfatara Crater 15 D3
Spiaggia del Castello 16 C3
Via Manzoni 17 F3
Villa Rosebery 18 F3

EATING 🍽 (pp115–26)
A Lampara 19 F3

ENTERTAINMENT 🎭 (pp127–36)
Freelovers @ Edenlandia .... (see 5)
L'Arenile di Bagnoli 20 E3
Lido L'Altro 21 E3
Nabilah 22 B3
Palapartenope 23 E3
Stadio San Paolo 24 F3
Vibes on the Beach 25 C4

SHOPPING 🛍 (pp137–44)
Mercatino di Posillipo .... (see 13)

SLEEPING 🛏 (pp145–54)
Hotel Terme Puteolane 26 D3
Il Casolare di Tobia 27 C3
Vulcano Solfatara 28 D3

287

POZZUOLI

0   200 m
0   0.1 miles

A   B   C   D

1

SIGHTS & ACTIVITIES	(pp63–106)
Anfiteatro Flavio	1 D4
Rione Terra	2 B6
Tempio di Serapide	3 B4

TRANSPORT	
Bus Station	4 A2
Ferry Terminal	5 A4

INFORMATION	
Tourist Office	6 C5

Via Campana

Via Domiziana - Campi Flegrei

2   4

Via Miliscola - Fasano

Corso Terracciano

Pozzuoli

3

Via Sacchini

3

1

Via Roma

4

Porto

Pozzuoli

Via Anfiteatro

Via del Carmine

Via Solfatara

Am
Au

Via Rosini

5

5

Via Cosenza

Via de Fraia

Corso Garibaldi

Corso E Piazza

Via Cavour

Cappuccini

6

2

6

Corso Matteotti

Corso Umberto